The Ancient Ways of Wessex

Travel and communication in an early medieval landscape

Alexander Langlands

Windgather Press is an imprint of Oxbow Books

Published in the United Kingdom in 2019 by
OXBOW BOOKS
The Old Music Hall, 106-108 Cowley Road, Oxford, OX4 1JE

and in the United States by
OXBOW BOOKS
1950 Lawrence Road, Havertown, PA 19083

© Windgather Press and the author 2019

Paperback Edition: 978-1-91118-851-3
Digital Edition: 978-1-91118-852-0

A CIP record for this book is available from the British Library

All rights reserved. No part of this book may be reproduced or transmitted in any form or by any means, electronic or mechanical including photocopying, recording or by any information storage and retrieval system, without permission from the publisher in writing.

Printed in the United Kingdom by Short Run Press

Typeset in India for Casemate Publishing Services.
www.casematepublishingservices.com

For a complete list of Windgather titles, please contact:

United Kingdom
OXBOW BOOKS
Telephone (01865) 241249
Fax (01865) 794449
Email: oxbow@oxbowbooks.com
www.oxbowbooks.com

United States of America
OXBOW BOOKS
Telephone (800) 791-9354
Fax (610) 853-9146
Email: queries@casemateacademic.com
www.casemateacademic.com/oxbow

Oxbow Books is part of the Casemate group

Cover photo: The view east from Melbury Beacon, Dorset © Alexander Langlands

Contents

List of figures and tables   v
Acknowledgements   viii
Introduction   ix

PART 1: LITERATURE REVIEW
1. The landscape of routes and communications   3
2. Travellers and journeys   29
3. From emporia to markets: trade networks in Wessex   48

PART 2: THE CASE STUDIES
4. A note on the evidence: Anglo-Saxon charters and Ordnance Survey maps   61
5. Hampshire   75
6. Devon   88
7. Dorset   100
8. Wiltshire   110

PART 3: DISCUSSION
9. Roman roads, wayside markers and gates   137
10. Bridges, herepaths, trade routes and the king's peace   164

Conclusion: Wessex and the early medieval world beyond   197
Appendix   208
Abbreviations   213
Bibliography   214

For Lynn and Jim

List of figures and tables

Figure 1   The 'old British way' snaking up the northern scarp slope of the Vale of Pewsey, either side of 'Woden's barrow'. © Clickos / Dreamstime.com

Figure 2   Ridgeways and earthworks of Wessex (Hippesley-Cox 1927, 20–21)

Figure 3   Co-axial landscapes on the Chiltern dip slope (Williamson 2008, 129, fig. 32)

Figure 4   The Roman roads of Wessex (Margary 1957, 76–77, fig. 3)

Figure 5   Major roads in Anglo-Saxon times (Hill 1981, 116, fig. 199)

Figure 6   The causeway and bridge across the Wylye valley between Stoford ('stone ford') and Great Wishford (see study area 8.1, SU03NE)

Figure 7   Water transport in medieval England (Blair 2007, 18, fig. 5)

Figure 8   Middle Anglo-Saxon trading sites and landing places recorded in tenth-century charters.

Figure 9   Anglo-Saxon illustrations of ox-carts (Hill 1998, fig. 1)

Figure 10   Minster Street and Market Place, Salisbury, in close proximity to the site of St Thomas's Church and a likely focus for activity prior to the foundation of the medieval city in 1220 (Langlands 2014)

Figure 11   Coin productive sites (excluding hoards) and Roman roads in Hampshire (Palmer 2003, 59, fig. 5.3, after Ulmscheider 2001, map 21)

Figure 12   Regression analysis of Hamwic coinage in Wessex (Metcalf 2003, 41, fig. 4.1)

Figure 13   The Scole-Dickleborough field system, an observation underpinned by the analysis of historic Ordnance Survey maps (Williamson 2008, 125, fig. 30)

Figure 14   Key to the study areas

Figure 15   The locations of study areas 1 to 10

Figure 16   Study area 1.1, The Harroway, Roman roads and other routes (Contains OS data © Crown copyright (2018))

Figure 17   [RR3] (see study area 1.1), a substantial way connecting the Silchester to Andover Roman Road to the Harroway

Figure 18   Study area 1.2, The Harroway study area (Contains OS data and OS 1st Edition Six Inch base map © Crown copyright and Landmark Information Group Limited (2018), all rights reserved)

Figure 19   Study area 1.3, Buttermere and 'Æscmere' (Contains OS data and OS 1st Edition Six Inch base map © Crown copyright and Landmark Information Group Limited (2018), all rights reserved)

Figure 20   Study area 2.1, Winchester and the Upper Itchen Valley (Contains OS data and OS 1st Edition Six Inch base map © Crown copyright and Landmark Information Group Limited (2018), all rights reserved)

Figure 21   Study area 2.2, Winchester and its north environs (Contains OS data and OS 1st Edition Six Inch base map © Crown copyright and Landmark Information Group Limited (2018), all rights reserved)

List of figures and tables

Figure 22 Study area 2.3, Alresford and the Upper Itchen (Contains OS data and OS 1st Edition Six Inch base map © Crown copyright and Landmark Information Group Limited (2018), all rights reserved)
Figure 23 Study area 3.1, Crediton and Exeter (Contains OS data and OS 1st Edition Six Inch base map © Crown copyright and Landmark Information Group Limited (2018), all rights reserved)
Figure 24 Study area 3.2, Crediton and Copplestone (Contains OS data and OS 1st Edition Six Inch base map © Crown copyright and Landmark Information Group Limited (2018), all rights reserved)
Figure 25 The crossroads location of the Copplestone Cross
Figure 26 Study area 4.1, The South Hams (Contains OS data and OS 1st Edition Six Inch base map © Crown copyright and Landmark Information Group Limited (2018), all rights reserved)
Figure 27 Bantham Beach, the site of a late Antique and early medieval beach market
Figure 28 Study area 4.2, Halwell, the herepaths and street (Contains OS data and OS 1st Edition Six Inch base map © Crown copyright and Landmark Information Group Limited (2018), all rights reserved)
Figure 29 Study area 5.1, The Isle of Purbeck (Contains OS data and OS 1st Edition Six Inch base map © Crown copyright and Landmark Information Group Limited (2018), all rights reserved)
Figure 30 Chapman's Pool © Kevin Eaves / Dreamstime.com
Figure 31 Study area 6.1, Shaftesbury's southern environs (Contains OS data and OS 1st Edition Six Inch base map © Crown copyright and Landmark Information Group Limited (2018), all rights reserved)
Figure 32 Study area 6.2, Lazerton and the old ford (Contains OS data and OS 1st Edition Six Inch base map © Crown copyright and Landmark Information Group Limited (2018), all rights reserved)
Figure 33 Study area 7.1, The Ebble Valley (Contains OS data and OS 1st Edition Six Inch base map © Crown copyright and Landmark Information Group Limited (2018), all rights reserved)
Figure 34 Study area 7.2, Winklebury and the upper Ebble Valley (Contains OS data and OS 1st Edition Six Inch base map © Crown copyright and Landmark Information Group Limited (2018), all rights reserved)
Figure 35 Study area 7.3, Bishopstone and the lower Ebble Valley (Contains OS data and OS 1st Edition Six Inch base map © Crown copyright and Landmark Information Group Limited (2018), all rights reserved)
Figure 36 Study area 7.4, The Downton herepaths (Contains OS data and OS 1st Edition Six Inch base map © Crown copyright and Landmark Information Group Limited (2018), all rights reserved)
Figure 37 Study area 8.1, Wilton and Old Sarum (Contains OS data and OS 1st Edition Six Inch base map © Crown copyright and Landmark Information Group Limited (2018), all rights reserved)
Figure 38 Study area 8.2, Laverstock and the 'Winterbourne' charter (Contains OS data and OS 1st Edition Six Inch base map © Crown copyright and Landmark Information Group Limited (2018), all rights reserved)

Figure 39　The Roman road from Winchester to Old Sarum, looking west as it passes Park Corner (the location of the now lost Beornwin's Stone), with Clarendon Park to the south

Figure 40　Study area 9.1, Bradford-on-Avon radiating routes (Contains OS data and OS 1st Edition Six Inch base map © Crown copyright and Landmark Information Group Limited (2018), all rights reserved)

Figure 41　The medieval bridge over the Avon at Bradford-on-Avon. © Kevin Eaves / Dreamstime.com

Figure 42　Study area 10.1, Kinwardstone, Wansdyke and the Bedwyn Dykes (Contains OS data and OS 1st Edition Six Inch base map © Crown copyright and Landmark Information Group Limited (2018), all rights reserved)

Figure 43　Study area 10.2, Wansdyke, Chisbury and the Bedwyn Dykes (Contains OS data and OS 1st Edition Six Inch base map © Crown copyright and Landmark Information Group Limited (2018), all rights reserved)

Figure 44　Study area 10.3, The Ham Dyke (Contains OS data and OS 1st Edition Six Inch base map © Crown copyright and Landmark Information Group Limited (2018), all rights reserved)

Figure 45　Roman roads in early medieval Wessex (Contains OS data © Crown copyright (2018))

Figure 46　'Hagas', 'Septi', gates and dykes (Contains OS data © Crown copyright (2018))

Figure 47　Stockbridge and Langport Compared (OS 1st Edition Six Inch base map: © Crown Copyright and Landmark Information Group Limited (2018), all rights reserved)

Figure 48　Winchester to Wilton, via Stockbridge (Contains OS data © Crown copyright (2018))

Figure 49　Somerton to Taunton, via Langport (Contains OS data © Crown copyright (2018))

Figure 50　The Street causeway, Somerset, showing method of construction (reproduced in Brunning 2010)

Figure 51　Wic herepaths and chapmen place names (Contains OS data © Crown copyright (2018))

Table 1　Study area 1 charter boundary clauses
Table 2　Study area 2 charter boundary clauses
Table 3　Study area 3 charter boundary clauses
Table 4　Study area 4 charter boundary clauses
Table 5　Study area 5 charter boundary clauses
Table 6　Study area 6 charter boundary clauses
Table 7　Study area 7 charter boundary clauses
Table 8　Differences in the Easton Bassett boundary clauses, S 630 and S 582
Table 9　Study area 8 charter boundary clauses
Table 10　Study area 9 charter boundary clauses
Table 11　Study area 10 charter boundary clauses

Acknowledgements

This book has been a long time in the making and reflects a life time of both amateur interest and academic study on the subject. As such, in the process, I have drawn on the wisdom of a vast number of people from a variety of fields. Barbara Yorke and Ryan Lavelle were fundamental in the marshalling of my early thoughts into the thesis that provided the underpinning structural integrity to this work. En route, Grenville Astill, Stuart Brookes, David Hinton, Wendy Davies, Julio Escalona, Sarah Semple, John Baker, Tim Tatton-Brown, Gus Milne, James Graham-Campbell and Martin Welch have all been instrumental in helping me to shape my ideas and refine my scholarship. The long-term support and on-going conversations with Andrew Reynolds provide continuous inspiration. A very special mention is reserved for Simon Roffey, an ever-present friend, mentor and backing vocalist, without whose early encouragement this volume would almost certainly have never seen the light of day. The kind patience and support of Julie Gardiner and the team at Oxbow Books is duly acknowledged.

The publication of full colour images throughout this volume was made possible through the generous donations made by the Marc Fitch Fund and Swansea University's College of Arts and Humanities Research Support Fund.

Introduction

Studies of travel and communication have become a standard feature in our understanding of modern historical periods. The impacts of the internal combustion engine, the advent of the railways, the developments in air freight and steam shipping, the stagecoaches and turnpikes, the network of inland-waterways and the digital revolution have all been heralded as central to the definition of the periods within which their impact was most keenly felt. Yet, for the early medieval period, commentary on the way in which individuals and groups communicated and moved around on the local, regional and national scale is sparse. Even if it is the case that further back into our past the interplay between the networks through which goods, people and ideas moved and the societies they were part of becomes less tangible, it is abundantly clear that the role of travel and communication was equally as important then as it is in our studies of more recent history. The concept of travel itself in the medieval period has received no shortage of attention through the eyes of the traveller, the notion of the journey and the historical evidence for long-distance communications (for some classic studies see Jusserand 1889; Newton 1930; Wade-Labarge 1982; Ohler 1989). Very often dismissed, even in more recent commentary, as 'a pale and ill-maintained shadow of its Roman predecessor' (Brooks 2002, 14) and as 'primitive, with many being poorly constructed and poorly maintained' (Newman 2011, 43), the exact physical edifices upon which people travelled and communicated in the medieval – and especially the early medieval period – have received very little attention.

It has for some time now been observed that scholarship of early medieval England has failed to seek topographical explanations for significant political, social and cultural developments in Anglo-Saxon history (Pelteret 1985). This circumstance, with a few notable exceptions (Chapter 1), pervades today and the impact of this oversight on the popular understanding of archaeological and historic periods has been that, for the general reader, there is a scarcity of accessible literature directly concerned with the interpretation of communications in historic landscapes (Muir 2000, 93). So, what do we know about Anglo-Saxon roads today?

David Harrison concluded in his study of medieval bridges that a majority of those that supported the economy of the fourteenth century were in existence by the end of the eleventh century and must therefore have formed part of a highly developed network of roads. He goes on to write that it is 'inherently implausible' to assume that investment was made in 'splendid' bridges whilst the roads and ways that connected them remained mere 'oceans of mud' (Harrison 2004, 222–223). For early medieval communications, mud is a popular theme with rural settlements 'scattered over hundreds of square miles, each at the end of a long muddy track' (Campbell 2000, 218), in a 'Muddy Age' (Robinson 1984, 749), 'still popularly imagined as one of muddy immobility' (Morris 2004, 10). Yet, some sense of the sophistication of the network is promoted through the view that alterations to it had been slight up until the advent of the seventeenth-century turnpikes (Taylor 1979, 110).

Anecdotal evidence has been used to illustrate the standards that late Anglo-Saxon road-building had attained. Oliver Rackham (1986, 257–259) points out that Harold's feat in 1066 of marching an army from London to York in four and a half days would seem to suggest that Anglo-Saxon roads were capable of carrying a large contingent of fighting men and their retinue at speeds similar to those achieved in the Roman period. Citing King Æthelstan's eight-day journey from Winchester to Nottingham, and the moving of Bishop Æthelwold's body from Beddington to Winchester (a distance of over sixty miles in two days), David Hill (1981, 115) suggests that such journeys 'could hardly have been undertaken by people creeping apologetically along the margins of irate peasant's fields, or blundering through trackless woods'. In a landmark paper that set out the maximum view for the Anglo-Saxon State, James Campbell (1995, 54) suggested a phase of economic development in the late Anglo-Saxon period arguably more significant than that of the sixteenth century. Essential to this economic success, in his eyes, was the maintenance of roads and bridges.

FIGURE 1. The 'old British way' snaking up the northern scarp slope of the Vale of Pewsey, either side of 'Woden's barrow'. © Clickos / Dreamstime.com.

The evidence, therefore, for a sophisticated network of maintained roads seems primarily to be indirect. The same circumstance can be observed in early medieval Ireland. Amongst the numerous historical source materials that survive for the period there is 'little mention of the first essential for transport – the road' (Lochlainn 1940, 465) in a world clearly where very many journeys of all kinds are being made (Doherty 2015, 30).

We may well have been guilty of not seeking to place travel and communication as a more central issue in our understanding of the Anglo-Saxon period, but this is not necessarily because of a lack of direct references to the theme. It is very much more the case that the material that lies at our disposal is of such a diverse nature. This is a view clearly shared by Norbert Ohler in his *Medieval Traveller*:

> We can get a fairly accurate idea of the stages of princely journeys from the places and dates listed in documents, annals and chronicles; but we do not know very much about the exact location and condition of the roads. There are many gaps in our knowledge and we have to fill in the picture by studying traces in the landscape, field-names, indicators of resting places or inns, archaeological remains, old maps, aerial photographs and other details. (Ohler 1989, 24)

Any approach, therefore, to the study of travel and communication in the landscape of Anglo-Saxon Wessex must fundamentally embrace interdisciplinarity, making use of historical, topographical, toponymic and archaeological evidence to gain a greater understanding of the route network of early medieval Wessex. The time is ripe for such an undertaking not least because of recent developments in our understanding of the middle Anglo-Saxon economy, the emergence of towns, the identification of a complex system of administration, justice and governance, a wider understanding of civil defence and clear evidence for an intensification of agricultural productivity in the later part of the period. How do the pattern of routes and the nexus of communications in the early medieval landscape serve as both a function of these processes and a contributor to them?

This relationship, a kind of iterative reciprocity, is a common theme amongst commentators on communications in archaeological and historical periods. Peter Fowler (1998, 25), for example, writes that, 'If landscape is not only the result of dynamics but is itself dynamic at any one time, then movement within and through it by people and their materials is both a lubricant and a product of those dynamics'. The same sentiments are expressed by Paul Hindle (1993, 11): 'Roads and tracks are important in that they have allowed virtually every other feature of the landscape to develop, and have themselves developed because of those features'. It is this dynamic between developments in communications and wider societal and economic transition that is so crucial to understand if we are to move beyond merely observing change to identifying why change takes place and, for our purposes, the role that evolving communications play.

This book is divided into three parts. Part 1 reviews much of what we already know about early medieval route networks and offers some synthesis of archaeological, historical and place-name evidence in a bid to draw together some coherent themes for further analysis. Chapter 1 considers the landscape of communications and explores not only the scholarship that has to date been undertaken on the early medieval route network but also the currently accepted views on what the prehistoric and Roman legacy was in terms of the roads, tracks and ways that survived into the Anglo-Saxon period. The current thinking on bridge building in the later Anglo-Saxon landscape is assessed along with recent work on the extent of early medieval waterways and the scale of water transportation in the period. The objective of this chapter is to establish what we know of early medieval overland and riverine communication networks in Wessex but crucially where there is scope and potential for in improved understanding. Equally, Chapter 2 sets out the current state of knowledge concerning the range and types of journeys that were made through the Anglo-Saxon landscape and considers why individuals and groups from every level of society had cause to travel. One of the main stimuli for travel and communication in the early medieval period was the need for the redistribution and exchange of goods and materials. With a particular focus on Wessex, Chapter 3 reviews the developments and changes in the Anglo-Saxon economy from the period of the eighth century through to the eleventh. The shift in trading practices, from an allocative economy to one based on price-making markets must be seen to have had an impact on the way goods of both a bulk and prestige variety were moved from place to place and via which routes.

Part 2 consists of five chapters. The first reviews the nature of the primary evidence used in the case studies: Anglo-Saxon charters and the first edition Ordnance Survey. The chapter examines the veracity of both data sources and demonstrates that, used collaboratively, they can be a powerful tool in the elucidation of the early medieval landscape. It also considers the debates surrounding the theoretical underpinnings of various approaches to historic and archaeological landscapes in Britain. The following four chapters each cover one of the four counties within which the ten case studies have been undertaken. The study areas were selected in an attempt to cover a range of differing geologies, terrains and geographical situations in southern England. In central Wessex, where the chalk downland predominates, Study areas 2 and 8 were selected in the lower valleys where the settlement pattern was more developed (Winchester and the Upper Itchen Valley and the Salisbury Basin). Parts of study areas 1 and 7 (The Harroway, Whitchurch, and the Bourne Rivulet and the Ebble Valley) provided coverage on the Upper Chalk where the settlement pattern was more dispersed and the land was used less intensively for arable cultivation. Study areas 3 and 4 were undertaken in Devon (Crediton and the South Hams) to observe what the charter evidence had to say of a landscape very different in its geological and agrarian character, and historical and cultural background, from the chalk heartlands of Wessex. Study areas 4 and 5 were undertaken in coastal zones to explore the arrangement of communications in conjunction with harbours, beaches and coastal look-outs (the South Hams and the Isle of Purbeck). The varying geology (Lower Oolite, Lias Clay and Lower Greensand) of study areas 6 and 9 (Shaftesbury's southern hinterland and Bradford-on-Avon and its environs) offer environmental comparison from within the Wessex heartlands but these studies were also selected because of the role that important early medieval central places had on the hinterland geography of routes. Finally, the Kinwardstone Hundred study area, 10, has been selected to explore how a frontier zone might impact on the configuration of routes. In each of the study areas certain themes predominate. For example, the commentary on the Crediton study area (3) is centred primarily on the evidence for the herepath network whilst the focus in the Kinwardstone Hundred study area (10) is necessarily on the numerous gates that are mentioned in the boundary clauses for the region.

In Part 3, consisting of Chapters 9 and 10, the observations made in Part 2 are used to address some of the key themes that emerged from the discussion in Part 1. Chapter 9 begins by addressing the issue of Roman roads and the degree to which they continued to function into the early medieval period. The chapter also summarises the evidence from the study areas for how the landscape, and particular routes, were inscribed with markers of both practical and ideological purpose and links this evidence with the current thinking on religious, political and judicial monumentalism in the landscape. In the final section to the chapter, the issue of how access was controlled in the landscape is covered in relation to both the frontier zone of the Kinwardstone Hundred area but also in the control and movement of livestock in upland zones. Chapter 10 employs the evidence from all ten study areas, in conjunction with outside examples, to address the early medieval route network in both its physical form and the evidence for the designated status and functions that certain roads enjoyed. It creates a link between what we know of bridge-building in the period and the ubiquitous 'herepath' to demonstrate that the people of Wessex took a conscious and proactive role in the functionality of the communication networks that connected their destinations of trade, governance, worship and work.

This research demonstrates that between the places of Anglo-Saxon Wessex lay anything but 'oceans of mud' and in doing so it illustrates that the means and the methods are there to reconstruct in some detail the routes that furnished a large part of the early medieval landscape of Wessex. As a sample, the ten study areas chosen for this project represents only a small part of the early medieval landscape that is documented through Anglo-Saxon charter boundary clauses. Yet, by modelling the patterns that emerge in these areas and employing such models in areas where charter data is lacking, in conjunction with place-name evidence and approaches from landscape archaeology, we can further fill out the landscape with a more comprehensive map of Anglo-

Saxon roads than that provided by the template of Roman roads. Indeed, this is a study for which the methodology could be extended to much of the post-Roman medieval world. It takes a step in that direction, and alongside drawing together some of the key findings discussed in Part 3, the conclusion will set about recommending avenues of future research whilst at the same time placing the study in the broader context of early medieval northern Europe.

Part 1
LITERATURE REVIEW

CHAPTER ONE

The landscape of routes and communications

Prehistoric trackways

The 'lost' or 'ancient' ways of Wessex and the wider landscape through which they pass have proven a popular subject for writers and publishers over the course of the last century (*e.g.* Belloc 1911; Cox 1927; Massingham 1936; Cochrane 1969; Timperley and Brill 1970; Bulfield 1972; Wright 1988, 10–32; Belsey 1998). With an appeal to a wide audience of ramblers and walkers with increasing access to the countryside, works such as *The Lost Roads of Wessex* (Cochrane 1969) and *The Ancient Trackways of Wessex* (Timperley and Brill 1970) tend now to sit more comfortably into an appreciation of landscape that owes more to the English landscape tradition of Wordsworth and W.G. Hoskins – with its Romantic undertones and nostalgic tendencies – than they do in the realms of the theory and practice that characterises modern interdisciplinary landscape studies (Johnson 2006, *passim*). Whilst many of the routes described in these books can be seen to traverse the landscape for considerable distances and are thus thought to be some of the primary features of our landscape, the common consensus currently amongst landscape archaeologists is that at best, such routes are notoriously difficult to date and at worst, they are entirely speculative as long-distance prehistoric routes (Taylor 1979, 12; Turner 1980, 2; Fowler 1998, 27; Harrison 2003). Paul Hindle, whose work is primarily focused on the post-Conquest period, views the numerous claims made that certain roads and tracks are of prehistoric origin as 'unsubstantiated' (1993, 17). Christopher Taylor in his *Roads and Tracks of Britain* warned against the desire to see obvious ridgeways as necessarily facilitating long-distance communication and was particularly dismissive of the so-called 'Jurassic Way' (1979, 34–37). John Barnatt has discredited the idea that a long distance Iron Age or Bronze Age route traversed the Peak District from the Trent Valley in a north-westerly direction (2002, 39–44). The North Downs Trackway is a route that today makes use of the ridge of chalk downland that traverses Kent on an east/west alignment. Although popularly referred to as the medieval 'Pilgrim's Way' in places, the likelihood that such a route existed in the pre-Roman period has been brought into question (Turner 1980). Similar concerns have been voiced for the Icknield Way, a route that at its maximum extent runs from the Wash in East Anglia via a crossing

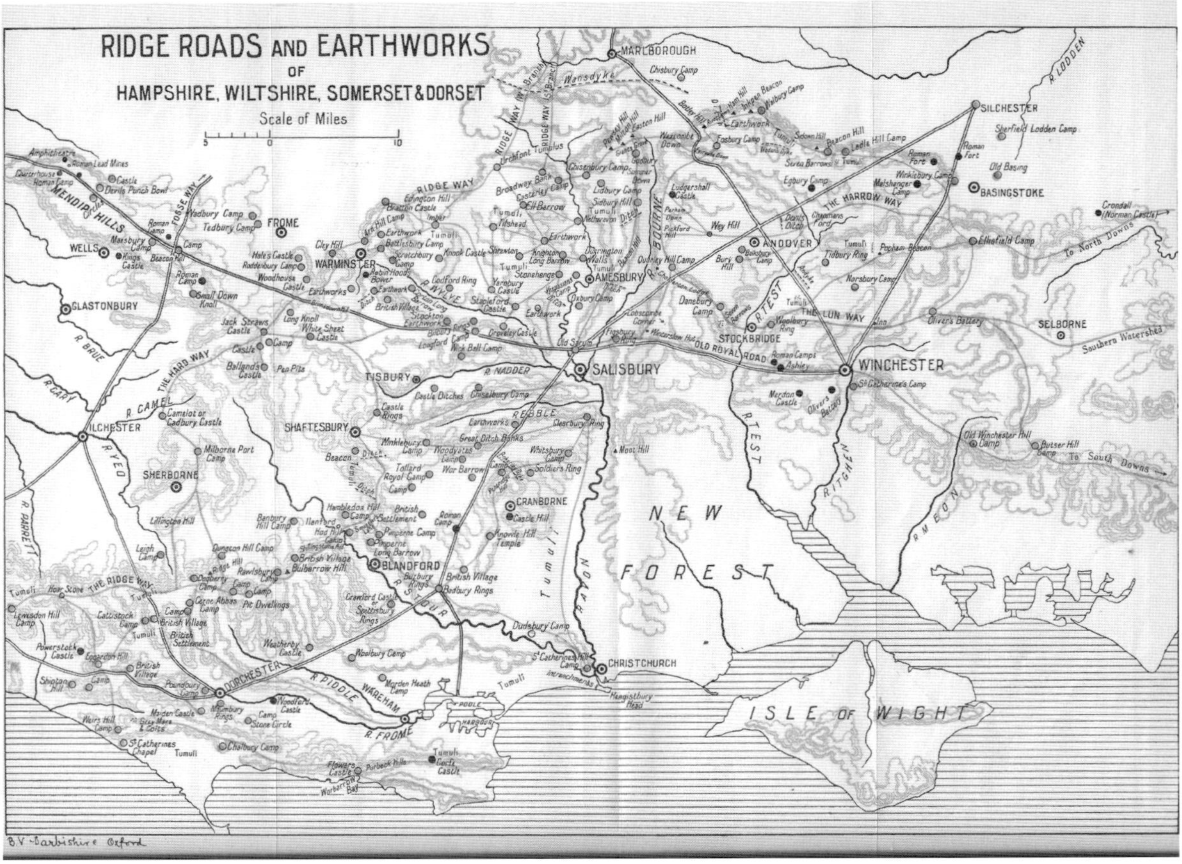

FIGURE 2. Ridgeways and earthworks of Wessex (Hippisley-Cox 1914, 20–21).

point of the Thames at Goring to the English Channel (Harrison 2003). Archaeological evidence would appear to substantiate these dismissive claims. Sarah Harrison draws attention to excavations undertaken at Aston Clinton (Bucks.) where the 'accepted' line of the Icknield Way slights features of early Iron Age to late Roman date (R.P.S. Consultants 2002; Harrison 2003, 11). P.J. Fowler observes the same relationship between 'The Ridgeway' (the definite article of which he takes issue with) and 'two axially arranged organised field systems' of late Iron Age/Romano-British origin on the Fyfield and Overton downs (Wilts.) (1998, 30). Further north of Fowler's study area, the same route passes Uffington Hill Fort near to which excavations revealed a layer of compacted chalk overlaying the fill of a late Bronze Age boundary ditch implying an Iron Age date at the earliest (Denison 1998b).

The presumption that our 'ancient' and 'lost' ways were in permanent and regular use as single long-distance trackways, connecting up far-flung parts of the British Isles is a notion, therefore, that is clearly refuted. But what if such routes hosted more intermittent usage, serving large-scale seasonal gatherings, or movements of livestock, and only the occasional long-distance communication? Such movement might not require a fixed, constrained and metalled surface but might rather be reflected, in Fowler's description of sections of The

Ridgeway, in a 'bundle of former track lines', sinuous and braided as they negotiate open country. From his analysis of Wansdyke in the southern parts of the parishes of Fyfield and West Overton, he considers the construction of the post-Roman bank and ditch and the regularity of original gates within the earthwork as a response to a 5 km (3.1 miles) wide corridor of movement that required marshalling (2001, 195). As early as 1951 W.F. Grimes demonstrated that the distribution of material culture along the line of a conjectural 'Jurassic Way' represented a 'corridor for traffic rather than a single track' and that it constituted what was in effect a 'Jurassic Zone' of movement as recent as the late Iron Age (1951, 158–171). So whilst convincing evidence for such ridgeways serving as regularly functioning socio-economic transport networks in prehistory (*i.e.* premeditated and planned highways) is lacking, as stretches of open (certainly by the late Bronze Age) and dry country they fundamentally allowed for ease of movement and therefore must have served as attractive thoroughfares – in any period of Britain's landscape history (Figure 2). It may not be specious to draw a comparison here with the most recent of overland transport networks. Only a very small percentage of travellers using a motorway travel its entire course. More frequently, sections of it facilitate movement on a much more local level. It is perhaps, then, in the sub-regional sphere that the study of the pattern of prehistoric route networks is likely to find itself on more solid ground.

Tom Williamson, in his most recent assessment of the longevity of prehistoric field systems, believed that the boundaries that constrained prehistoric fields – particularly those on the long axes that created the courses of their 'slightly wavy brickwork' appearance in plan form – may actually have been, in their first incarnation, ways that served communities within valleys by running at right-angles to a parallel banding of resources. These routes allowed the people dwelling in the valleys access to woodland, summer pasture, arable fields and alluvial meadows and their continued use throughout the Romano-British period, early medieval period and beyond represents, in Williamson's words, 'a response to similar environmental circumstances' (2008, 130–132).

In Wessex, Fowler, like Williamson, suggests that the earliest lines in the landscape of West Overton and Fyfield are the trackways allowing access to woodland and downland pasture and that these go on to form the main axes of later field systems (1998, 26–32). In the Romano-British period they were, he states, 'already old' and that 'they contributed to the shaping of the land units, the tithings and the parishes and goodness knows what before them' (1998, 40). A further characteristic of these field systems is that their long axes (*i.e.* those that run from the valley bottom to the higher ground) tend to terminate at watersheds (Williamson 2003, 40). Of the Scole-Dickleborough field system for example, the long axes appear to terminate at a 'traverse element which was variously a watershed trackway, a parish boundary and a hundred boundary', and the same relationship occurs in two examples of co-axial field systems identified in Hertfordshire (see Figure 3). Despite scepticism over the extensiveness of individual long-distance tracks, the local approach to route

6 Alexander Langlands

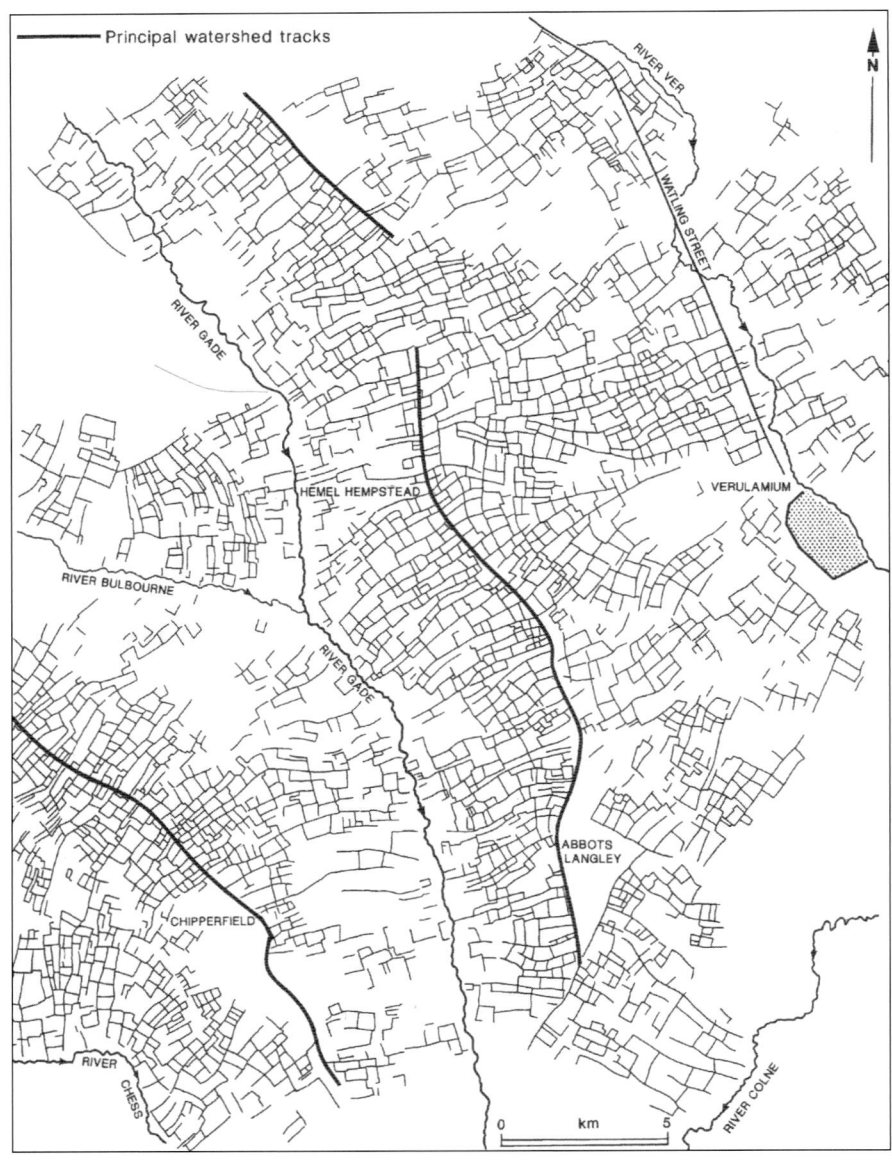

FIGURE 3. Co-axial landscapes in the Chiltern dip slope (Williamson 2008, 129, fig. 32).

ways, one that carefully examines their relationship with field systems, presents good evidence for a network of ways, tracks and paths serving, certainly by the late Iron Age, and especially in the south-east of Britain, a relatively dense settlement pattern (Cunliffe 1974, 153–179).

Roman roads

Very often the network of major Roman roads in Britain identified by the likes of Thomas Codrington (1903), G.M. Boumphrey (1935, 216) and Ivan Margary

(1948; 1957; 1973) is used to furnish the distribution and location maps of historical and archaeological studies of the early medieval period (Figure 4). Without wishing to single out any one study, in the employment of what is essentially a very specific topographical construct there is an implicit assumption that the entire Roman road network continued in use from the Roman through to the medieval period. The extent, however, to which it survived the ravages of time and impacted upon the development of post-Roman society in Britain has yet to come under closer scrutiny and has resulted, even in most recent scholarship, in opposing generalisations. On the one hand, there is a continuing temptation to see the orbit of movement in the early medieval period as being in some way less expansive than in the Roman, thus impacting upon the survival of the Roman networks as a device for long distance communication. Most recently, 'the travelling needs of the Saxon settlers' have been considered to be so local they resulted in 'the long stretches of Roman road [breaking] into shorter stretches of continuous road' (Allen and Evans 2016, 12). Yet, on the flip side, echoing Frank Stenton's observation that Ogilby's map of 1675 preserves 'in essence' the situation as it was in fifth century (1936, 1), Hindle summarises that 'many of these roads clearly remained in use, providing a basic network' (2016, 34).

On the evolution of the road network in early medieval Europe, Albert Leighton suggests that Roman roads had become something of a liability during the period, serving better the marauders and plunderers of the migration and invasion period and stretching beyond the horizons of the political and geographical zones of the day. Put literally, 'they no longer led where people wanted to go' (1972, 52). Similarly, Norbert Ohler (1989, 22) draws attention to the anachronistic character of Roman roads after the fall of the empire. They were, he argues, designed for military purposes and to get the quickest and most effective action from the smallest amount of troops. By the middle centuries of the first millennium they had in his view become defunct. Their fate, however, was variable. Some found themselves robbed, some abandoned, some formed boundaries (as they may well have done during active service) and others, whilst experiencing continuing usage, would have suffered through lack of maintenance. It has been estimated that Roman roads would have stood up under the onslaught of iron-shod and iron-tyred wheels for no more than seventy to one hundred years (Forbes 1955, 159), and for those that clearly had no immediate requirement as a means of communication, evidence from the continent demonstrates their use as quarries for the construction of local buildings (Schreiber 1962, 156–157). Maintenance would have undoubtedly been costly and it has been proposed that keeping Roman roads in a serviceable condition was even beyond the financial capabilities of the Byzantine and Islamic Empires of the eastern Mediterranean (White 1967, 66–67).

This view is contrasted with the accepted view on the survival of Roman roads in Britain where it appears, certainly from analysis of later medieval maps that, 'many Roman roads remained in use' into and beyond the post-

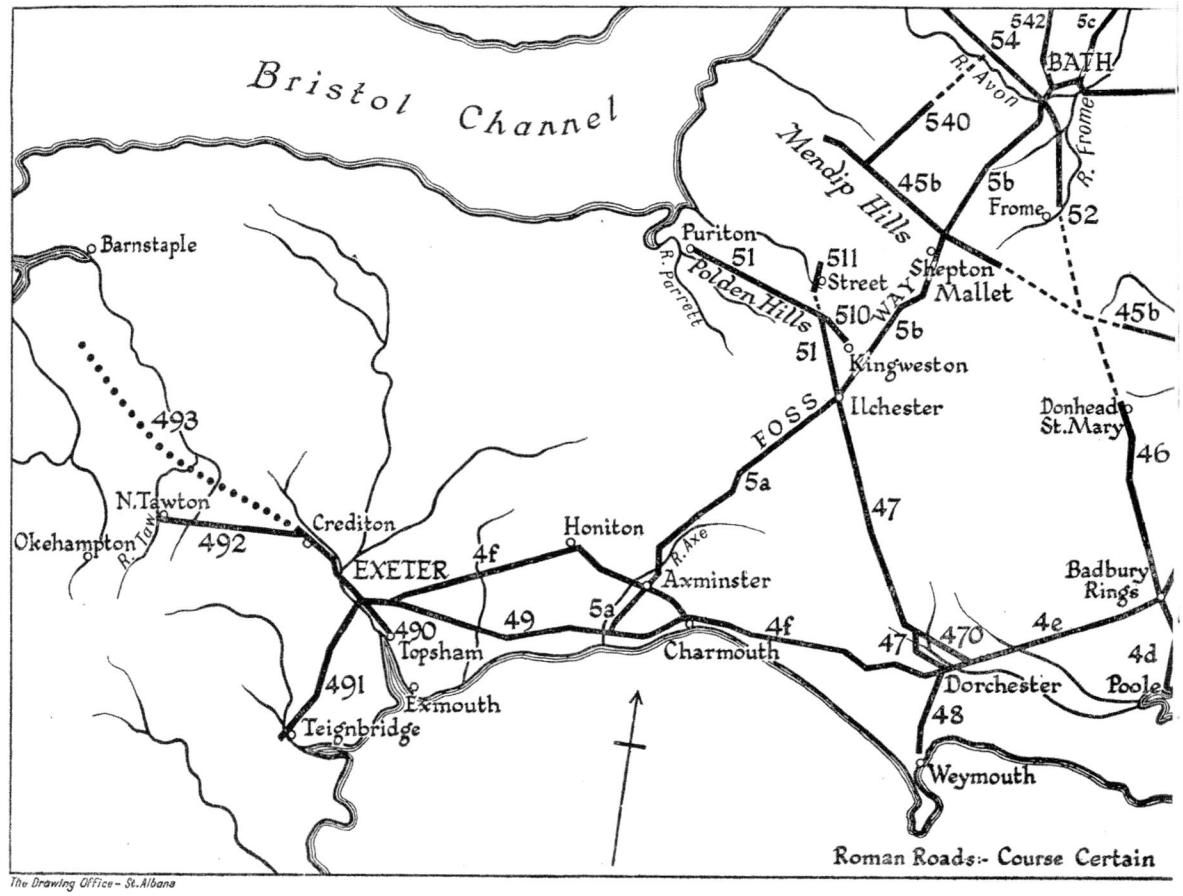

FIGURE 4. *(top & opposite)*. The Roman roads of Wessex (Margary 1957, 76–77, fig. 3).

Conquest period (Hindle 1976; 1982a; Edwards and Hindle 1991, 124). Many studies too of the early medieval period imply that the Roman road network was a functioning entity. For example, Anne Cole's recent assessment (2007) of water transport in early medieval England has identified a series of place-names which indicate early ports and harbours and a key shared characteristic of these sites is their apparent proximity to Roman roads. Likewise, Leigh Symonds and R.J. Ling's representation of socio-geographical concepts of time and travel in early medieval England suggests that the Roman roads of the Lincolnshire area survived as viable routes through which to conduct trade and communicate (Symonds and Ling 2002; Symonds 2003, 135, 161, 168, 224). Although Katharina Ulmschneider is reserved in her assessment of the proximity of single coin finds of the middle Anglo-Saxon period to Roman roads, her distribution map demonstrates that, 'Roman roads are clearly important in the distribution of coinage' (2000, 100, map 21; see also Palmer 2003, 58–59, fig. 5.3). There is always a danger, however, that the interrelationships presented in such studies are the results of the accidents of geography: the fact that Roman roads might occupy and connect the corridors of landscape most conducive to centres of occupation and settlement spanning

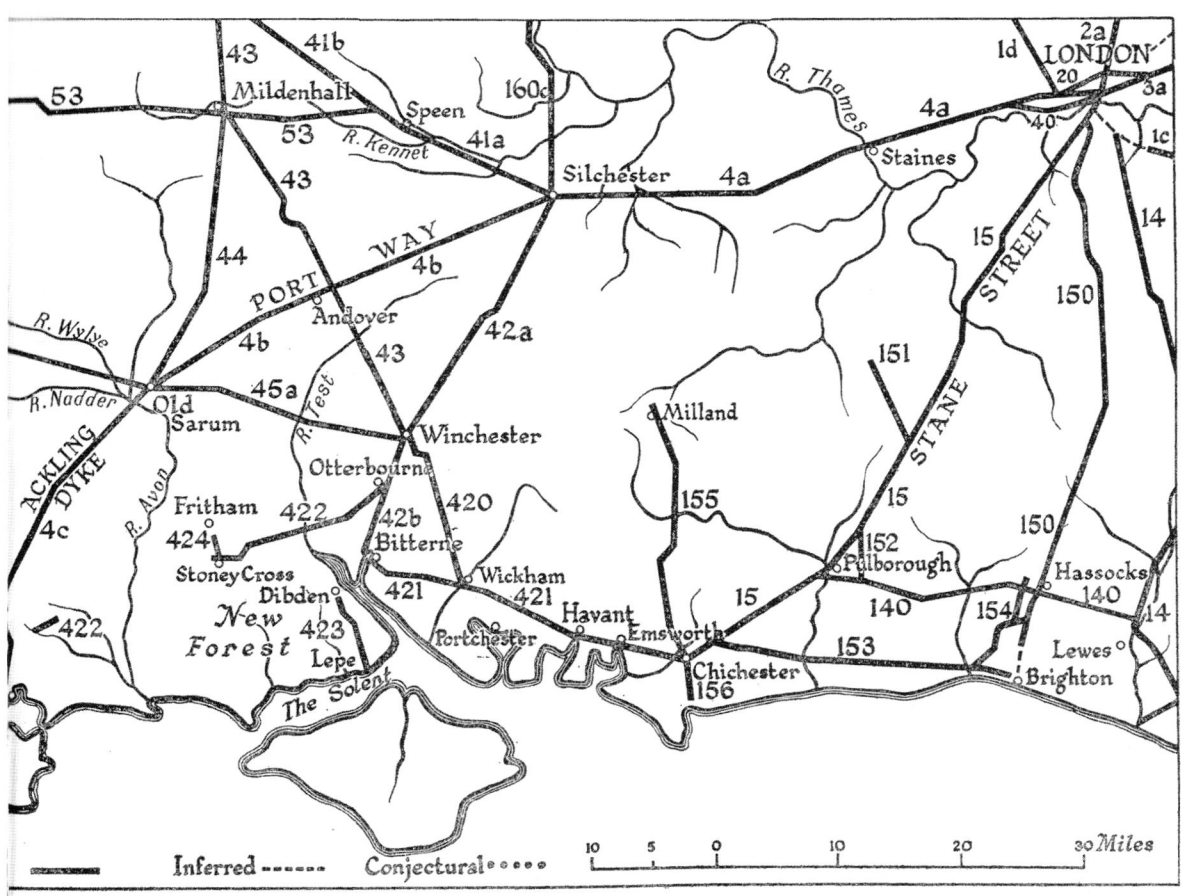

multiple time frames. Keith Briggs (2009, 44) has demonstrated that without rigorous statistical analysis we ought to be careful of how assured we are of any apparent positive correlations between certain place-names and Roman roads.

It is also clear that in some places Roman roads fell almost entirely out of use. O.G.S. Crawford's (1953, 67–73) study of the London to Bath Roman road demonstrated the complete abandonment of the Roman roads in favour of higher ground and river crossings better suited to fording than those crossing points determined by the trajectories of Roman roads. Although an absolute chronology for the abandonment of the Roman road remains elusive, elsewhere the early failure of all Roman *urbs* in an east–west belt through central southern England has been observed (Reynolds and Langlands 2006, 42). It therefore seems highly likely that the London to Bath Roman roads, via Silchester, fell out of use soon after the demise of the towns and cities they served.

Christopher Taylor's study of the local road network around Stamford illustrates how when the Roman bridge over the River Welland on Ermine Street fell out of use, a fording place further east was favoured and the course of the road subsequently diverted (1979, 97–101). A second shift however is observed further east to a bridging of the river at 'Danish Fort' (north of Welland) and 'English Fort' built by Edward the Elder in 918. Significantly, Taylor's case study illustrates parallels with that of Crawford, in that for Roman roads, the loss of a crossing point could impact upon the wider use of the road. Della Hooke observes a similar situation at Stratford-upon-Avon in her study of a route that runs parallel to the Roman road (1977, 214–215). Key places such as the ford itself, a pagan Saxon cemetery, and a site of Romano-British occupation are used to suggest an apparent shift away from an ancient route and crossing of the Avon to the course of the Roman road. However, the presence of a minster church and assembly place on the course of the ancient route might yet suggest a reversion to that thoroughfare in the mid-to-later Anglo-Saxon period.

Tim Tatton-Brown has observed that from the outset there was 'good evidence' to suggest that in the early Anglo-Saxon period, much of the Watling Street route through northern Kent was probably not used at all and that 'only in the late Anglo-Saxon period' did it once again become an overland route between Canterbury and London (2001, 121–122). However, when this route did come back into existence, few stretches respected the alignment of the original Roman road, which itself survived only as parish boundaries, hedgerows and local tracks. It was not until the building of the A2 in 1924, Tatton-Brown observes, that the line of the original course of the Roman road was once again taken up.

Analysis of excavation reports of Roman roads might help us to understand the variable histories many roads enjoyed. But without sophisticated scientific dating techniques, it is notoriously difficult to date road surfaces and to refine chronologies sufficiently to identify particular periods of use and abandonment. A good example of this is the Roman road from Silchester to Winchester in the location of East Stratton, which in the mid-1970s was subjected to analytical earthwork survey prior to a number of cuttings being made through the projected course (Fasham 1981). In one cutting, a phase of activity characterised by a humus and phosphate-rich dark soil overlay the first two phases of road construction that were believed to be of the Roman period. Thirty-seven sherds of pottery recovered from this 20 cm thick dark soil yielded a date range from the sixth to seventh century and this deposit was interpreted as a mid-Saxon occupation layer. 'Period 3', as it was designated, was in turn overlain by a layer of flint cobbles believed to correspond to a phase of 'late Saxon road building' (Fasham 1981, 167–172).

Whilst the evidence from Stratton Park suggests that the Roman road may have very naturally slipped into redundancy, the desire to restrict free movement along the course of Roman roads must be considered as evidence of their continued use. This is best illustrated by excavations undertaken at Bokerley Dyke where successive blockings and re-openings of the course of the Roman road from Old Sarum to Badbury Rings were in evidence from the fourth century and later (Eagles 1994, 17). The iconic network of straight Roman roads throughout Britain was clearly subject to variable conditions that impacted upon its survival. Even where a Roman road exists as an operating road in the landscape of today, the possibility must be entertained that it may have been brought back in to service, after a period of redundancy, by a later period of road construction and may not have enjoyed a continuous operational status from the first and second centuries through to the present.

Another problem with the tendency of early medieval scholars to use only the pattern of Roman roads to furnish their distribution maps is that as a consequence, the dense network of prehistoric routes that had serviced a blossoming economy in late Iron Age Britain are ignored. Where are these – the 'Romanised roads' – in Ivan Margery's maps? Roman road hunting can be, quite literally, a straightforward pursuit, but finding the Romanised roads, the late Iron Age routes that provided the warp through which the weft of later Roman roads passed is not so easy. As Richard Muir states: 'the straight roads of the textbooks were only the top status elements in a system that also included un-surfaced routes, winding tracks and pre-existing route ways' (2000, 100). Archaeological evidence suggests that the Romans were not the first to introduce sophisticated road-surfacing techniques to the British Isles. Very recently, thermoluminescent dating of sediments recovered from successive surfaces of a road excavated in Shropshire suggest that phases of gravel resurfacing and cobbling are dated to the late Iron Age. At 95% probability, the first phase of the Iron Age droveway falls in the period 200–205 cal BC, with the successive road constructions at 125 cal BC–cal AD 35, 110 cal BC–cal AD 70, and 105 cal BC–cal AD 105 for the final phase: *i.e.* an 82% probability, using Bayesian modelling, that this last event was also Iron Age rather than Roman (Malim and Hayes 2011). If the metalled surface of limestone fragments and quartzite pebbles recovered from a site at Yarnton, near Oxford, and dating to the Bronze Age is anything to go by, constructed road surfaces of prehistoric date may be far more ubiquitous than we have lead ourselves to believe (Denison 1998a).

In summary, these studies all illustrate that a much more critical perspective needs to be adopted on the issue of the survival and subsequent impact of the Roman road network in the early medieval period. Not only do we need to evaluate how the top tier of Roman roads were affected by the apparent collapse of the Romano-British infrastructure, but the degree to which a lower level of routes still functioned and the level at which local people had recourse to ridgeways for the purposes of long-distance movements, must also come under scrutiny. Ridgeways, or 'watersheds', by their very nature require much less maintenance and upkeep than the kerbed, gravelled and cobbled Roman roads that occupied the valley bottoms. As romantic and confused in its grasp of the chronology of British prehistory as Hippisley-Cox's *Green Roads of England* (1914) may be, it is a work that demonstrates a very simple premise that, irrespective of whether they served as corollaries of long-distance contact in prehistory, we must consider ridgeways and watersheds as viable alternatives to the dilapidating Roman roads of post-Roman age (Figure 2). What, then, was the travel and communication network – the physical means of moving around the landscape – that early medieval Wessex inherited from the Romano-British and prehistoric periods? Which elements of it fell redundant and which elements went on to impact upon the dynamics of emerging social and economic structures?

Medieval ways and paths

If the study of the early medieval road network of Wessex involves in the first instance establishing what can be brought forward from the prehistoric and Roman periods, the parallel challenge is that of attempting to project back from what emerges in the post-Conquest period in the network of medieval and early modern roads that can be found in cartographic sources such as the *Gough Map* (*c*. 1360), John Ogilby's *Britannia Atlas* (1675) and John Speed's county maps (1610/11). Stenton (1936) made extensive use of the *Gough Map* in his study of the character of the medieval road network and, by comparison to the network he identified for the thirteenth century onwards, he ultimately arrived at a quite disparaging view of Anglo-Saxon roads. Since, with regards to the post-Conquest road network, it is to Paul Hindle that our greatest debt is owed (1976; 1978; 1982a; 1982b). Through the 1970s and 1980s, his work on medieval roads established that a developed system of communications existed in much of lowland Britain from at least the thirteenth century onwards. Much of his work was derived from the analysis of early maps, used in conjunction with various documentary sources that enabled commentary on the processes of construction, condition and the maintenance of a hierarchy of both local and national route ways. There was clearly an expectation, on both the local level and amongst the ruling elites in the thirteenth and fourteenth centuries, for a standard of roads to serve not only the economic and social needs of the period but also, in the borderlands of Wales and Scotland, to support military campaigning and subjugation.

What elements we can take from this portrayal of a road network and retrospectively impose on the Anglo-Saxon period it is difficult to know. There does seem to be a consensus amongst some commentators that an earlier developed network of roads provided the foundations for this later medieval system. There are, however, few studies devoted specifically to early medieval roads. Hill's *Atlas of Anglo-Saxon England* reconstructed some of the major arterial route ways including the four royal roads (Figure 5) and a handful of other significant routes (Hill 1981, 115–116, fig. 199).

These included Della Hooke's network of ways servicing the Droitwich salt industry and an inset of Hampshire roads from F.R. Aldsworth's B.A. dissertation (Aldsworth 1973; Hooke 1977, 213; 1981c). If anything, this map serves better to illustrate how little was known, back in 1981, of the early medieval route networks throughout England. Four years later, David Pelteret (1985) set out the situation, highlighting our failure to consider the importance of understanding systems of travel and communication in the period whilst at

FIGURE 5 *(opposite)*. Major roads in Anglo-Saxon times (Hill 1981, 116, fig. 199).

1. *The landscape of routes and communications*   13

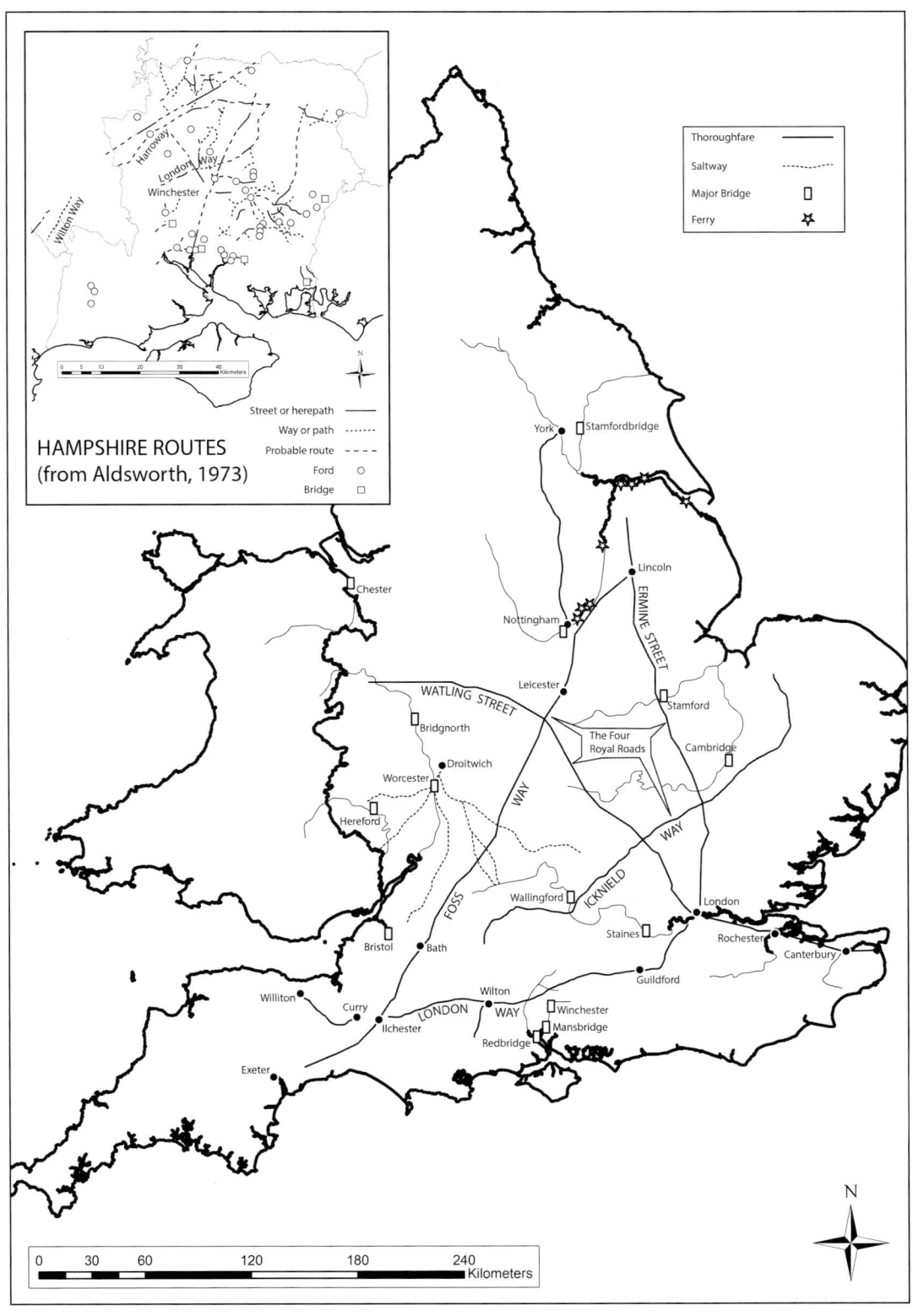

the same time, setting out profitable avenues of enquiry. Chiefly, references to the communications network in Anglo-Saxon charter boundary clauses, as used by Aldsworth, was prominent in his review acknowledging, in the process, the work of G.B. Grundy who dedicated many years to exploring and publishing the charter boundary clause evidence for the shires of Wessex. Grundy's first publications of this material were concerned with what he termed the 'Ancient road system' or 'Ancient highways and tracks' as described in the charter boundary evidence (1917; 1918; 1939a). In his second of three papers published on the subject, he offers a classification for the main types of roads and notes the various terms applied to them in Saxon times (1918, 70–72). To date, this stands as one of the best assessments of the nature of Anglo-Saxon communications in Wessex and many of Grundy's conclusions are broadly concurred with by later commentators. His comments are reprinted here in full:

A. Pre-Roman roads

(1) *Ridgeways*: They are really watershed ways; and in the case of the larger watersheds of this country, may be traced for miles through county after county. Their importance as lines of communication made their character well known to the Saxons, who usually called them by the name *Hrycgweg*. Even quite short stretches of ridgeway were called by this name. For example, the road from Faringdon to Wantage in Berkshire is only a watershed way for the first few miles out of Faringdon; but it is called *Hrycgweg* in a Berkshire charter.

But, as these ridgeways were mostly through-roads, the Saxons sometimes applied to them the more generic term Herepath, which means literally 'army way', but is obviously used in the modern sense of 'highway' or 'through-road'.

The ridgeway owes its genesis to the necessity of avoiding streams, which, even if small, would in the winter have quagmires in their neighbourhood, or deeply cut channels difficult of passage.

This leads to the second type of pre-Roman road.

(2) The *Summerway*. This type has not been recognised; but it is represented again and again among the present highways of the country. In the summer season the upper waters of streams, especially in the chalk districts, tend to run dry, and so during this season it was not necessary for the traveller to climb to the actual top of the ridge, for he could make his way unimpeded by quaggy ground along the lower slopes of it. Nearly every one of the great ridgeways has its accompanying summerway. The Saxons did not distinguish this as a special type of road; but, inasmuch as such roads were nearly always through-roads, they frequently applied the term Herepath to them.

B. Roads of the Romano-British age

(1) *Roman roads*. To these the Saxon nearly always applied the term *Straet*, 'street' or 'made road'. Not having the method or money to 'make'

roads himself, he was keen to notice the presence of 'making' in a road. Sometimes, though rarely, he may apply the term Herepath to them, as being through-roads.

It is, of course, known that, apart from the great Roman roads, there existed short stretches of vicinal way running from these roads to Villas. No instance occurs in the Hampshire, Berkshire or Wiltshire charters in which the term Straet may be suspected to be applied to such a way.

(2) *Romanised Roads.* These are really earlier roads in a modified form, *i.e.* ridgeways or summerways which have been 'made' in some way, either by both metalling and straightening, or by metalling only. Examples of straightening are to be found on the Icknield Way in Berkshire, on the same road in Oxfordshire, on a piece of road in Meon, Hampshire, and on a piece of road in Farnborough, Berkshire.

C. *Roads of Saxon age*

(1) The Saxon developed new through-tracks, to which the term Herepath, 'highway', is commonly applied.
(2) *Weg,* 'way', is a generic term which may be applied loosely to all kinds of roads, but is usually used of purely local roads, probably the tracks from the village to its outlying lands.

Grundy numbered the various routes he identified from the charters and described their course through the shires of Berkshire, Hampshire, Somerset and Wiltshire, and it is easy to see why, of all of the landscape phenomena described in charter boundary clauses, he went first to the theme of highways and tracks. In his introduction to his 1918 study of ancient highways he remarked how, 'It will be seen that the charters are sufficiently thickly distributed about the county [Wiltshire] for them to intercept at some point or other most of the main lines of communication' (1918, 70). He went on to say the same thing about the system in Hampshire: 'It is fortunate that the charters are distributed fairly evenly over the whole of the county area, because that renders it probable that they give information of some kind with regard to all the *main* lines of communication within the county' (1918, 175). This opportunity, clearly taken up by Aldsworth (1976), has most recently been pointed out by Oliver Rackham who identified that one in six of the features mentioned in English charter boundary clauses are concerned with communications (Rackham 1986, 259). A total of 1654 streets, ways and paths are mentioned, making up 11.6 per cent of all English boundary features and that these outnumber every other class of man-made landscape feature. What is more, references to fords and bridges make up a further 4.6 per cent of features.

Della Hooke went on to publish widely on Anglo-Saxon charter boundary clauses (reviewed in Chapter 4) but some of her first publications dealing with this material concerned the reconstruction of route ways in the West Midlands and more locally in the hinterland of Worcester (1977; 1980). Her later study of the Droitwich salt industry drew on the same evidence and here she demonstrated the significance of understanding the network of roads dedicated to serving what was an important industry of the time. The various 'salt' roads referred to in charters were clearly not mere byways but the major 'made-up' route ways of the day (1981c, 134). Already, from these studies it is clear that a complex hierarchy of routes existed in the Anglo-Saxon landscape and that charter boundary clauses could further comment on the function of some routes. Returning to Wessex, in a short piece on 'Communications' in a paper employing charters as evidence for settlement in the tenth century, Michael Costen develops the idea of three groupings of routes (1994, 104–106). The first category he describes consists of major routes that carried communications between significant political, religious and trade centres. The second category he suggests is comprised of local routes between central places and finally, a third category describes routes that link smaller dependent and tributary estates. A similar ranking of routes has been suggested by Andrew Reynolds who employs the useful device of letters 'A', 'B' and 'C' (broadly comparable to Costen's ranking) to indicate the relative hierarchy between routes in the early medieval landscape (Reynolds 2009b).

In Grundy's classification there are incidences when what he calls the 'generic' term herepath was applied to ridgeways, summerways and Roman roads but that the term, translated by him as 'army path', was most commonly applied to 'new' Saxon through-tracks. The term itself has divided opinion amongst scholars but has curiously, in view of its ubiquity in the charter boundary material, only recently garnered systematic analysis (Baker and Brookes 2013a, 143–149). Oliver Rackham seems to have gone furthest in attempting to quantify the evidence for herepaths and in the first instance has observed that the term occurs 221 times in the charters. He also observes that they rarely have proper names and that there is a regional difference in their distribution: 'In the Midlands, north-east England and Kent', he states, '*strǣt* is the commoner term and is used for almost all main roads. In Wessex and Devon most main roads were called *herepað*' (Rackham 1986, 259). The incidences where the term appears as a place-name further confirm their confinement to Wessex and the south-west Midlands (Baker and Brookes 2013a, 144).

On the term itself, although Margaret Gelling and Anne Cole simply see it as a West Saxon term for a 'main road' (Gelling and Cole 2000, 90), most commentators are in agreement that herepaths have some kind of role associated with military activity (see, for example, Hindle 2016, 37). Christopher Taylor favours a track employed primarily for military purposes but he also suggests a role in the governance of the realm in stating that they were so named because they were 'followed by government administrators travelling with armed escorts'. He observes a further characteristic of herepaths as enabling the wider populace to travel distances beyond the normal limits of local economic and social demand but warns against the 'dangers of linking up isolated occurrences of the name [herepath] and so producing spurious major route ways' (1979, 93). The herepath running through the late Anglo-Saxon residence at Yatesbury is considered by Andrew Reynolds to play 'a significant local role in civil defence' and he further observes that it was spurred into parts of the Roman road network that were still in use and that they comprised, along with beacons, a 'parallel means of communication' (1999, 93–94).

Justification for those interpretations which see the *here-* element associated with a defensive military force can be found in a set of laws dated to the immediate post-Conquest period (discussed in more detail below) within which we are told that 'the royal road should be wide enough for two ox carts to pass each other, and the drivers to touch their goads at full length, and for sixteen armed knights to ride side-by-side' (Downer 1972, ch. 10.2). The latter requirement led Rackham to put forward the possible definition of a herepath as being a path wide enough for an army (1986, 259). Yet, he goes on to observe that they, 'usually turn out to be ordinary roads without apparent military importance' and a further reflection of this is found, he believes, in the observation that when Latin terminology is used, *via publica*, 'possibly meaning a road maintained at public expense' is used in preference to the expected *via militaris*. On *here-*, therefore, we arrive at the position where the term denotes either roads of purposeful construction for military endeavours or the suitability of the roads or fords for the passage of an army (Brookes 2013, 49).

Alan Cooper draws attention to the consistency with which the word *here* is used in the Anglo-Saxon Chronicle to refer to the Viking armies and raiding bands and this justifies his translation of 'hostile-raiding-party path' (2002, 59). Cooper's discussion of Anglo-Saxon highway law is reviewed in more detail below but as part of his study he is keen to promote the idea that there was a suspicion and general distrust of strangers in the Anglo-Saxon period. He therefore attaches to the use of the term hostile connotations and urges against it implying a highway as something useful for the movement of armies for the common defence of the realm. 'On the contrary,' he says, 'it is a further indication of the fear with which the highway could be regarded'. This interpretation confirms his general observation made of attitudes to the highway whereby the term herepath 'is reminiscent of the distrust of strangers expressed in the law codes' (2002, 63).

That herepaths therefore represented the routes travelled by armies, and on the basis of the *here-* element, probably offensive armies, seems now to have become widely accepted along with a likely administrative function on the local level (Halsall 2003, 148, 222). However, a more detailed analysis of the network on the ground and in relation to other elements of the West Saxon landscape of civil defence puts this assumption to the test. John Baker and Stuart Brookes' study of the Kennet Valley and Avebury region represents the first concerted attempt to set out to analyse and interpret herepaths in a wider landscape context (Baker and Brookes 2011). Building on the work of Andrew Reynolds (1995; 1999, 93–94), they employ archaeological, historical (in the form of charter boundary clauses) and place-name evidence to reconstruct the pattern of communications in an area of north Wiltshire. To characterise the routes in this region, they carried out a friction surface test to model the suggested isotopic energetic costs of moving across different slopes. Elsewhere this method of 'least-cost' path analysis has been employed, in the context of military logistics, in the prediction of optimum communication routes through a landscape and whilst the results of such analysis are necessarily of a deterministic type, the independent data set that is created can be demonstrated to improve analytical and historical investigations (Bellavia 2006). Baker and Brookes' model found a negative correlation with those routes described as herepaths in the place-name and documentary record and this led them to observe that, in fact, herepaths appear to link together the natural or 'best-fit' paths rather than be themselves the optimum routes through a landscape. Alongside this, they observed that herepaths also provided the primary link between static defences in the region. The implication of their analysis was an interpretation of the term that, in contrast to Guy Halsall for example, implies that such routes were not the most likely/direct routes that a harrying army (*i.e.* a *here*) might adopt (Halsall 2003, 148, 222). Significantly, Baker and Brookes present, on a scale beyond Reynolds' study of the Yatesbury/Avebury herepath, the first key study to link the herepath network with a system of defensive forts allowing both to be analysed as dual characteristics of the same coherent system. This study prompted Baker and Brookes to conclude that, 'the use of *here* in the *Chronicle* to describe Viking hosts should not be seen as relevant to the meaning of herepath' and this therefore pulls the interpretation of the term back towards a definition wherein the *here-* element is seen as generically referring to armies of either a defensive or offensive character (Baker and Brookes 2013a, 256).

We are left then with a confusing and potentially unresolved enigma. It seems likely that a herepath was a fairly major road and that it played a role if not for a local militia then for hostile raiding parties or both. Of all our roads, however, the herepath alone stands out as a distinctly Anglo-Saxon (perhaps even more specifically West Saxon) creation notionally as well as physically. Grundy demonstrates how the notion of a herepath can overlay what might otherwise have been called a ridgeway, summerway or Roman road and alongside this primacy of the term when applied to existing routes, the possibility clearly exists for new roads to have been laid out in the period. It is reiterated here that despite the frequency with which the term is used in Anglo-Saxon charter boundaries, there has clearly been a failure to apply more scrutiny to these roads and the role they played over the region in which references to them are most numerous. Can, contrary to Taylor's views, their courses be traced for some distance? What character do they take in the landscape? How are they associated with other travel and communication features such as bridges, fords and gates? And perhaps most importantly, what types of settlement do herepaths connect – where do they actually run from and to?

Bridges and fords

Few structures in the landscape can be seen to alter so significantly the geography of movement and the flow of traffic than the construction of a bridge. The profound effect of medieval bridges and their impact on the societies and settlements of medieval Britain has been explored recently in two key studies (Harrison 2004; Cooper 2006). In both, the consensus is that the beginnings of the medieval bridge building programme can be found in the late Anglo-Saxon period. Alan Cooper writes: 'The conclusion to be drawn from the charter bounds, place-names and narrative evidence is that there were few bridges in England before the tenth century, and that the great period of the building of bridges at points previously un-bridged was between 900 and 1200' (2006, 15). This is a view broadly shared by David Harrison, and like Cooper he draws attention to records in Anglo-Saxon charters of the period to the obligation placed on estates to construct and repair bridges. This obligation is one of three, including service in the army and work on forts that has come to be known as the *Trinoda Necessitas* (Stevenson 1914). However, the frequency of the occurrence of this clause in ninth- and early tenth-century charters and the seeming lack of bridges prior to the mid-tenth century presents us with a curious paradox. There is an apparent delay between when the obligation to build bridges is reserved in charters and the first documentary references for bridges.

The relative increase in bridge numbers suggested by charters of the mid-tenth century seems to find corroboration in the fact that the terminology of the bridge obligation in the *Trinoda Necessitas* changes to reflect an emphasis on 'repair' rather than 'building' beyond the mid-tenth century (Cooper 2006, 10). Harrison is wary of the statistics borne out of the charter evidence and suggests that, as early bridges invariably only appear in one written source, more written sources might easily point us towards more bridges (2004, 27). An early to mid-eighth-century bridge recovered in excavations at Cromwell, alongside the Trent in Nottinghamshire, is an important reminder that a reliance on the surviving historical evidence is risky in the extreme (Salisbury 1995). The location of the bridge is not, as one might think, placed to serve a major highway but rather a spur road from the Fosse Way cutting back across the Trent, some five miles north of Newark, in the direction of the 'Great North Road' and a crossing of the River Maun at Ollerton.

There is undoubtedly a marked increase in charters from the ninth to the tenth centuries and this must be kept in mind when proffering any potential increase in bridges. Furthermore, it should be observed that boundary clauses get progressively more detailed during the tenth century and therefore present us with a risky bias. Harrison also draws attention to John Blair's work on Anglo-Saxon Oxfordshire where in a comparatively small but well documented study area numerous bridges are recorded crossing smaller streams and brooks (Blair 1994, 130–132; Harrison 2004, 27). Where Cooper and Harrison do agree, broadly speaking, is in the place-name evidence suggesting an increase, progressively, in 'bridge' elements against the number of 'ford' places and furthermore, Cooper observes that the term 'old ford' does not appear in a single set of bounds prior to 945 but appears in thirteen sets after that date (2006, 8–9). Ultimately it seems likely that as we move through the centuries of the early middle ages, in line with rising economic growth, more and more bridges are replacing fords as crossing points on rivers and streams. What seems in dispute is the chronology and pace of change.

Cooper puts the stimulus for this campaign of bridge building down to changes and developments in the wider landscape such as the alteration in river courses, speed of flow caused by programmes of drainage, embankments and other reclamation in the period. Woodland clearance would no doubt, he argues, have created a greater run off with mill races, mill ponds, weirs and dams all making fords unusable – or at least less reliable (2006, 18, although see p. 25 for how weirs may have actually formed part of composite river-crossing and mill structures). We should also, however, consider the financial benefits of building bridges and, despite some of the effects on the landscape stressed by Cooper, even in the best of conditions, fording rivers was never without risk. If we do see a rise in economic activity in the late Anglo-Saxon period in Wessex, we must surely anticipate an increase in traffic reliant on carting, which in turn would impact upon the continued viability of using fords for crossing rivers. Put simply, if the economy of early medieval England was to experience any form of growth, it needed to know that produce, goods and commodities could move freely between markets without fear of both seasonal and non-seasonal weather conditions determining which rivers were and were not traversable. David Harrison suggests that an increase in prosperity was one of the major factors behind the programme of bridge building in the medieval period that, from both his and Cooper's numbers, would seem to have started in the pre-Conquest period (1992; 2004, 2).

The character and function of the bridges described in this period of bridge-building defined by Cooper and Harrison requires some analysis. Until recently, the greater emphasis in the study of military obligations has been placed on the requirement to build forts and towards the defensive character of the bridges that might be associated with such structures. Nicholas Brooks' in-depth study of Rochester Bridge found clear evidence that different estates and administrative areas (socio-political units) were responsible for different sections of the bridge (1994; reprinted in 2000b). This study was to confirm a view extolled in his seminal work on military obligations where he was drawn to the conclusion that fort and bridge should be seen as a 'single military unit' (1971, 71–72). Much therefore has been made of the connection between bridges and forts and how the two were part of the same strategy and a scheme of defence implemented by Alfred (and possibly earlier in Mercia by Offa) to ward off the threat posed by the Vikings (Brooks 1964; Haslam 1987; Hill and Rumble 1996). Certainly, Charles the Bald met with a degree of success when implementing this strategy in Francia in the 860s and this may have influenced Alfred's adoption of the policy (Hassall and Hill 1970). David Harrison draws attention to possible Alfredian examples of fort and bridge at Wareham, Exeter, in the Anglo-Saxon Chronicle's record of the events on the River Lea, and Asser's account of the bridge connecting two fortresses built at Athelney (2004, 41). A similar scenario is described in the

Anglo-Saxon Chronicle for Edward the Elder's capture of Nottingham from the Danes when, in 920, he is recorded as building a stronghold to the south of the river and a bridge between it and the existing town (Swanton 1996, 104). As discussed earlier at Stamford, forts either side of the River Welland would have served the same purpose in 918, and such a design is envisaged for both London Bridge and at Bristol in the eleventh century (Watson 2001; Leech 2009). So, when bridge-work is being referred to as an obligation in Anglo-Saxon charters it has overwhelmingly been associated with large defensive structures over major navigable rivers and in conjunction with forts.

Archaeological evidence, however, conflicts with the idea that the bridges referred to in the *Trinoda Necessitas* are of the 'double-burh'/'bridgehead' type. John Baker and Stuart Brookes note that with the exception of Rochester, 'there is no *archaeological* [my italics] support in England before the late tenth century for a model of deliberate construction of strongholds and bridges, sited to stop movement up-river and to hinder advances along major waterways' (2013a, 109–110). It is in the mid-ninth century that the first genuine Wessex charters including military obligations appear (Brooks 1971, 81). So, if bridge-work is not referring to large defensive bridgeheads which don't apparently appear in the historical and archaeological record for the best part of another seventy years, what kind of work is it referring to? The excavation of a landmark

FIGURE 6. The causeway and bridge across the Wylye valley between Stoford ('stone ford') and Great Wishford (see Study Area 8.1, SU03NE).

recorded in the boundary clauses of charters granting land at Ducklington and Witney (Oxon.) may give some indication as to what this form of bridge-work entailed (S 678, S 771, Blair and Millard 1992). The landmark in question is referred to as a *stanford* in the Ducklington charter of 958 and because the same landmark is referred to as a *stan bricge* in the later Witney charter of 969, it might reasonably be concluded that between these dates a bridge was built to replace the ford. However, excavations revealed a stone-paved surface linking a rubble-built causeway across what was once a much wider streambed. This led the excavators to conclude that in this instance the term 'bridge' and 'ford' were synonymous and the interchangeability of the words in the epic poem *The Battle of Maldon* (in lines 74 and 88) is cited as supporting evidence (Blair and Millard 1992, 348). In a broadly reliable charter of 944 recording King Edmund's grant of land in Northamptonshire to Ælfic, Bishop of Ramsbury, a *stan bricgge* has been confidently identified with a location which has no obvious credentials as a major thoroughfare (S 495; Keays-Young 1930, 274, 279).

Localised case studies may, therefore, have much to offer in terms of both identifying and characterising early medieval river-crossings and the impact they had on the wider landscape of rural and urban development. By closer analysis of bridges referred to in both charters and place-names in relation to the route networks they were part of, it should be possible to cast more light on the purported phases of bridge-building identified by Harrison and Cooper.

Waterways and water transport

In the 1990s, a series of papers debated the extent and functionality of the medieval inland waterways network, its interconnectivity with the medieval road network and the subsequent contribution it made to the economy of the thirteenth and fourteenth centuries (Edwards and Hindle 1991; 1993; Langdon 1993; Jones 2000). A key area of analysis was the role that navigable rivers played in the growth of an integrated transport network to serve a rise in medieval towns from the fifty or so recorded in Domesday Book to the 500 to 600 in existence in the early fourteenth century (Edwards and Hindle 1991, 123). The conclusions drawn from this initial study, the full extent of inland waterway transportation and the degree to which it contributed to economic growth in the twelfth to fifteenth centuries was thought by John Langdon to have been overstated (1993, 1) and, off the back of a robust defence of the original study, a conciliatory tone was adopted that acknowledged that the use of different sources ultimately lead to the differing theories presented by both parties (Edwards and Hindle 1993, 14). Nonetheless, the impression given from this debate, alongside a further review of the source material, is one very much of a long-term decline in water transport over the wider medieval period (Jones 2000).

The implications of this are that, at an earlier stage, the waterways of England enjoyed a 'heyday' when 'there had been more incentive to invest in water' (Blair 2007a, 1). From a series of more recent landscape studies of wetlands

1. The landscape of routes and communications 23

and river passages throughout England, it has become increasingly apparent that vast engineering works were well within the capabilities of early medieval institutions. In John Blair's introduction to the *Waterways and Canal Building in Medieval England* (2007) two maps of England are compiled from a range of data used by scholars contributing to the book. The first depicted place-name elements for waterways set against twelfth- and thirteenth-century purveyance account loads, coin loss during the period 950 to 1180 and selected Roman roads (Blair 2007a, 16, fig. 4). The second represented a speculative attempt to interpret the data (Figure 7).

The conclusion to be drawn from these maps is that whilst navigable rivers and known watercourses appear to service the hinterlands of major rivers such as the Thames, the Severn and the Wash, Wessex seems not to have been similarly penetrated inland by navigable rivers. The Itchen is depicted as navigable only as far as Winchester and the Avon, not necessarily even as

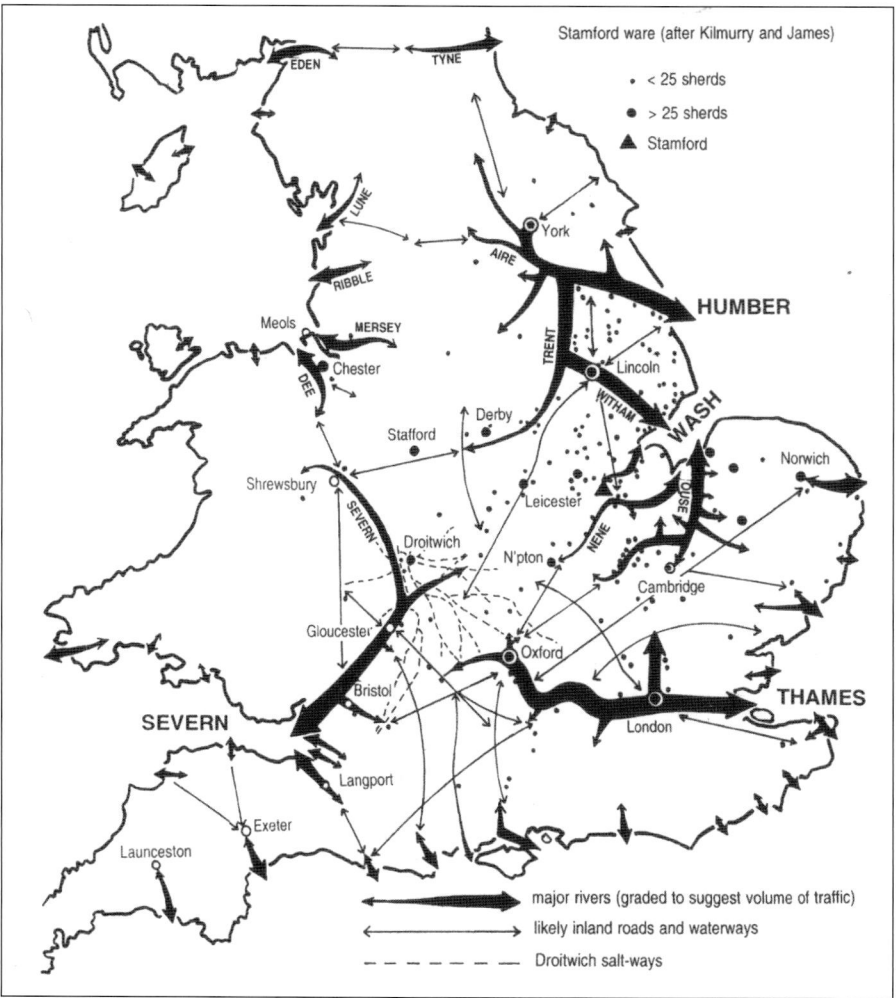

FIGURE 7. Water transport in medieval England (Blair 2007, 18, fig. 5).

far as Old Sarum, whilst the River Frome does not extend beyond Wareham. Further evidence for the lack of activity on Wessex's rivers comes from the analysis of certain place-names associated with water transport. Anne Cole's paper in the same volume looks at the evidence for water transport in the pre-Conquest period through the distribution of *port*, *hȳð*, *ēa-tun*, *lād* and *stæð* elements and in particular the Thames stands out as a major arterial waterway along with those of eastern England (2007, 83, fig. 19). For Wessex, a complete lack of *hȳð*s away from the coast and into the chalkland areas is thought to indicate the seasonal nature of rivers over this geology (Cole 2007, 84), a fact that prompts us to question the importance of waterborne transport to the economic development of the area.

The limited geographical range of Wessex's navigable waterways has therefore impacted upon the extent to which this study has explored the role of river communications and their influence on the wider landscape. Only two study areas were selected from coastal zones (South Hams in Devon and the Isle of Purbeck in Dorset) and for the most part, the focus has been on inland areas beyond the reach of the navigable rivers identified by Blair. This review will therefore restrict itself to considering Christopher Currie's identification of an early medieval watercourse on the Itchen (Hants.) and the limited charter boundary clause evidence for similar structures and arrangements of water transport in the region. It will also consider briefly how the lack of navigable waterways in the Wessex region might have impacted upon the distribution of wealth throughout the kingdom in the middle Anglo-Saxon period and how processes of landscape change in the later Saxon period may further have blighted the viability of river transportation throughout the region. Ultimately, if water transport was geographically limited in Wessex from the outset, irrespective of further hindrances, developments in overland transport might be more identifiable and may well be seen to have played a more vital role in the growth of the economy in later Anglo-Saxon southern England.

First identified in an analysis of the landscape evolution of the south-central Hampshire Basin and subsequently discussed in two papers, Christopher Currie employed evidence from charter boundary clauses and field survey to identify a possible canal cut to improve navigation up the River Itchen in the direction of Winchester (1994, 112–113; 1997; 2007). Two sets of charters survive for an estate at South Stoneham dating to 990 × 992 and 1045 (S 944, S 1012). In the boundary clause of the later charter, a reference is made to a *niwan ea* (a new river), a boundary mark that does not feature in the boundary clause of the earlier charter. Currie took this to suggest that an alteration was made to the course of the Itchen between the granting of the two charters and he uses map regression and landscape analysis to identify a man-made channel cut between two mills. The suggestion from Currie's findings is that navigation at least as far as Bishopstoke (from where cargoes could have been moved onto Winchester by road) was being either maintained or inaugurated at this point and a tentative link is made between this undertaking and the migration of functions upstream to Winchester from the declining settlement at *Hamwic* (Morton 1992, 75; Currie 2007, 251).

A similar reference can be observed in the charter boundary clause for Romsey (dated 967 × 975) suggesting an alteration of the course of the River Test (S 812). Here it is not a new river that is being referred to but rather an old one as the boundary is recorded as running, 'From hunter's island into the old Test (*alde tersten)*, along the old Test (*ealde terste*) until it comes to the street where the Test (*þurstan*) runs'. Analysis of the landscape around Romsey in a bid to identify where the 'old Test' runs in relation to the present course, may go some way to determine its character and function. But in both the Romsey and South Stoneham cases, it may be that navigation further upstream is a concern of canal builders and this is suggested by instances of the term *stæð* that appear in charter boundary clauses for estates granted up-river. Currie observes the reference to a *stæð* that appears in the charter for Bishopstoke dated to 960 (S 683). Although there is some suggestion that at this date, this element meant 'bank' or 'shore', the preferred interpretation amongst place-name scholars is 'landing-place' (Smith 1956 (reprinted 2008), 142; Mills 1991, 305; Gelling and Cole 2000). A complicated arrangement of water management consisting of two *stæð*s, a 'beam weir' and two fords is referred to in a charter for St Mary Bourne and Hurstbourne Priors (S 359), where the boundary is recorded as running 'out to the Test to the southern *stæð*, then along the *stæð* that is beneath the beam weir to the northern *stæð*, along the *stæð* back to the two fords'. Such an arrangement suggests a degree of construction – not least if we see fords, in Blair and Millard's (1992) view, as constructed causeways – and this all occurs at the confluence of the Bourne Rivulet and the River Test, upstream of Romsey's 'old Test' (Map 1.2, SU44NW). Other examples of *stæð*s appear in the Wessex study area where the *æfene stæþe* is found on the Wiltshire Avon (S 348), a *noddre stape* is recorded near Wilton on the River Nadder (S 438, S 493) and a *pilig stæþ* is recorded on the River Wylye (S 469).

Another option for exploring early medieval river navigation in Wessex, as with the road network, is to work forward from what is known archaeologically from earlier periods. Drawing attention to Andrew Sherratt's map of major navigable waterways of late Prehistory, Blair suggests that the 'size and shape' of early medieval riverine transport may have more in common with the main arterial waterways of a *longue durée* from the late Iron Age onwards (Sherratt 1996, 212–213; Blair 2007a, 13; and for an eighteenth-century map of navigable waterways see also: Armstrong 1989, 97). In Sherratt's map, the rivers of Wessex are not seen to penetrate much beyond the coastal fringe with the exception of the Hampshire and Wiltshire Avon, which, he suggests, was navigable as far as the Amesbury area. Ben Palmer redraws this prehistoric network of rivers for the purposes of his analysis of the hinterland of *Hamwic* in the middle Anglo-Saxon period (Palmer 2003, 52). He argues that the lack of waterway transport in the region was, in part, responsible for the lack of sites producing metalwork and coin finds of the seventh and eighth centuries (discussed below) (Blackburn 2003, 35–36; Palmer 2003, 52, 58).

26 *Alexander Langlands*

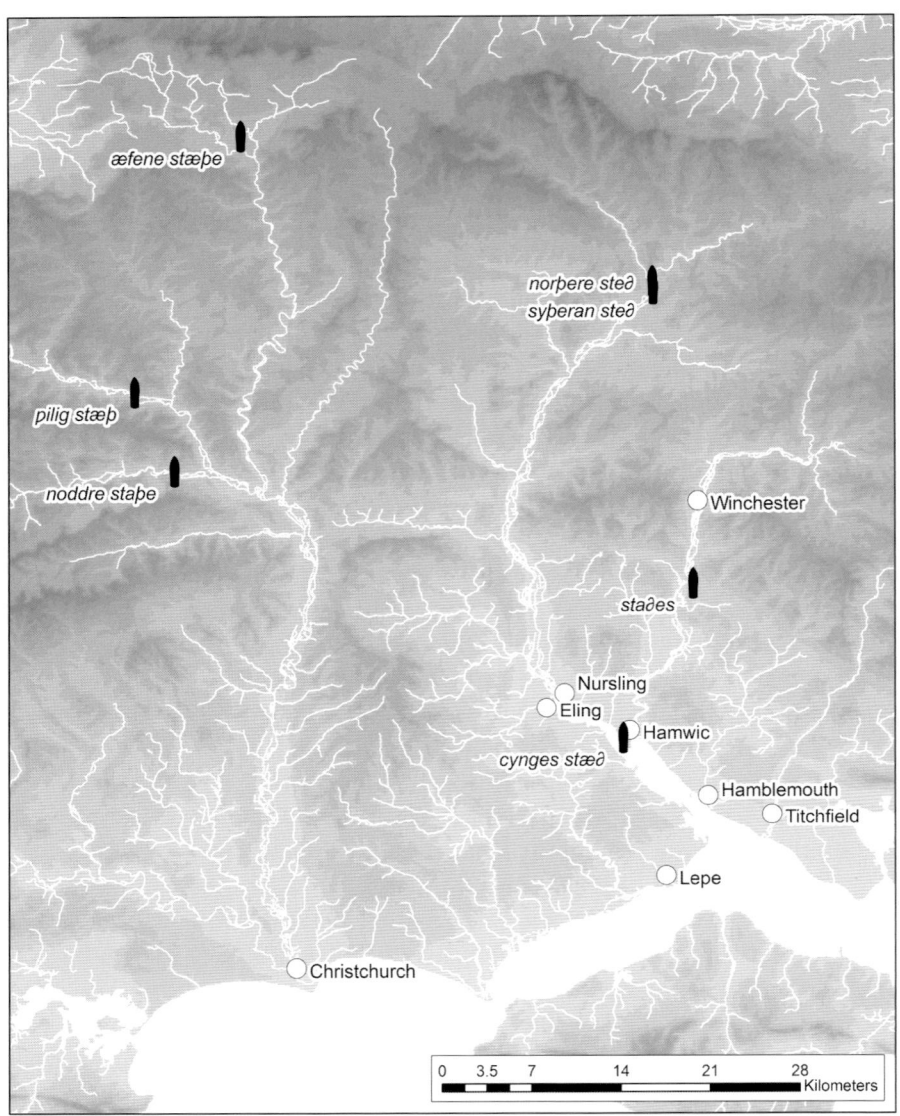

FIGURE 8. Middle Anglo-Saxon trading sites and landing places recorded in tenth-century charters.

A key question that arises out of the Wessex evidence is what we consider 'navigable' to mean. There can be no doubt that floating bulk goods down river was inordinately easier than attempting to pilot the same goods up river and we therefore have to envisage a situation where voluminous and potentially heavy goods (bulk items) are moving primarily in one direction; being floated down stream to commercial centres in coastal locations for redistribution and consumption. It may very well have been the case that the load capacity of river vessels meant that only when they were empty could they be successfully hauled, rowed or sailed upstream. Anecdotal evidence of the relative time taken to navigate up and down river is provided by Albert Leighton who observed that flatboats took 2–5 days to float down the Rhône from Lyon to Avignon but took almost a month to return needing several animals to tow (1972, 126). Norbert Ohler draws attention to Frederik Barbarossa's (1152 × 1190) attempt to foster trade along the course of the Rhine where in a law code it states, 'no one should hinder the merchants who travel up the Rhine or who pull a tow rope along the bank, which is acknowledged to be the King's Highway, on the pretext of demanding a toll or in any other way' (1989, 36). Returning to the 1990s debate on later medieval water transport, Langdon considered that a system dependent on hauling empty vessels upstream on the river Thames could not be seen as an economically viable proposition (1993, 6). Whilst no attempts have been made to identify towpaths in early medieval Wessex, Christopher Currie did observe a path (designated a 'pathway' in a tithe map and award for South Stoneham) alongside the artificial water channel at Stoneham that he thought might possibly represent the remnants of one (2007, 249). Many more such paths may have existed alongside short sections of adapted and constructed watercourses and it stands to reason that in the process of excavating a large channel, up-cast riverine deposits might feasibly be used to create a corresponding bank. Early medieval polities clearly had the administrative networks and ambitions to take on really rather large engineering projects (Squatriti 2002) but, Currie's observations aside, positing this level of watercourse management for Wessex in the eighth to tenth centuries would be dependent only upon the results of specialised field investigations.

What complicates the issue further is the growing evidence for a whole range of other industries that were making use of waterpower in early medieval England and the possibility that many would come into direct competition with those using rivers for transport (Hooke 2007). Alongside the documentary references, there is growing archaeological evidence in support of watermills from as early as the seventh century on sites throughout England (Wilson and Hurst 1958, 183–185; Hinton 1992, 258–259; Rahtz and Meeson 1992; Jackson 2000; Buss 2002; S 25). Six thousand and eighty two mills are recorded in Domesday Book but because the survey is incomplete, John Langdon and Martin Watts have argued that this figure should be much higher (Darby 1977, 272, appendix 14 at 361; Langdon 2004, 9; Watts 2006, 7; and see Crossley 1997, 115, who suggests that 5,624 mills are indicated in Domesday Book). The view from the editor and various contributors to *Waterways and Canal Building in Medieval England* is positive in the sense that despite the growing number of mills and the increasingly sophisticated and ubiquitous fisheries of the period, it was, in Della Hooke's words, 'unlikely that enormous problems were created for shipping' (2007, 53–54). Blair suggests too that, providing the incentives were there, we should expect human effort to overcome the physical obstacles provided by changes in river conditions (2007b, 255). Of the later medieval rivers of the Humber Estuary, Edwards and Hindle see the numerous inquisitions relating to the obstructions and complaints about hindrances to navigation as evidence of their continuing importance and the many examples of man-made watercourses discussed in *Waterways and Canal Building* are surely evidence of the value placed on waterborne transport (Edwards and Hindle 1991, 126).

Yet, is it the case that the demise of inland water transport identified in the post-Conquest period might actually have started, as part of a longer-term process, in the early medieval period and are not the canal-building endeavours described in *Waterways and Canal Building* also a reflection of increasing problems? Other factors may well have taken their toll on the viability of water transport in England and the effects of economic development on the environment and in particular the intensification of agricultural production from the ninth to the thirteenth centuries (together termed 'the second landscape Evolution') might very well have had an impact (Taylor 1988b, 42; 1988a, 67). In the late ninth and tenth centuries, for example, the middle section of the Thames valley exhibits increasing evidence for alluviation, silting and sedimentation, a clear indication of an increased level of arable cultivation (Robinson 1992; Robinson and Wilkinson 2003, 79–81). Deforestation can also be seen as a major contributor to soil erosion and there is a broad consensus that the period spanning the ninth to thirteenth centuries was also characterised by a phase of woodland clearance (Darby 1956, 190–192). Although Rackham writes that Anglo-Saxons, in the course of 600 years did not 'radically reorganise the wooded landscape', he does suggest that woodland shrank from 15 per cent in 1086 to perhaps 10 per cent by 1350 (1997, 84, 88).

In summary, it is clear that Wessex's rivers never really enjoyed the same level of navigability as the Thames, the Severn and those in eastern England. Even if we adopt the least conservative view that the Itchen was navigable as far as Winchester, and the Avon as far as Amesbury, goods seem likely to have been moving only in one direction – towards the coast. As will be illustrated in Chapter 3, it may be that the locations of Christchurch, *Hamwic* and the *mercatorium* located at Hamblemouth are a result of this pattern and we must therefore envisage, with the growth of the economy in the tenth and eleventh centuries and the rising wealth on inland sites, a shift in how and where goods were being moved about the landscape. It is therefore re-iterated that because of the existing limitations in water transport in Wessex, developments in overland transport might be more identifiable and may well be seen to have played a more vital role than they did elsewhere in the growth of the economy in later Anglo-Saxon southern England.

CHAPTER TWO

Travellers and journeys

Rad byþ on recyde   rinca gehwylcum
Sefte, and swiþhwæt   ðam ðe sitteþ
Onufan meare mægenheardum   ofer milpaþas

Riding, in the hall, for each person,
Is sweet, yet severe for him that sits
Upon a sturdy mare over miles-long pathways
Old English Rune Poem (translated in Griffiths 1996, 206)

The following chapter, through the analysis of existing research and scholarship, will profile the range of journeys and the types of travellers that would have moved through the landscape of early medieval Wessex. As the *Old English Rune Poem* states, travelling was arduous and not to be undertaken lightly, but the opportunities for advancement, knowledge and worldly experience made it an important and rewarding endeavour. Reviewing this material is important because it can serve as a useful way to frame the manoeuvres, journeying and itineraries of agencies and actors, and force us to consider how the landscape was constituted to accommodate them. How in practice were these journeys committed and how was the landscape altered and inscribed to create a conceptual geography in the minds of the medieval traveller?

Pilgrimages

Pilgrims represent the most renowned group of medieval travellers and many of the stories associated with the lives and miracles of the saints, and the pilgrims who journeyed long distances to worship at their shrines, provide us with colourful insights into life on the road. There is a degree of sophistication suggested by the account of the pilgrimage to Jerusalem made by Willibald and his company in the eighth century, where ship travel, tolls, customs and fares are all mentioned. Early missionaries enjoyed a high level of mobility and individuals like Boniface were known to have travelled at least on three occasions to Rome, a popular destination for pilgrimages of the seventh and eighth centuries (Talbot 1954). It is clear that Ceolfrith set about making extensive preparations for his journey to Rome, including hiring a ship, collecting gifts and having good letters of introduction (Wood 1995, 15). All of these examples suggest that, in the early days, such pilgrimages required the very highest levels of affluence and influence in order to be successfully undertaken.

For the later Anglo-Saxon period, however, we witness the rise in popular pilgrimages and a growing culture of saint worship amongst the lower orders of the social hierarchy (Rollason 1989, 187). The *Translatio et Miracula S. Swithuni*, for example, provides us with a fascinating insight into life on the road in Anglo-Saxon Wessex for a range of individuals from varying backgrounds. The document is a record of the miracles performed posthumously by St Swithun in the later tenth century (Lapidge 2003, 217–331). St Swithun's relics were translated from a tomb outside the west door to the chancel on 15th July 971 and Lantfred's account is thought to have been written a short while afterwards. The *Translatio et Miracula S. Swithuni* describes aspects of journeys made to Winchester from near and far. For the most part travellers are the infirm, the visually impaired or the physically disabled journeying to the tomb of St Swithun in search of a miracle cure. The emphasis of the work is very much on the role of St Swithun and each chapter is rhetorically loaded to persuasively elaborate on the power of the English saint as a force for righteousness and the restoration of health. In some aspects, therefore, the document is problematic, as the focus is not necessarily on providing accurate accounts of the exact nature of each journey.

Lantfred's account is, however, useful in illustrating the varied provenances of people journeying to visit Winchester in the tenth century. Locally, we are told of people travelling from the province of 'Ham' (Hampshire), Collingbourne (Wilts.) and the Isle of Wight. Yet, further afield individuals and groups were travelling from Bedfordshire, London, Rochester, *Hunum* (? Huntingdonshire), 'far away areas to the west' and 'various regions of England'. In one account a thief awaiting the death penalty in France hears of St Swithun's miracles through merchants who were crossing the Channel (Lapidge 2003, 323). St Swithun was clearly beginning to have a European-wide draw and it is evident that the roads in and out of the city of Winchester would have been well trodden by the feet of pilgrims seeking out the tomb of the popular saint. Of particular interest in the *Translatio et Miracula S. Swithuni* is the frequent mention of guides, particularly young boys, for the blind and infirm. Clearly, those that could not see would have been in need of help in finding their way through the landscape of Wessex to the city of Winchester. In one instance, three blind women travelling from the Isle of Wight are furnished by their lord with a mute man of 'about 20 years of age' who leads them to Winchester 'by a winding road' (Lapidge 2003, 289). Another story is especially insightful for our purposes when we are told that a blind woman and her mute female companion travelled together from 'far away areas to the west' and whilst the mute one guided the blind one, the latter 'asked directions of passers-by for her guide' (Lapidge 2003, 305). It is tantalising to think of what directions were verbally conveyed and the kinds of landmarks that were being listed *en route* to the holy site. One story gives an insight into the types of monuments that may have marked out such a journey. In it, a blind man is guided by a young boy, both from a remote part of England and, we are told by Lantfred, they rest at a large stone cross some three miles out of Winchester (Lapidge 2003, 318). In this final incident we are invited to consider the types of monuments and signs that will have been used to inscribe a landscape and to communicate with travellers local and foreign.

Clerics and the mobility of the church

Whilst the popularity of pilgrimages was growing, there continued the need for members of the church to travel so that it could maintain its influence in the wider world and administer care to its people. Pastoral care carried out in the Anglo-Saxon period – particularly during the period within which the minster system predominated – consisted of members or groups of secular clergy travelling from a central church throughout large, expansive minster *parochia* carrying out such duties as preaching, performing baptisms, celebrating mass, prescribing penance and caring for the sick – duties that would require them to travel regularly and to lesser and perhaps isolated settlements (Thacker 1992). In return though, parishioners would be required to visit the places of worship to receive basic religious rites. Not all of the emerging manorial parish churches of the tenth and eleventh centuries would have had graveyards, as is clear from the laws of Edgar which stipulate that tithes should be paid according to whether or not a thegn's church had a graveyard (Robertson 1925; Blair 1985, 119; 1988b, 57; Morris 1989, 228). It is therefore important to consider the network of roads that would have served local and minster churches and the very real need to deliver recently deceased family members to burial grounds and newly born babies to baptismal fonts.

Such were the concerns at the very local level for ensuring safe passage to and from lesser religious centres but for the bishops and abbots of cathedral and monastic foundations, a different range of travelling issues existed. Bishops and archbishops with important roles in the affairs of the state travelled, probably with considerable retinues, to attend council meetings and are attested in the witness lists of charters issued at such events (Keynes 2002). Catherine Cubitt has assembled a list of church councils for the period 650 to 850 with not only dates and locations of where the meetings were held but also a discussion on attendees (Cubitt 1995, 22–23, 297–321). Her work clearly indicates that the Christian church in Anglo-Saxon England was dependent on individuals and groups from institutions throughout Britain journeying, on occasions, considerable distances to carry out their work. Religious and institutional travellers of this nature must therefore have represented a significant, if not the most adept, group of travellers in Anglo-Saxon England. If disease was 'one of the most influential medieval travellers', it says something of the mobility of the monks, clerics and other church offices that they were the most susceptible to epidemics (Leighton 1972, 46).

How can this level of movement on the part of institutions whose effectiveness was dependent on travelling have influenced the pattern of routes in the landscape, and furthermore, is that influence detectable? A charter from the early ninth century gives us an insight into how such retinues may have provided for themselves whilst on the road. Bishop Ealmund of Winchester granted an estate at Farnham, Surrey, to Brihthelm in exchange for four estates in Wiltshire but retained the right to two nights of hospitality in Farnham each year (S 1263). Farnham is located at approximately the half-way point on the road, via Alresford and Alton, from Winchester to London and it is likely that this charter reflects the needs of the bishop to enjoy secure and fitting hospitality whilst on business to London. That the entertainment of a Bishop and his retinue could be an onerous commitment is suggested by a charter purporting to date from the reign of King Ine (688 × 726) but likely to be a later forgery, possibly of the twelfth century (S 250; Finberg 1964, 113–114; Abrams 1996, 46, 128). The charter grants a range of privileges to the Abbey at Glastonbury and amongst the many obligations of which the Abbey was to be free was the uninvited visitation of the bishop who, when he had been invited, was to limit his retinue to three or four men and stay in one of only two lodgings in *Poelt* (Pilton). Although in essence a spurious charter, it seems likely that it represents the desires, at the very least, of the forgers who themselves had an aversion to overbearing hospitality demands being placed on them.

The distributions of apparently isolated and remote estates belonging to large ecclesiastical foundations has been used in some instances to reconstruct the pattern of communications and the likely routes employed by bishops as they attended councils and synods throughout the kingdom and administered within their own dioceses. It seems likely that an importance was placed by the bishops of Lindisfarne on the acquisition of properties connecting to the Roman road network so that easier access and overnight accommodation would be provided for journeys to the episcopal centre of the shire (Cambridge 1989, 380–384). A similar scenario is observed in Kent where the archbishop of Canterbury obtained various properties that would have enabled movement throughout Kent but also along the Thames Estuary coastline to conduct business in London (Brooks 1984, 101, 106–107, 129–131, 144, 233, 284).

For the West Midlands, the evidence for 'way-stations', in the form of estates held in the ownership of the bishops of Worcester, allows for the reconstruction of the likely routes by which the bishop and his retinue would travel to conduct business in London (Barrow 2012, 557–559). A particular group of properties under the ownership of the church of Hereford goes even further in illustrating that the changing values of such places over time can indicate changes in journey patterns (Barrow 2012, 559–565). In Wessex, the Domesday properties of the bishops of Winchester at Downton (Wilts.), Fonthill (Wilts.) and Rimpton (Som.) serve as a chain of estates that would have facilitated journeys from Hampshire towards the large episcopal estate at Taunton (Barrow 2012, 553, footnote 23). Whilst there can be no doubt that the acquisition of these properties provided sumptuous accommodation for a bishop on the road and out ministering to his flock, the motivation for their purchase may have lain just as much in the ability to move produce derived from different ecological zones widely and securely over a landscape, all under the auspices of the one institution. In some ways, the string of properties from Winchester to Taunton also served as a self-supporting network of estates where specialised produce moving from the wetlands of Somerset could be, *en route* to the estate centre at Winchester, distributed amongst other properties from which other specialised produce could be collected. A similar situation might be envisaged for the Worcester 'way-stations' where produce brought into London from the continent, recorded as remitted from tolls in the eighth century S 98, could be moved (and distributed) securely from way-station to way-station *en route* to Worcester. Such 'way-stations' therefore also have the capacity to enable us to reconstruct a certain type of trade route – one that reflects the internal economy of monastic houses and large ecclesiastic institutions.

Both the *Regularis Concordia* and the *Benedictine Rule* detail the correct conduct of monks should they gain permission to travel. Colourful insights are provided on the reservations churchmen had in letting clergy travel far from the sanctuary of the monastic compound. For example, in the *Regularis Concordia*, a rule of the tenth-century Benedictine reform movement, it is stipulated that travelling bishops were not to take in their retinue youths but rather 'grown-up persons from whose conversation they may take profit' (Symons 1953, 7, ch. II). Monks too were not permitted to travel without permission, for experience of the secular world was clearly deemed to have a negative effect on the wider monastic community:

> When brethren return from a journey, let them on the day they return, at the end of each canonical Hour of the Work of God, lie prostrate on the floor of the oratory and ask the prayers of all on account of any faults that may have surprised them on the road, by the seeing or hearing of something evil, or by idle talk. Nor let anyone presume to tell another what he has seen or heard outside the monastery, because this causes great harm. (McCann 1952, 153–154, ch. 67)

Clearly, those churchmen travelling between the way-stations and to synods and councils beyond were subject to a set of strict guidelines, but one stipulation in particular is of relevance to our study of the early medieval landscape of Wessex. In the *Benedictine Rule*, monks are urged to celebrate masses at the usual hours when away, and a similar expectation is made in the *Regularis Concordia* which further recommends engagement in the singing of psalms or other necessary business (McCann 1952, 117, 125, chs 50, 51, 55; Symons 1953, 7, ch. II). In service to these needs we might begin to envisage a role for roadside stone and timber crosses. Such monuments survive as standing remains, relocated fragments of stone (usually in churches), in place-names and in charter boundary clauses. Alexander Rumble has interpreted their functions variably as 'wayside edifices at which travellers pray to Christ', and those 'sited on significant hills or on coastal promontories' as 'landmarks for travellers' as well as 'Christian Symbols in the landscape' (2006, 39). Sam Turner makes the point that these were monuments 'whose impact would have been maximised when viewed by as many passers-by as possible' supporting the view that roadside locations were important factors in their distribution in the landscape (2006, 168). Although those recorded in Anglo-Saxon charter boundary clauses by their very nature fall on significant early medieval boundaries, John Blair has stressed that crosses are not to be seen in the first instance as boundary markers but rather roadside monuments (2005, 479).

In summary, of the types of travelling and journeying by both those in service to the church and by those in pursuit of the church's services, there appear two areas within which a landscape approach may contribute. The first of these is in the inscribing of landscapes – particularly with Christian iconography. It might be argued that of all the many travellers reviewed in this chapter, pilgrims represent the first group travelling without any prior knowledge of long distance routes. Can it therefore be posited that a rise in signposting and inscription within the landscape was intended to meet with the rise in popular pilgrimages in the late ninth and tenth centuries? Was this form of sign-posting as much a means by which roadside prayer could be facilitated as it was the desire within the established church of this period to make Christianity more a part of daily life? (pers. comm. Barbara Yorke). Pilgrims as well as churchmen would have prayed at roadside edifices and this study can set about identifying crosses, roods and stones and characterising the distribution of such monuments in a landscape context to gain a greater understanding of which routes might have served these purposes. The second area to which a landscape approach can contribute is in identifying the route ways that would have served the internal economies of major ecclesiastic centres. We might see these economies as having a vested interest in the maintenance and clear passage of routes between their estates and it certainly seems clear that a regular form of travelling and transportation would have existed between ecclesiastical centres and their distant estates.

Messengers

Undoubtedly, the church would have required a considerably complicated network of messengers to carry out its work throughout Europe and beyond and the overwhelming number of individuals listed as 'messengers' in the *Prosopography of Anglo-Saxon England* are recorded as carrying out the work of the Christian mission. The *Prosopography* is a web-based resource providing access to structured information on all of the recorded inhabitants of Anglo-Saxon England from the late sixth to the end of the eleventh century and of the 127 individuals listed as 'messengers', 101 remain anonymous whilst 26 are referred to as named individuals (www.pase.ac.uk). The kinds of messages being conveyed under this list include everything from Gregory I's first 'message', sent via Augustine, to the English people through to the messengers sent out by Cnut in 1017 in search of a wife (Campbell and Keynes 1998, 4–52).

It is clear from an analysis of the various offices of the state that mobility was a crucial factor in the governance of state-affairs (Campbell 1987). Where the burden of obligation to perform this service lay in secular society is indicated in a letter sent to King Edgar within which Oswald, Bishop of Worcester, set out the conditions in which leases were granted and stipulated that certain men of a noble class were expected to perform specific services including riding to deliver the bishop's messages (S 1368). At other levels of society, however, it is clear that the maintenance of communications was of the greatest importance. An eleventh-century estate comprised of dispersed holdings (*i.e.* the kind observed throughout Domesday Book), was, James Campbell argued, 'a constellation of settlements which could not simply be left in the hands of peasants and village reeves', but one that needed some kind of highly mobile system of control and exploitation (1987, 212).

The legal compilation of status entitled *Geþyncðo* (Dignities) dated to the first quarter of the eleventh century, lists the term of service *Radstefn* (riding persons/force) (Whitelock 1979, 468). A similar term is found in the Domesday Book where there are approximately 583 references to *radmanni* and *radchenistre* (riders or riding men) to be found in a band of counties stretching from Cheshire, along the western border of England to the English Channel (Cathers 2001, 197). The exact functions of this position and the service it renders are not entirely obvious from the 1086 survey. The term itself might suggest the role of a bodyguard and proximity to the Welsh border might have required an extra level of vigilance for elites and the king, but Dorothy Whitelock and Frank Stenton have also drawn parallels with the position of the *geneat* in the *Rectitudines Singularum Personarum*, a list of the 'rights and ranks' of people, drafted in the eleventh century (Harvey 1983). Amongst the many services placed on the shoulders of the *geneat*, the care of horses, acting as a guard to the lord and riding are stipulations alongside the duty to *ærendian fyr swa nyr, swa hwyder swa him man to tæcð* (carry messages far and near wheresoever he is directed) (Douglas and Greenway 1953, 875). The *geneat* and *Radstefn* were therefore likely to have played a crucial role in the linking of the manor with the wider world. Whilst the provision of horse and carts and the obligation to ride and provide carrying service may have kept the *geneat* within the orbit of daily affairs (discussed below), it seems likely that in the delivering of messages 'near and far', he may very well have been taken to more remote parts where directions and guidance were required. It is likely that the same types of landscape monuments used by pilgrims and churchmen will have helped in the orientation of long distance travelling *geneat*s, helping them to form a mental map of where they were and where they needed to get to. If entirely lost on the road, they would very likely have been intercepted by other local *geneat*s whose further obligation it was to 'bring strangers to the village'.

Landscapes of governance

The mobility of the Anglo-Saxon kings is best illustrated in David Hill's *Atlas of Anglo-Saxon England* (1981) and it would seem, especially from the reigns of Æthelstan, Edgar and Æthelred, that key to the success of ruling elites in the early medieval period was the ability to both see and be seen.

Levi Roach (2011) has recently presented the case for the importance of the *iter regis* and the constitutional role played by a charismatic king conducting face-to-face business throughout his kingdom. Drawing primarily from hagiographical works of the tenth and early eleventh centuries, Roach identifies royal visitations and the pomp and ritual that was a part of them as crucial both to king and kingdom in obtaining harmony, justice and political stability. Asser gives us an insight into how such royal retinues may have been comprised, explaining that the king's followers were divided into three groups which rotated service in the court, dividing their time between support of the king and their own estates (Stevenson 1904, ch. 100). Thus, a large retinue of fighting men and councillors would always be in attendance with either the king's household or that of his closest family. The witness lists of Anglo-Saxon charters record some of the people present at the king's court when charters were issued. Whilst at great councils a larger number of dignitaries might be expected to attend, for lesser meetings, charters can provide us with information about the composition of the court. Bernard Reilly's work on late eleventh-century Léon-Castilla serves as a good model on which to base this kind of study. In an attempt to discover just how many people travelled with King Alfonso VI from Léon to Santiago de Compostela, to Oviedo, back to Léon and on to Burgos in Castilla during a period of five months in 1075, Reilly analysed the witness lists and locations at which charters were signed (1988, 148–149). He went on to conclude that at any one time the king might be travelling with a retinue of over 220 people, 51 carts and more than 200 animals (1988, 155). His work involves a degree of extrapolation from the known dignitaries mentioned in the witness lists of charters to a conjectural body of people including servants, men at arms and other courtly figures such as falconers and masters of hounds. What is clear, however, from Reilly's work is that a not inconsiderable train of vehicles, riders and people would be using the route ways of northern Spain to transport the king and his court.

Whilst Anglo-Saxon charters do not provide quite the same level of detail as their counterparts from northern Spain, they say enough to give us some idea of the sizes of retinues and travelling parties either with the king or *en route* to meet with him for council duties. The work of Simon Keynes (1980; 2002) has illustrated that witness lists from authentic charters of King Æthelred II record actual attendance at the exaction of their issue and Jennifer MacDonald (2001, 131), working from Keynes' tables, identifies that on average around thirty high status individuals were attending these meetings. Reilly calculated that between eight and nine dignitaries travelled with Alfonso VI, leading him to the overall numbers in the concomitant retinue stated above. MacDonald draws our attention to the sixty-four dignitaries that witnessed the granting of land at Downton and Ebblesbourne (Wilts.) by charter in 997, but even with the average number of witnesses from Æthelred II's charters at about thirty, the sizes of the parties travelling and converging on these high-status official meetings would have been considerable – if we work to Reilly's calculations (S 981). A factor not often considered in relation to assemblies like this was the state of the roads and, as John Maddicott has observed, 'only by circumstances which favoured relatively speedy and direct travel' were the great gatherings of the tenth century made possible (2010, 17). He goes on: 'That English rulers could bring men together from so far away was a tribute not only to their political enterprise and authority but also to the English travelling conditions, for which they too may have been partly responsible' (2010, 18).

We now turn to the travel requirements of those committed to attendance at local assemblies. For this, more comparative work of continental practice is useful. In a chapter entitled 'Mobility' in Wendy Davies's *Small Worlds: The Village Community in Early Medieval Brittany*, the witness lists of charters and the locations of issue are examined to determine the orbits of local dignitaries and *plebenses* (members of the village community) (1988, 105–133). The community of the *plebs* is explicitly referred to in a set of unique ninth-century texts that detail membership, transactions and social developments that would affect the group. Davies's approach helps us to get closer to 'ground level' and understand a more localised pattern of movement within rural communities. The majority of *plebenses* found cause only within the courts of their own *plebs* but it is clear that some notable individuals, trustworthy but not necessarily wealthy peasants, travelled further afield – sometimes distances of up to 30 km (18.6 miles) – to witness transactions and serve on juries in two, or in some cases three, neighbouring *plebs*. Documents recording at this level of detail the workings of the hundred, or even shire court, do not exist for Anglo-Saxon England and it might be contentious to uncritically transpose a pattern of early medieval Breton mobility on to the landscape of Wessex in the same period. It is clear however, from the *Hundred Ordinance*, a set of laws laid down between *c*. 939 to 961 (Whitelock 1979, 429–430, cat. no. 39), that in the obligation for dignitaries 'to assemble every four weeks and each man is to do justice to another' lies a regularity of local meetings on a scale similar to that in Brittany. Given the distances of some ecological resources from their estate centres (discussed below), 30 km in the early medieval landsacpe of Wessex would be entirely appropriate for representatives to travel in the collective management of common rights to grazing, timber and other resources in distant wood pastures, marshlands and upland areas.

Archaeological and place-name studies of meeting places in Anglo-Saxon England also illustrate that local governance was formalised, highly organised and structured around a dense network of designated muster points (Adkins and Petchey 1985; Meaney 1995; Pantos 2004; Pantos and Semple 2004; Semple 2004). Assembly sites have come under increasing analysis and their distribution throughout the landscape and in relation to administrative units, such as hundreds and shires, is beginning to contribute to our broader understanding of the administration and governance of late Anglo-Saxon England (Baker *et al.* 2011; Baker and Brookes 2013b; 2013c; 2015a). What is clear, from place-name evidence, however, is that an earlier tier of meeting places more idiosyncratically arranged to meet judicial needs in a less formalised structure of administration existed prior to the hundredal system (Meaney 1995). It might therefore be countenanced that a shift in assembly sites, in accordance with new administrative arrangements, might be both a response to changes in patterns of movement through a landscape as well as an influence in the subsequent patterns of connectivity on a local level. To date, in only a very local study has the siting of an early medieval meeting place been considered in relation to the major routes through the valley in which it is located (Semple and Langlands 2001), but this promises to be a fruitful area of study. For example, a topographical characteristic of John Baker and Stuart Brookes's 'hanging-promontory' type of meeting place is their location immediately adjacent to well-worn hollow ways (Baker and Brookes 2013b).

Other categories of site concerned with acts of governance that warrant mention are execution sites and their concomitant cemeteries. Recent studies of the distribution of execution sites in relation to other landscape phenomena have done much to contribute to our understanding of the landscape context of Anglo-Saxon justice (Reynolds 1997; 2002b). Boundary locations seem to be important, in particular those in prominent and highly visible locations, and association with earlier monuments such as prehistoric barrows (as is the case with some assembly sites) and linear earthworks appears to be significant. From the earliest known examples, proximity to a major highway was also of major concern (Reynolds 2008, 25–43). At recent excavations of execution burial sites, the immediate proximity of a major thoroughfare has been observed (Pitts *et al.* 2002; Hayman and Reynolds 2005; Buckberry and Hadley 2007; Cessford *et al.* 2007), and whilst boundary locations for burials might be articulating the exclusion of social deviants and a consignment to a conceptual 'underworld' (Reynolds 2002b, 188), it was the passing through such locations by travellers in the landscape of the living where the message of law and order was most clearly articulated. Execution sites in prominent locations highly visible to passers-by served this purpose and – as with the case of assembly sites – the examination of the networks of routes that existed in the hinterlands within which these judicial processes were taking place will only contribute to our understanding of developments in governance and judicial practice over time.

To conclude then, the early medieval network of travel and communication would have played host to a range of mobilities in service to both the emerging Anglo-Saxon state, and the conducting of judicial and government affairs on the regional and local level. On occasions, this network clearly had to accommodate the large retinues of high status individuals travelling to councils and assemblies that the king, bishops and ruling elites would have attended. More regularly though, individuals and small groups would have travelled to hundred and shire assembly sites. Travel in the service of local and national administration would clearly have been instrumental to the development of the institutions of government in Anglo-Saxon England and it seems inconceivable that care would not have been taken to ensure at all times safe and assured passage through the landscape. The level of mobility that must be posited for the successful running of the country – not least a country at war – makes it especially important to identify more specifically the types of route, their character and the extent of the early medieval network.

An Anglo-Saxon highway code

A review of execution sites and cemeteries runs us neatly into the subject of how movement through the landscape was monitored, protected and ultimately valued by both wider society and the institutions of power. These elements manifest themselves most clearly in the evidence for an emerging medieval highway code in the laws of the twelfth century. For the Anglo-Saxon period the law codes with specific references to the highway are few, but significant gains have been made in our understanding of late Anglo-Saxon attitudes to highway law through the analysis of immediate post-Conquest laws and in part, through analysis of a wider European legal tradition (Cooper 2000; 2002). It is clear that late Roman legal ideas across the continent set the foundation for the early medieval notion of a 'highway' or a *via regia* (royal way) and although direct influence is hard to ascertain, Anglo-Saxon law appears to have developed along parallel lines with early medieval European legislation (Cooper 2002, 40).

Alan Cooper's careful analysis of the *Leges Henrici Primi* has demonstrated that many of the laws concerning highways in this legal treatise composed in the early twelfth century can be seen to have their origins in the Anglo-Saxon period (2002). If we take a look at the evidence for execution in the laws of Henry I there is an explicit link with the king's highway. A prefatory note describing the king's rights stresses that:

> All *herestrete* [army streets] pertain wholly to the king, and all *qualstowa*, that is places of execution, pertain totally to the king and are in his soke. (Downer 1972, ch. 10.2)

Archaeological evidence confirms the association between 'killing-places' and major highways and furthermore enables that link to be pushed back into the Anglo-Saxon period. As early as 1937, the location of four excavated execution cemeteries at Meon Hill, Stockbridge Down, Roche Court Down and Old Sarum, all on the main Winchester to Old Sarum route, was believed to indicate royal control (Hill 1937, 258). Recent analysis of the same sites and the individuals interred therein has demonstrated that they all fit squarely into a tradition of judicial execution present in Anglo-Saxon England (Reynolds 1997). This link between highways and execution sites, evidenced in both the documentary sources and archaeology, implies that where archaeological or place-name evidence for an execution site or cemetery exists, we must suppose the existence of a fairly significant thoroughfare and perhaps one which enjoyed a form of legal status under the protection of the king.

The *Leges Henrici Primi* offer a legal definition of a *via regia*, a royal way, as a route that runs from 'burh to burh' and one justification for projecting this definition back into the late Anglo-Saxon period is founded on the restriction of trade to royal boroughs in laws of Edward the Elder and Æthelstan I (I Edw 1; II As 13, 13.1). Furthermore, it has been observed how certain terms in the *Leges Henrici Primi* have a distinctly Anglo-Saxon ring to them. For example, the crime of *Stretebroche* is the illegal obstruction or 'breaking' of a road, an offence punishable by a fine of 100s to the king (Hn 80.5, 80.5a). The Domesday Book for Kent includes similar laws:

> If anyone has made a fence or ditch whereby the King's public road is narrowed, or has felled into the road a tree that stood outside the road, and has carried off branch or foliage from it; for each of these offences he shall pay 100s to the King. (Williams and Martin 1992, 3)

Again, when concerned with laws relating to the roads in and out of the city of Canterbury:

> If anyone digs or fixes a post within these public roads within the City or outside it, the King's reeve follows him wherever he has gone, and receives the fine for the King's works. (Williams and Martin 1992, 5)

Finally, on the road from Nottingham to York:

> If anyone ploughs or makes a ditch within 2 perches of the King's road, he has to pay a fine of £8. (Williams and Martin 1992, 757)

It is clear then, certainly by the late eleventh century, that the physical structure of the highway enjoyed a degree of royal protection. Ease of passage was clearly valued by the king and the physical surface of the highway itself was not to be tampered with. But what of those who used the highways? Most of the continental law codes of the period extend protection to women and strangers on the highways and it seems likely that in Anglo-Saxon England similar steps were taken to ensure safe passage for all (Cooper 2002, 42–43). One of the earliest direct references to the safety a stranger might enjoy whilst travelling on designated highways can be found in the laws of King Wihtrid of Kent and Ine of Wessex. The respective clauses in each law code are in fact so similar that they suggest a degree of co-operation between these loosely allied kings and detail how, *Gif feorcund mon oððe fremde butan wege geond wudu gonge and ne hrieme ne horn blawe, ðeof he bið to profianne: oððe to sleanne oððe to áliesanne* (If a man from afar, or a stranger, quits the road (*wege*), and neither shouts, nor blows a horn, he shall be assumed to be a thief, [and as such] may be either slain or put to ransom) (Wi 28; Wi 25, 26; Ine 20). This law implies that whilst on the road, individuals enjoyed the protection of the law, yet this is all we have to support the back-projection of a king's 'peace' into the late-seventh century.

In later law codes, however, chapters covering the reservation of protection to foreigners, strangers and 'men from afar' are more regular. Alfred's code, for example, stipulates that: *Utan cumene and elðeodige ne geswence ðu no* (Do not harass foreigners and visitors from abroad), although such protection is not specific to the highway (Af. 34; see also ECf. 15.7). That Emperor Justinian's sixth-century 'presumption of innocence' existed as a concept in the Anglo-Saxon period is implied in the laws of Cnut (1020–1023) where the king's protection is extended to those on their way to assemblies (Digest of Justinian 22.3.2; II Cn 82.). The highway was clearly intended to provide sanctuary to those whose guilt had yet to be proven. In the Domesday Book, we find similar assurances given that whilst on the road, the protection of the king could be enjoyed. The men of the lathes of east Kent agree on a set of royal laws within which it stipulates:

> On breach of the peace, if anyone commits it and is charged on the road or attached he shall pay a fine of £8 to the King. (Williams and Martin 1992, 3)

This study offers the opportunity to explore some of these concepts in the landscape of early medieval Wessex. By looking at the language used in Anglo-Saxon charter boundary clauses to describe different types of routes, is the notion of a legally defined highway – a type of public space – whereon people could travel in peace, borne out? Can we identify the burh to burh routes and if so, what is their character and how are they described? Can we find further evidence to help project back into the Anglo-Saxon period the notion of a highway code as evidenced in Henry I's laws?

Driving droves and leading loads

Alongside the plethora of routes within the immediate vicinity of the estate centres, longer distance routes must have existed to enable these places to effectively exploit the detached parcels of land that provided seasonal grazing and resources such as wood and hay (Faith 1997, 109–110). For the purposes of seasonal grazing, transportation is a fairly straightforward affair; the beasts themselves are driven, seasonally, between summer pastures and winter pounds (for studies of Anglo-Saxon transhumance see Fox 2006; 2012). The hay harvest, as well as bean and cereal harvests, would also have commanded only the seasonal use of a route. The transportation of timber, however, as well as repeated visits to more regular markets, would have required accessible thoroughfares at more regular intervals in the calendar year. In particular, whilst the transportation of beans and cereals may have been achievable through the carrying of pack-animals, the transportation of timber and other bulky resources will have required the use of wheeled vehicles. It may be that our understanding of the growth of the early medieval economy is dependent on the critical issue of how prevalent carts were during the period and, perhaps more importantly, whether we can hypothesise an increased use in wheeled transportation from the eighth through to the eleventh century. The evidence from documentary sources and illustrations suggests a varied use for wheeled vehicles in the period. Evidence for increased usage is, however, like the evidence for an increased number of bridges, encumbered by the fact that an increasing number of documentary sources (and therefore more references) exist for later periods.

The salt routes identified by Della Hooke were clearly capable of carrying carts or 'wains' as a charter dated to the 880s records the granting of rights to the church at Worcester specifying that, *buton þæt se wægnscilling and se seampending gonge to ðæs cyninges handa swa he ealning dyde æt Saltwíc* (the wagon-shilling and the load-penny at Droitwich go to the king as they have always done)

(S 223; Harmer 1914, 22–23, 54–55; Whitelock 1979, 540; Kelly 1992, 17). It seems that so developed was this system of long-distance transportation that as early as the ninth century, the obligation had been commuted to a cash render. That carts were being used to undertake basic functions in the agricultural economy on a local level also seems likely from a reference in a tenth-century riddle from the Exeter Book (Fell 2007). The riddle is widely believed to be referring to a plough that is, at one point, referred to as being *wegen on wægne* (carried on a 'wain') suggesting that at the time the riddle was composed, such a role for a cart was not considered out of the ordinary (Krapp and Dobbie 1961, Riddle 21). Further evidence for regular use of wheeled vehicles comes from the *Laws of the Northumbrian Priest* where there is a section that forbids assemblies, all work and the carrying of goods, whether by wagon or by horse or on one's back (Whitelock 1979, 438). Carrying and carting were duties placed upon the *geneat*, a manorial steward or bailiff recorded in the *Rectitudines Singularum Personarum*. In the same document, however, the *gebur*'s obligations (a hierarchical tier below the *geneat*) are restricted to only carrying (using pack animals) (Douglas and Greenway 1953, 875–876, cat. no. 172). This may be an indication of the levels of proliferation of carts in Anglo-Saxon England as much as it is an insight into who in the manorial hierarchy had access to them. The obligation for cart provision may share a common origin with a reference in Charlemagne's *Capitulare 'de villis'* where the onus was placed on royal estates to construct carts to support armies in the field (Loyn *et al.* 1975, 72). This obligation finds itself repeated in 869 in the levies raised by Charles the Bald (King of West Francia, 840 × 877) where we are told that *de mille mansis unum carrum cum duobus bobus* (from each thousand *mansi*, one cart with two oxen) must be supplied to fulfil manpower and equipment requirements for the building of the Pont de l'Arche (Grat *et al.* 1964, 152–153). Similar explicit references to the provision of carts for military service are absent from Anglo-Saxon sources but despite this, evidence suggests that carts were used to support military campaigning in the ninth century (Lavelle 2010, 208, 337). So wheeled vehicles appear to be in use for the purposes of industrial transportation – in this case salt – funded in part, as suggested by the Worcester charter, by cash renders. They are conducting day-to-day operations around the estate under the auspices of the *geneat* and in service to the army presumably as part of the military obligations owed by manorial estates. But what form did these vehicles take?

David Hill has analysed manuscript illustrations of Anglo-Saxon carts and drawn ethnographic parallels of their construction with those observed in service to the rural economy of twentieth-century Portugal (Hill 1998) (Figure 9). In *Cotton Claudius B. iv, 67r*, two teams of oxen are illustrated pulling a cart where the driver is stood at the back of the vehicle with a goad. Detail on the wheel construction is lacking and the vehicle is 'gated' whereby a single rail holds in place the heads of the uprights that form the 'carriage'. A similar arrangement regarding the superstructure of the carriage can be observed in both *Cotton Julius A. iv, fo. 5v* and *Cotton Tiberius B. v, fo. 6* (not pictured). Similarities in the scenes depicted in each manuscript indicate a

FIGURE 9. Anglo-Saxon illustrations of ox-carts (Hill 1998, fig. 1).

common provenance and in both cases the carts are being used to carry timber. Two beams running the length of the chassis and also comprising the draw bar are coupled together at the point where they are attached to the yoke. In *Cotton Julius A. iv, fo. 6v* the cart is depicted with a similar chassis to the two mentioned above but it is clear that a retaining wattle wall has been woven through the uprights of the carriage. In this instance, the labourers are transporting sheaves of grain crops.

Iron tyres are used to hold together the structure of modern cartwheels, being heated up and then cooled onto the frame of felloes, spokes and hubs to draw the structure fast together. Further iron bands are shrunk on to the hubs to prevent splitting under shock. It is just possible that these Anglo-Saxon carts could be constructed without the use of such techniques but even in the event of iron tyring, when the cart had reached the end of its serviceable life, such a vital material would hardly be discarded for the benefit of future archaeologists. So whilst the documentary evidence for cart use in early medieval England is anecdotal, direct archaeological evidence for carts would theoretically be extremely hard to identify (although dateable cart ruts might offer a glimmer of hope). Commentary on any increase in the usage and abundance of carts in the period must therefore remain hypothetical.

The obligations placed on the *geneat* in the *Rectitudines Singularum Personarum* find parallels in two other documents of the period, a customary for an estate at Tidenham (Gloucs.) and a statement of services rendered at Hurstbourne Priors (Hants.) (S 359; Faith 1994, 39). All three documents have been used to suggest that by the tenth century a model concept for how an estate should be run was in circulation (Harvey 1983). In the *Rectitudines*, one of the *geneat*'s roles was to *ridan and auerian and lade lædan* (ride, and carry [?with pack animals] and lead loads) and in the Tidenham customary to these roles is added the term, *drafe drifan* (drive droves) (S 1555). All these functions are considered of importance not only to the internal economy of the estate but as Rosamond Faith has argued, in the long-distance trade that gave the eighth century the name 'the age of emporia' (1997, 109–110).

To gain some idea of how ubiquitous carting was by the twelfth century, estate records that deal with the conveyance of produce from outlying estates to estate centres can provide some insights. What emerges in the Glastonbury records of 1135 to 1201, and those from Shaftesbury and Burton Abbeys a generation earlier, is clear evidence of the level of obligation placed on manors to provide carrying services and the importance of this service to the management of large dispersed estates (Douglas and Greenway 1953, 884–885; Farmer 1989; Stacey 2001; 2006). Records include the carting of wood, hay, corn, beans, dung, lime and peat – obligations that could also be commuted to cash renders. Due to the paucity of direct references, projecting this level of mobility back to the eleventh century and beyond becomes problematic. However, from some of the earliest documentary sources and from place-name evidence, it seems that institutions were exploiting different ecological resources at considerable distances from estate centres. Timber for building, cooking, brewing, baking and heating would clearly have been one of the key resources in demand in early medieval England and the collection of this raw material in bulk, illustrated in the manuscript evidence above, was dependent on carts. The best evidence of woodland exploitation comes from Kent where place-names and some of our earliest reliable charters allow us to identify the rights estates based on the coast had to ownership of woodland as far south as the later boundary between the shires of Kent and Sussex (Boulay 1961, 141–180; Everitt 1986, 36–48). Frank Stenton observed that the early forms of the place-name Tenterden, *Tenetwaradenn*, implies a *denn* (woodland) belonging to the men of Thanet and the two places are nearly 65 km apart (1971, 280). Similar arrangements can be observed in a charter dated to 724, where the *Limenwearawalde* and *Weowerawealde* can be seen to belong to the respective 'lathes' of Lyminge and Wye (S 1180; Witney 1976, 272; Hooke 1989b, 113; Kelly 1995, 163–165). Elsewhere Wychwood may have been the wood of the Kingdom of the *Hwicce* and the prevalence more widely of '-ingfield' place-names are believed to be an indication of the ownership and rights of early kin-groups to detached woodland resources in potentially very early periods (Gelling 1984, 244; Hooke 1985a, 14–15).

In Wessex, the evidence for such wood transportation is not dated as early as it is for Kent. A charter, purporting to date to 909, recording the grant of Overton by Edward the Elder to Winchester Cathedral, with attached hidages of woodland at Tadley, North Waltham and Bradley indicate that the same arrangements were desirous in Wessex in at least the eleventh century, the likely period of its forgery (S 377; Hart 1970, 29). The Domesday entry for South Newton (north of Wilton, Wilts.) records how belonging to the manor was a customary due from Melchet Forest of eighty cartloads of timber (along with fodder for eighty pigs and 'what was needed for the repairing of houses and fences') (Williams and Martin 1992, 172). This customary due is recorded in an earlier charter for South Newton, dated to 943, where attached woodland is described as at *fyrste felda*, a place-name that survives only as Frustfield Hundred which itself contained a large tract of Melchet Forest (S 492). Domesday Book also records an identical customary due for a manor at Washern immediately south of Wilton (Williams and Martin 1992, 172) and in both this, and the case of South Newton, a total of 160 cartloads of timber per year passed between the two manors and their outlying woodland. Clearly, there existed a need to move timber resources from distant woodlands to points of consumption and carts must have fulfilled this role. What route did the wood-carters take between Wilton and Melchet? Did an existing route allow these kinds of grants to be made, or in issuing the grant, was it foreseen that a serviceable route between the two would be maintained?

There is another reason, however, as to why these detached and distant parcels of woodland were of interest to early medieval institutions and this lies in their use as woodland pasture for pigs and cattle. It may very well have been the case that it was not just loads of wood that were being moved the 65 km (40.4 miles) from Tenterden to Thanet and that in fact, large herds of pigs and cattle were also being driven between the two places. References to attached pasturage, and more explicitly swine-pasture, are common occurrences in grants of land conveyed by charter and the driving of livestock over considerable distances and their management in pastoral areas will undoubtedly have had an effect on the structure of landscape (S 21; S 24; S 25; S 30; S 181; S 323; S 572; S 1181; S 1215; S 1220; S 1403; S 1437; S 1441; S 1611; S 1623 of which S 1181; S 1215; S 1220; S 1437; S 1441 refer explicitly to swine pasture).

Transhumance and its impact on the landscape of early medieval south-western England has been explored in detail by both Harold Fox and Susan Pearce (Pearce 1985; 2004; Fox 2006, 50–64; 2012). Using post-Conquest source material, Anglo-Saxon charters, place-name evidence and topographical analysis, Fox has made a convincing case for projecting a well-recorded medieval system of transhumance in Devon back into the pre-Conquest period. Tenurial arrangements recorded in Domesday Book and other later documentary sources provide a link between low-lying coastal estate centres and upland pastures on Dartmoor. In the example of Cockington, which is recorded in 1086 as having an outlying pasture at Dewdon on Dartmoor, the place-name Cockingford on a direct route between the two places establishes a physical link that may place this arrangement in the pre-Conquest period (2006, 84). In another example, Fox made the case for the extensive tract of land on the high moorland of Dartmoor, recorded in an undated boundary clause for land at *Peadington*, representing the summer pastures appurtenant to the coastal town of Paignton (2006, 90–92). These connections between the higher ground of Dartmoor and the settlements on the coast and in the surrounding river valleys are made explicit in a boundary clause from a charter for land at Meavy (S 963). Here the boundary is recorded as passing along the *boc sætena hig wege*, translated as 'the people of Buckland's high way' (Finberg 1970, 31). Both Finberg and Susan Pearce favour an identification with a route that runs from the settlement of Buckland Monachorum up on to the moor in the direction of Princetown (Pearce 1985, 16–17, 55). Della Hooke prefers to translate *hig* as 'hay (?waggon)', suggests a slightly alternative route and believes, like Fox, that this is evidence of summer grazing rights on the moor belonging to Buckland (Hooke 1994b,

199; Fox 2006, 97). In the early medieval period mowing and reaping of hay formed part of the 'rustic labours' owed as a customary rent by most ranks of society from *thegn*s downwards (Faith 1997, 110–112), and this route may just as well have been the means by which hay owed to the landowning abbey was conveyed to the manorial centre at the bottom of the valley for consumption during the winter months. Meadow grasses were a crucial resource in the rural economy of early medieval England and where an estate granted by charter was located in land unsuitable for hay-making, meadowland elsewhere would be needed. Detached meadows are another common occurrence in the charters and we must suppose that cartloads of this important resource would also have been moved, if only seasonally, from summer cutting grounds to winter storage (S 321; S 350; S 403; S 492; S 771; S 786; S 842; S 845; S 874; S 1180; S 1280; S 1310; S 1358; S 1369; S 1403; S 1477; S 1654).

It is likely that Dartmoor generated its own unique set of circumstances that impacted upon the pattern of exploitation and subsequent tenurial arrangements, but in other parts of the west of Britain, similar arrangements have been observed. In Somerset, for example, a system as large, as complex and with roots as ancient as those on Dartmoor has been proposed (Rippon 1994; Pearce 2004, 61). In Cornwall, place-name evidence can be seen to indicate a system of transhumance that goes back into the early medieval period, if not further (Pounds 1942; Herring 1996). The place-name evidence has been used to suggest similar systems in the Black Mountains of Wales whilst more widely in Wales, the pattern of *commote* boundaries across large tracts of uplands suggest division between valley communities in the Roman and pre-Roman periods (Jones 1972, 294; Ward 1999, 346).

Harold Fox (2008) had extended his interest in transhumance beyond the south-west and most recently, through the analysis of *smeoru* (smear/grease/butter), *butere* (butter) and *wīc* (dairy farm) elements in place-names, has identified evidence for transhumance in regions as diverse as Cornwall, Wales, Derbyshire, Gloucestershire and the Isle of Wight. In Hampshire, Christopher Currie has identified areas of common pasture and their concomitant drove roads through analysis of the boundary clauses describing the limits of estates at North and South Stoneham, Bishopstoke and Durley (Currie 1994, 115–118). The presence of gateways in the boundary clauses lead Currie to conclude that areas now known as Southampton Common, Horton Heath and tracts of land in Allington, Shamblehurst and Townhill manors were all enclosed wood-pastures where a system of grazing existed similar to that operating in the New Forest as recently as the nineteenth century (Currie 1994, 116–117). Further analysis of the drove ways, as identified on early edition Ordnance Survey maps, suggests provisioning routes, from these identified pastures, leading directly to *Hamwic*. Currie's work on these wood pastures and his suggestion that the same arrangement existed in the New Forest finds support in the analysis of the faunal remains from *Hamwic*, which have demonstrated that a well-managed and 'productive' hinterland was serving the *emporium* with a large number of high quality beasts for slaughter and processing (Bourdillon 1988, 193; 1994, 122–123).

The point of covering all of this information is that it forces us to project on to the early medieval landscape a pattern of routes constituted to deal with the exploitation of varied resources and the drawing of such resources to estate centres. Whilst the droving of animals such as swine, cattle and sheep to summer pastures, markets and fairs may have required only the most basic of passage to be provided, it is important to consider how this movement was managed in the landscape. Christopher Currie draws attention to the importance of gates as an indication of enclosures to keep livestock from wandering onto precious arable land and in the moving of larger herds, clearly the routes taken must have sought to avoid any areas where damage may have been incurred by errant beasts. The regularity with which timber, grain, hay and other crucial resources were moved from outlying manors and detached woodland and meadow, to places of consumption and sale raises not just the possibility but the *necessity* for serviceable route ways upon which heavily laden carts could safely travel – potentially all year round. Given the recent importance attached to the 'economically crucial level of bulk goods' moving around early medieval Europe, this study becomes all the more important (Wickham 2005, 701). If we are to suppose any form of economic growth or 'take-off' – even a 'take-off in embryo' – for the early medieval period, we simply have to posit the existence of a proactive attitude to the manner and means with which basic but vital goods were moved around (Langdon 1995).

CHAPTER THREE

From *emporia* to markets: trade networks in Wessex

From a broader European perspective, the lack of explicit historical references to trade and commerce in the early medieval period has served as a hindrance to understanding its role in the wider communications of society (McCormick 2001, 3). In Anglo-Saxon England, this dearth in the documentary record is best illustrated by the paucity of direct references to merchants. It is clear from the archaeological record (discussed below) that commercial exchange was commonplace in the later Anglo-Saxon landscape and recent studies now suggest, tentatively, that neutral exchange, supported by a cash-nexus, was in evidence in Wessex in the eighth and ninth centuries (Costen and Costen 2016). It is enigmatic then that a mere eight specific references to merchants are listed in *The Prosopography of Anglo-Saxon England* (www.pase.ac.uk). Furthermore, those references that we do have, for the most part, are incidental to a narrative rather than being in any way descriptive of the conduct and mechanisms of exchange. A good example of this is the occasion when, having humbly fled from his election to the papacy in 590, Gregory I (590 × 604) took refuge in the company of merchants. Benedict Biscop (*c.* 628–690), founder and abbot of the monastery at Monkwearmouth and Jarrow, on his third visit to Rome commandeered the services of a merchant ship to provide him with safe passage from Lérins (Farmer 1983; Colgrave 1985, 73–139). Charlemagne's correspondence with Offa raises his concern that merchants are masquerading as pilgrims and details the proper conduct of individuals engaged in trade (Whitelock 1979, 848–849, cat. no. 197). Irrespective of whether these arrangements represent a formal trade agreement (Story 2003, 184–188, 195–199), this is clearly a reflection of the desire on the part of both rulers that such activity was permitted only by royal control. In the same period, the royal overseeing and promotion of trade is suggested by the evidence for tolls. Susan Kelly (1992) examined a group of ten documents concerned with the remission of tolls on ships owned by ecclesiastic communities in the North Kent and Thames Estuary area. Although it is difficult to say how reflective this small group is of a more widespread practice, it is thought that they represent a fairly short-lived tradition introduced in the eighth century, seemingly abandoned relatively quickly, and pertaining to coastal and overseas commerce.

Royal control of trading – or, at least, the royal ambition to control trade – is also suggested by evidence from the law codes (Sawyer 1977). A brief exploration of some of the references to trade and traders in law codes is warranted because a shift in the geography of trade in Wessex is just about detectable from the laws of Ine to those of Edward the Elder and Æthelstan. As early as the seventh century, in the codes of Wihtred and Ine, we learn of 'men from afar' and 'strangers'; people who were very likely to have been engaged in trade. Equally, the Kentish laws of Hlothære and Eadric inform us that households were to be responsible for the conduct of merchants and men who come from over the border (Wi 28; Ine 20; Hl 15). Such groups were likely to have been made up of men from all of the English kingdoms as well as men from overseas, particularly Frisians who were well attested in many parts of northern Europe in the eighth and ninth centuries (Sawyer 1977, 151). Finds from the middle Anglo-Saxon *emporia* of *Hamwic*, Ipswich and London, especially imported pottery, confirm strong links with the Rhineland and the Low Countries and the likely presence of overseas traders (Scull 1997, 275–280). The references in these early codes to where such people might travel to is of particular interest here. In Ine's code (688 × 694), for example, we learn *Be ciepemonna fore uppe on londe* (Of traders travelling up inland) and are told *Gif ciepemon uppe on folce ceapie, do þæt beforan gewitnessum* (If a trader [makes his way] up amongst the folk, and [proceeds to] traffic, he shall do so before witnesses) (Ine 25). The suggestion here is that traders are departing from the more usual coastal trading location to travel inland to conduct their business. In the laws of King Alfred (*c.* 880s), traders were obliged to bring before the king's reeve, at a public meeting, those individuals they were taking 'up with him'. The law states: *Éac is ciepemonnum gereht: ða men ðe hie up mid him læden, gebrengen beforan kyninges gerefan on folcgemote* (Also it is laid down for traders: those men that they are taking inland with them, should be brought before the king's reeve at the folk assembly) (Af 34). Bill Griffiths has translated *up* in this instance as short hand for 'inland', a sense in accordance with Ine's laws (Other examples of *uppe* used in conjunction with *on londe* can be found in Bosworth and Toller 1898, 1141; Griffiths 1995, 69). So in Alfred's time we might also assume that to travel inland is to remove oneself from the usual sphere of commerce, requiring prior permissions granted by the king's reeve. In both instances, the suggestion here is that merchants are normally engaged in trade at coastal locations and that travelling into the country required quite specific legislation. In the laws of the tenth-century kings, however, there is an unwritten recognition that trade is occurring 'inland', especially in the instance of Edward the Elder (*c.* 874 × 924) and Æthelstan (*c.* 893 × 939), where it is being restricted to the emerging towns (I Edw 1; II As 12, 13.1; Attenborough 1922, 114–115, 134, 134–135). Are these laws therefore very broadly describing the same processes witnessed in the archaeological record of a shift from *emporia* – sites at coastal locations – to a nexus of trading sites reliant on inland trade in the tenth century?

Emporia, minsters and 'productive' sites

One of the fastest growing fields of study of the early medieval period is in trade and exchange and this is in no small measure as a consequence of the huge

FIGURE 10. Minster Street and Market Place, Salisbury, in close proximity to the site of St Thomas's Church, a possible minster and the likely focus for activity prior to the foundation of the medieval city in 1220 (Langlands 2014).

increase of data that has been brought about by metal detectorist finds and the *Portable Antiquities Scheme* (PAS, www.finds.org.uk) (Ulmschneider and Pestell 2003, 4). The dataset of the PAS has forced a rethink on the traditional emphasis placed on *emporia*, which, it has been argued, have skewed our understanding of the significance of production in the late seventh and early eighth centuries and masked the fact that rising economic growth is reflected at sites throughout the country (Morland 2000). It would seem that other locales and type-sites within which significant developments in production and commerce took place co-existed with the *emporia* and were part of a wider network of exchange (Scull 1997; Anderton 1999; Ulmschneider and Pestell 2003). In particular, the recent upsurge of coin finds means that 'hot-spots' have been identified and these have themselves prompted interesting questions about trade routes and the way money was transferred into the region (Ulmschneider and Pestell 2003, 5; Costen and Costen 2016).

The *emporia* therefore sit at the top of a hierarchy of trading sites in the eighth century, although characterising that hierarchy with any degree of certainty has proved elusive. One particular type-site of the period has been easier to identify than others and John Blair has demonstrated that minsters founded in the late seventh century were the focus of 'commercial activity' and the likely settings for markets (Figure 10). By drawing attention to their provisioning needs and disposable surpluses, Blair has made a strong case for such sites playing a crucial role in town origins (Blair 1988b, 47–48; 2000, 250–251). It is apparent, however, that minsters were located in highly accessible places in the landscape – most frequently at the intersections of major routes and the crossing points of rivers (Hase 1994, 58). It is important to consider therefore how the location as much as the institution governed later growth. Are we looking at markets at the gates of minsters or minsters at the gates of markets?

Royal estate centres – some of which were granted for the foundation of minsters (Yorke 1995, 306–307) – have also been seen as important places in eighth-century Wessex and likewise sit in similar central locations in the landscape. The documentary evidence for royal *tun*s as central places from which local areas were administered make them the likely places for the collection of rents, renders and surplus agricultural produce and thus also candidates for commercial activity (Sawyer 1983, 281). To these sites though, a looser and perhaps more idiosyncratic network of trading sites must be conjectured. As Chris Scull writes: 'any development model [of urbanism] should therefore take account of diversity of site character and trajectory of development' and he goes on to suggest that further distinctions need to be made – particularly of the middle Anglo-Saxon period – between periodic activity at single function sites and seasonal activity at or near permanent settlements (Scull 1997, 290). It may very well be the case that the *sceatta* coin finds that have turned up at a range of locations such as road and river crossings and hillfort sites relate to a more idiosyncratic distribution of trading in the period of a type Scull is referring to (Metcalf 1984a).

Seeking to find the central places of middle Anglo-Saxon Wessex is not easy, due, in part, to an archaeological paucity. Whilst minster churches theoretically occupied a role in a system that saw regional focal points acting as religious or administrative centres with economic functions, evidence, both archaeological and documentary, is in short supply for the period between foundation, in the seventh and eighth centuries, and what emerges in the eleventh century (Astill 2006, 238–240; 2011, 259–260). In Hampshire, those minsters – the likely centres of consumption and wealth – that on documentary evidence can be closely dated to the late seventh and eighth centuries are all to be found around the Solent basin (Hase 1988, 46). This geographical limitation is also reflected in the archaeological evidence of the period. Elsewhere throughout England, what seems important in the determining geographical factors of 'productive' sites is their access to maritime and riverine communications – a factor that undoubtedly had an influence in the developments of these trading centres (Ulmschneider and Pestell 2003, 7). As has already been observed (pp. 22–24), Wessex is poorly served by navigable waterways and this has been seen to explain, to a certain extent, the lack of any inland 'productive' sites, and the small number of sites overall in Wessex (Blackburn 2003, 22). Whilst Kent, East Anglia, Lincolnshire and Yorkshire are well furnished, only *Hamwic* and Carisbrooke feature as significant 'productive' sites in Wessex (Figure 11)

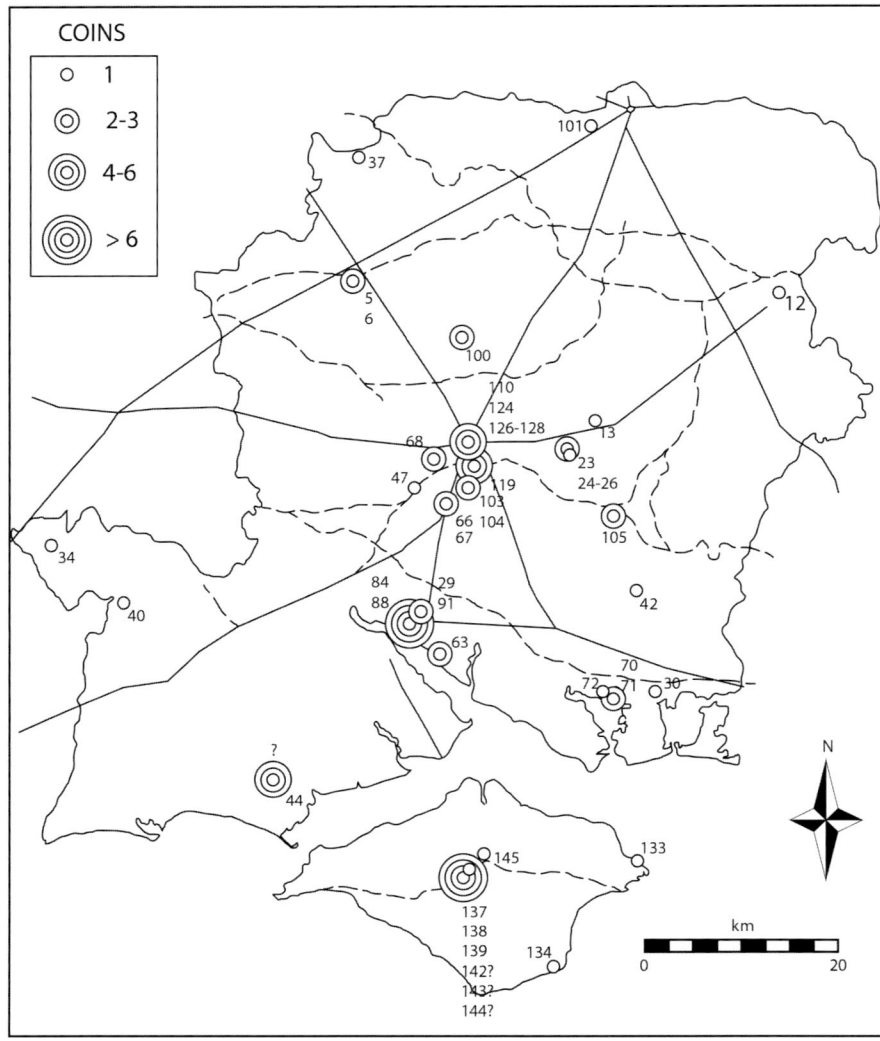

FIGURE 11. Coin productive sites (excluding hoards) and Roman roads in Hampshire (redrawn from Palmer 2003, p. 59, fig. 5.3, after Ulmschneider 2001, map 21).

(Ulmschneider 2003, 79). So, in general, those trading sites in Wessex that we have both archaeological and documentary evidence for in the eighth century seem to be restricted to locations where they share coastal and riverine connections.

Throughout the ninth century, trade and exchange between England and the continent appears to have been in decline and recent attempts to understand this process of 'deceleration' in *Francia* have suggested that the limitations of a 'command' economy, one sanctioned and controlled by elites and major ecclesiastical foundations, was as much responsible as the low level of agricultural efficiency of the emerging bipartite manorial system of the ninth century (Henning 2007). Whatever the reasons for this contraction on the continent, by the end of the eighth century, it was certainly hastened by Viking raiding throughout northern Europe (Hinton 1986, 18). In Wessex this resulted in the demise of *Hamwic* as a major trading centre and the sharp fall in single coin loss during these decades suggests that the economy based on coastal trading with the continent and employing the use of *sceatta* coinage was in decline. Is it the case though, that another economy co-existed and was in part integrated with that of the *emporia*? Can we posit a rural-based economy that was resilient to the change in fortunes in the wider continental economy and one which carried different archaeological signatures? Despite the prolific coinage in the eighth century suggesting socially embedded exchange and a high-level integration in places like East Anglia and Kent, Grenville Astill has drawn attention to non-coin using areas and has suggested that two models of exchange co-existed – a monetary economy and a form of non-coin using exchange (Astill 2011, 259). John Blair, in his introduction to *Waterways and Canal Building in Medieval England*, drew attention to the same issue suggesting that coin and metalwork loss may not be a true reflection of the movement of bulk goods (Blair 2007a, 14–15). As late as the eleventh century, where in Domesday Book 300 *mitts* (c. 30 tons) of salt are recorded as payment in return for 300 wagon loads of wood, it appears that large and important transactions of bulk goods could take place without money changing hands (Sawyer 1977, 147). Is it therefore likely that larger scale transactions of lucrative agricultural and industrial produce were changing hands in the eighth century outside of the *emporia* and without the need for silver coinage?

That this rural economy carried different archaeological signatures to those of the *emporia* and the trade in precious metals is perhaps apparent at an even earlier period. John Maddicott contrasted the wealth of Northumbria with the apparent poverty of Wessex in the seventh century and argued that the wealth that we see travelling westwards during this period, from the estuarine coastlands of the Rhine, 'failed entirely to reach the south-west'. Furthermore, he argues that, 'If the South-West was an economic backwater when the West Saxons moved in, so it remained throughout the seventh and eighth centuries' (Maddicott 2000, 43). Despite this relative inequality in wealth, however, Maddicott contrasts the more immediate profitability of Northumbria with the more lasting legacy of West Saxon expansionism. Was this lasting legacy founded in part upon an economy based on the production and movement of rural bulk goods, an economy that isn't so easily detectable in the archaeological record?

In Ben Palmer's analysis of the hinterlands of three major *emporia* he has identified what he termed 'substantially different trends' in the *Hamwic* hinterland, in differential terms, from the hinterlands of Ipswich and London (Palmer 2003, 58). In Hampshire he suggests that a manorial system of royal estates, one that he believes the West Saxon kingdom was first to organise its lands around, can be linked with the evidence. Ryan Lavelle's analysis of the customary 'farm of one night', recorded as a levy on some estates listed in Domesday Book, and its link to patterns of landholding in the pre-Conquest periods illustrates that royal estates were part of the development of a conscious landholding strategy in the mid to late Anglo-Saxon period and a crucial part of the state's power base (Lavelle 2007). Land, rather than precious metals and a circulating coinage, seems to be the wealth indicator in middle Anglo-Saxon Wessex. In general, the few imported goods of this period recovered from rural sites in Hampshire suggest that 'monetary transaction had not spread into the hinterland' (Palmer 2003, 58–60). This is perhaps best illustrated at Romsey where the current absence of coin finds of this period from the town is seen by Katharina Ulmschneider, in view of the clear evidence for eighth-century iron production, as 'intriguing' (Scott 1993, 18, 47; 1996, 9, 11; Ulmschneider 2000, 39). Do we have an economy in Wessex then based on landed wealth, one that profited from *emporia*-orientated continental trade but was not necessarily reliant on it? It is widely thought that *Hamwic* was the product of royal establishment and Barbara Yorke has drawn attention to the likelihood that the *emporium* served as a convenient place for the West Saxon kings and elites to exploit the agricultural surpluses from their estates, in return for a slice of the cross-channel trade that other regions in early medieval England were enjoying (Yorke 1995, 306–307). There has been a marked shift since the 1990s in the approach to *emporia* sites and in both England and on the Continent there is an increasing desire to direct the focus away from their role in long-distance trade and towards their significance in the creation of regional production and distribution (Hodges 2000, 9; Hamerow 2007). Placing *emporia* in a regional setting presupposes lines of communication by which goods moved between these large commercial centres and their agricultural hinterlands.

One of the factors behind the identification of 'productive' sites as early as the 1980s, along with the large scale of coinage recovered, was their identification along the main lines of transport and communication (Metcalf 1984a, 27, 41). This appears especially to be the case in Wessex and in particular in Hampshire and the Solent basin where a theoretical network of trading routes can be put forward: What is most apparent from middle Anglo-Saxon trading sites in the region is access to the coast and maritime transport. Although the riverine geography of Wessex is limited, all of the documented minsters of the eighth century and other trading sites sit at the mouths of rivers: Christchurch on the Avon, Nursling and Eling on the Test, *Hamwic* on the Test and Itchen, a *mercimonium* (mentioned in Hugeburc's *Vita Wynnebaldi*) (Bauch 1984, 136–137; considered at length in Morton 1992, 59–62; Ulmschneider 2003, 81), at the mouth of the River Hamble and finally, Titchfield on the River Meon. They would all thus be well placed to receive bulk goods floated down-river from estates deep in the Wessex heartlands (see pp. 25–26, Figure 8 for a discussion of *stæð*s (landing-places) for the possible entrepots from which collected goods were launched). Yet, to what extent were these sites also served by overland communications? Elsewhere, good access to major routes of communications has been identified for other inland 'productive' sites such as, South Newbald (Yorks.), Melton Ross (Lincs.) and Hollingbourne (Kent) (Leahy 2000; 2003, 148; Brookes 2003, 95). Whilst at present evidence for inland 'productive' sites is

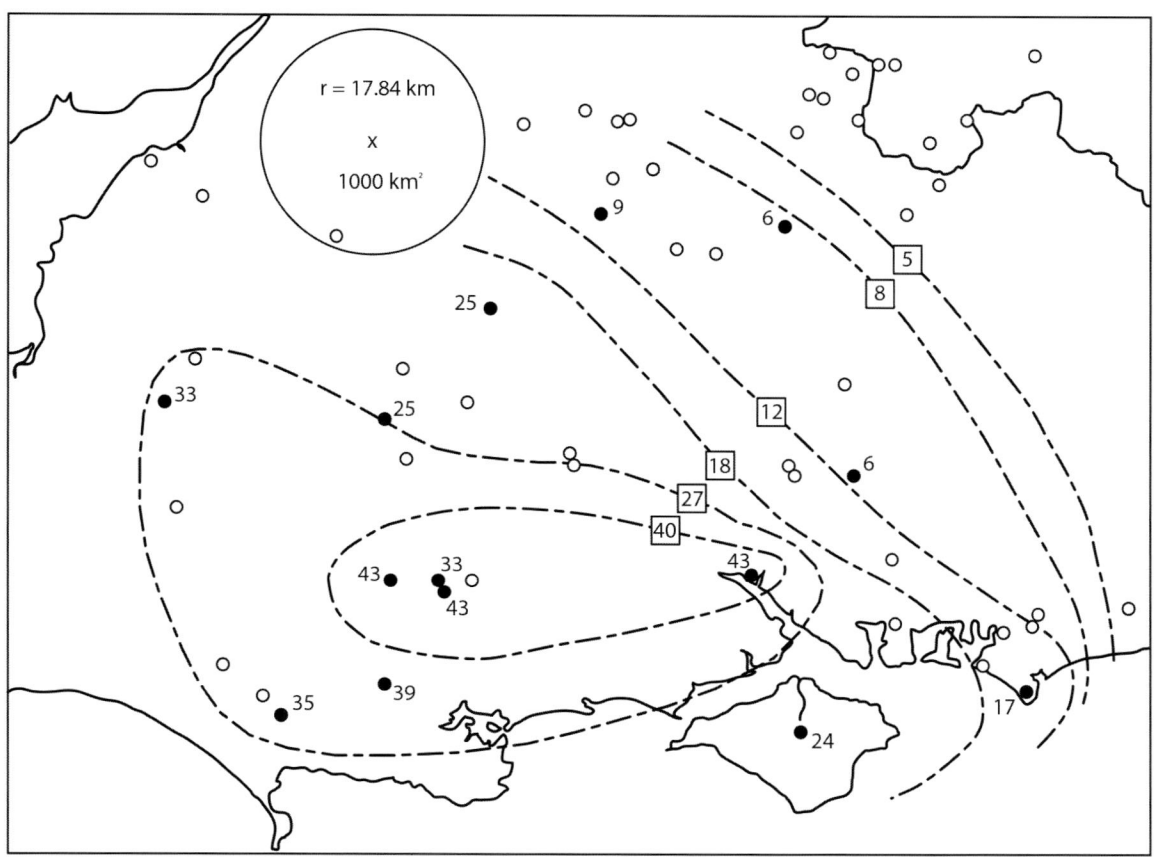

FIGURE 12. Regression analysis of Hamwic coinage in Wessex (redrawn from Metcalf 2003, 41, fig. 4.1).

lacking for Wessex, *sceat* coin finds of a type U and J recovered from excavations in *Hamwic* have been suggested to indicate a north–south route to a minting place in the upper Thames Valley (Metcalf 1988, 21–22; 1994, 559). Furthermore, Series J *sceattas* have been recovered from excavations and metal detected sites at and around Winchester and are thought to suggest access to this same trade route (Ulmschneider 2000, 43). Most recently, the patterns of coin loss from the period *c.* 600–780 in the west of Anglo-Saxon Wessex have been used to suggest both that foreign trade was not necessarily being mediated through *Hamwic* and also that an older trade system is evident, one in which hill-forts and other open sites were important (Costen and Costen 2016). Central to this hypothesis is the character of the riverine geography of the kingdom and the relative paucity of coin finds from Devon and Somerset are seen as a result of the south and south-western-facing river systems upon which these areas were dependent (Costen and Costen 2016, 3). The law codes discussed above seem to suggest that middle Anglo-Saxon Wessex had overland routes upon which traders were travelling *uppe on lande*, so despite the apparent importance of riverine communications in the 'age of emporia', there must have been arterial overland trade routes.

The emergence of a market-based economy

One of the main complications in attempting to map the transition from an economic model that was probably more allocative and redistributive to one better characterised by a market-based system lies in separating out the political and military objectives that lay behind the construction of fortified sites throughout the region in the ninth and tenth centuries (Yorke 1995, 309). The study of urban development during this period – particularly in Wessex – is intricately bound up with the study of the West Saxon kings' strategy of burh building throughout the kingdom in order to counter the Viking threat. A series of excavations in Winchester in the 1960s and into the early 1970s coupled with renewed interest in the *Burghal Hidage* gave birth to a debate that sought to tease out the economic origins of the urban centres of the tenth century from the military requirements of a nation under siege (Brooks 1964; 1979; Hill 1969). Whilst the defensive functions of the West Saxon burhs is undeniably a primary factor in their creation, the regular planned gridded street systems evident at Winchester during the early tenth century were believed to serve as an index of the economic aspirations of the time (Biddle and Hill 1971; Loyn 1971; Biddle 1976a; Hill 1978a). More recently, the appropriateness of assigning the socio-economic successes of urbanisation in Wessex to purely political endeavour has been brought in to question (Palmer 2003, 50) and it seems clear that those towns that 'succeeded' in the tenth to eleventh centuries were already well connected in terms of communications, and had existing minsters founded in the eighth and ninth centuries. This is a view shared by Grenville Astill who suggests that an older, pre-burh pattern of trading and assembly places (one linked to minsters and royal *vill*s), 'despite royal efforts to the contrary, continued to determine the social and economic relationships of the majority of the population'(2006, 240–250, 254).

In general, more recently, there has been a greater recognition of the need to identify the mercantile aspirations of the burhs, and Astill goes on to offer a model of urbanisation from the ninth to the eleventh centuries where sites can be seen to be the product of either a 'short' or 'long' chronology of development (2006, 235–236; and for a review of the non-military functions in this process, see Williams 2013). Winchester in the ninth century clearly experienced a phase of population growth and a rise in commercial activity, demonstrating a 'short' chronology of urban growth. Similar late ninth- and early tenth-century growth appears to be the interpretation of the archaeological evidence in the case of the main urban centres of England such as London, Gloucester, Exeter, Canterbury and Oxford with the hierarchical structure of towns taking shape throughout the tenth century (Hodges 1989, 156). However, Winchester, perhaps the most archaeologically studied of all burhs, could be seen as exceptional on the basis of clear evidence for both royal and ecclesiastical interests playing a major part in its development (Yorke 1984). For the majority of other burhs in southern England the evidence appears to be extremely limited for urban development until the late tenth century and for these sites a 'long chronology' is proposed (Astill 2006, 235–236).

Studies of urban plan forms, and the identification of a 'high street' type burh, convincingly suggest an intention, from the very start, for a permanent population as part of a plan of urban formation (Haslam 2015). However, if there were economic aspirations in the implementation of the *burghal* system, they were not realised for at least a generation later as the general picture painted by archaeological evidence is one of slow urban growth in the first half of the tenth century (Hinton 2000, 230). It is in the last third of the tenth century that urban centres experience a period of rapid expansion with many towns benefiting from new trading opportunities, a greater access to silver supplies and coinage reform. Archaeologically, street frontages – a sure sign of competition for space – become identifiable and cellared buildings indicate the need for the storage of surplus for redistribution (Hinton 2000, 230–235). This widespread growth is also evident in the topography of the emerging towns: the laying out of gridded streets and tenement properties, the metalling of streets and the refurbishment of walls (Palliser *et al.* 2000; for Wessex see the various contributions to Haslam 1984a). It is also reflected in the increase in the range of craft production and the distribution of the pottery types of the main economic centres of production. Leatherworking, woodworking, pottery, metalworking, bone-working and textile production are all represented at archaeological excavations in the major urban centres of the later tenth century.

This later (than Winchester) urban development is seen by some as part of a 'massive leap forward' and the result of a 'step-change' wherein a dramatic shift in the economic organisation and political development of Wessex is paralleled by increased cereal growing, the fragmentation of estates, the rise of a lesser nobility, the creation of open fields and further changes in the countryside that had a dramatic effect on the level and scale of agricultural production (Hodges 1989, 155–166; Astill 2011, 269–272). Instead of large regional 'monopolistic' centres like *Hamwic*, what emerges is, in Richard Hodges's view, a ranked hierarchy of competitive markets with places like Winchester at the top, sites like Chichester and Southampton representing middle ranking centres of limited craft-production until the mid-to-late tenth century, and lower-order markets in this hierarchy equating to locales of 'sub-regional trade in surplus commodities' (Hodges 1989, 156).

Whilst this is not the place to explore in great detail the reasons behind the apparent growth in the later tenth century of urban centres, it is the place to raise the possibility that changes in the networks of travel and communication may have affected, and been affected by, these significant shifts in production and consumption. Crucially, Astill does not see the step changes identified as being necessarily part of an evolutionary sequence nor one directly related to state development but rather a result in a 'shift from long-distance trade to regional trade'. The urban development in the tenth century, in contrast to that of the eighth, was unrelated to long-distance trade and a response to regional developments in the socio-economic structure of the countryside (*i.e.* developments to an existing rural economy based on royal estates, strategic landholding with central places (minster/royal *tuns*) exhibiting proto-urban functions) (Astill 2011, 269–272). In Astill's model, it is not until the later tenth century and into the eleventh century that long-distance trade picks up again (2000, 37–38).

So, can we see this shift in trade patterns articulated in the route networks of early medieval Wessex? Theoretically, a network of trading routes in the eighth century consisted of coastal connections, down-river transportation of bulk goods and limited overland routes. As we shall see, the evidence from charter boundary clauses is at its most abundant and most reliable in the middle decades of the tenth century, that is, before the rapid urban development towards the end of the century. So whilst this source might be restricted in its capacity to help elucidate the inland geography of routes in the eighth century, it will be in a position, in part, to help bridge the gap between the decline of middle Anglo-Saxon coastal trading in Wessex and the rise of a network of inland market towns in the late Anglo-Saxon period. Furthermore, as the relative abundance of detailed boundary clauses (compared to the eighth and ninth centuries) continues into the eleventh century, the opportunity is provided to detect any developments in concurrence with the re-establishment of long-distance trade in that period and to assess how this may further have affected the networks of travel and communication in the late Anglo-Saxon landscape of Wessex.

Part 2

THE CASE STUDIES

CHAPTER FOUR

A note on the evidence: Anglo-Saxon charters and Ordnance Survey maps

Anglo-Saxon charters

Two key sources of evidence have been used as the primary means with which to reconstruct the early medieval landscape across the ten study areas in Part 2. Whilst LiDAR data, aerial photography, archaeological evidence, stray finds (recorded on the Portable Antiquities Scheme, www.finds.org.uk), place-names, earlier tithe and estate maps and later historical sources have all been variously consulted in order to interrogate aspects of each study area, the principal geographical framework for each has been derived from the rich topographical information contained in Anglo-Saxon charter boundary clauses being plotted against first edition Ordnance Survey (OS) maps; both County Series at 1:2500 (1853–1904) and 1:10560 (1846–1969). Elsewhere the veracity of the detailed local knowledge of landscape contained in Anglo-Saxon charter boundary clauses has been reviewed for its use as a means to reconstruct elements of the early medieval landscape and patterns of land holding (Langlands in press). Anglo-Saxon charters record grants or leases of land made by the king, bishop or some other dignitary, to their subjects and usually contain a section detailing the nature of the grant and the dues dependent on it, a witness list and an indication of where the boundaries of the estate in question lie. It is the latter of these that is of most importance to this study. Within these 'boundary clauses', written in Old English, is contained an incredibly rich level of topographical detail in the form of individual boundary marks. These can comprise natural or human-made features and many of them can be located in the present day landscape, or by reference to cartographic evidence of the nineteenth and earlier centuries.

There is huge variation in the tradition of Anglo-Saxon charters, a corpus that spans a four-hundred-year period, and this is not the place to provide a detailed review. The reader is advised, in the first instance, to familiarise themselves with P.H. Sawyer's *Anglo-Saxon Charters: An Annotated List and Bibliography* which, now available as an updated on-line resource, serves as an indispensable aid in navigating the idiosyncrasies of what is a highly complex body of material (Sawyer 1968, www.esawyer.org.uk). Critical editions of the cartularies of early medieval ecclesiastic houses, from which many Anglo-Saxon charters derive, have been published in a series of volumes funded by the British Academy and these are vital to understanding the complexities of individual documents and their scriptorial and diplomatic contexts (Campbell 1973; Sawyer 1979; O'Donovan 1988; Kelly 1995; 1996; 1998; 2000; 2001; Miller 2001; Kelly 2004; 2005; Crick 2007; Kelly 2007; 2012; Brooks and Kelly 2013). There is also an extremely useful guide for the translations of some boundary clauses to be found on *Langscape*, a web-based resource that explores *The Language of Landscape: Reading the Anglo-Saxon Countryside* (www.langscape.org.uk). For now, it is important to highlight that what complicates the issue of using Anglo-Saxon charters is that many cannot be taken at face value. Less than 20 per cent of the 1,500 or so documents that exist survive in the form of original single sheet diplomas. Anachronisms and later interpolations undermine the credibility of the remaining 1,200 which survive principally as copies made into cartularies. Boundary clauses feature in around 50 per cent of the overall corpus but where they appear in purportedly earlier charters, it is clear that they are later interpolations or appendages (figures quoted in Kelly 1990, 39). How, then, can we reliably use this kind of topographical detail when it derives from such problematic contexts?

There is also a chronological bias in the nature of the material with the overwhelming majority of detailed vernacular boundary indications originating in the early to mid-tenth century. We are, therefore, very much being presented with a description of the later Anglo-Saxon landscape scene. Their inclusion may represent a shift in function for the charter itself and the concept and tradition of granting land by 'bookright', reflecting the increasing role of the written word in framing proprietorial arrangements (Kelly 1990, 46). As evidentiary documents they would need to function at, presumably, shire and hundred court level and it is for this reason that, even in the most outrageous of forgeries, there was perhaps a requirement for the boundaries to be as accurately recorded as possible (Langlands in press). Indeed, this may reflect 'a practical benefit' of King Alfred's educational programme implemented a generation before, placing in the hands of an increasingly literate middle order a powerful tool that had hitherto been the preserve of the ecclesiastical classes (Keynes 1990, 231). It is within this level of literacy amongst an emergent and landed thegnly class that we might seek a social context for the detailed vernacular boundary clause and that a number survive as standalone documents suggests that surveys may have been undertaken in the field and consigned to the written word at the point of capture (Lowe 1998, 65).

Various landscape historians and archaeologists have, therefore, confidently employed the rich and detailed topographical information bound up in the vast corpus of Anglo-Saxon charters in a range of academic enquiry, informing studies of settlement (Costen 1994), industry (Hooke 1981c), judicial practices (Reynolds 1997; 2002b), assemblies and meeting places (Pantos and Semple 2004), hydronymic features (Jacobsson 1997), the ideology of middle and late Anglo-Saxon England (Semple 1998) and dialectical variations of Old English

4. A note on the evidence: Anglo-Saxon charters and Ordnance Survey maps

(Kitson 1995). Equally, it has proven popular to provide 'solutions' to individual boundary clauses, and many of these can be found in county journals and publications relating to local history (They are far too many to list here, but the following provide some useful examples: Brown *et al.* 1977; Reed 1979; Hooke 1994b). An outstanding contributor to the study of Anglo-Saxon charter boundary clauses is Della Hooke whose work focused initially on the charter evidence for the West Midlands (1981a; 1982). Thus, the counties of Staffordshire (1983), Worcestershire (1990) and Warwickshire (1999) have received attention in individual volumes as have, from outside her original area of study, Devon and Cornwall (1994b). She developed her study of the topographical detail to address themes such as Anglo-Saxon woodland management (1978; 1989b), the salt industry (1981c), open field systems (1981d; 1988), communications (1977; 1980), burials (1981b), administrative frameworks (1994a), settlement patterns (1989a), village nucleation (1985b) and early units of government (1992). The historically defined territories of the Kingdom of the *Hwicce* and the Western Marches of Mercia are also scrutinised through the analysis of charter boundaries (1985a; 1986). Hooke stresses that a combined historical, archaeological and geographical approach should be adopted in order that this historical data could be 'spatially related to the physical and man-made environment' (1977, 219). This is a key tenet of *The Ancient Ways of Wessex*; that the rich topographical information contained in Anglo-Saxon boundary clauses can be used independently of the documents within which it resides and examined within what might be considered its primary context (*i.e.* the landscape). As O.G.S. Crawford noted over fifty years ago (1953, 41), 'Objects should be capable of being marshalled spatially, that is to say geographically, so as to yield new knowledge'.

Crawford himself was a pioneer in identifying the boundary marks recorded in Anglo-Saxon charters and his study of the Andover area (1922) serves as a benchmark for the level of confidence we can frequently have in placing one-thousand-year-old landmarks within the contemporary landscape. Crawford was, however, an inveterate field archaeologist and spent a good deal of his life on-foot within the very landscapes that were his object of study. Elsewhere, the same level of rigour is advised, and access to landscapes is deemed of practical importance so that boundary solutions can be provided off the back of 'repeated walking in various seasons and weathers' (Brooks 1974, 224). Much of what Crawford achieved, however, could not have been accomplished without being guided by a resource that has proven invaluable to the study of field archaeology, local history and historical geography since its widespread availability in the early twentieth century. I am writing, of course, about the first edition OS sheets, published from 1846 onwards. It is this resource that G.B. Grundy made such extensive use of in a series of publications that provided solutions for the southern counties of England. Wiltshire (1919; 1920), Hampshire (1921; 1924b; 1926b; 1927b; 1928c), Dorset (1933a; 1934; 1935a; 1936; 1937; 1938; 1939b), Somerset (1935b), Berkshire (1922–3; 1924a; 1925; 1926a; 1927a; 1928a),

Oxfordshire (1933b), Gloucestershire (1935–6), and Worcestershire (1928b) all received Grundy's attention in a series of studies that systematically related the individual landmarks recorded in Anglo-Saxon charter boundary clauses to topographical data recorded on the first edition OS. Grundy's approach, although unlike Crawford's in his failure to undertake elucidation in the field, was a comprehensive coverage of the material (at least in Wessex) which to this day serves as an excellent desk-based assessment. Although some of his translations of individual boundary marks are found wanting by the standards of today's scholarship, on reflection, Grundy successfully demonstrated one crucial piece of information: Anglo-Saxon estate boundaries, as recorded in charters, follow very closely the lines of parish boundaries recorded in the first edition OS. This priceless observation is largely what supports the degree of confidence this, and other studies, can have in placing landmarks recorded over a millennium ago in the landscape of today.

The Ordnance Survey and the theory and practice of landscape archaeology

> By the time one has scrambled over hedges, leapt across boggy streams in deep woods, traversed narrow green lanes all but blocked with brambles and the luxuriant vegetation of wet summers, not to mention walked along airy ridges on a day of tumultuous blue-and-white skies with magnificent views of deep country all round – by the time one has done this, armed with a copy of a Saxon charter and the 2½-inch [Ordnance Survey] maps, the topography of some few miles of the English landscape is indelibly printed on the mind and heart. (Hoskins 1955, 66–67).

The above paragraph encapsulates what some have seen as both the strengths and weaknesses of W.G. Hoskins's method: the underlying theoretical discontents of the Romantic movement (Johnson 2006, 36–40). Recent commentaries have put the 'lukewarm' reception to his work by professional historians and archaeologists down, in part, to 'the emotional tenor of the writing' and increasingly, Hoskins is being seen as a product of his times, writing within a very specific post-War social and economic context (Meinig 1979, 209; Matless 1998, 274–279; Wylie 2007, 35). On a factual level, Hoskins's *The Making of the English Landscape* has garnered debate and on the 'origins' of the English landscape, open-field systems and village nucleation, it has proven to be both incorrect and over-simplified (Taylor 1980; Aston 1983). Hoskins's approach was one where extended narratives depended upon 'argument by example', where the personal and individual meaning of the 'local' was of importance and where 'shallow-brained' theory had little role to play (Hoskins 1959, 6–7). Its underlying approach has maintained its appeal. Maurice Beresford in the preface to *The Medieval Landscape of Wessex* (Aston and Lewis 1994), for example, when describing his annual 'escape' from the Midlands to the 'hills of the holiday counties', recalled how his mind responded more to Belloc's sentiments rather than the 'now-forgotten Keats, Shelley and Wordsworth' (1994, vii–viii). He went on to assert that it was the nature of landscape history to be comprised of 'an accumulated record of single and small observations'. This 'inductive' and 'historicist' nature meant that, like the study of archaeology more generally in the 1950s and 60s, this form of landscape study (or appreciation) became subject to the criticisms of the 'processual' school of archaeologists characterised in British archaeology by the work of David Clarke (1973; 1978) and, in a 'spatial' context, by Ian Hodder and Clive Orton's *Spatial Analysis in Archaeology* (1976). The 'New Archaeology' as it came to be known cautioned against empiricism, imploring all archaeologists to adopt the rigorous scientific framework of hypothesis and deduction to test ideas and theories.

At this juncture, traditional landscape history/archaeology and theoretical archaeology seemed to have gone their separate ways. A second generation of traditionalists took the lead of Hoskins and the themes of field systems, village origins and historical landscapes in general continued to be debated in the particularistic vein (Aston and Rowley 1974; Rowley 1981; Aston 1985; Lewis *et al.* 1997). In landscape archaeology more generally discomfort with the 'processual' school began to surface with many of the criticisms levied at the New Archaeology equally applicable to the method of 'traditional' landscape archaeology. In essence, statistical, quantitative and scientific approaches to landscapes were seen to have removed people from the analysis and the 'top-down' approach of the traditional school was seen as constraining human action via a series of 'titanic' forces (such as population growth, climate, land use patterns and settlement patterns/foci) over which the society being studied had no concept (see, for example, Thomas 1993, 19–48 for a critique of Aston 1985). Whilst these methods were all ways in which to generate datasets or 'evidence', 'post-processualists' as they came to be known, implored landscape archaeologists to be both conscious of their subjectivity and to 'go beyond the evidence' in our interpretations of the past (Bender 1993, 7–8). The link between the concept of landscape and the rise of capitalism as observed in approaches used in cultural geography exposed traditional landscape archaeology as an extension of the preserve of the privileged (Cosgrove 1984; Thomas 1993, 21–29). In place of the landscape painting, an articulation of the Western 'new politics of vision', field archaeologists had the aerial photo, satellite imagery and Geographic Information System, as a means with which to control, monitor and discipline the past, reflecting the 'sectional interests of the powerful' (Fleming 2006). So whilst 'positivist' approaches to landscape were in danger of hiding behind scientific objectivity (Pearson and Shanks 2001, 158, 162), the most obvious criticism of the 'traditional' school was concerned with the flaws of back-projecting contemporary concerns with social hierarchy and territoriality – concerns that may not have existed in pre-Enlightenment cultures. Post-processual landscape archaeologists expressed a concerted desire to explore the worlds of past societies from the 'dwelling perspective' and to adopt an 'archaeology of inhabitation' as an antidote to approaches wholly dependent on the constraints of positivist, top-down and distinctly Cartesian analytical tools – such as the OS map (Thomas 1993, 21–29).

Out of these criticisms arose new ways of looking at landscape and drawing on the ideas of Heidegger (1927) and Merleau-Ponty (1945) amongst others, post-processualists began to apply to their subject matter the branch of philosophy known as phenomenology (Bender 1993; Tilley 1994; Bender 1998; Tilley 1999; 2004a; 2004b). Phenomenologists wanted to see human action and agency as central to the understanding of past landscapes and set out to describe the character of human experience via our own apprehension of the material world. In breaking down the subject–object divide that characterised post-Enlightenment thought, phenomenology was seen to provide an antidote to the abstract models generated through both traditional and positivist approaches to landscape.

For the most part, these approaches have found themselves to have had the greatest impact on the study of the remoter periods of British prehistory and, in particular, in approaches to the Neolithic. Yet, their findings and the accusations they make of traditional 'investigative' approaches to landscapes have not themselves been without criticism. In the first instance it has been questioned whether at all it is possible to apply the character of human experience specific to the Western world to conceptions of the world by past societies (Gosden 1996; Fleming 1999; Brück 2005). In one of the most sustained critiques of post-processual approaches to landscape, Andrew Fleming has also concluded that these new approaches are more problematic than their proponents have allowed themselves to accept. Furthermore, in a defence of 'conventional' landscape archaeology, Fleming suggests that the priorities for the landscape archaeologist lie not in 'hyper-interpretative' writing or 'experiential treatments' but on grounded arguments and in weighing evidence dispassionately (Fleming 2006, 279).

One of the key aspects of these theoretical and conceptual shifts is that much of the debate surrounded the study of prehistoric landscapes. The archaeology of historic and proto-historic landscapes seems to have either been ignored by the theoreticians or its proponents have carried on oblivious of these wider theoretical debates. *The Medieval Landscape of Wessex* (Aston and Lewis 1994), for example, appears unacquainted with the debates concerning theory and practice taking place in contemporary approaches to archaeological landscapes and, more recently, it has been accepted that the discipline of medieval archaeology has been slow to embrace archaeological theory even if this should, at least, be set against the major contribution that practitioners of the discipline have made to the advancement of methodology (Jones and Hooke 2003, 31). Further criticism of the 'traditional' school of landscape archaeology suggests that it has always suffered from the 'disciplinary subordination' that characterised archaeology of the 1960s and 1970s (Johnson 2006, 59). The main criticism from a landscape perspective was that archaeologists were going out to create an uncritical link between historical terms, such as 'manor', 'village' and 'open-field system' and their objects of study, without first setting out to describe in physical terms the entities they were reporting on, that is, characterising them *archaeologically*. It was clear by the late-1980s that medieval archaeology had to set out its own agenda, one with its own archaeological discourse founded on its own epistemology and data and one wherein the written record forms part of a wider suite of evidence (Driscoll 1988; Austin 1990). In some ways then this interdisciplinary doctrine set the study of prehistoric landscapes apart from the study of historic landscapes. Fleming draws attention to the fact that re-peopling the landscape – *i.e.* putting the humans that scientific methods had removed, back into the landscape – was enabled through 'text-aided' horizons. Documents allow us to write, in his words, 'imaginatively about named individuals' without having recourse to 'hyper-interpretive' methods (Fleming 2006, 277). David Austin, in his 'Proper Study' of medieval archaeology also drew attention to the fact that documents had the capacity to provide 'insights into the past's own self-awareness' (Austin 1990, 12). In many ways, this is where the Anglo-Saxon charter boundary clauses can come in to their own as a source for understanding the landscape in both a 'top-down' manner and from the 'dwelling perspective'. Yes, we can put dots on maps, indicate where roads, woodland and fields existed. But these references to landmarks – places – also allow us to explore the lived experience, and provide us with a window into a 'local sense of place', illustrating what those who were tied to the land 'thought of the landscape in which they lived' (Howe 2008, 31–32).

Ever since Frederic W. Maitland likened the OS map to a palimpsest, the metaphor has proven a popular vehicle through which to conceptualise change in archaeological and historical approaches to landscapes (Maitland 1897, 15; Wilson 1987; Johnson 2006, 55–58). In particular, the notion that a landscape could be read, especially through the maps of the OS, has gained popular currency amongst archaeologists, historians and historical geographers (Martin 1968; Bender 1998, 25–38; Muir 2000; Yarnham 2010). Hoskins, writing of Maitland's comments on the OS, implored us to 'decipher' the OS map, and to see the landscape as 'an equally revealing document, equally full of significant detail, and equally difficult to interpret aright' (Hoskins 1952, 289; Rippon 2008, 1). Putting aside the inherent problems in identifying what is a 'right' and 'wrong' interpretation of a landscape, the idea of seeing landscape as a 'document' and something that can be 'read' has been popular amongst commentators and analysts of the British landscape for well over half a century. O.G.S. Crawford also made use of the metaphor describing the 'surface of England' as a 'document that has been written on and erased over and over again' (1953, 51–59). The parallel between such a parchment or tablet and the man-made landscape is, remarked David Wilson, 'so evident that it scarcely needs to be spelled out in detail' (1987, 5). Crawford's rationale for its use undoubtedly lies in the vision of the British landscape he gained from undertaking aerial photography (Crawford 1924; Crawford and Keiller 1928). What he saw so clearly from above was not just landscape phenomena that made up the content of the OS, but the shadow, frost and crop marks of whole field systems and settlements that had been literally wiped from the surface by centuries of arable agriculture. This is where the palimpsest paradigm and its relationship to the OS warrants reconsideration because so much has not been wiped from the tablet but has actually influenced later formations. Wilson admits that under scrutiny the parallel between palimpsest and landscape begins to break down and more recently, the application of the metaphor has been questioned on the grounds that it sometimes fails to take into account temporality or the 'time dynamic' (Cosgrove and Daniels 1988, 8; Lucas 2005, 37–43; Bailey 2007). For example, Gavin Lucas, whilst not entirely dispensing with the idea, prefers rather to see a 'messier affair' of temporality, multiple events and multiple timescales overlaying each other, rather than a simple reduction to chronological sequence (Lucas 2005, 37). The palimpsest therefore becomes an ongoing process where different time scales and their constituent landscape phenomena co-exist.

Perhaps then, rather than seeing the landscape as something that is recurrently wiped clean and re-inscribed, we should, sticking with the notion of something that can be read, see it as a document that requires 'editing' if it is to be truly understood chronologically and with all the complexities of various time scales. In such a scenario, we might envisage some text being entirely removed whilst other text is re-worked into new passages. Extending the metaphor, meaning within the text could be lost or re-interpreted and old text could be interpolated with new. The issue arises, however, about how exactly this document can be 'edited' and how the landscape historian and archaeologist can draw out meaning from the various phases of writing and rewriting. Put literally, how exactly can we separate out the chronological relationships between various landscape features, establish the level of continuity and change, and identify re-use and redundancy?

As an approach, horizontal stratigraphy has yet to earn formal recognition of its validity in the same way vertical stratigraphy and, for example, the Harris matrix has (Harris 1989; Harris *et al.* 1993; Roskams 2000). Yet, in many ways, the principles of stratigraphy as applied to the relationships between discrete archaeological features in open area excavations are the same as those that can be applied to the relationships between topographical phenomena over much larger areas. By analysing the stratigraphic relationships therefore between various landscape features, theoretically, we can draw out a relative chronology between the earliest and latest elements. It is perhaps best to begin with the exact object of study in all of the enquiries that employ horizontal stratigraphy as a method. These are 'lines' in the landscape. As Peter Fowler remarked, 'the skein of complexity on the ground seems to be held together by linear features' (Fowler 1998, 28). He identifies three types of line: field boundaries, tracks and ditches. To these should be added the various administrative boundaries that we have good evidence for by the late Anglo-Saxon period. Certain sites in the landscape can also be employed in the elucidation of relative chronologies between these lines. For example, execution cemeteries appear to have been located on or close to boundaries and the location of high status barrow burials seems dependent on proximity to major arterial route ways (Williams 1999; Reynolds 2002b; Brookes 2007). It is logical, therefore, that in both situations the line had to be already in existence to serve as the focus for the burial practices. Thus, a relative chronology exists between line and site and this, in essence, is the method of horizontal stratigraphy. In theory the interrelationships between the various lines that create the 'skein' of the landscape can be mapped and ordered in such a way as to enable retrogressive analysis of the landscape. Clearly, later layers of lines can be peeled away to reveal progressively earlier time slices wherein the earliest network of lines can be explored for the influence they may have had on the structure of the later landscape.

The method of horizontal stratigraphy is most regularly applied in the analysis of field systems and in Eastern England in particular it has led to suggestions that patterns of field boundaries mapped in the nineteenth century can be projected back into prehistory. In one of the first studies to propose the survival of early relict field systems, Warwick Rodwell and Paul Drury identified an alignment of linear field boundaries in Essex that appeared to extend beyond the limits of manorial estates (Drury and Rodwell 1978; Rodwell 1978). They were thus deemed to be earlier than the medieval manorial boundaries and earlier too than the course of a Roman road that appeared to slice through them. A similar situation was observed in the Scole-Dickleborough area of East Anglia where Tom Williamson drew attention to the manner in which a Roman road appeared to cut through an earlier field system identified through the drawing out of landscape lines from nineteenth-century editions of the OS (Figure 13).

Parts of the field system that Williamson had identified were still in modern use and were thus seen as a 'relict' or survival from pre-Roman times. The term now widely used to describe these field systems is 'co-axial' and in plan form they tend to take the appearance of 'slightly wavy brickwork' (2008, 123). Successive studies in Norfolk (Figure 13) (Davison 1990; Hesse 1992), Cambridgeshire (Oosthuizen 1998; Harrison 2002; Oosthuizen 2003; Percival and Williamson 2005) and Hertfordshire (Figure 3) (Williamson 2008, 126–127) have found similar evidence for the apparent survival of these 'co-axial' field systems existing as part of later medieval and present day field systems. Co-axial fields seem not to be restricted to the east of England though. Examples have turned up in Herefordshire (White 2003, 45), and on Dartmoor they survive as an archaeological entity rather than a 'relict' system (Fleming 1988). In Wessex, we not only have Fowler's (2000) Fyfield and Overton research area but also a number of examples identified by Simon Draper, particularly in north Wiltshire where co-axial systems appear overlain by Roman roads (Draper 2006, 91–93). In the parish of Crudwell, landscape features on a north–south axis underlie the Fosse Way where it forms the county boundary between Wiltshire and Gloucestershire and at Calcutt near

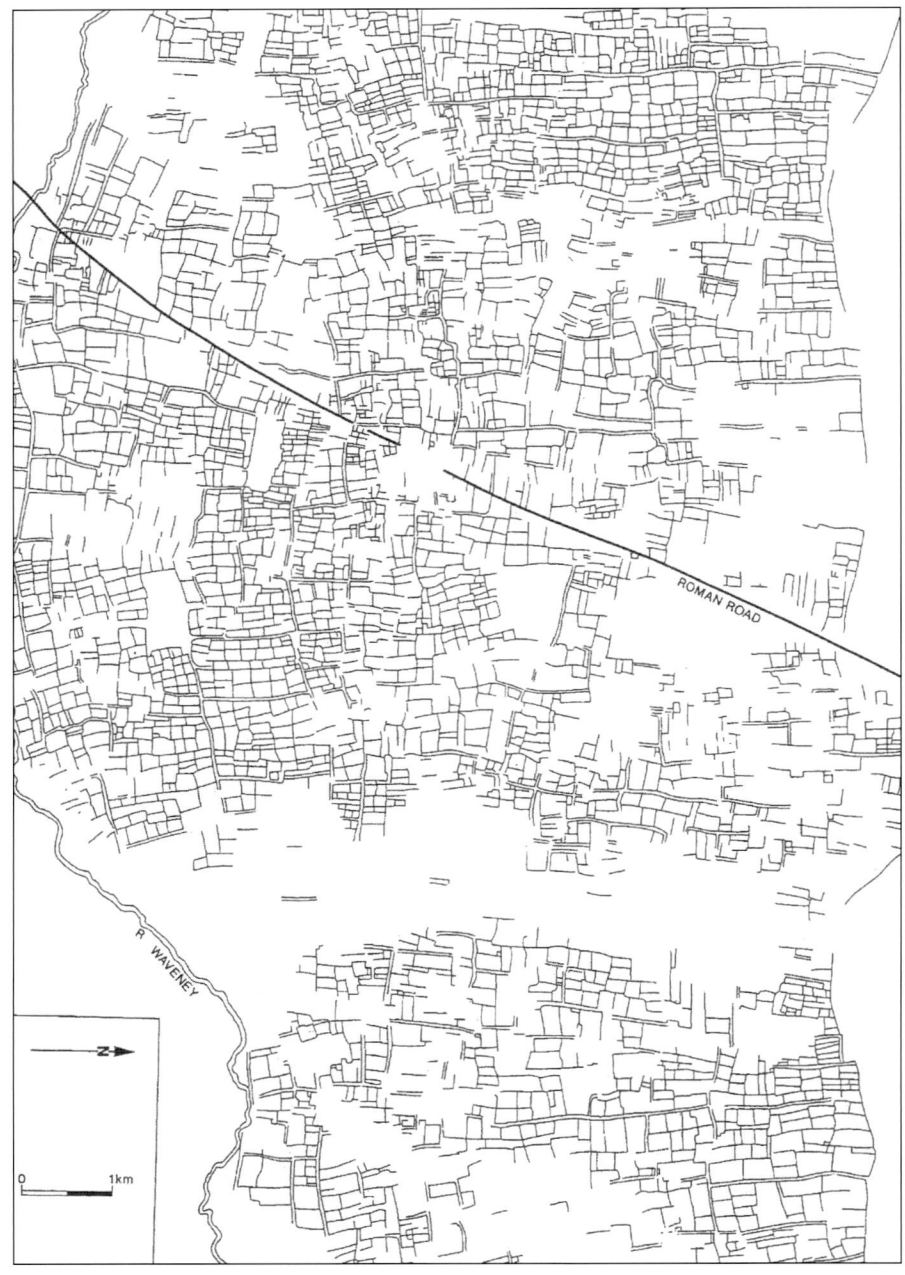

FIGURE 13. The Scole-Dickleborough field system, an observation underpinned by the analysis of historic OS maps (Williamson 2008, 125, fig. 30).

Cricklade, the Roman Ermine Street is seen to slice obliquely across a north–south field system. Echoing the descriptive terminology of Williamson, he describes 'the somewhat wobbly outlines of a sort of grid', the major arterial axes of which he believed were already old in the Romano-British countryside (Fowler 1998, 28).

The wholesale survival of such field systems has at times been met with a degree of scepticism which cautions against the tendency to overstate the case through a selective use of landscape lines and an over-reliance on OS map data (Hinton 1997; Martin 1999). However, under closer scrutiny and with a more critical approach it appears that whilst such field systems are not entirely comprised of prehistoric and/or Romano-British ditches and that some axes are of more recent dating, the main lines of the systems can be traced back to prehistory (Rippon 1991; Williamson 1998; Percival and Williamson 2005; and for a continental study see Vermeulen and Antrop 2001). Stephen Rippon, for example, re-examined the evidence from Essex and established that whilst not all elements of the field system could be pushed back into prehistory, some elements were potentially very early in date (1991). Williamson also returned to the Scole-Dickleborough case study of 1987 (Figure 13) and cited a number of examples in Hertfordshire (Figure 3), Shropshire and Norfolk where archaeological evidence has also confirmed only partial rather than comprehensive survival of prehistoric field systems (2008, 132–134). As a consequence, he now opts for a process of continuous development, and the infilling over time of what was originally a much sparser pattern of parallel boundaries.

In all of these studies, the main subject of analysis has been the various lines as they are configured in cartographic form and these have been used to propose the identification, essentially through a form of morphology, of an early field system type. It is primarily the horizontally stratigraphic relationship with Roman roads and the shared characteristics (*i.e.* co-axial) of the field systems that have enabled their projection back into prehistory. Studies employing horizontal stratigraphy in the analysis of another type of line – routes – are less prevalent. John Baker and Stuart Brookes set out a methodology, in their study of the communications network of the Kennet Valley, to examine the topology of routes. In their view, analysis should be attempted on two levels prior to the integration of evidence from documentary sources. The first stage is the retrogressive analysis of cartographic sources; peeling off the known recent additions to a landscape to reveal a network of communications of some antiquity. Next, they advocate assessing the stratigraphic relationships between the remaining routes identifying where routes overlay, abut or cut each other as indications of their relative date. By doing this, they argue, a matrix of route-way relationships can be arrived at where it is possible 'to determine the relative chronology of road construction' (Baker and Brookes 2013a, 172–173, but see also Deacon 1994). Elsewhere, the importance of identifying routes, their primacy in the landscape and their subsequent influence has been commented on but with little further attempt to refine an approach. Christopher Taylor has observed more generally that the pre-village layout of tracks in an area very often conditioned the form of villages when they finally appeared (1979, 104). Fowler's study area demonstrates how 'the presence and use of tracks at different times have influenced the formation of the historical landscape and, arguably, at least some strands of the tenurial framework within which it developed' (1998, 27).

Route ways appear clearly, therefore, to be important in the formation of a landscape and in many cases, may represent the primary lines.

Of all the studies discussed as part of this chapter, it is difficult to overstate the role early editions of OS maps have played, if not in just the provision of contextual spatial data, then in underpinning entire studies. Brian Roberts and Stuart Wrathmell's *Atlas of Rural Settlement*, for example, took as its starting point the pattern of settlement as identified in the first edition OS maps of Great Britain and their subjective grading of type-sites allowed them to divide England into three zones of settlement believed to be of great antiquity (Roberts and Wrathmell 2000). In a recent study of the fieldscape of late Roman and early medieval Britain, the first edition OS has been used as a 'historic landscape' horizon and in many cases, archaeological field boundaries can be demonstrated to align with linear features recorded by the surveyors of nineteenth-century Britain (Rippon *et al.* 2015). Elsewhere, because the early OS employed detailed mapping at large scales, adhering to common cartographic principles, plans of medieval towns can be elucidated for the further analysis of urban morphological and development (Lilley 2000; Haslam 2016; Lilley 2017).

Earlier cartography could have been used in the ten case studies presented in this volume but what is of critical importance is that the OS of the nineteenth century was concerned with topography rather than property and therefore represents, certainly in the second edition series, the first attempt to provide accurate topographical data for the requirements of a fast industrialising nation. Through the 'primary levelling of Great Britain', a campaign to measure all altitudes from a standard position, the demands of railway engineers were met and the adoption of a finer scale (in some places 25 inches to a mile) meant that the rapidly expanding industrial centres could be mapped and socially catered for (Hewitt 2010, 289–307). In both these requirements, the OS was essentially to come of age and to produce, in scientific terms, a level of recording comprehensive in its detail. The accuracy, and crucially, the uniformity of nineteenth-century OS maps across the entire nation is in part the attraction for their use amongst landscape historians and archaeologists and their various studies illustrate that the information recorded by the surveying techniques of late eighteenth- and nineteenth-century European cartographers can be studied for what it can reliably say about a much earlier state of affairs.

We have seen how Maitland was first to draw attention to the notion that the OS was a palimpsest that could be read, and he eulogised how 'two little fragments of the original one-inch OS Map will be more eloquent than would be many paragraphs of written discourse'. But he was also prophetic in his suggestion that, 'A century hence the student's materials will not be in the shape he finds them in now … instead of a few photographed village maps, there will be many; the history of land measures and the field systems will have been elaborated' (1897, 596). The OS has played no small part in these advances and

4. *A note on the evidence: Anglo-Saxon charters and Ordnance Survey maps* 73

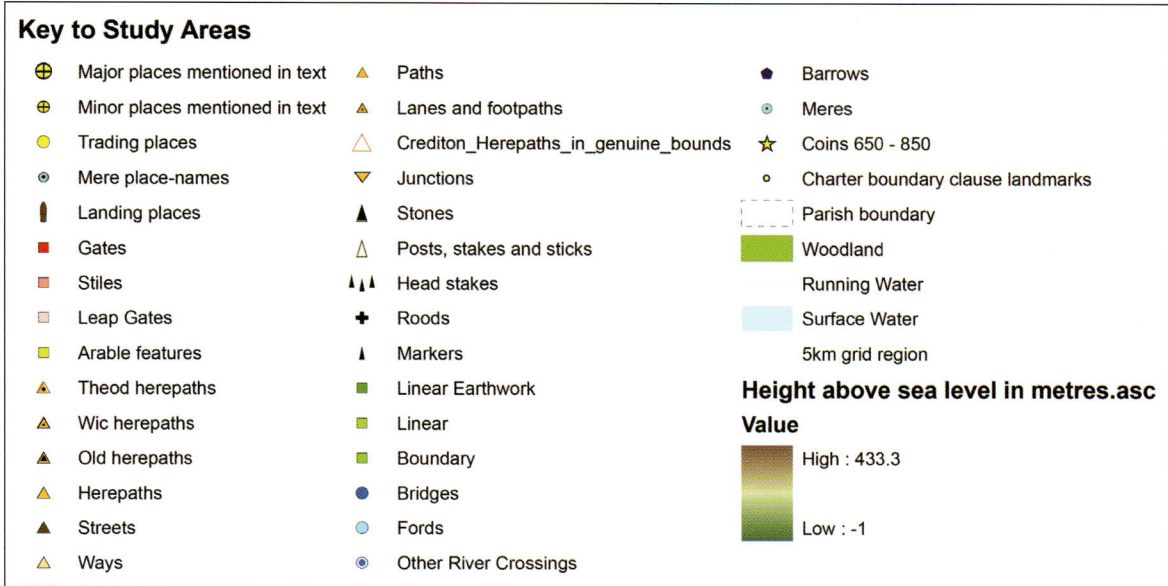

FIGURE 14. Key to the study areas.

it is hoped it will be demonstrated here that it will serve as an appropriate and sufficient back-drop to explore the lines of communication of early medieval Wessex and the detailed topographical information found in Anglo-Saxon charter boundary clauses.

The text for the following ten study areas (Figure 15) should be read in conjunction with the maps and key provided (Figure 14). The Anglo-Saxon charters examined for each study area can be found in a series of tables in the appendix. Having located the various landmarks referred to in Anglo-Saxon boundary clauses, a set of symbols were applied to features deemed relevant to discussion. In particular, priority was given to routes, river crossings, access points (such as gates and stiles) and markers (such as stones, roods and posts). Five-kilometre grid squares have been applied to the maps and labelled with their OS tile data reference number (*e.g.* SU89SE). The grid provides both scale and directional information whilst also allowing landmarks, routes and places mentioned in the text to be located by the reader with a greater degree of ease.

A number of maps have been reproduced for different study areas. Commentary is by no means comprehensive in its discussion of the early medieval contextual data of each area, in the same way that the maps are selective and not comprehensive in their inclusion of early medieval historical and archaeological data. Both the text and study area maps have naturally gravitated towards particular themes. For example, in study area 3, herepaths predominate and have therefore guided the discussion.

The selection of some supporting data is intended only as a guide: woodland coverage and surface and running water is derived from modern OS digital data (© Crown Copyright 2019). Ancient parish boundaries (*i.e.* pre-1974)

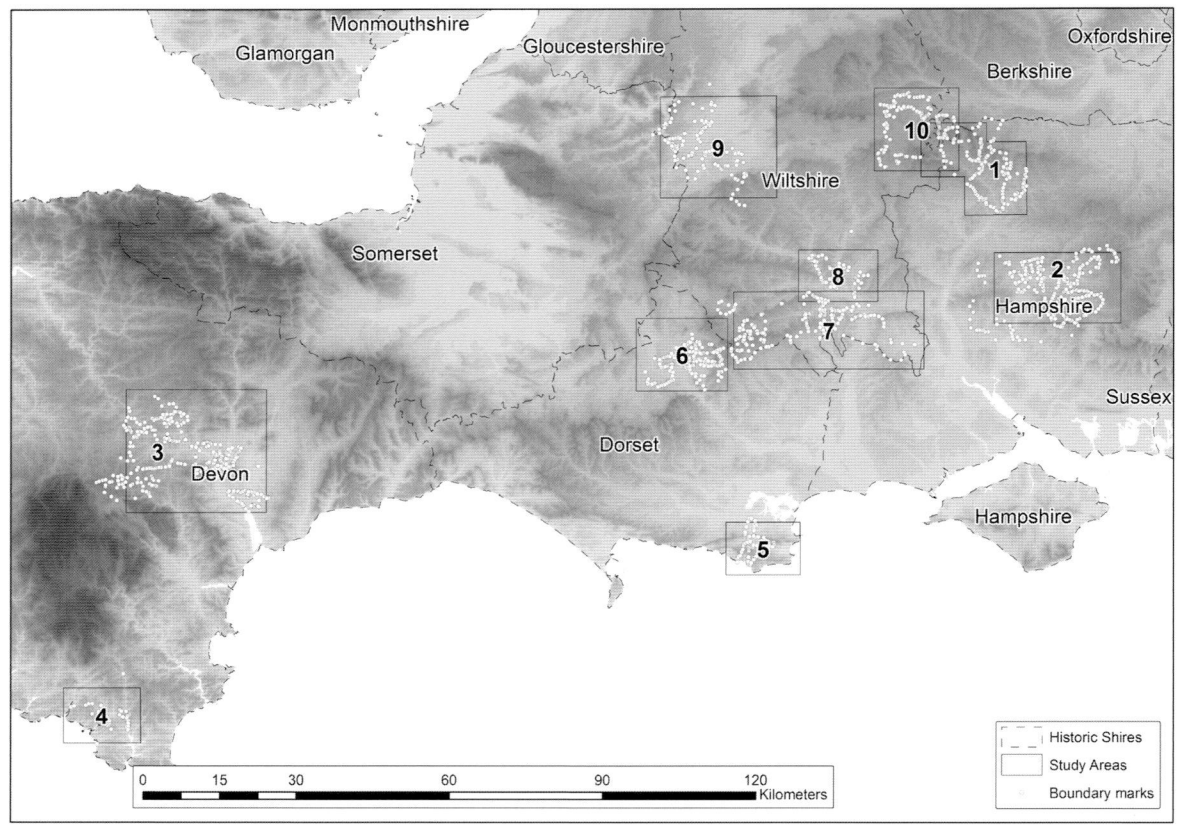

FIGURE 15. The locations of study areas 1 to 10.

were taken from the *Historic Parishes of England and Wales: An Electronic Map of Boundaries before 1850* (https://discover.ukdataservice.ac.uk) and have been included to aid in the location of boundary features. Some caution is therefore needed in the reading of this geographical data. In most cases, an attempt has been made to sketch in the likely routes by which early medieval society moved through the landscape, however, it is clear that a vast array of possibilities existed for crossing certain landscapes, be they downland or river valley. So other interpretations are possible. It is felt, however, that the main lines of communication in the later Anglo-Saxon period, through the various study areas, have been achieved.

The record of the distribution of coins is built around selective use of the data from the *Early Medieval Coins* register, the *Portable Antiquities Scheme* and examples recorded in county archaeological journals and other publications. The chronological distribution has been limited to the period 650–850 and is intended mainly for discussion in Part 3. Major and minor places that have been mentioned in the text have also been illustrated and underlying each study area, to help provide even more contextual data, are copies of late nineteenth-century first edition OS maps (OS 1st Edition Six Inch base map: © Crown Copyright and Landmark Information Group Limited (2018), all rights reserved).

CHAPTER FIVE

Hampshire

Study area 1: the Harroway, Whitchurch and the Bourne Rivulet Valley

The exact meaning of the *harro-* element in Harroway is uncertain. Leslie Grinsell suggested that it could have derived from any of *har* (hoary [with age]), *hereweg* (military road), and *hearg weg* (the way to the shrine or holy place) (1958, 298). Of the latter he suggests 'doubtfully' that it applies to Stonehenge, yet elsewhere it has been argued that because the course of the Harroway passes this exceptional monument *en route* to the west of England, it is inconceivable that it did not play some role in the conceptual landscape of Old English speakers as they moved through the south of England (Reynolds and Langlands 2011, 417). In such a scenario, its nomenclature is likely to have followed the same etymological rules that governed the formation of Harrow-on-the-Hill (Middx.) and Harrow Hill (Suss.) and is therefore likely to have derived from *hearg* (shrine, temple) (Mawer and Stenton 1929–30, 165; Ekwall 1947, 211). Recently, the archaeological and topographic context of the term *hearg* has been examined in relation to a number of sites and it seems likely that the traditional definition applied to the term as a place of pagan worship of the fifth to seventh centuries should be eschewed in favour of a longer-lived, localised cult practice peaking in the late Iron Age and Romano-British periods (Semple 2007). Such a definition certainly fits with the recorded archaeological activity at Stonehenge where many sherds of third- to fourth-century pottery indicate a high point of activity in the late Roman period prior to a lull in the fifth century and onwards (Parker-Pearson 2012, 312). Thus, it seems reasonable to assume that a route, perhaps of prehistoric origin, was functioning at the point it was assigned an Old English name and it most probably represents a major east–west 'Romanised' road (Crawford 1922, 34–35; Cochrane 1969, 12; Timperley and Brill 1970, 81–91; Belsey 1998, 32).

Recent commentary has, however, questioned this interpretation, favouring, on onomastic grounds alone, a derivation from *here-weg* (Baker and Brookes 2013a, 149). This compound is extremely rare, surviving in only two known examples, both from the cartulary of Shaftesbury Abbey, where one appears in a reliable charter of the very early eleventh, and the other in what seems likely to be an eleventh century fabrication (S 899 and S 630; Kelly 1996, 86–92). Observations on the character of herepaths would seem also to stand against the *here* interpretation. The herepaths of the Kennet area appear 'primarily to link together the static defences of the region rather

76 *Alexander Langlands*

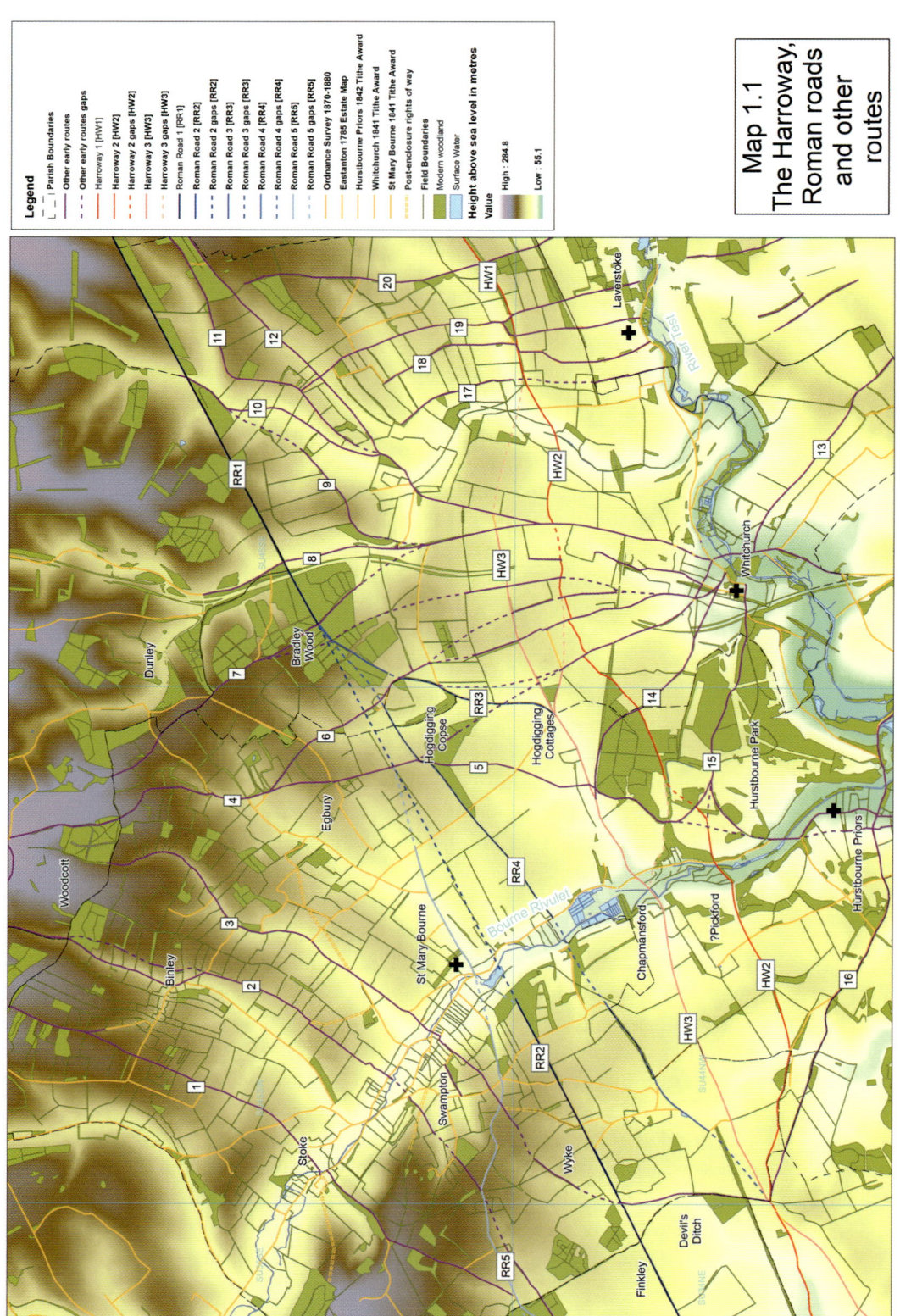

Map 1.1 The Harroway, Roman roads and other routes

than reflecting natural corridors of movement as defined by the regional topography' (Baker and Brookes 2013a, 258). The Harroway very definitely fits into the latter category and finds better parallels in the Icknield Way, and putative Jurassic Way as a corridor of movement, making best use of natural watersheds. Furthermore, in Chapter 10 it is argued that the compounding of *here* almost uniquely with path is of significance in itself. Were the Harroway designated *here-* status we might also expect it to be described so in contemporary boundary clauses, yet it is not. In the boundary clause of a clearly forged charter for land at Whitchurch, it is termed the *horo weg* S 378 (Keynes 1994, 1145). This form, the first documented reference to the route, suggests a different etymological route from that which is recorded on the nineteenth-century OS and late eighteenth-century estate map for Enham, Eaststanton, Finkley and Doles (1785, H.R.O. cat. no. 9M84/1). A similar form can be found in a charter purporting to record a grant in 900, by the king to New Minster, of land at Micheldever some eight miles to the north-north-east of Winchester (S 360). That this document is unreliable in its present form is founded on the observation that the script and diplomatic form both derive from the eleventh century (Brooks 2000a; Rumble 2001, 231; 2002, no. XVIII). In this charter it is recorded as *horpeges norð ende* (the north end of the Harroway). These first documented references to the road do little to help in the interpretation of the *Harro-* element and suggest that by the time of the eleventh-century forgeries, the meaning of the term had become obscure to the forgers. This may indicate a relative antiquity, and might therefore, as might be expected for one of the most enigmatic prehistoric temple sites of Northern Europe, place the first use of the term used to describe it in the earliest period of Anglo-Saxon migration and settlement.

The Silchester to Old Sarum Roman road [RR1] (1.1) is referred to in the charter perambulations on three occasions (1.2) and is used as a boundary. [RR2], the original continuation of [RR1], may have fallen out of use at a very early period. No trace of the road can be observed on the east bank of the Bourne Rivulet (SU45SW), nor in the historic maps and LiDAR data for the region. It may have been systematically robbed, ploughed out or, perhaps, never existed on this line but made use of an earlier crossing further upstream. It seems likely that [RR2] was surpassed by [RR4] which adopts a course that connects it to the Harroway at an entrance in the Devil's Ditch through which a number of routes coalesce. On this line, it is followed by the parish boundary too and both of these observations might suggest an early medieval date. [RR3], a (?later) deviation from the course of the Roman road to a junction with the Harroway at Hogdigging Cottages, perhaps to make use of the latter's crossing of the Bourne Rivulet at Chapmansford, is referred to as a 'way' (1.2, SU45SW), thereby bracketing a conjectural sequence of [RR1]+[RR2] → [RR1]+[RR4] → [RR1]+[RR3] between the date of first construction (presumably in the late first to early second century) and the possible tenth-century (but more likely eleventh-century) dating of the Whitchurch charter (Figure 17).

FIGURE 16 *(opposite)*. Study area 1.1, the Harroway, Roman roads and other routes (contains OS data © Crown copyright (2018)).

FIGURE 17. [RR3] (see study area 1.1), a substantial way connecting the Silchester to Andover Roman Road to the Harroway.

The boundary to the Stoke estate circumnavigates Harewood (SU44NW) where it makes use of a 'way' [16] (1.1), and then crosses another two ways. The continued course of the Harroway is used for a short stretch as the boundary in this location. The perambulation then proceeds north-west where it is referred to as the 'boundary way' (Figure 18, 1.2). A further reference to a boundary way is made on the course of the conjectural route connecting Winchester with the Upper Thames and via a crossing of the Test at Whitchurch (SU45SE). However, no further reference is made to this route or a likely north/south alternative via a crossing at Hurstbourne Priors. Running across the top of the entire study area is a pronounced ridgeway, with a recognised importance in the early medieval period (Grundy 1918, 164–169; Ulmschneider 2000, 45–50, map 18), which passes through the hillfort of Walbury. The charter for Crux Easton provides a rare opportunity to examine the landscape of an earlier period as it is one of four charters where detailed directional terminology in the boundary clause is written in Latin and the landmarks in Old English (Langlands in press). In this case, the ridgeway is referred to as a *via publica* in a charter reliably dated to 801. However, in the next reliable charter, dated to 931, it is termed a herepath. Finally, in a charter that purports to date to 909, but likely to be a forgery of the late tenth to eleventh century, it is called a 'way'.

The 'chapmen's dell' is recorded in three charter boundary clauses (1.2, SU45NE). In the study area we are told that the boundary runs

FIGURE 18 *(opposite)*. Study area 1.2, the Harroway study area (contains OS data and OS 1st Edition Six Inch base map © Crown copyright and Landmark Information Group Limited (2018), all rights reserved).

5. Hampshire

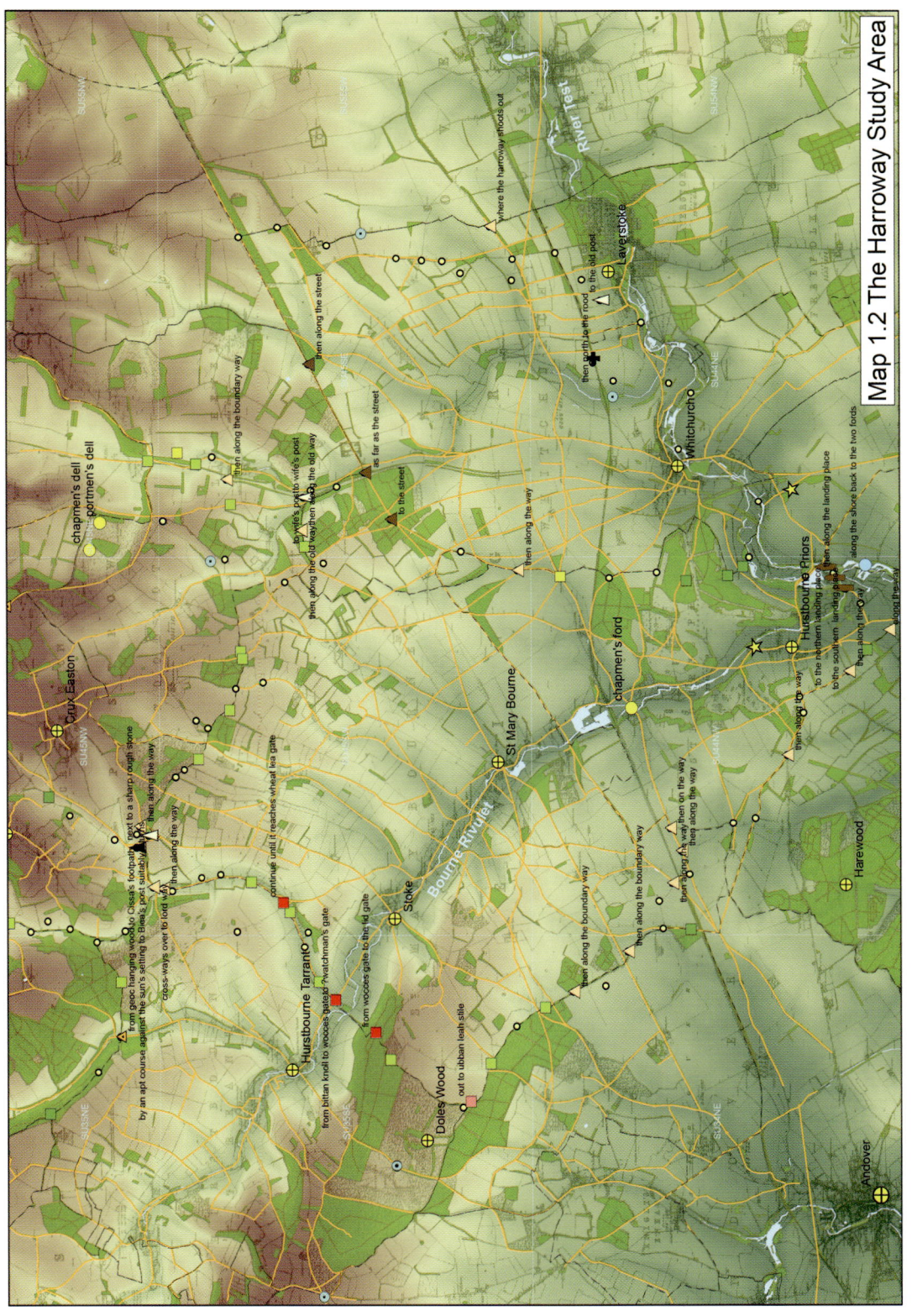

Map 1.2 The Harroway Study Area

oð ceapmanna del, of ceapmanna dele þæt on portmanna del (as far as the chapmen's dell, from the chapmen's dell then to the portmen's dell) and illustrates that there was clearly a distinction at this time between a chapman and a portman, both with their respective 'dells'. What is of further interest is that in a contiguous charter (not covered in the study area and dating to 955) the boundary runs in the reverse order *of scipdelle. on cypmanna dell* (from the sheep dell to the chapmen's dell) (S 565). Clearly this crossroads location, overlooked as it is by the hillfort at Burghclere, was an important site for trading with the likely objects of exchange the livestock reared in the surrounding areas of expansive open downland (Figure 19).

The north-west boundary of the Stoke estate is marked by a *haga* (hedge) within which four access points are referred to (1.3, SU35SE/SU45SW). These consist of three gates and a stile and together it is likely that these represent an important division in land use between arable agriculture in the valley bottom and pasture land on the open downland. This division is made explicit in the name of the 'wheat lea gate' and this reference suggests that elements of the field system identified on the north-eastern valley slopes above Stoke and St Mary Bourne (SU45SW) can be pushed back at least to the eleventh century. To the north-west of the *haga*, the landscape is characterised by dry open downland from which the headwaters of the Bourne Rivulet spring. A distinctive characteristic of this landscape is the prevalence of dew ponds of which seven have been identified from the charter boundary clause evidence, a further eight are recorded as place-names whilst numerous unnamed lentic systems are recorded in modern OS digital data (1.3). Of significance is the name *Butermere* given to the area recorded in a grant of 863, which says something of how the stretch of open downland was perceived and used in the ninth century. Another three gates are recorded in boundary clauses on the fringes of this area of downland whilst a 'horse path gate' indicates an internal division. 'Ashbert's gate' and 'Æmbriht's gate' potentially indicate responsibility over, and rights to, this managed landscape of upland grazing with all the evidence of dew ponds, *hagas*, gates and the butter place-name suggesting a form of transhumance and dairying of the like described by Harold Fox (2008).

Study area 2: Winchester and the Upper Itchen Valley

With the exception of a charter for Martyr Worthy (S 340) dated to 868, until the tenth century the charters for this study area are all apparent forgeries. Attempts therefore to study aspects of change in this landscape from the ninth century onwards are compromised by the difficulty in securely dating the boundary clauses attached to forged documents. This study area, by necessity, is limited to presenting a generic tenth- and eleventh-century landscape within which a total number of 497 boundary features have been recorded (2.1).

Around the Worthy place-names (Headbourne, Kings, Martyr and Abbots) and Easton a number of linear features (dykes and lynchets) imply a working

FIGURE 19 *(opposite)*. Study area 1.3, Buttermere and 'Æscmere' (contains OS data and OS 1st Edition Six Inch base map © Crown copyright and Landmark Information Group Limited (2018), all rights reserved).

5. Hampshire

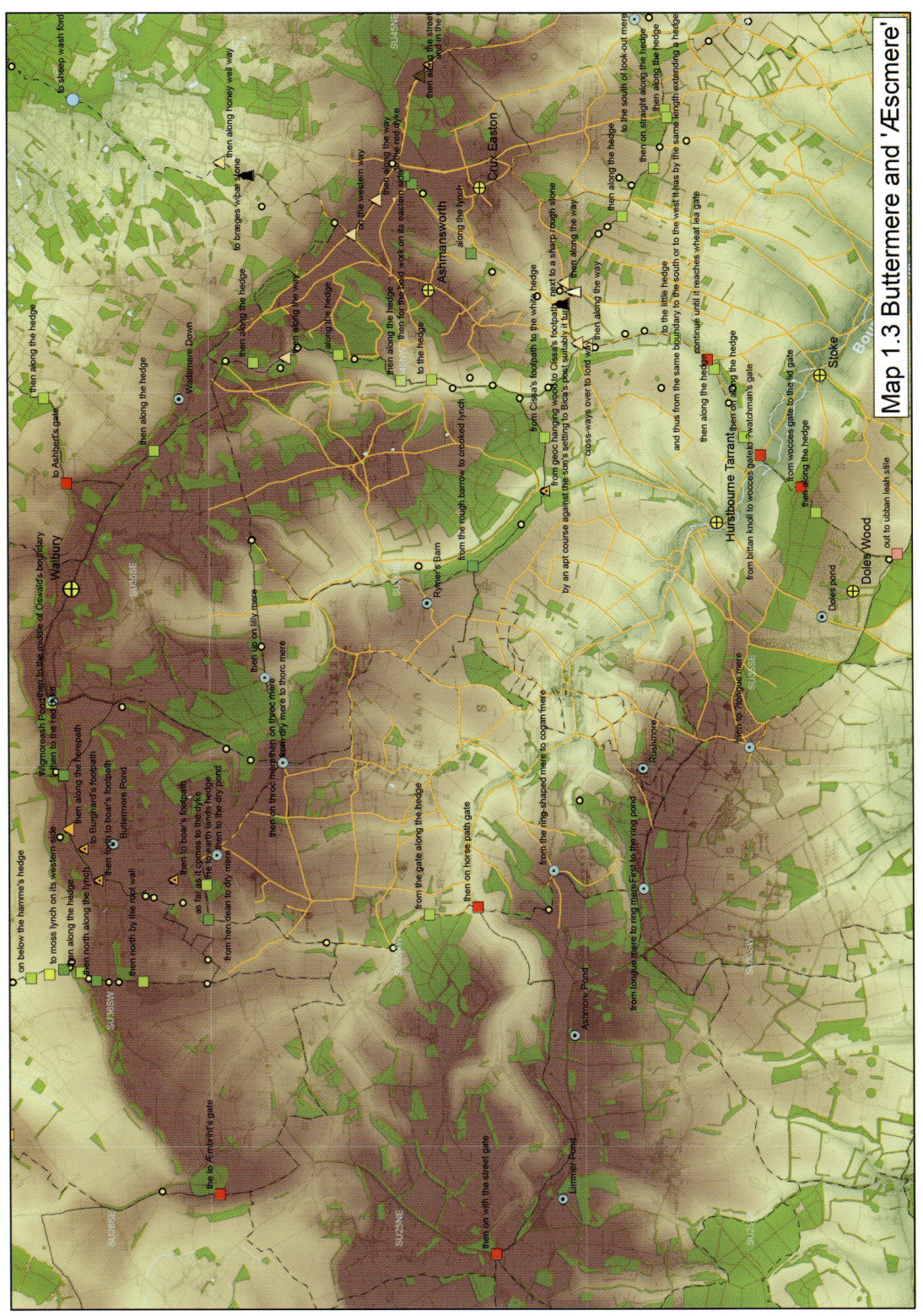

Map 1.3 Buttermere and 'Æscmere'

and subdivided landscape and references to arable features (furrows, furlongs and acres) mentioned on the internal boundary between Headbourne and Kings Worthy suggest cropping (2.1, 2.2, SU43SE/SU53SW). References to headlands and acres in the Ovington and Itchen Stoke area suggest that similar land use extended up the valley as far as Kilmeston where a further 'six acres' are referred to (2.3, SU53SE/SU52NE).

The references to three *lið* gates throughout the study area suggest a certain type of gate (2.1, SU42SE, SU52SE and SU53SW) is in operation. A literal translation of 'ship gate' seems obscure but the same mechanism by which a ship's sails are operated might give some indication as to how these gates were opened and closed. The *tyrngeate* [turn gate] in the vicinity of Tichbourne is a more obvious indication of the opening mechanism and in all, such gates may have controlled access through a busy agricultural landscape for the many people travelling to and from Winchester. These gates are to be contrasted with the gates recorded in the far east of the study area which bound an area described by the East Hampshire Survey, through the lack of archaeological finds, as being remote and characterised by scattered settlement in a landscape dominated by woodland (Shennan *et al.* 1985, 89–91, fig. 8.1). A further four gates are recorded in the study area charters to the east of Map 2.1 (just outside the area covered by the map) and in each case, they are compounded with -*mere* elements (*grenmeres stigele*, *lammeres geate*, *bocmeres stigele* and *bealmmeres geate*) suggesting the internal divisions of wood pasture and the controlling of access to watering holes.

On the course of the South Downs Way, the ridgeway that runs due east-south-east from Winchester, there is a reference to a herepath running in the direction of a crossing of the Meon river at Warnford. This herepath is intersected by a route running due south-west from Cheriton which is also called a herepath (2.1, SU52SE). Otherwise, however, where referred to by charter boundary clauses, routes across this area of downland are generally termed 'ways'. The area to the north of Winchester provides a better opportunity to explore the character of Anglo-Saxon roads as a little more detail is given concerning function (2.2). The Roman road running due north-west from Winchester towards Cirencester via Mildenhall is referred to as a 'street' in the location of the *fulan flode* and the *heafod stoccan* and as both places survive into the modern period as Fulflood and Harestock, these references can be closely located to within a few miles of Winchester. Further out from the city, however, the terminology used to describe the Roman road changes. The use of the road as a boundary along much of its length in the study area gives justification for placing the two references to herepaths on its course. What is important here is that, in being designated a 'herepath', what is being suggested is that it is not merely a physical description that is being alluded to but perhaps one that highlights a certain status. The importance of this route's status as a herepath transcends its appearance as a 'street'.

Close analysis of the Headbourne Worthy boundary clause in this area allows a previously un-located landmark of considerable importance to be placed in the landscape with a degree of certainty. After the reference to the street at Harestock, the boundary passes a thorn tree and a deep dell before reaching

FIGURE 20 *(opposite)*. Study area 2.1, Winchester and the Upper Itchen Valley (contains OS data and OS 1st Edition Six Inch base map © Crown copyright and Landmark Information Group Limited (2018), all rights reserved).

5. Hampshire 83

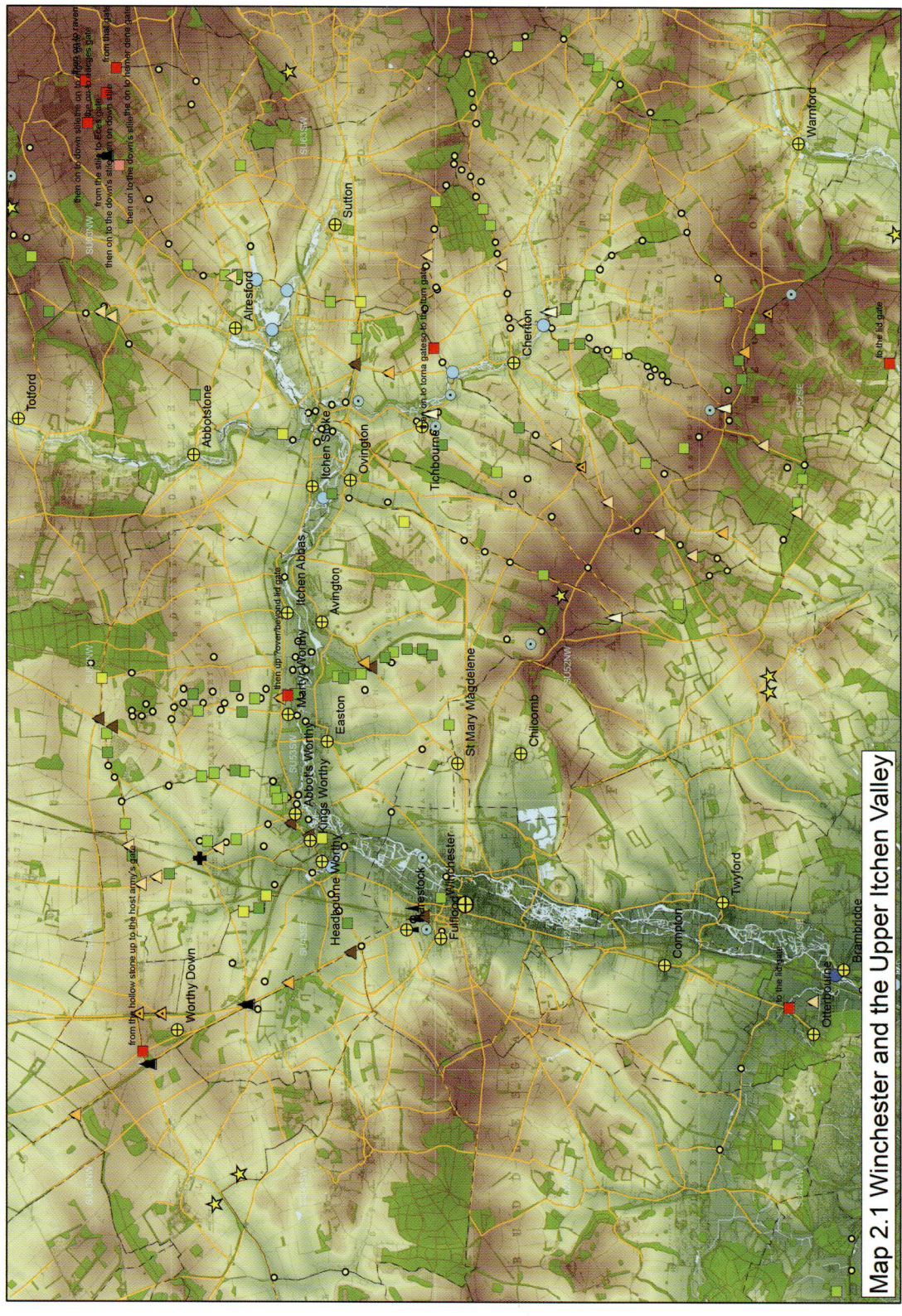

Map 2.1 Winchester and the Upper Itchen Valley

Map 2.2 Winchester and North Environs

the *kinges stane* (2.2, SU43SE). In the section on Pilgrimages in Chapter 2 we learnt of the stone cross that Lantfred, writing in the late tenth century, tells us a blind man and his young guide stopped at, three miles out of Winchester. However, in a later version of these events, Wulfstan's *Narratio Metrica de S. Swithuno*, we are told that at this resting place there stood, '*uexillum quoniam de rupe uestusto erectus sublime crucis*' (a replica in ancient stone of the sublime cross). However, Wulfstan elaborates further and informs us that this was a cross, '*quem lingua 'Petram' uocat Anglia 'Regis*'' (which the English tongue calls the King's Stone) (Lapidge 2003, 319). The relevant section of the Headbourne Worthy charter boundary clause details:

> up to kinges stane. from kincges stane. up to holan stane. of holan stane. up to fyrd geate. of fyrd geate. to wic herpaðe. and lang wic herpæðes. æft to kynges stane [up to the king's stone, from the king's stone, up to the hollow stone, from the hollow stone, up to the host army gate, from the host army gate to the *wic* herepath, along the *wic* herepath, back to the king's stone]

So the boundary clause, in returning to the king's stone, describes an essentially detached piece of downland and this has been interpreted as the triangle of land bounded by the Roman road to the west, the London Way to the north, the *wic* herepath to the east and known as Worthy Down today (2.2, SU43NE/SU43SE). This places the king's stone at the point where the *wic* herepath parts company with the Roman road heading north out of the city of Winchester, a location that in the nineteenth century was marked by a mile stone indicating a distance of three miles to Winchester. Michael Lapidge, in his discussion of Wulfstan's 'king's stone', suggested that such a monument may have been a boundary marker on the limits of the *territorium* of the Roman city and draws attention to the ancient Chilcomb estate, which in the tenth century was a suburb of the city (Biddle 1976b, 256–257; Lapidge 2003, 529, n. 715). However, he was clearly unaware of the boundary mark in the Headbourne Worthy charter and likewise, G.B. Grundy was unaware that in his analysis of this boundary clause he might have wanted to consider Lantfred's information that it lay some three miles out from the city (Grundy 1926b, 127–130). Of course, stones may have announced the intersection of the *territorium* boundary with all the major roads running into the Roman city. Yet, crucially, this monument is not simply a stone. It is also a cross and the location at the junction of the *wic* herepath and the Roman road suggests relevance in an early medieval rather than a Romano-British context (it should also be noted that the *niwan stan* ('new stone') recorded in the boundary of Crawley, in a spurious document recording a confirmation made by King Edward to Winchester Cathedral, is very likely in this location (see S 381)). The importance of two near contemporary sources referring to a monument as both a 'stone' and a 'cross' has implications for how we perceive other stones referred to in both charter boundary clauses and place-names, all of which will be discussed in Chapter 9.

The 'hollow stone' has been placed at the north-west corner of the Worthy Down triangle on the crossing point of the Roman road with the London Way, and the 'host army gate' (2.2 SU43NE) has been placed on a route that

FIGURE 21 *(opposite)*. Study area 2.2, Winchester and its north environs (contains OS data and OS 1st Edition Six Inch base map © Crown copyright and Landmark Information Group Limited (2018), all rights reserved).

deviates from the Roman road in a north-north-west direction. This route, and one deviating from it in a west-north-west direction (beyond the map limits), are likely to have been favoured over the Roman road as routes with which to cross the Rivers Dever and Test. The former can cross the Test at Middleton, the latter at Wherwell whilst no evidence in the form of settlements or place-names exists to suggest a crossing of the Test on the trajectory prescribed by the course of the Roman road. The *wic* herepath can be seen to pass north, on a course broadly commensurate with that of the modern A34 that connects Winchester to Oxford via a crossing of the Test at Whitchurch. The London Way is referred to twice in the same document (SU43NE) and in being told that at one point the boundary passes along its course, we are able to associate these references to the line of a route that passes across the top of the study area, effectively bypassing Winchester and its environs, on a trajectory from the south-west of England to London. East from the charter references, it crosses the Silchester to Winchester Roman road and passes through Micheldever Wood beyond which it appears to divide. A northern course crosses the Candover at Totford and can be traced as an almost continuous line through Bentworth, Long Sutton and Crondall to Farnborough (2.1, SU53NE). The southern variant crosses the Candover below Abbotstone and joins the Alton/Farnham route to London (SU53SE).

At Martyr Worthy (2.2, SU53SW) there is a rare occurrence in the charter boundary clauses of when we are told explicitly the destination of a route. In this instance, *a braðan herpað ðer ged to worði forda and to alresforda* (a broad herepath that goes to Worthy ford and to Alresford) is described and is likely to make use of the same ford as the 'street' referred to in Kings Worthy, Abbots Worthy and at the junction with the London Way.

The street referred to in the southern environs of Alresford may be alluding to the course of a Roman road that connected Winchester directly with London, *via* Alton and Neatham. Yet, locating this reference with any certainty is problematic. It may also be the same route that is referred to as a herepath and perhaps the same herepath that passes from the south-west, up through Cheriton and crosses *cuthaenes ford* to Alresford (2.3, SU53SE). Finally, attention should be drawn to one other route that is described differently in the boundary for the contiguous estates of Easton and Avington. In the Easton charter, the boundary is recorded as passing *of þam æpenan byrigelsan and lang mearce to þære port stret andlang smalan dune* (from the heathen burials, along the boundary to the *port* street and along a small down). The same features occur in the Avington charter in reverse order: *andlang smalan dune on þone herpað . of þam herpaðe 7lang mearce to ðam hæpænan byrigelsan* although in this instance, in place of the *port* street we are told that the route is a herepath. Whilst there appears to be no reason to doubt the authenticity of the Easton charter (Rumble 2002, no. XXII), the formulation of the Avington document is thought to derive from Æthelstan's reign (924 × 939, Whitelock 1966, 103) and the original (and its boundary clause) therefore date to a generation earlier than the Easton charter of 961. Thus, the term herepath can be seen to predate the use of the term '*port* street' to describe the route that passes from Winchester on a course to Alresford *via* Avington and Ovington.

FIGURE 22 *(opposite)*. Study area 2.3, Alresford and the Upper Itchen (contains OS data and OS 1st Edition Six Inch base map © Crown copyright and Landmark Information Group Limited (2018), all rights reserved).

5. Hampshire

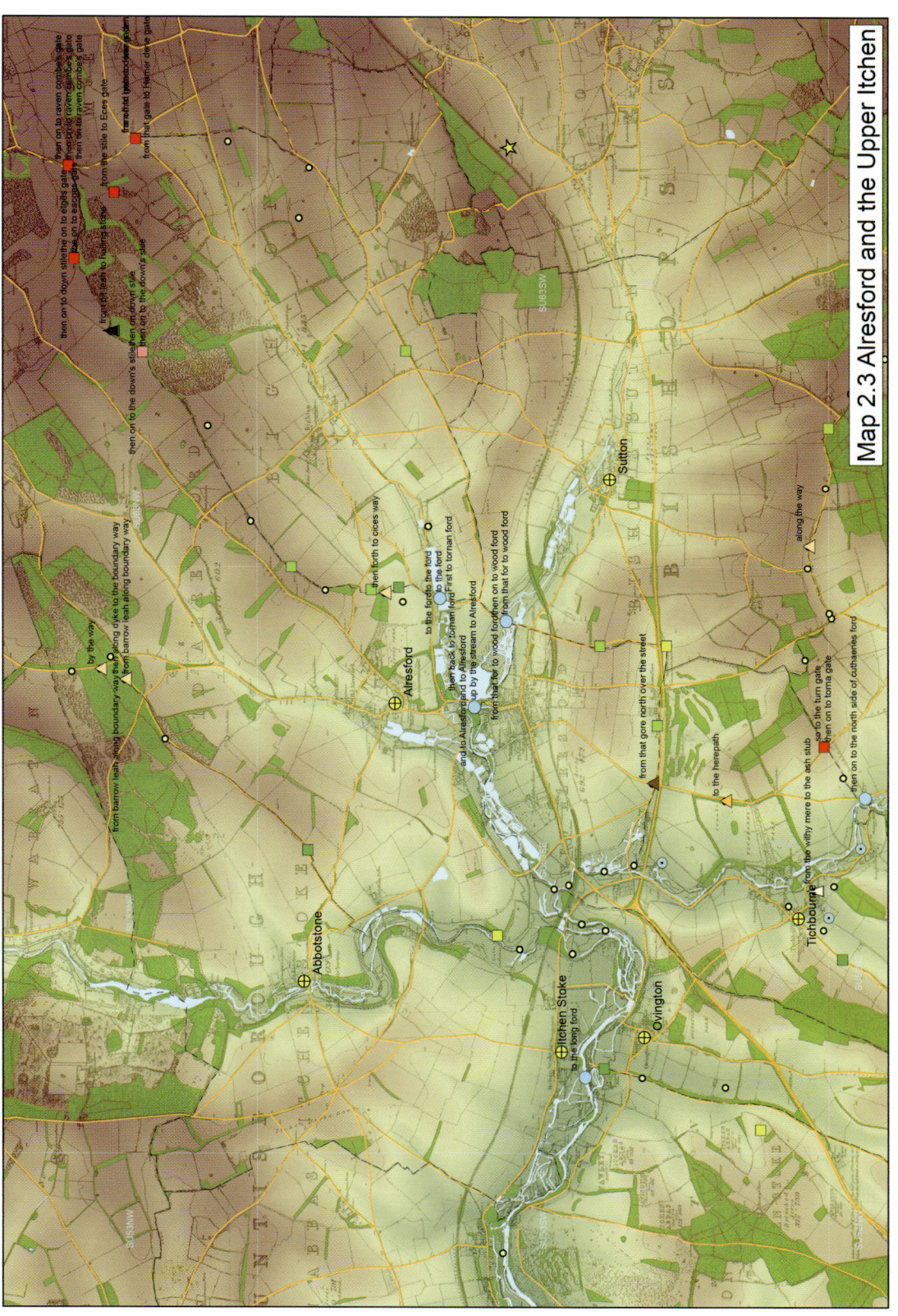

Map 2.3 Alresford and the Upper Itchen

CHAPTER SIX

Devon

Study area 3: Crediton

Devonshire boasts a greater number of streams, streamlets and rivers than both Hampshire and Wiltshire and this is reflected in the Crediton area in the many fords that feature in boundary perambulations (20 in 3.1 alone). These provide evidence, along with place-names, of a dense network of routes. It is, however, the numerous references to herepaths that deserves special attention in this study area for, in an area no greater than 20 × 15 km, there are no fewer than twenty references to herepaths. Of these, thirteen lie within a 19 km stretch of a particular route, allowing the detailed reconstruction of a herepath as it works its way from Stoke Canon in the east, through the estates at Brampford Speke, Shobrooke and Creedy Barton, across the Creedy Bridge, into Crediton, to Copplestone and beyond (3.1). This herepath functioned undoubtedly as a major arterial route and is likely to have played a role in connecting Crediton with settlements to the east and west. In the bounds of Wyke in Shobrooke, there is a mention of *þone þeod herpað* (the people's herepath) (3.1, SX89NE). It is possible that this is a reference to a herepath running on a north–south axis and crossing the major east–west herepath. In which case, it would connect Exwick/Exeter to the settlements of Stockleigh, Cadbury and Cheriton (Fitzpaine) to the north. However, the language used in the boundary clause makes it difficult to be certain exactly which route is being referred to. The course the major east–west herepath takes east of Creedy Bridge crosses the low ground of the Creedy and Exe flood plain and it is across this type of landscape that any route would be in need of constant maintenance. The *sulhford* (?ploughed up/sullied ford) and *foulanford* (foul ford) give an indication of how difficult the going would be in periods of inclement weather (SX99NW).

To the west of Creedy Bridge the herepath runs across the top of Crediton along the ridge of high ground and out towards Copplestone, which takes its name from a highly decorated granite cross-shaft, with evidence of Scandinavian influences (Cramp 2006, 82–83), that is also recorded in an original charter of 974 (Figure 25, 3.1, 3.2 SS70SE). The crossroads location of this monument has been discussed in detail elsewhere (Reynolds and Langlands 2011, 420) but it is also interesting to note the ambiguity in the terminology used to describe this landmark. Today only the shaft of the cross survives and this situation may have been the case in the tenth century when the name was assigned – perhaps

FIGURE 23 *(opposite)*. Study area 3.1, Crediton and Exeter (contains OS data and OS 1st Edition Six Inch base map © Crown copyright and Landmark Information Group Limited (2018), all rights reserved).

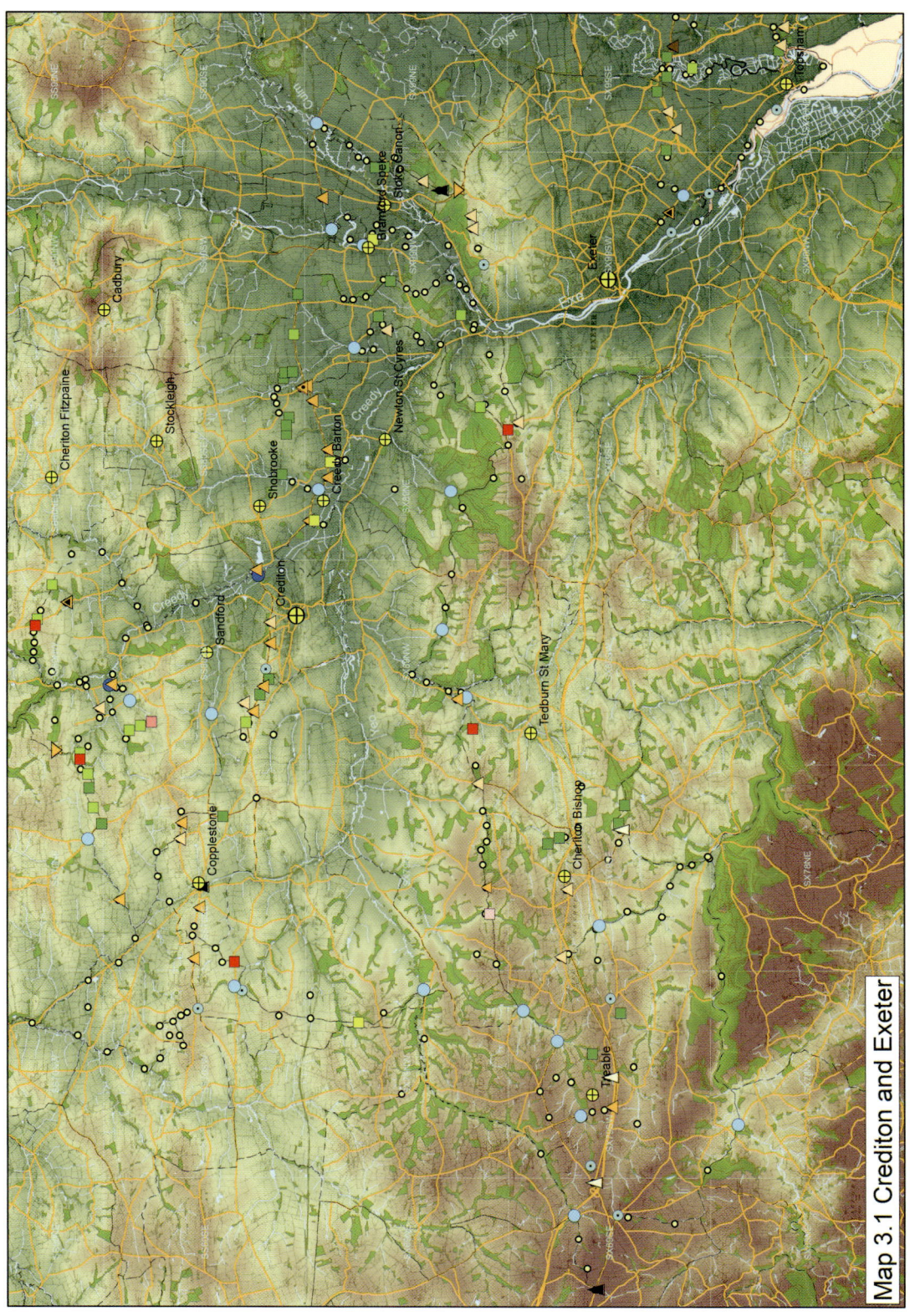

Map 3.1 Crediton and Exeter

deriving from Old English *coppedan* (having the top cut off, polled) (Simpson and Weiner 1989b, 907). However, as the boundary clause runs *Ærest on copelan stan* (First to the Copplestone), in similar fashion to the 'king's stone' of the Headbourne Worthy charter, the Copplestone cross is referred to only as a stone and not explicitly a cross. This monument is sited at a major junction and clearly played an important role in articulating passage through the landscape of central Devon and the lower ground between the massifs of Dartmoor to the south and Exmoor to the north (3.2) (Figure 25). From here, to the west, one could head out in all directions; north-west to Bideford and Barnstaple (likely to be the course of Margary 1973, no. 493), west to Bude and south-west to Okehampton, Tavistock and to Cornwall beyond. In fact, Copplestone sits on the crossing point of the major north-east/south-west and south-east/north-west axes of central Devon and these routes connect, respectively, Tiverton and north Somerset to the south-west of England, and Exeter to Barnstaple.

The remaining seven references to herepaths in this study area illustrate how widely and regularly they are adopted as boundary features. It seems reasonable to assume that in areas for which we do not have charter evidence, other routes that share the characteristics of our named herepaths would have shared their status too. One herepath is recorded as running east-north-east from Copplestone on a course, via the 'planked' bridge, towards Tiverton (3.2, SS70SE). Another heads due north from Crediton, again to the same bridge, on a course towards South Molton. The four priests recorded at South Molton in Domesday Book as holding one *virgate* of land in alms (*c*. 30 acres but also a unit for the assignment of obligations), in accordance with the criteria set out by John Blair, suggests the presence of a minster church (1985, 105–106; DB Dev. 13a, 1). The nucleated settlement pattern and extensive field system, comparable with the topography of Lydford, also suggest an important early central place (Ravenhill 1986, 40–41, figs 3 and 4). The place-name Thelbridge on the same route but further north than our boundary clause *thel brycge* indicates that this herepath was well furnished with bridges of a particular type at river crossings (Gover *et al.* 1931, 395). To the south, reference is made to a herepath on the course of a route from Crediton to Tedburn St Mary whilst a similar path radiates out from Crediton towards Cheriton (3.1, SX89NW, SX79NE). To the south-west of Treable, a herepath is recorded on the line of the modern A30, a major route connecting west Devon and Cornwall with Exeter and a likely candidate for Margary's Roman road number 492 (1973). It is perhaps logical to assume that similar routes connecting the main centres of administration, finance and settlement would have been described in the same fashion (such as the Crediton to Tiverton route for which we have no charter evidence).

Two herepaths are worthy of discussion on the basis that they are described as 'old'. The first of these appears in a grant of one hide at Topsham (S 433) and may reflect the continuing importance of the Roman road that connected the natural beaching port of Topsham with the Roman walled city of Exeter (3.1). Excavated Roman remains of military and civilian occupation at the

FIGURE 24 *(opposite)*. Study area 3.2, Crediton and Copplestone (contains OS data and OS 1st Edition Six Inch base map © Crown copyright and Landmark Information Group Limited (2018), all rights reserved).

Map 3.2 Crediton and Copplestone

FIGURE 25. The crossroads location of the Copplestone Cross.

site are testament to its importance in the third and fourth centuries and the documentary evidence for well-established trading activity of the twelfth century has been argued by Andrew Jackson to reflect an earlier significant coastal trading site (1972; Jarvis and Maxfield 1975; Sage and Allan 2004; Higham 2008, 169).

The second 'old' herepath is a route that runs along the higher ground to the east of the Creedy and it is difficult to say exactly which places this herepath is connecting and indeed, why it was, by the eleventh century, being considered 'old'. The two bridges of the study area charters are here relevant to the discussion, as they may well have had a significant impact on the fate of this route. It is broadly accepted that despite the eighth-century date of the Crediton charter, the bounds attached to it are eleventh-century (Brooks 1971, 75–76; Edwards 1988, 255–258). Thus, the Creedy Bridge (and the old herepath mentioned above) is only safely placed in a much later landscape. The same rule may apply to the *ðelbrycge* (planked bridge) as its appearance in a document of dubious integrity might place it more accurately in the eleventh century rather than to the ascribed date of 930 in the charter (Keynes 1991, 8–9). Perhaps, however, the construction of these bridges (and we can postulate that similar bridges served the other main routes into the town) made passing through Crediton and taking the herepath running north from the town the more attractive option for those travelling on a north-north-west/south-south-east alignment. This may have led to the redundancy of the old herepath or at least to it being considered 'old'. Two further possibilities exist: in the first instance, as in the case for the Topsham charter, when the phrase 'old herepath' is employed by boundary surveyors, it may be that it is being purposely applied to Roman roads. The second is that because both 'old' herepaths appear in eleventh-century charters, it may be that, perhaps a century or more after their period of initiation, these routes as 'herepaths' are already considered to be of some antiquity.

Whatever the impact of the planked and Creedy bridges, their relationship to the herepaths is of note. Whilst Thelbridge provides passage for the Crediton/South Molton herepath across a fairly minor tributary of the River Dart, the *ðel* bridge of the charter and the Creedy Bridge sit at key places on the route network of the region. The Creedy Bridge serves Crediton with all traffic from the west and the planked bridge facilitates traffic from Crediton (and presumably Exeter) to South Molton and the north Devon coast beyond whilst also allowing traffic from Tiverton to Copplestone to take a more direct route (without passing through Crediton) (3.1, 3.2).

In no other study area are herepaths quite so numerous and outnumber other types of route. By contrast, a mere ten 'ways' are referred to in the same 20 × 15 km area. We should perhaps be wary about reading too much into this simply because many of the charters from the Exeter archive purporting to date to the reign of Æthelstan have clearly been forged by the same hand in the eleventh century (Chaplais 1966, nos 1, 2, 4–6, 11, 22). Although it is not necessarily the case that the forger himself favoured the use of herepath to describe major routes, the shared provenance of this group might suggest a preference within the church at Exeter for the term over and above 'way' or 'street'. The ubiquity of the term in this area and the regularity with which it features throughout the Crediton and Exeter hinterlands presents a forceful case for herepaths being of greater importance in this part of Wessex.

Study area 4: South Hams

The overlap between charters for the South Hams and Sorley in south Devon provides an insight into the development of the area around Kingsbridge between the mid-ninth and the mid-tenth centuries. The former charter is an important document in that it survives in an original, or at least a near contemporary copy, and contains the earliest detailed vernacular boundary clause in perambulatory form (Stenton 1971, 308; Reed 1984, 269; Lowe 1998, 82). Because the town or burh of Kingsbridge is mentioned in the later charter and not in the earlier document the implications are that the settlement's origins as an Anglo-Saxon fortified site derive from this period (Haslam 1984b, 271–273). However, other observations on the development of this area over a hundred-year period can be made by analysis of the landmarks referred to in the two documents.

This study area is also relevant because in the vernacular set of bounds for the South Hams charter appears one of the first references we have in the historical sources to a herepath. It is important therefore to consider the character and function of this route in the landscape. Although Della Hooke is uncertain of the location (Hooke 1994b, 109), where the bounds of both charters are coterminous, certain recorded features can be associated with each other (SX74NW). The *pealpeg* and *ðone stan* (British way and stone) from the earlier document appears as the *ealdan pege* and *grǣwan stane* (old way and grey stone) in the latter. As we shall see, this way is likely to be a major route by which produce was brought to and from the late- and post-Roman trading site at Bantham (Figure 27), but it means that a likely association can be made between the next landmark in the South Hams charter – the herepath – and the route running due north out of Kingsbridge where it crosses the parish boundary.

This route would go on to become the High Street of what is believed to be a burh and bridge fortification constructed in the reign of Edward the Elder (Haslam 1984b, 273–275). Two further references in the Sorley charter dated to 962 suggest that an urban topography was emerging during the tenth century. Firstly, another ford, likely to be downstream of the *wealdene* ford but upstream from the king's bridge, is referred to as *manning ford*. Whilst this may relate to the personal name *Manna*, it could feasibly have derived from the Old English verb *mannian*, to garrison. Secondly, the single reference we have in all study areas to a 'lane' features as the boundary rises up from the ford *op eorþburg* (as far as the earth burh).

If herepaths represent one element of a coherent strategy of civil defence (including bridges, beacons and burhs) (this will be argued in Chapter 10, but see also Baker and Brookes 2013a, 176), this mid-ninth-century reference to a herepath on a course to a location whose strategic qualities are clearly in evidence would seem to suggest co-ordinated defensive steps carried out a generation before those implemented by King Alfred and his heirs. Map 4.2 (Figure 28) presents the relationship between the early herepath and Kingsbridge and the location of Halwell – a fort recorded in the *Burghal Hidage*. Halwell's location is clearly commanding in both its centrality to the region but also through the inter-visibility it enjoys with other Iron Age forts (Slater 1991, 76–77). Whether or not the site had a similar role as a sanctuary in a prehistoric and Romano-British landscape as part of a strategy of coastal defence must remain speculative, but in a comparison of its scale and location with other *Burghal Hidage* forts, Baker and Brookes suggest that it is more correctly interpreted as a temporary refuge for the surrounding countryside and as a consequence, it may hark back to an older system of civil defence (2013a, 89). In any event it was replaced (or perhaps surpassed) in the late Anglo-Saxon scheme by Totnes – a location with far better commercial potential – in the first quarter of the tenth century (Hill and Rumble 1996, 213–214).

In no other study area is the pattern of routes through the landscape so determined by natural topography and geological relief (4.2) (for an excellent

FIGURE 26 *(opposite)*. Study area 4.1, the South Hams (contains OS data and OS 1st Edition Six Inch base map © Crown copyright and Landmark Information Group Limited (2018), all rights reserved).

6. Devon 95

Map 4.1 The South Hams

review of the routes of communication in the area around Halwell see Slater 1991, 71–74). The many streams and rivulets that have carved through the fertile Devonian sandstones of the South Hams coast have created steep-sided valleys that have in turn dictated that travel of any distance must utilise the numerous ridgeways and water-sheds throughout the region. A character emerges to some of these ridgeways as they clearly serve the inlets and natural harbours of the coastline with access to and from the inland areas and presumably the moors beyond. One route in particular is picked up in both the ninth- and the tenth-century charter and differences in the way it is described in each document shed some light on its relationship with the important Romano-British and early medieval coastal trading site of Bantham and its apparent demise in the sixth century (Figure 27) (Griffith and Reed 1998; Reed *et al.* 2011). Mentioned above, the *pealpeg* (British way) of the South Hams charter is described in the later Sorley charter as the *ealdan pege* (old way). The *pealh-* element appears in two other landmarks as *wealdenes ford* and *wealding ford* (the same location). Della Hooke has offered 'wall' as the first element in 'wall-way' but suggests that *wealdene* is a personal name (1994b, 105–112). In such close proximity both in spatial and documentary terms it seems more likely that the *weal-* elements in both phrases are consistent with each other and refer to the 'British dene' (a type of valley) and their 'way'. The term *wealweg* or *walweg* appears not infrequently in charter bounds and its application to strands of the great Wessex Ridgeway in the Burbage and Bedwyn charters (S 688 and S 756, study area 10) and Alton Priors charter (S 272) suggest a perception on the part of Anglo-Saxon surveyors of a route of antiquity once trodden by the native British people. In the case of this Devonian example, the association may be less generic and its use in the South Hams charter may imply a recognition of the once vibrant trade that passed along this road to and from Bantham (Figure 27), a trade that had long since declined by the date of the Sorley charter where the way is twice referred to as being 'old'. A route, constrained by valleys and ridgeways can be identified running on a similar axis from Mothecombe where another coastal trading site with an archaeological date range from the fifth to eighth centuries has been identified (Turner 2004; Turner and Gerrard 2004).

One landmark in the charter boundary evidence for this study area is of particular interest as it represents an extremely rare example of a reference in the Anglo-Saxon documentary record to work being undertaken on roads. In the mid-ninth century charter for South Hams, we are informed that the boundary runs *on ðone torr æt mercecumbes æwielme ðonne on dene paldes stan ðonne on ðone dic ðær Esne ðone weg fordealf* (to the tor at the boundary combe spring, then to Denewald's stone, then to the dyke where the serfs dug the way). The boundary combe is clearly the valley within which the present parish boundary follows the course of the stream (4.1, SX64NW). Denewald's stone may sit at the junction of the parish boundary with a route running north-west, but might equally mark the crossroads at the highest point of this ridge. Either way, the 'dyke where the serfs dug the way' is undoubtedly to be associated with a route

FIGURE 27. Bantham Beach, the site of a late Antique and early medieval beach market.

that passes round the north-east ditch of a univallate hillfort of possible Iron Age date (4.1, SX64NE) (SMR Monument Number 440954). This route connects the manorial centres of Kingston and Bigbury with a Modbury/Halwell route (4.2). The place-name Kingston is likely to have arisen as a result of the grant of South Hams by king Æthelwulf to himself and Bigbury may represent a settlement of similar size and function and one perhaps even fortified with a burh (Griffith and Wilkes 2006; DB Dev. 15, 44). Some analysis of the term *esne* is required here as it impacts, to a certain extent, on how this route is perceived. It first appears in the laws of Æthelberht of Kent (*c.* 602–603) and whilst *mannes esne* (a man's serf) suggests that the status is one that is owned, that an *esne* enjoys some marriage rights and was subject to fines, suggests a status above that of a slave and one that had financial means (Abt 85, 86, 87 and 88; Liebermann 1903–1916, 8; Griffiths 1995, 42). This is in part the justification for the translation of 'serf' rather than 'slave', however, closer to the period

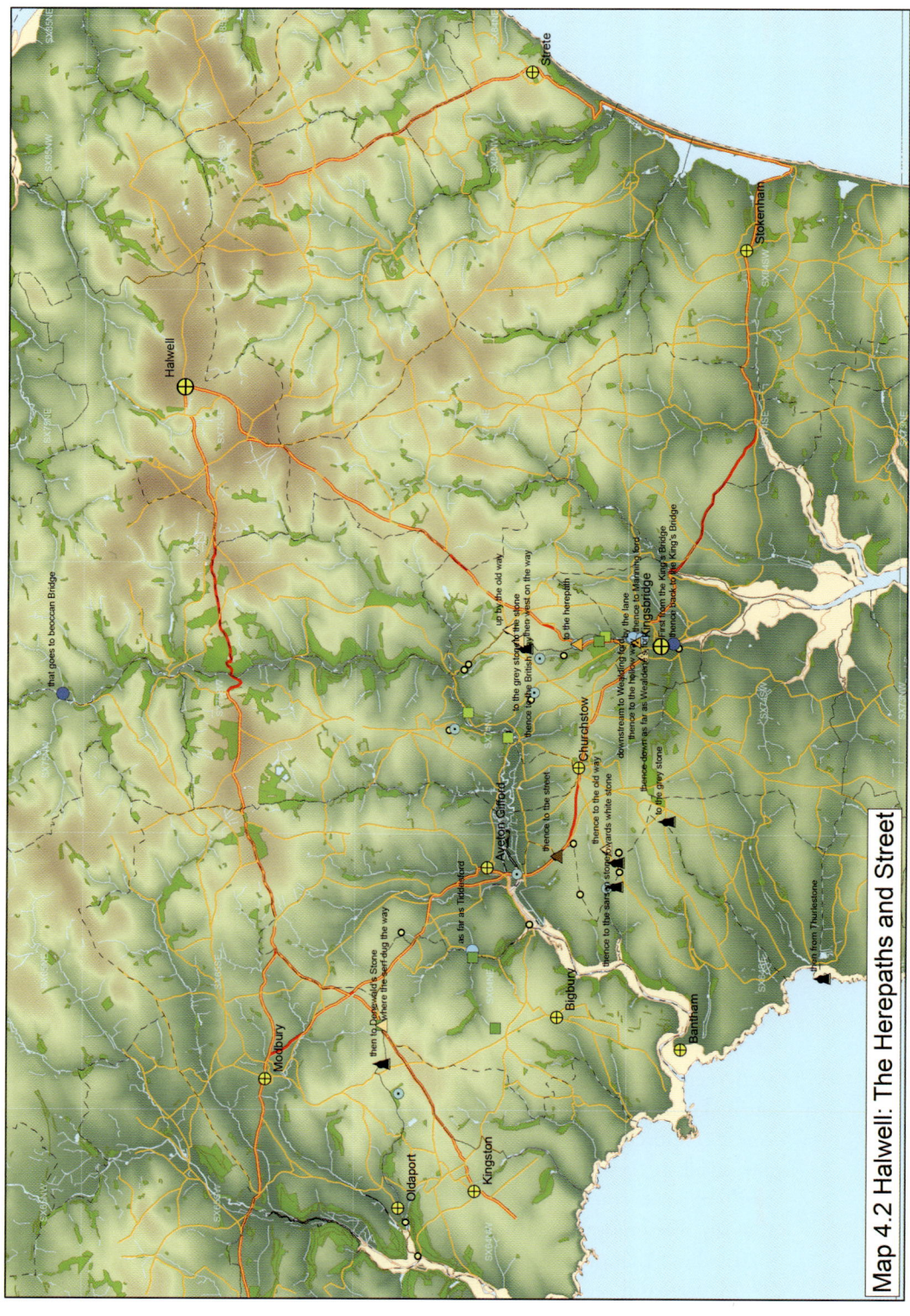

Map 4.2 Halwell: The Herepaths and Street

of the South Hams charter is the phrase in Alfred's lawcode of *esnewyrhtan*, directly translated as 'unfree workers', 'hired labourers' or 'servile workers' (Af 43; Griffiths 1995, 75; Pelteret 1995, 84; Nelson 2004, 12). This reference, along with the evidence for status derived from Æthelberht's laws, led David Pelteret to speculate that the term was used to refer to someone 'whose legal position somewhat blurred the formerly clear legal distinctions between slaves and *ceorlas*' (1995, 85). The work being undertaken by the *esne* on the South Hams way was evidently in a bid to improve communications between these manorial centres and the fort at Halwell. Although not termed a herepath, this route bears the hallmarks of one, being set out to connect significant manorial centres with a strategically placed fort. Coming as it does in a reference of mid-ninth century date, it further helps to push back to an earlier date a strategy of coastal defence of which the fort at Halwell and the Kingsbridge herepath were early facets, and one which involved the coercion or 'hiring' of a certain type of labour to undertake the task.

Finally, in this coastal area of Devon, there is a reference to a 'street' (4.1, SX64NE). The existence of few Roman roads has been proven in southern Devon and those known penetrate little further south-west than Exeter (Margary 1973, nos 491–493). This 'street' is referring to a route that broadly conforms with the modern A379 passing from Elburton (south of Plympton and Plymouth) to Churchstow (immediately north-west of Kingsbridge), running parallel to the coastline, crossing the Yealm, Erme and Avon rivers just above their tidal reaches. Eastwards beyond Kingsbridge it is likely that this route, where it is used by a parish boundary, runs towards Stokenham and beyond to Slapton Sands along whose course access to the village of Strete is provided. First recorded in 1194 as *Streta* (Ekwall 1947, 429) this may represent further evidence of a route used during the Romano-British period to convey processed soft metal ingots (or unprocessed mineral-rich ores) along the coastline between various harbouring points before trans-shipment. Modbury, which is first recorded in Domesday Book as *Motberia*, deriving from the Old English *gemōt burg* (meeting place burh) (Gover, Mawer and Stenton 1931, 279; Ekwall 1947, 313), sits in a strategic location that connects Halwell and Oldaport, but crucially defends this 'street', the major east–west route through the region. An Accelerator Mass Spectrometry (AMS) date derived from the mortar of a cross-spur wall on the promontory site of Oldaport yielded a date range from between the late ninth and the early eleventh century, and is thought to suggest a construction designed to repel Viking attacks during the reign of Æthelred II (Rainbird 1998; Rainbird and Druce 2004). Although Oldaport is not referred to in the bounds of the South Hams charter, the AMS date was taken from the most recent phase of defensive ditch (Phase 2, Farley and Little 1968), and the earlier phase may be contemporary with a mid-ninth-century plan of strategic defence in the region suggested by the South Hams herepath and the way dug by the serfs.

FIGURE 28 *(opposite)*. Study area 4.2, Halwell, the herepaths and street (contains OS data and OS 1st Edition Six Inch base map © Crown copyright and Landmark Information Group Limited (2018), all rights reserved).

CHAPTER SEVEN

Dorset

Study area 5: Isle of Purbeck

The Isle of Purbeck provides a further opportunity to explore the network of routes in a coastal zone. Parallels can be drawn between this study area and the South Hams. In the first instance, the link between the referenced herepath and the Kingston place-name illustrates the desire to see a significant manorial centre interconnected with warning stations, beaches and a central refuge (5.1, SY97NE). A herepath is mentioned to the immediate west of Kingston where it leads to Swyre Head, a promontory that takes its name from Old English *sweora* (neck). Although there is no place-name record of a look-out at this location (as in Worbarrow Tout and Houns-Tout, both on the same coastline) the location commands a 360-degree viewshed and almost certainly provided early warning to the settlements on the peninsular and to the *Burghal Hidage* fort at Wareham beyond (5.2). From such a vantage point it is easy to see how the *thegn* and the *cottar* in the *Rectitudines Singularum Personarum* might have carried out their duty to guard and watch the coast, an obligation also recorded in a genuine charter of 977 for St Keverne for which a 360-degree viewshed is provided from Keverne Beacon (S 832; Douglas and Greenway 1953, 813–814; Hill and Sharp 1997, 158–161; Lavelle 2010, 179, fig. 5.1).

Kingston first appears in the documentary sources as *Chingestone* in Domesday Book wherein an exchange between King William and Shaftesbury Abbey is recorded. In return for one hide of land in the manor (upon which to build Corfe Castle), the King makes a gift of the church of Gillingham (DB Dors. 19, 10). The *king-* element is very likely however to have derived from when the land was in the ownership of the Anglo-Saxon kings before King Eadred's grant to Ælfthryth. There is some evidence to suggest Kingston's early importance and David Hinton has made the case for a possible 'minster' site (Hinton and Webster 1987, 51). It is also thought to be the site of the church founded, according to William of Malmesbury, by Aldhelm in the seventh century (Keen 1984, 213; Winterbottom and Thomson 2007, 363, book V, ch. 217). To the east, the herepath connects Kingston along a High Street that passes through Langton Matravers, to the High Street of Swanage and the site of the parish church of St Mary's. In 877 the *Anglo-Saxon Chronicle* informs us that 120 Danish ships were washed up somewhere on the shores of *Swanawic* (the *wic* of the herds) and, although 'dairy farm' of the herdsmen seems to be the preferred interpretation (Mills 1977, 52), it is possible that the sheltered harbour

FIGURE 29 *(opposite)*. Study area 5.1, the Isle of Purbeck (contains OS data and OS 1st Edition Six Inch base map © Crown copyright and Landmark Information Group Limited (2018), all rights reserved).

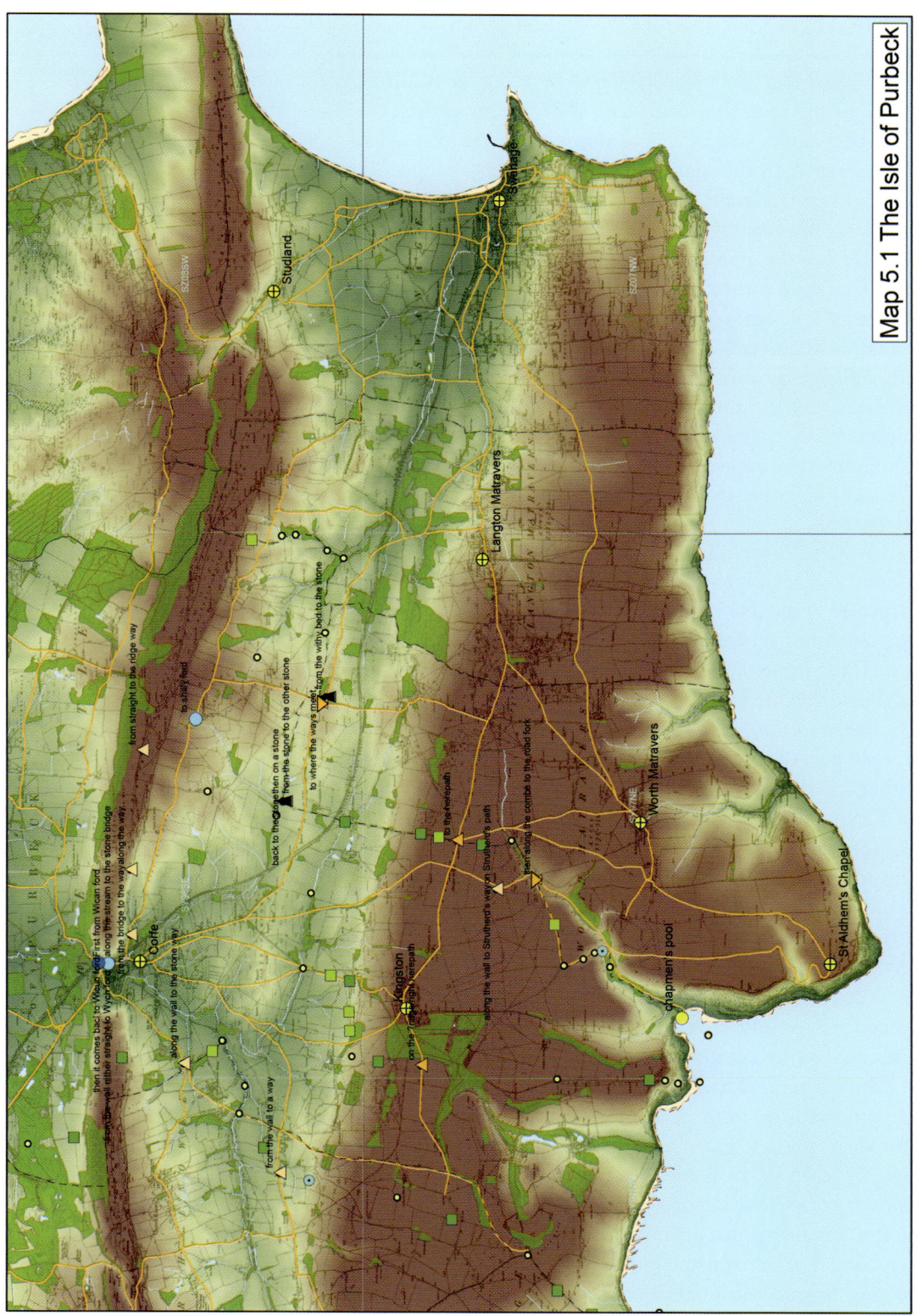

Map 5.1 The Isle of Purbeck

provided by the bay and the surrounding peninsula made for an attractive *wic* site in the middle Anglo-Saxon period. Radio-carbon dating of burials from an inhumation cemetery of fifty-eight graves at nearby Ulwell yielded a date range in the seventh century and it may be that these individuals represented members of this coastal *wic* community of herdsmen (Cox 1988).

References in the charters to lynchets, walls, hedges, dykes and rows suggest an enclosed landscape suited to the management of livestock. The place-name Studland (the land where horses were kept) (Ekwall 1947, 430) and *þon ealdan stodfald* (to the immediate north of Kingston) indicate that horse breeding may well have formed a part of the economy here. On the nineteenth-century OS maps a system of parallel field boundaries (most strikingly in the parish of Langton Matravers) divides up the downland landscape. No charter references are available for this area of the peninsula, so it is not feasible on documentary evidence alone to project this arrangement back into the early medieval period. However, the system was clearly laid out in respect of 'The Priest's Way', a route that runs east–west between Swanage, Worth Matravers and St Aldhelm's Chapel suggesting that at the time it was laid down, it made its way over open downland.

With its square floor plan, irregular orientation and lack of *piscina* and altar, it has been questioned whether St Aldhelm's Chapel represents a religious structure at all (Newman and Pevsner 1972, 16). The doorway is Norman and the remaining stonework can be reliably dated to the twelfth century with the structure sitting in what is thought to be an earlier 'Christian' sub-circular enclosure defined by a bank (RCHME 1970, 411–412). In considering the landscape location of the structure, it seems likely that its role as a chapel was a small part of its overall function and that its key role lay in aiding navigation either around the promontory on which it is situated or into the safe haven of Chapman's Pool (Figure 30). Excavation alone might confirm its role as a lighthouse or beacon in earlier periods but some chance finds in and around the location of Chapman's Pool go some way to confirming the location's importance to maritime trade. Shale, a substitute for jet, was important to cross-channel trade in the Iron Age and Romano-British period and a significant shale-working site on the shores of Chapman's Pool attest to its earlier viability as a coastal trading site (Calkin 1953). A Durotrigian 'stater' and a coin of Theodosius found at locations along the combe that runs down to the bay indicate further commercial activity (Farrar 1974; Keen 1979c).

The current place-name of Chapman's Pool, like 'chapmen's dell' and Chapmansford, implies a continued trade into the Anglo-Saxon period. However, the references to it in the charter boundary clauses are confusingly enigmatic. In the earlier (and more reliable) charter, it is referred to as the *schort mannes pol* and the later rendering of *seortmannes pol* seems a likely scribal error in the copying of this document to produce a conflated charter. 'Sc(e)ort-' may represent a personal name but the use of the definite article *þe* might mean that *mannes* reflects Old English *ge-mænnes* (community) and because the boundary effectively divides the pool it might suggest an appropriate translation of 'the small pool in common ownership'. It is next recorded as *Shortmanpole* in 1489 and then *Shipman(')s Pool(e)* in 1575 but interestingly the surname *Chapman* is recorded in the parish as early as 1321 (Mills 1977, 64).

Routes radiate south from the 'gate' in the Purbeck Hills within which Corfe is located and strip plots associated with the later borough, in respecting the courses of these ways, indicate their primacy. It is possible that the current site of Corfe Castle was the location described as the *Corfegeat* where King Edward was murdered in 978 and evidence for a high-status residence – either a *hospitum* belonging to Shaftesbury Abbey or a royal residence – was recovered in archaeological excavations (Penn 1982, 44–45). That the flow of traffic funnelled through this break in the natural geology created the need for an improved thoroughfare is suggested by the presence of a *stanene bregge* (5.1, SY98SE). It is tempting to speculate that this bridge is a relic of the Romano-British landscape and served the land to the south of the Purbeck Hills with assured passage over the Wych stream to the *civitas* at Dorchester. The numerous Romano-British inhumations and cist burials around the Swanage area point to occupation and perhaps a beaching port in the late Roman period (HER Monument Numbers 457451; 457630; 457471; 457463; 457433; Farrar 1962, 116). Furthermore, the stones mentioned on the valley bottom *en route* between Swanage and Corfe

FIGURE 30. Chapman's Pool © Kevin Eaves / Dreamstime.com.

may also represent stone relics of the same period marking the route from harbour to *civitas*. However, the form of *bregge* is late, it appears only in the conflated charter of 956 and, if Susan Kelly is correct in her analysis (1996, 82), this document may well have been devised at the point of William I's exchange with the church at Shaftesbury. In the two other charters relating to this study area, a *Wican forde* is described in the same location suggesting that the bridge was a construction of the eleventh century.

Study area 6: Shaftesbury's southern hinterland

Susan Kelly's rejection of the charter within which Iwerne Minster and Compton Abbas are recorded as the property of Shaftesbury Abbey is based on the fact that in a contiguous perambulation for lands at East Orchard dated to 963, the boundary is described as running *oð kinghes imare* (as far as the king's boundary) at precisely the point it hits the boundary of Iwerne Minster (ST81NW). Thus, if the boundary surveyors and scribe of the East Orchard charter are to be believed, Iwerne Minster cannot have been in Shaftesbury's hands in 956. In its present form Kelly argues that it belongs to a period rather later than the purported date and has been reworked to include property that came to the nuns at a later date (1996, 87–88). It is interesting then to consider the use of the term *hereweg* which appears in only one other instance in the charter boundary clauses of the entire corpus of Anglo-Saxon charters. This is in the grant by Æthelred II of a *cenobium* at Bradford-on-Avon dated to 1001, also to be found in the Shaftesbury cartulary (S 899 and discussed later in study area 9). In the immediate vicinity of the *hereweg* of the Compton Abbas bounds, a *snelles hamme weghe* is recorded in the Fontmell charter but it is difficult to reconcile the two (6.1, ST81NE). 'Snell's *hamme* way' may be referring to another local way and the term *Hereweg* may genuinely be referring to a route running south, from Shaftesbury, *via* Okeford (6.1, ST81SW) on a course to Okeford Hill where it connects with what is today known as the Wessex Ridgeway, a route which takes a near-direct course to Dorchester. Elsewhere, the Fontmell charter boundary clause refers to an 'old' herepath which further along its course to the south-west, is described simply as a herepath. Further south-west, on the same trajectory of this route, there is a mention of a *hegen pað* (all in 6.1, ST81NW). This translates directly as the 'hedge (or enclosure) path' and coming immediately after the landmark *panne on þe hegen* would appear to make sense. However, it is clearly unwise to rely too heavily on the orthography of a late manuscript where the vernacular elements have clearly been corrupted by heavy modernisation (Kelly 1996, 35). Thus, it may be that the late copyist has erroneously placed the *hegen* of the previous landmark in place of the *here-* element. The fact that the term 'hedge path' does not feature in any other boundary clause from the entire corpus of Anglo-Saxon charters does not necessarily stand against the veracity of this unique usage. However, the course of this route goes some way to supporting the suggestion of a later copyist error. Not only does it connect Sturminster Newton with the burh at Shaftesbury, but beyond this likely minster site (Hase 1994, 53; Hall 2000, 100), it continues to Kingston in the parish of

FIGURE 31 *(opposite)*. Study area 6.1, Shaftesbury's southern environs (contains OS data and OS 1st Edition Six Inch base map © Crown copyright and Landmark Information Group Limited (2018), all rights reserved).

7. Dorset

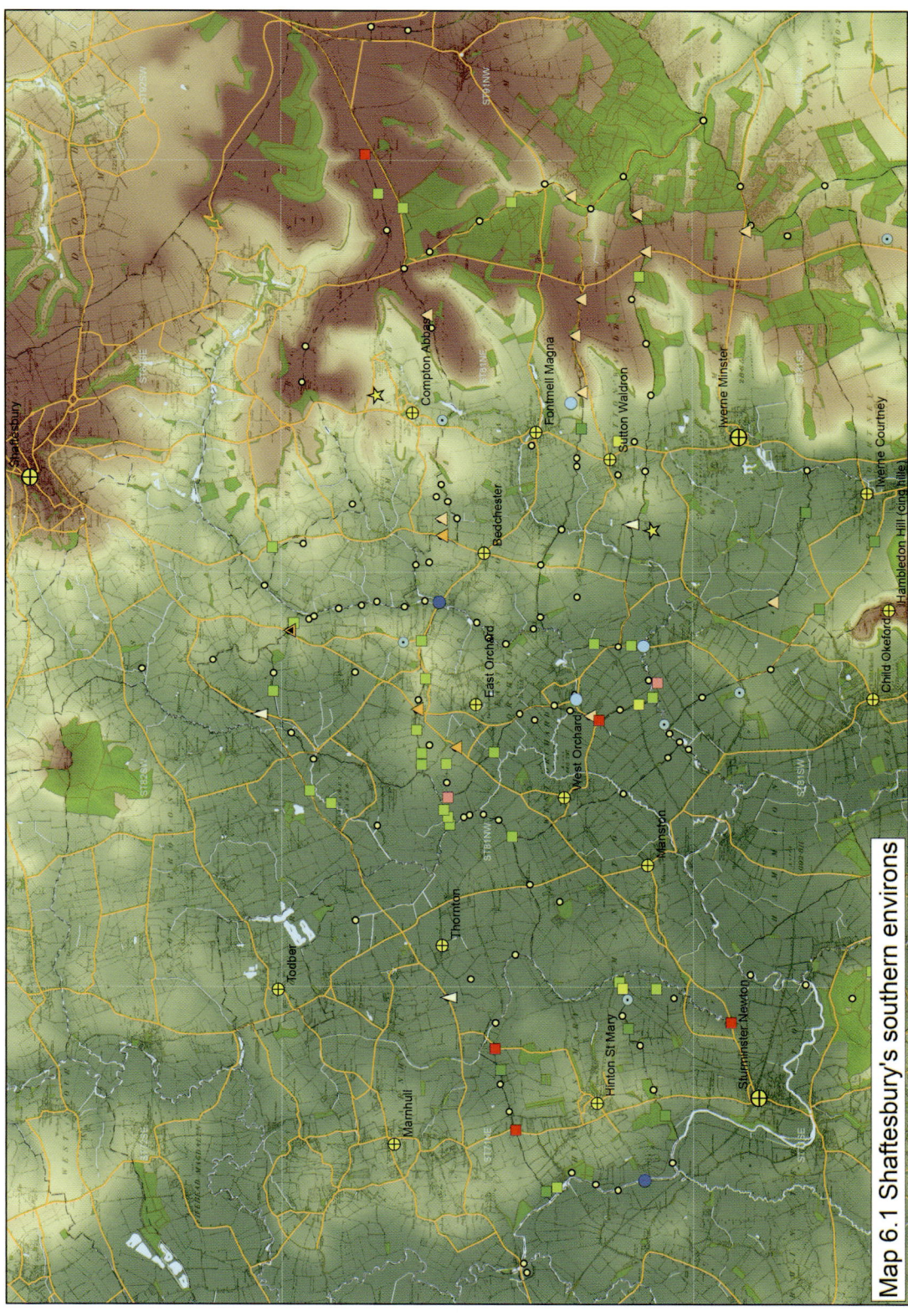

Map 6.1 Shaftesbury's southern environs

Hazelbury Bryant. Thus, it bears the hallmarks of a herepath, connecting the major centres of the Shaftesbury hinterland with a fortified refuge.

This herepath and the *here weg* are two of a number of routes that visibly radiate out from Shaftesbury illustrating the central importance of this place during the early medieval period. Whilst it might be expected that at least some of these routes have their origins in an earlier period (linked to a likely early minster site, Hase 1994, 53), evidence of previous occupation on the hill-top site of Shaftesbury is limited. Prehistoric activity is suggested from the recovery, to the immediate east of the medieval town, of multi-phase pits yielding early Bronze to late Iron Age finds (Teulon-Porter 1950). Surface pottery found in the location of the abbey fishponds indicates a Romano-British presence and a settlement of the same period is suggested by the presence of coins and architectural fragments recovered from a site on Barton Hill, again to the immediate east of the town (Teulon-Porter 1949; RCHME 1974, 76).

Whatever the earlier occupation on the site, Shaftesbury was likely to have been the location of a minster community that perhaps served as the focus for Alfred's foundation of a nunnery for his daughter Æthelgifu (Keynes and Lapidge 1983, 105, 107; Keen 1984, 230, 241). If William of Malmesbury's account of a fragment of inscribed stone recovered in the late tenth to early eleventh century is to be believed, a burh was established at the site in 880, and the fort is recorded in the *Burghal Hidage* as having a 700-hide hinterland from which to draw provisions and labour for the upkeep of its walls (Hill 1969; Cramp 2006, 111–112). For much of the early medieval period, Shaftesbury's status rose as both a focus for religious activity and a defensive stronghold for the region. This central importance may well have generated the pattern of routes that radiate out from the site and these in turn are likely to have experienced a heightened level of commercial traffic with the establishment of a mint in the reign of Æthelstan (Keen 1984, 241).

References to these routes, other than the herepath and *hereway*, are few in the charter boundary clauses for the area. The seven references to ways in the eastern part of the study area are the clearest indication yet that this term is favoured for the description of routes over open downland. 'Hollow' and 'boundary' ways attest to the already ancient appearance of some of these routes as they served as primary features against which to draw up estate boundaries. A 'green' way – perhaps denoting encroaching foliage – suggests a lack of use and can be associated with the route that runs south-south-east out of Shaftesbury heading due south over the higher ground *en route* to Blandford Forum. It is possible that this lack of use is as a consequence of the route that runs parallel through the valley bottom and passes through all the manorial settlements at the foot of the scarp slope. This is a route of undoubted importance during the late Anglo-Saxon period but the boundary clauses remain frustratingly silent over its function.

Another radiating route is marked by a *wigheardes stapele* (Wigherd's post) in the Fontmell charter (6.1, ST82SW). This landmark is referred to again in the charter for land at Thornton but the distance between the two estate centres and

FIGURE 32 *(opposite)*. Study area 6.2, Lazerton and the old ford (contains OS data and OS 1st Edition Six Inch base map © Crown copyright and Landmark Information Group Limited (2018), all rights reserved).

7. Dorset 107

Map 6.2 Lazarton and the Old Ford

the order of the landmarks in their respective perambulations makes it difficult to place the landmark in the same place (see, therefore, the one placed in 6.1 at ST71NE). Either the surveyors of the Thornton or Fontmell bounds are mistaken or there are two posts belonging to Wigherd. In support of the latter suggestion, they both sit on a route that runs between Shaftesbury and Sherborne via the *Stapulbreicge* ('post bridge' known today as Stalbridge) recorded in a charter of 998 (S 895). In study area 8 we shall see that the use of the term *stan stapol* (stone post) is suggestive of Roman milestones but here it is pertinent to draw attention to the fact that a 'post' can equally be construed as a 'column'. Thus, Wigheard's columns could feasibly be stone markers (perhaps reusing earlier milestones) on what would have been an important route between two major ecclesiastical centres. It is possible that the fragment of late tenth-century stone block incorporated into a later churchyard cross at Todber, sitting on another route radiating out of Shaftesbury, has its origins in a similar monument (6.1, ST82SW) (Cramp 2006, 114–116). Equally, another fragment of a cross shaft dated to the ninth/tenth century was recovered during the demolition of a house in East Stour (Cramp 1975, 189–190; Cramp 2006, 101–102).

The 'old ford' is located at the point where what is today referred to as the Wessex Ridgeway crosses the Iwerne river before rising up to pass between Hod Hill and Hambledon hill fort, crossing the Stour at Hanford and continuing on a more or less direct course to Dorchester (6.2, ST81SW/SE). In close proximity to this ford, numerous finds of Saxon *sceattas*, an early seventh-century forged *tremissis* and a silver penny of Offa attest to the location's importance in respect of both national and international trade (Keen 1979a; 1979b; 1983; Metcalf 1984b, no. 5; Challis and Cook 1987, no. 36). In total, these finds, the hillforts (one of which is referred to as *cing hille* in S 630) and the location on a major ridgeway all suggest the presence of a trading site, perhaps a 'productive' site, and a significant trade route. It may be that the demolished church of St Andrew's at Lazarton and the deserted settlement that once occupied the valley bottom aside the old ford was a relic of an earlier geography of settlement dependent on this trade route. That the location of Shaftesbury fits within this early geography is suggested by finds of a Series C *sceatta* from Compton Abbas dated to *c.* 700–710 and a Series H from Iwerne Minster (finds.org.uk, SOMDOR-9BF885 and DOR-44C847). Whilst the former of these coins suggests a link with the vibrant trade of the Thames Estuary, Series H were almost certainly minted in *Hamwic* and indicate a regional or 'kingdom' level of commerce (Stewart 1984, 10, 13).

Two further observations are of note from this study area, beginning with the character of the two bridges that are referred to, their function and locations. The *oxene bricge* is likely to have allowed traffic coming from Sherborne via Stalbridge in the west to access Hinton St Mary without having to loop down via a crossing of the Stour at Sturminster Newton (6.1, ST71NE). The *W(u) de bricge* will have allowed the estate centre of Fontmell access, through the deserted settlement of Bedchester (Good 1979, 44), to its resources in the more remote parts of its estate where *wigheardes stapele* represents one of its most western boundary marks (6.1, ST81NW). Woodbridge, after its mention in boundary clauses of tenth-century date, does not appear in the place-name record again until the seventeenth century (Mills 1977, 105). Both bridges are associated with local access and if resources could be found for structures of such mundane purpose, it seems highly likely that other bridges, especially on important routes, may very well have existed at crossing points not covered by charter boundary clauses (*i.e.* at much more central locations).

Finally, a *higweges* is referred to in the bounds of West Orchard (6.1, ST81NW). In Chapter 2, attention was drawn to this term in the bounds of land at Meavy, Devon (S 963). H.P.R. Finberg's translation of the *hig-* element, in accordance with the views of the *Place-Names of Devon* was 'high' as in 'high way' (Finberg 1970, 31). Della Hooke, however, opted for 'hay' as the translation and associated the way with access to summer grazing on Dartmoor (1994b, 199). In the case of the West Orchard example it would appear that 'hay way' is the more appropriate interpretation. The route seems to be fairly minor in its course and it runs, via a *lipgete* (leap gate), into what the Anglo-Saxons usually refer to as a *hamme* – an area of 'hemmed in' meadow/pasture land and perhaps the *hamm* of *Archethamm*, the name of West Orchard in the title of the charter. On the nineteenth-century OS map a road sweeping through the spine of the *hamme* is referred to as the Mower's Lane, reflecting its suitability for haymaking. This interpretation has important implications, however, for the origins of the ubiquitous later medieval term 'highway'. The accepted origins of 'highway' in the Oxford English Dictionary are to be found in an original charter of 859 and Alan Cooper suggests that both *higweg* and *heahstrǣt* are indicative of 'exalted status', as in 'high king' (S 1196; Simpson and Weiner 1989c, 233; Cooper 2002, 61). Cooper notes the term's first appearance in the West Orchard bounds (evidently unaware of the 859 document) and informs us that it is referred to on a further fourteen occasions. In view of both the Meavy and West Orchard examples, however, it may be that *higweg* needs separating from *heahweg* (or *strǣt*) in its meaning, with the origins of the later legalised term 'highway' being sought in the instances where the *heah-* element prevails.

CHAPTER EIGHT

Wiltshire

Study area 7: the Ebble Valley

A group of eight charters describe land granted in the Ebble Valley from its upper reaches on the border with Dorset in the west down to the confluence of the Ebble with the Avon (7.1) (Langlands in press). The final charter in Table 7 (see Appendix) (S 891) is preceded by four forged charters which have been largely ignored in this study as a consequence of the similarities in the boundary clauses (S 299; S 275; S 393; S 540). The 997 charter is a 100 hide grant of land at 'Downton and Ebblesbourne' and the 30 hides at Ebblesbourne have been identified with the modern parish of Bishopstone (Hill 1910; Grundy 1920, 145–148). The northern half of Bishopstone parish (*i.e.* the part north of the river Ebble) is also represented by two further charters (S 522, S 640) where again they are described as land 'at Ebblesbourne'. Three further grants of land also titled 'Ebblesbourne' are represented by the parishes of Stratford Tony (S 861), Coombe Bissett (S 696) and Homington (S 635). These last five charters are widely accepted as authentic documents and, dating from between 928 and 986, they go on to form the Domesday hundred of Cawdon. The grant of 100 hides at Chalke includes the manors of Broad Chalke, Bower Chalke, Ebbesborne Wake, Alvediston, Berwick St John and Tollard Royal, which all go on to form the later hundred of Chalke. Like the Shaftesbury charter for Compton Abbas and Iwerne Minster (S 630 – which also covers land at Donhead, Easton Bassett and Sixpenny Handley), the authenticity of this charter is suspect and the nature of both documents, the fact that they describe two large contiguous blocks of land each interspersed with each other's outlying manors, suggests some collusion between the draftsmen (or perhaps, draftswomen) of each document. Like the Shaftesbury Abbey charter, therefore, the grant of Chalke to the nuns of Wilton possibly represents an eleventh-century fabrication (Kelly 1996, 88).

The manor of Easton Bassett, by virtue of the fact that it was held by Shaftesbury but sits entirely surrounded in the Ebble Valley by the Chalke manors, is perambulated in both charters and the bounds as recorded in each document have been listed in Table 8 in the appendix. It is possible that the respective surveys were conducted on separate occasions and that this explains the differences between the two. The number of variations, both in the relative number of features mentioned and the alternative spellings would suggest that the level of collusion alluded to by Kelly between the houses of Shaftesbury and Wilton was not so close that they both shared access to the same boundary survey.

FIGURE 33 *(opposite)*. Study area 7.1, the Ebble Valley (contains OS data and OS 1st Edition Six Inch base map © Crown copyright and Landmark Information Group Limited (2018), all rights reserved).

8. Wiltshire 111

Map 7.1 The Ebble Valley

The directional terminology S 582 takes through Maple tree comb and the repeated mention in the overall boundary clause for Chalke of the head stakes as a landmark that is being returned to, suggests a text that is rather more closer to a physical perambulation than the list-like landmarks of S 630. This might suggest that the boundary marks in the latter document have been verbally relayed, which in turn may have caused the confusion over the *elchene seað* and the *miclen diches*. However, the inclusion of a *bican pet* in S 630 suggests a separate provenance and the *empenbeorch* is less obscure as 'imps' barrow' than it is as *ippan beorge*. The 'stone that lies on the street' in S 582 is important because, as we shall see from study area 8, the occurrence of stones on Roman roads may suggest survival into the early medieval period of Roman milestones. However, frustratingly, the bounds of S 630 refer to a stone *scylien*, an enigmatic phrase that, translated literally, means 'stone shaling/shaley' (Bosworth and Toller 1898, 912). The phrase appears in only one other text, the *Gospel of St Mark*, where it is glossed as *super petrosa* (Skeat 1871, 28–30). Perhaps then the 'stone that lies on the street' is, by the time of S 630, literally lying over; a monument that once stood erect now lying fractured on the ground.

Most frustratingly, the references to the various routes in each charter conflict to a degree that either the exact status and names of routes mattered little to surveyors of boundary clauses or, more likely, that the survey of S 630 really is a garbled second-hand account of either S 582 or of a separate field survey, but one conducted, perhaps, with the same local contacts. Fieldwalking and analysis of LiDAR data can find no trace of a Bica's pit between the imps' barrow and the head of the thorn spring. It may even be that a *bican setle* (Bica's settlement or seat) mentioned much earlier in the Chalke perambulation has caused further confusion. So the discrepancies between the two surveys seem likely to be as a consequence of S 630's dubious character and the boundary clause for Chalke is otherwise in a charter that other commentators are content to grade as authentic (Keynes 1980, 49–50; Lapidge 1993, 289–290). Analysis of charter boundary clauses on this level – *i.e.* studying the spatial relationships between landmarks and how the same marks are described in different charters – can only help to contribute to the assessment of a charter's authenticity and can furthermore help us to understand the processes by which the custom of perambulating boundaries in the landscape comes to be articulated textually as a clause in a legal document.

Taking the references to routes in the Chalke charter, we can identify a herepath that runs east–west through the valley and the parish of Alvediston. It may be that the course of this route passed north of Windmill Hill as *sceattas* of Series H, N and B recovered from the fields to the west of Norrington manor have been recently registered through the *Portable Antiquities Scheme*. Both Series H and N are the only groups with a determinable southern origin, with *Hamwic* the likely minting place of Series H (Stewart 1984, 13–14). A further Series D has been recovered in close proximity to the ridgeway to the south (the street on which the fallen stone lies) and these coin finds may be a further

FIGURE 34 *(opposite)*. Study area 7.2, Winklebury and the upper Ebble Valley (contains OS data and OS 1st Edition Six Inch base map © Crown copyright and Landmark Information Group Limited (2018), all rights reserved).

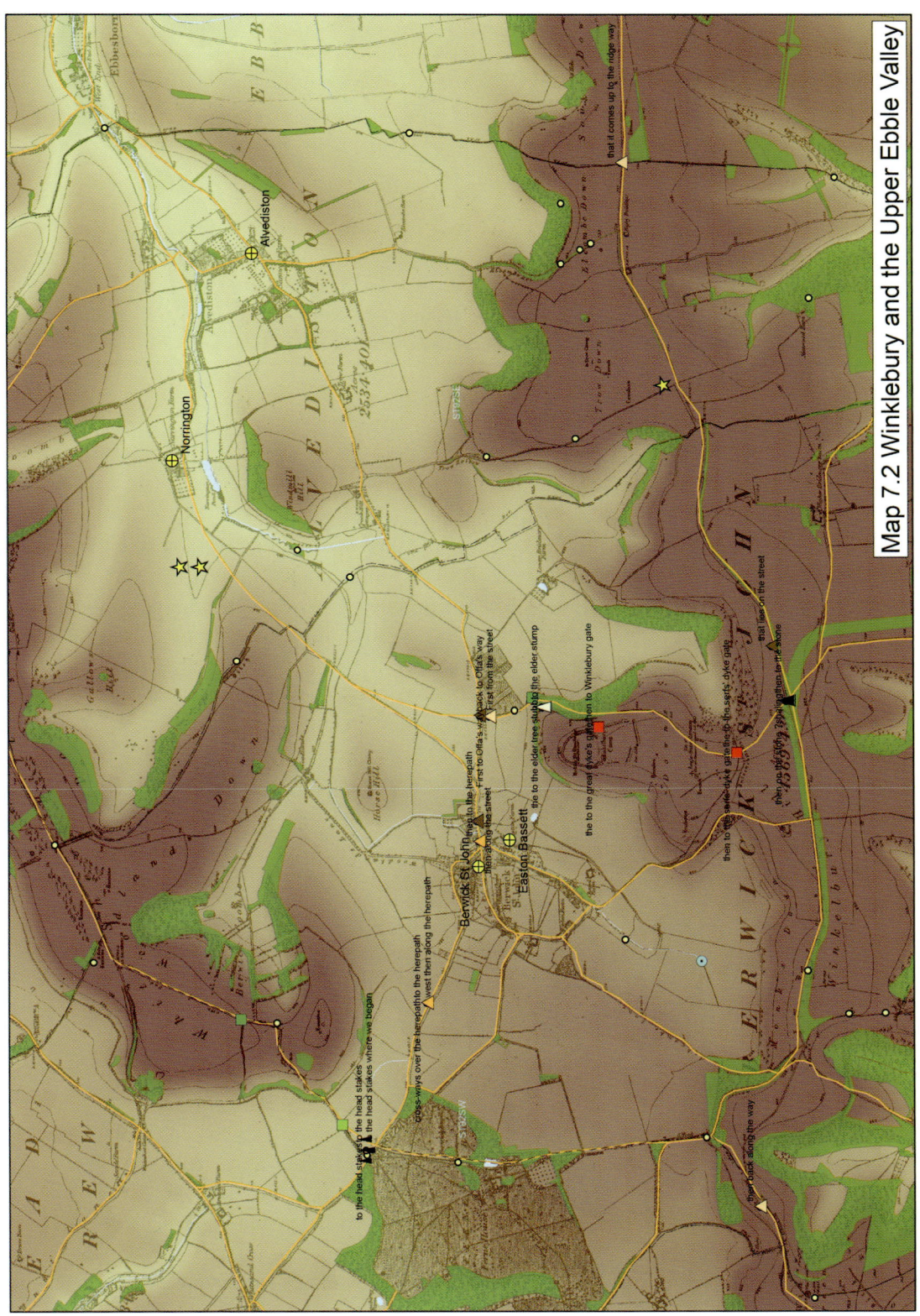

Map 7.2 Winklebury and the Upper Ebble Valley

indication of a middle Anglo-Saxon trade route (as in study area 6) making use of the ridges that bound the Ebble valley to the north and south (finds.org. uk, SOM-9BD402; SOM-7F2004; SOM-7E5141L). There are numerous lines, drove roads and ditches that run perpendicular to the axis of the valley and the *sceat* coin finds at these locations may well reflect a north–south route passing through the parish *en route* to Tisbury where an abbot and *familia* is recorded in a mid-eighth century charter (S 1256).

The 'street' of S 582 referred to as Offa's way in S 630 would appear to be the deep hollow way that runs up the east side of Winklebury Hill. A translation derived from *of-ferian* [to bear off] might suggest that this route did not continue to the north of the herepath and was spurred off at this point. The boundary then passes through the gate in what is referred to as the *winterburge* before continuing through the *esnadiche geate* (serfs' dyke gate) (7.2, ST92SE). Winklebury hillfort was excavated in 1881 by General Pitt-Rivers and the ceramics, worked metals and several phases of construction have been dated to the Iron Age (Hogg 1979, 206). It may be then that the serfs' dyke is actually an undated cross dyke blocking access to the Winklebury promontory (Colt-Hoare 1812, map on 236–237). Similar undated dykes can be seen serving the same purpose on the downs to the north and south of the valley with a marked cluster on the ridgeway to the north of Alvediston and on White Sheet Hill (Fowler 1964). Such dykes, if also built (or improved) by serfs in living memory of the Chalke charter date, may reflect a desire to control and monitor movement along these ridgeways.

At the very western end of the study area, the herepath passes through the *heafod stoccan*, a phrase that represents the location of stakes set up for the display of the heads of executed criminals (7.2, ST92SW) (Reynolds 2009a, 31, 169). As has been noted (Chapter 2), both a boundary location and proximity to a major thoroughfare are important factors in the siting of Anglo-Saxon execution cemeteries (Reynolds 2008, 25–43; Cubitt 2009, 1027). It may be too that the significance of this location is as a result of the crossing of the herepath that runs through the Ebble Valley with the major ridgeway that to the south-west connects (via study area 6) with the Wessex Ridgeway which heads to Dorchester. This crossroads location is then likely to be communicating to both a local and regional level of traffic using the herepath to connect the valley manors with Shaftesbury to the west and Wilton to the east and a national and international level of traffic using a major trade route connecting the shire capital of Dorset with its counterpart in Wiltshire.

Further east along the valley, the east–west herepath can be picked up in the bounds for Bishopstone and numerous other herepaths are referred to on both north and south ridgeways and along the course of the Roman road (7.3, SU02NE, SU02SE). Above, mention was made of the fact that the grouping of estates at Bishopstone, Stratford Tony, Coombe Bissett, Homington and Odstock all go on to form, along with Britford (for which no charter survives), the hundred of Cawdon. They are all (except the king's property at

Britford) recorded as being in the hands of secular individuals in the tenth century. Chapter 10 will discuss the fact that the references to herepaths in this area are replaced with references to 'ways' and 'ridgeways' in later charters where the church is the beneficiary. References to the Roman road where it runs through the valley of this hundred, survive only in conjunction with a 'ford' and it is difficult to know whether what is being referred to here is a 'ford where the Roman road crosses' or the settlement of Stratford Tony as both sites sit over 500 m apart (7.3, SU02NE). The issue is confused by a reference to *stret ford* in the Coombe Bissett charter on the eastern boundary of Stratford Tony – the opposite side of the estate from where the Roman road crosses the Ebble. In the immediate vicinity of the settlement of Stratford Tony (at the centre of the strip estate) a deep holloway passes around the back of the church, heading west to Bishopstone, and a further hollow way runs south-west up on to the spur of downland to the south upon which a *witan weg* is recorded. A literal translation of this term would read 'white way' but the route is picked up in a charter for Damerham to the south where it is referred to as the *piltenepeie* (Wilton Way) (S 513). This may reflect the fact that the crossing of the Ebble of the Roman road was rejected in favour of a more suitable – and perhaps pre-existing – crossing at the location that went on to become the site of the parish church of Stratford Tony. Much depends, however, on the survival of the Roman road's crossing of the Nadder to the north-east, and in this study area alone further insights can only be provided by the reference to a *bican bricge* (Bica's Bridge) in Bishopstone which is very likely to have provided access for traffic coming from the south-west (including that using the Roman road) to Wilton. This may further have impacted upon the popularity of a crossing of the Ebble on the trajectory of the Roman road.

Finally, attention is drawn to the *wic* herepath that is referred to in the bounds of Odstock and the herepaths that are mentioned in the north and south of the estate at Downton. Tracing the course of the *wic* herepath to the south (SU12SE), it can either run due south with the Avon valley or cross the river at Downton and head in a south-west direction. At Downton archaeological evidence of substantial Roman occupation has been recovered with villa remains, a corn dryer and bath house all part of a significant settlement to the immediate south of the current town. To the west of this site, on Castle Meadow, two intersecting Roman roads were also observed in excavations (Rahtz 1961). Pottery dated to the seventh/eighth centuries was recovered from the base of a large gravel-extraction pit in the Castle Meadow excavations. The up-cast gravel was believed to have been required for a hard building surface for construction on the soft alluvium of the Avon flood plain (Rahtz 1964). It may be, however, that the gravel was required for the construction (or repair) of a causeway across the Avon. The parish (and Anglo-Saxon estate) of Downton straddles the river, with significant territory on both sides. This suggests that at the time this boundary was laid out, access across the river was not only possible but unproblematic. Some 2 km (1.2 miles) south of the reference to

116　*Alexander Langlands*

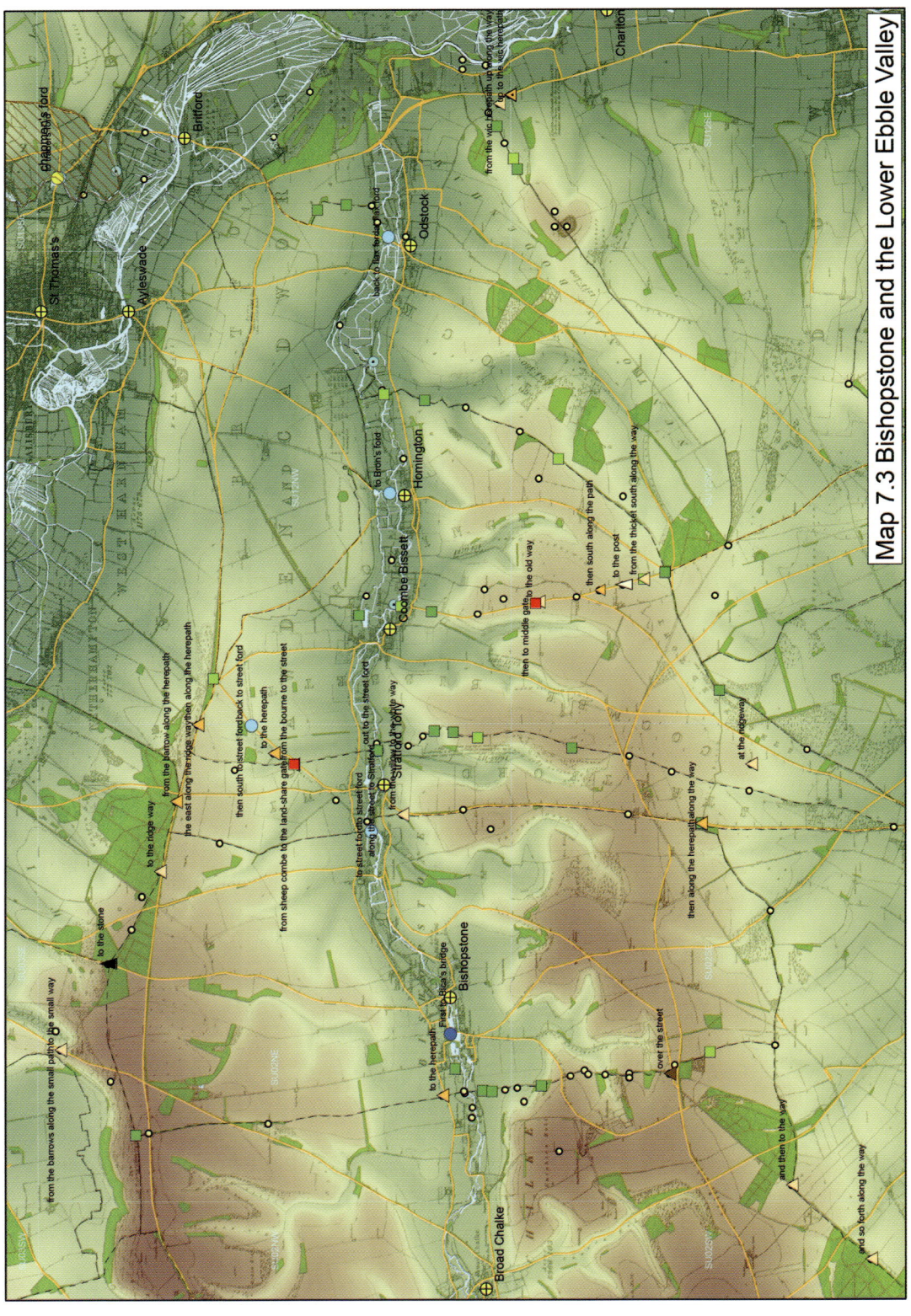

Map 7.3 Bishopstone and the Lower Ebble Valley

the *wic* herepath (now the A338 from Salisbury to Bournemouth) a significant fork off of the main road and running down towards the Avon in the direction of Downton is encountered opposite Barford. This suggests an alternative, more direct route, by which traffic crossing the Avon at Downton would have travelled north to crossings further upstream at Ayleswade (*en route* to Old Sarum) or Wilton.

In a later discussion, the significance of the *wic* herepaths will be covered in more depth but the possible destinations of the routes that are passing through this *wic* herepath should be highlighted here. Firstly, heading due south-south-east and crossing the Avon at Barford/Downton, a further two references to a herepath are picked up in the southern bounds of Downton (7.3, SU21NW). A *stenenan stapul* (stone post) is mentioned on the course of this route and, as will be demonstrated in study area 8, this term in particular is likely to be indicative of a Roman milestone. In which case, this route may well be making its way to the south-east corner of the New Forest and likely candidates for its destination could be either Hythe (perhaps the *Portmonna Hyðe* of S 701), Lepe or a site known as 'South Hampshire' in the list of 'productive' sites which Katharina Ulmschneider places in the New Forest Area (Ulmschneider 2003, 79). Whether crossing the Avon at Barford/Downton or staying on the west bank of the river, a route taken directly south runs to the harbour of Christchurch. So in both options, the continuation of the *wic* herepath takes the traveller in the direction of middle Anglo-Saxon trading sites. A second herepath is mentioned in the Downton perambulation on the line of what has gone on to become the A36, the main Salisbury to Southampton road. In the early medieval period this would have been the likely route by which traffic travelled between Wilton/Old Sarum and Hamwic/Southampton and a number of coin finds including a possible penny of Alfred, a penny of Ecgbert, two Series H and two Series J *sceattas*, would seem to confirm that trade was moving along this corridor (finds.org.uk, WILT-D6BD68; WILT-8D6931; WILT-30D3D6; WILT-C697D2; WILT-29EE75).

Study area 8: the Salisbury Basin

The herepath mentioned on the northern boundary of the Downton perambulation, on the course of the Salisbury to Southampton road, can be seen to continue to a crossing of the Bourne River at the *cypmanna ford* of the Laverstock charter (8.1, 8.2 SU12NE). Prior to this river-crossing, however, this herepath crosses a north–south route that passes from Britford to the south. The exceptionally fine carvings of plant-scrolls on the archway to the north *porticus* of Britford church demonstrate influences from contemporary Italian work and these architectural fragments have therefore been assigned an early ninth-century date (Gem 1991, 185–188; Cramp 2006, 206–208). Thus, it is likely that this church sat at a ford on an important early route. The presence of *byrhtferþes hlæwe* (Byrtferth's mound) somewhere to the north of Britford and Byrtferth's

FIGURE 35 *(opposite)*. Study area 7.3, Bishopstone and the lower Ebble Valley (contains OS data and OS 1st Edition Six Inch base map © Crown copyright and Landmark Information Group Limited (2018), all rights reserved).

118 *Alexander Langlands*

Map 7.4 The Downton Herepaths

estate in Odstock to the south (7.3, SU12NE, discussed in Chapter 4), is a suggestion of an active crossing in the tenth century (and earlier). It may have been this north–south route and the aforementioned herepath that provided the focus for an extensive early Saxon inhumation cemetery recovered at this location (and possibly the location of *byrhtferpes hlæwe*?) and trial trenches cut at Milford farm between this crossroads and the *cypmanna ford* yielded pottery with a fifth- to seventh-century date range (Leeds and Shortt 1953; Moore and Algar 1968; Algar and Hill 1973).

Having crossed the Bourne at the *cypmanna ford*, the herepath splits to take a course to either Old Sarum or Wilton. Jeremy Haslam has stressed that these two sites cannot be studied independently of each other as they appear to share urban functions in the early medieval period (1984c, 122–128). For example, the apparently inadequate defences and exposed location of the Wilton site led Haslam to speculate that the fort of Wilton mentioned in the *Burghal Hidage*, with its attached 1,400 hides, actually had its defences in the site of Old Sarum (1984c, 124). Recent archaeological evaluations conducted in the area of St John's Hospital at Wilton have, however, established that defences of Wilton in this period consisted of a substantial bank and ditch upon which, at a later date, a stonewall was constructed (Wessex Archaeology 1993; 1996a). There is clear evidence then that attempts were made in the early medieval period to fortify the valley bottom site, to control the crossing of the Nadder and Wylye rivers and to protect the major nunnery that had been established there by the tenth century. Furthermore, despite the defensive qualities of the Old Sarum site, archaeological evidence for occupation during the Anglo-Saxon period is limited and David Hill's case for the burh church and 'town' actually lying outside the walls of the hillfort, although yet to be substantiated on archaeological grounds, remains a viable proposition (1978b, 223).

It is likely that the hill-top site of Old Sarum at least fulfilled the functions of an 'emergency burh' with coins of Æthelstan and Edgar attesting to commercial activity at this time, along with the relocation of the Wilton moneyers in the eleventh century (Haslam 1984c, 128). The 'emergency burh' status is perhaps supported by the survival in the charter boundary evidence of a *peod* herepath interconnecting Wilton with Old Sarum (8.1, SU13SW). Analysis of this route in the field suggests two options. Firstly, having made use of the Avon river crossing at Stratford-sub-Castle, it could have turned due south-west and climbed the scarp slope where, at the point it coincides with the parish boundary, a purpose-built causeway levelling the steep hill slope can be observed (SU 412132). Having crossed the ridge it then skirts the north-west edge of Bemerton Heath where it is referred to in the charter for Bemerton (surviving today as a public footpath), before dropping down on to the valley road to Wilton. Alternatively, following a crop mark that rises up, due west from Avon Bridge, it rises up over the ridge, connecting with a well-established hedgerow on a course that sees it join up with the 'Kingsway' that itself drops down toward Wilton, entering it from the north. In either case, using the crossing of the Avon at Stratford-Sub-Castle,

FIGURE 36 *(opposite)*. Study area 7.4, the Downton herepaths (contains OS data and OS 1st Edition Six Inch base map © Crown copyright and Landmark Information Group Limited (2018), all rights reserved).

120 Alexander Langlands

Map 8.1 Wilton and Old Sarum

both paths take a more direct route between the two settlements and almost certainly represent a communication laid out to connect the two centres. That it existed in the mid-tenth century suggests that Old Sarum played some role in the protection and refuge-provision for the community based at Wilton and is another supporting factor in the case made by Haslam for Old Sarum serving, in part, as Wilton's fortification. Indeed, it may very well have gone on to serve this purpose as the route by which the þeod (people) fled the ravaging and burning of Wilton by King Swein in 1003 (ASC 1003).

The existence of a 'Kingsbridge Meadow', referred to in a map of 1793 detailing the freehold burgages of Stratford-sub-Castle (Wiltshire Records Office cc/chapter/14/2; cc/chapter/14/6), at exactly the place where the Roman road crosses the Avon to the south-west of Old Sarum complicates the issue somewhat in that, if of early medieval date, a bridge here would have provided even quicker access between Old Sarum and Wilton. Relating more to the geography of the hill-top site and associated settlements than to the later city of the valley floor, it seems likely to predate the purported shift of urban functions to the cathedral city of the early thirteenth century. If parallels were to be drawn with the nomenclature of the South Hams Kingsbridge then it might be seen to fit into a mid-tenth-century context. In providing a more direct passage between Old Sarum and Wilton (than the þeod herepath), it may have been constructed to further improve access between the two sites.

Both the charter boundary clause and place-name evidence for routes and river-crossings in this study area create a configuration of thoroughfares that allows for the topography of the alluvial plain, on to which the later city of Salisbury was placed, to be tentatively projected. The chapmen's ford allows a crossing of the Bourne for two major routes from the east and south-east. The route from the east, known today as the Clarendon Way, connects Winchester, via Romsey, to the Salisbury Basin (Beaumont-James and Gerrard 2007, 12). That it survives as the only public right of way through the forest of Clarendon tentatively suggests that it was in existence as a major thoroughfare before the establishment of the royal hunting ground in the post-Conquest (if not earlier) period. The route from the south-east, as we have seen in study area 7, comes from the Southampton area. Having combined to cross the Bourne at the *cypmanna ford*, a route heading north takes the traveller to the gates of Old Sarum whilst a route west takes the traveller across the floodplain towards Wilton. This east–west route is crossed by a north–south route that crosses the Avon at the location of a fording place indicated by the later street name 'Ayleswade', and then continuing north along the High Street before becoming Minster Street (SU13SW/SU12NW) (Chandler 1983, 22). From then on, it splits to go either side of Old Sarum but it is at the point where it intersects the east–west route that is of interest here (Cave-Penney 2004, fig. 12). The crossroads is marked by St Thomas's church, a building whose earliest architectural fragments date to the thirteenth century (Tatton-Brown 1997). However, circumstantial evidence suggests that this site may have been the focus for earlier activity (Langlands 2014). In the first instance, the topographical

FIGURE 37 *(opposite)*. Study area 8.1, Wilton and Old Sarum (contains OS data and OS 1st Edition Six Inch base map © Crown copyright and Landmark Information Group Limited (2018), all rights reserved).

location bears all the hallmarks of those sites that we know other Wessex minster churches occupy: low ground, proximity to running water, alongside good communications and a mile or two from a hillfort (Hase 1994, 54–60). The 'Minster Street' to the immediate east of St Thomas's church and the name that used to apply to the route running north from this location (before it became Castle Street), may well refer to the later cathedral site to the immediate south, but 'minster' is a term that, certainly by the early thirteenth century (*i.e.* the date of the cathedral foundation), had slipped from common usage with the minster system of parochial care already well subsumed into a local parochial system by the late twelfth century (Blair 1988a, 10–13). John Blair has demonstrated that minsters founded in the late seventh century were the focus of 'commercial activity' and the likely settings for markets (1988b, 47–48) and this crossroads location, the site of the later church of St Thomas (and the likely location for one of Salisbury's Domesday mills, DB Wilts. 3, 4), also goes on to become the medieval market place for the cathedral city (Figure 10). From the only excavations to date made within a 100 m radius of this crossroads, at the site of the Old George Mall immediately to the south, pottery of the sixth to eighth century was recovered from pre-structural horizons (Wessex Archaeology 1996b).

To the immediate west of St Thomas's church, and the market place, Bridge Street carries traffic across the Avon to Wilton but also in a north-west direction by a ridgeway route presumably of some antiquity. Support for this comes from the references to a *bradan herpaþ* (broad) and, on two occasions, an *ealdan herpaðe* (old). Elsewhere (study area 3), we saw how the use of the term 'old' herepath was applied to the course of a Roman road and it may be that this was the route by which Old Sarum was connected with the Romano-British town of *Verlucio*. Along the course of this route, three *stænan stapol*s (stone posts) are recorded and although each stone can be placed only very approximately, they appear to sit apart at a distance that suggests their function as milestones.

Beornwin's stone sits again on the trajectory of a Roman road (Figure 39) and is perhaps marking a significant crossroads to the immediate south-west of Figsbury (8.1, 8.2, SU13SE). A stone is also recorded on the ridgeway to the south of Burcombe (SU02NE) and it seems likely that this landmark is the stone being referred to as *beornolfes stan* (Beornwulf's stone) in a charter for land at *Pyrigean*, identified as an estate to the immediate south-west of Wilton (S 586 – not covered in the study area charters; Grundy 1919, 293–295)

Finally, from this study area, attention should be drawn to the *wic* herepath to the immediate east of Stapleford, the 'ford marked by a post' (SU03NE) (Gover *et al.* 1939, 229; Ekwall 1947, 418). Heading east, this route dips to the south and crosses the Avon at the *ealdan wuduforda* that Desmond Bonney (1969) has placed at the site of Lower Woodford. From here it can either head off towards Beornwin's stone in the direction of Romsey or due south to Old Sarum. From Old Sarum, those travelling further south could cross the Avon at Ayleswade and join the *wic* herepath mentioned in the Odstock boundary on a course towards Christchurch or the New Forest (discussed in study area 7).

FIGURE 38 *(opposite)*. Study area 8.2, Laverstock and the 'Winterbourne' charter (contains OS data and OS 1st Edition Six Inch base map © Crown copyright and Landmark Information Group Limited (2018), all rights reserved).

8. Wiltshire   123

Map 8.2 Laverstock and the 'Winterbourne' Charter

Or, a crossing of the Bourne at the chapmen's ford could be chosen in the direction of Southampton/*Hamwic*. To the west of Stapleford, this route continues up the Wylye valley in the direction of Warminster, the likely site of a *villa regalis* and minster church (Haslam 1984c, 118). The *wic* herepaths in study areas 7 and 8 seem, therefore, to be connecting the coastal trading sites in the Solent area with a *Hamwic* hinterland that Michael Metcalf has identified through the employment of geographical regression analysis to single finds of *Hamwic*'s Series H *sceattas* (Metcalf 2003, 41, fig. 4.1). In this model money is clearly being diffused westwards from the middle Anglo-Saxon trading emporium and it may be that the *wic* herepaths in this area served the purpose of carrying the trade that is archaeologically articulated through Metcalf's distribution (Figure 12).

Study area 9: Bradford-on-Avon and its hinterland

Topographically, Bradford-on-Avon represents an important crossing point of a major river and as a consequence, routes radiate out from the ford in all directions. It is likely to be the site of the battle of Bradford recorded in the *Anglo-Saxon Chronicle* for the year 652 and an Elbridge Lane, derived from OE *pel* (planked) bridge, suggests that a timber bridge existed from an early medieval date (Figure 41) (Gover *et al.* 1939, 117; Haslam 1984c, 90–94). Bradford-on-Avon's centrality may have played a role in the founding, according to William of Malmesbury, of a minster church and a community on the site as early as the late seventh century (Winterbottom and Thomson 2007, v.198.1). The '*cenobium*' of Bradford-on-Avon and its appurtenant lands were granted by Æthelred in 1001 to the nuns of Shaftesbury as a refuge (*confugium*) for the community and its relics presumably after some kind of catastrophe – perhaps Viking related – forced their temporary relocation (S 899; Kelly 1996, no. 29, 114–122). The other three charters in the group describe land to the south of Bradford-on-Avon at Steeple Ashton (S 727), Edington (S 765) and Westwood (S 867). All of the charters are believed to be authentic although the choice of the term *greatan hlywan* (great refuge) in the boundary clause of the Westwood charter of 987 to describe the church

FIGURE 39. The Roman road from Winchester to Old Sarum, looking west as it passes Park Corner (the location of the now lost Beornwin's Stone), with Clarendon Park to the south.

FIGURE 40 *(opposite)*. Study area 9.1, Bradford-on-Avon radiating routes (contains OS data and OS 1st Edition Six Inch base map © Crown copyright and Landmark Information Group Limited (2018), all rights reserved).

8. Wiltshire

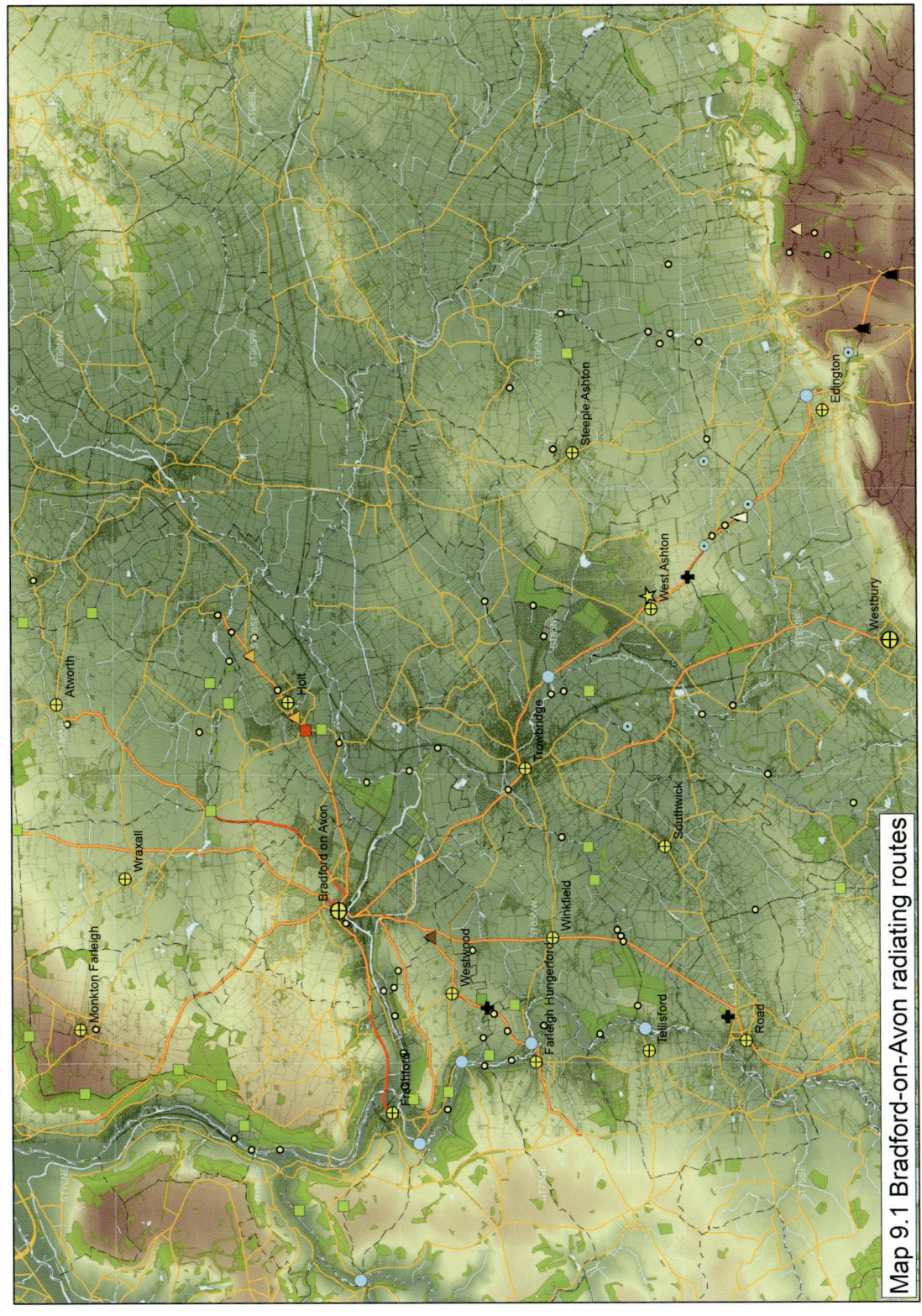

Map 9.1 Bradford-on-Avon radiating routes

at Bradford-on-Avon may be alluding to the church's role after Æthelred's grant in 1001 and so could suggest that the Westwood boundary clause was added after this date.

Despite the numerous routes that radiate out from the 'broad ford' in all directions to contemporary regional centres (such as Bath, Frome, Shepton Mallet, Westbury, Warminster, Melksham, Malmesbury and Chippenham) there are few references to routes in the boundary clauses of the charters for grants in this area (9.1). The boundary clause for Æthelred's grant in 1001 to the nuns of Shaftesbury seems mainly to refer to well-known boundaries belonging to local dignitaries in the immediate vicinity. For example, along its northern extent the perambulation goes *swa be þes abbotes imare to alfgares imare at Farnleghe, forð be is imare oð þat it cumet to þe kinges imare at Heselberi, forð be þes kinges imare þat it cumet to alfgares imare at Attenwrthe* (so by the Abbot's boundary to Alfgar's boundary at Farnleigh, forth by his boundary until it comes to the King's boundary at Hazelbury, forth by the King's boundary till it comes to Alfgar's boundary at Attworth). This marks this boundary clause out as unusual, perhaps as a result of the charter's unique circumstances. Yet, because little mention is made of the types of landscape features that characterise most boundary clauses, only three routes are referred to in the entire study area. The first of these is mentioned twice in the opening lines of the 1001 boundary clause where the term *herewai* is used to describe the route that makes its way from Bradford-on-Avon to Melksham to the east-north-east (ST86SE). As we have seen, the only other use of this term comes from a document of similar provenance and corresponds to land at Compton Abbas (S 630). A *hegweige* (?hay or 'high' way) is recorded in King Edgar's grant to Romsey Abbey of land at Edington in the south-east of the study area (ST95SW) but it is difficult to ascertain exactly which route it is referring to. It may be one that skirts the upper edge of the chalk downland in contrast to a summer way along the foot of the scarp slopes but it may also, like the *boc sætena hig wege* (the people of Buckland's high/hay way) on the fringes of Dartmoor, be referring to the route by which hay was seasonally carted from the upland areas down to the valley settlements.

Finally, a street is referred to in an apparently authentic grant of three hides made in 987 by King Æthelred to Leofwine at Westwood (ST85NW). The exact phrase from the boundary clause reads *suð to ðære strǣt on ða greatan hlywan* (south to the street to the great refuge) which heads in a south-west direction to cross the river Frome at Stanford. Three other fords are recorded crossing the Frome. From Stanford, the perambulation for Westwood goes *andlang streamæs on Igford* (along the stream to island ford) which survives as modern-day Iford. *Fersefordem* survives as a modern place-name Freshford and is the point at which the Frome joins the Avon (ST75NE). Routes west and south-west from Bradford would use this ford before then crossing the Midford Brook at Mitford (also mentioned in the charter of 1001). Finally, further upstream towards Frome, the boundary is recorded as passing '*inne Tefleforde*' (to ?game ford) which again survives in the modern place-name Tellisford (ST85NW). It is tempting to think of this last ford, like the *fegerhilde* (fair battle) *forde* (S 891) and *hildes* (battles)

FIGURE 41. The medieval bridge over the Avon at Bradford-on-Avon. © Kevin Eaves / Dreamstime.com.

ford (S 1547), as being indicative of a folk tradition of sparring combat held at fords. The prevalence of fords in this study area indicates that passage over this ground required negotiating the many streamlets that fed the headwaters of the Frome and Avon. A particular landmark that helped travellers to pick their way through this low-lying ground is also in evidence from the boundary clauses of this study area.

In a grant King Edgar makes out to himself of land at Steeple Ashton, a *rodestan* (rood stone) is referred to and by reference to Rood Ashton Farm, which appears on the nineteenth-century OS maps, this feature can be placed with a fair degree of certainty on a low rise on the alluvial plain (ST85SE). The rood stone is in a prominent position, visible especially to those approaching from the downlands to the south-east. There is good evidence for other possible roods in this study area but we are conscious of the caution that must be exercised in the interpretation of this place-name element. As Alexander Rumble has pointed out (2006, 29), the Old English *hrēod* (reed), *rōd* (a 'rod of land') and *rod* (clearing) all look and sound similar.

The landscape characteristics of the *rodestan* (*i.e.* highly visible and on a significant route) are shared by *burgredes rode* (Burgred's rood) which features later in the same boundary clause and appears to have given its name to Rode Hill and Road, recorded as *Rodehethe* in 1491 (ST85SW) (Gover *et al.* 1939, 145). Here traffic crossing the upper reaches of the Frome might be guided by a monument to the safest passage onwards to the refuge at Bradford-on-Avon. In this instance it seems unlikely that a 'rod of land' is being referred to in a landscape that is otherwise characterised by open country (*i.e.* heath), evidenced by the reference in the previous line of the boundary clause to the *wuntfeld* and the place-name Wingfield to the north. Equally, over such terrain, the interpretation of 'clearing' seems ill-fitting and as has been demonstrated from previous study areas, personal names are commonly associated with markers such as posts and stones. *Rodæ* (roods) are referred to in Æthelred's grant to Leofwine at Westwood (ST85NW). In the rubric of the same charter Æthelred gives also three *gyrda æt Fearnlege* (across the river Frome in Farleigh) and here a different spelling for 'rod', in this case inferring a measure of land, would suggest that the 'roods' imply an altogether different feature. Again, the *Rodæ* feature in a prominent location and may be directing traffic to Bradford-on-Avon along the aforementioned *stræt on ða greatan hlywan* on which they are located. Two further markers deserve mention. The first of these is on a continuation of the route out of Bradford-on-Avon, over Tibba's ford, past the rood stone mentioned earlier and up on to the downs where *on redestan* is recorded in the boundary for Edgar's grant at Edington (ST95SW). Here the form of the term is so similar to *rodestan* that a simple scribal or copyist's error could be suggested. On chalk downland it is highly unlikely that residual outcrops of natural red stone would be found. However, it may be that a red coloration is a deliberate, perhaps painted, feature of this marker stone as a *readan rode* (red rood) is referred to in a grant covering land on chalk downland in Hampshire (S 376) along with a *red stan* [red stone] on the chalk downland at Liddington (S 459). The *padecanstan* (?cloaked stone) occupies a similar position on the downland to the *redestan* in that it too sits on a high point alongside a significant route traversing the chalk downland and both these stones, along with the various roods above, all seem to be marking routes (as well as boundaries).

The *rodestan*, *redestan* and *padecanstan* all sit on a route radiating out from Bradford-on-Avon to the south-east, a route that other circumstantial evidence suggests is of some importance both in the middle and late Anglo-Saxon periods. In the first instance, the place-name Trowbridge ('tree' or 'wooden' bridge) suggests that another timber bridge served traffic travelling to and from Bradford-on-Avon (Gover *et al.* 1939, 133; Ekwall 1947, 458–459). The site is not described in the boundary clauses but archaeological evidence for middle-Anglo-Saxon occupation and a late Anglo-Saxon settlement supporting a Saxo-Norman church suggest a location of some importance in the early medieval period and a possible thegnly residence (Graham and Davis 1993, 146). Proximity of the ditched and banked enclosure of the later Anglo-Saxon phases to the major thoroughfare that passes through the settlement suggests that control of this route, as well as one that passes east–west through the site, was important. Finds in the parish of West Ashton of a *sceatta* Series H and continental Series E, dating from the early to mid-eighth century, indicate a possible trade route connecting this area with the south-east (finds.org.uk, WILT-D3B061; WILT-D38FA1). To the south-

FIGURE 42 *(opposite)*. Study area 10.1, Kinwardstone, Wansdyke and the Bedwyn Dykes (contains OS data and OS 1st Edition Six Inch base map © Crown copyright and Landmark Information Group Limited (2018), all rights reserved).

8. Wiltshire   129

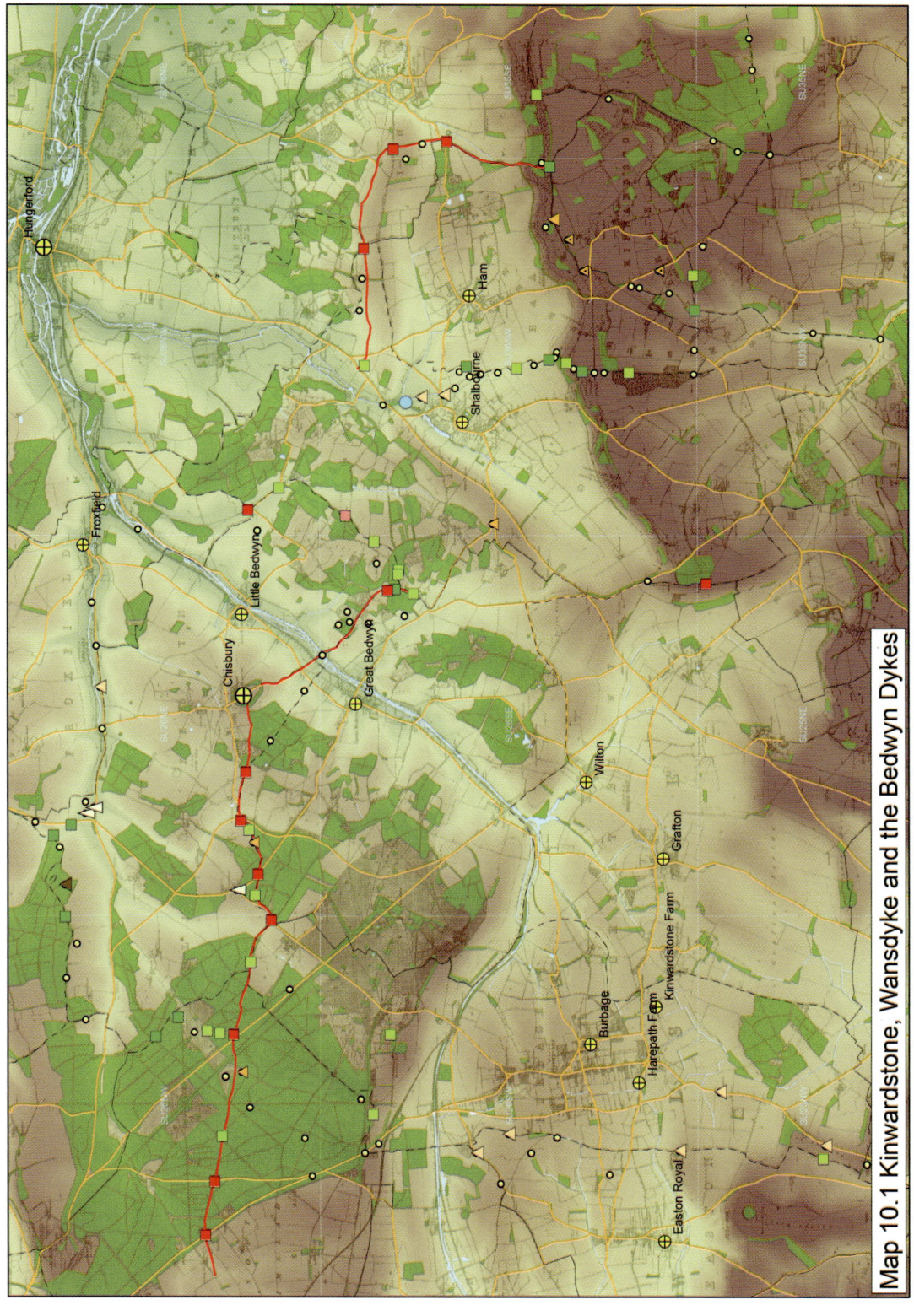

Map 10.1 Kinwardstone, Wansdyke and the Bedwyn Dykes

130 Alexander Langlands

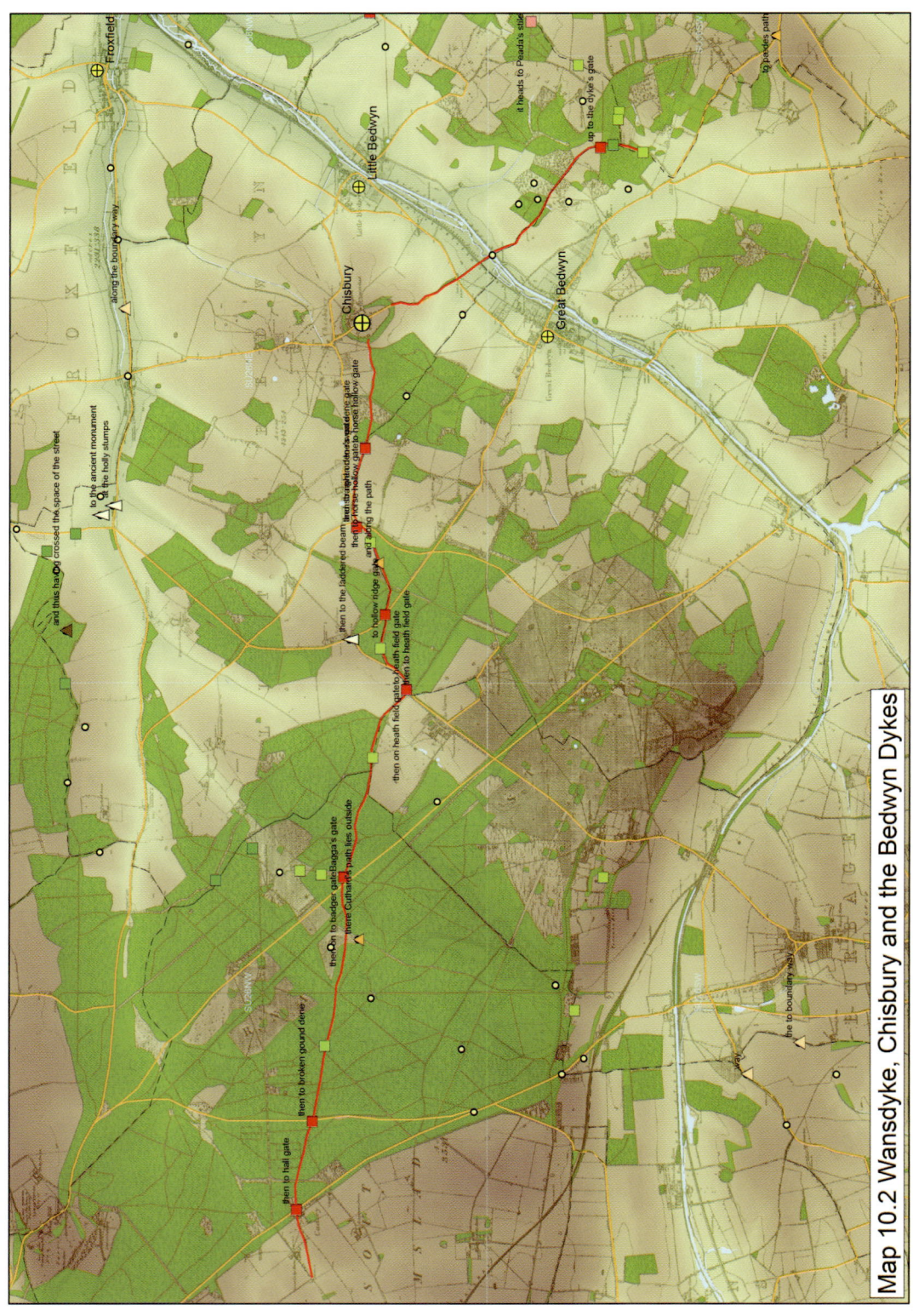

Map 10.2 Wansdyke, Chisbury and the Bedwyn Dykes

east of this study area, this route can be traced across Salisbury Plain ultimately as far as Stapleford and the *wic* herepath of study area 8, further illustrating the physical corollary by which Series H *sceattas* penetrated the *Hamwic* hinterland.

Study area 10: Kinwardstone Hundred

This area represents a large geographically coherent group of parishes situated on the eastern edge of mid-Wiltshire bordering both Berkshire and Hampshire. Assessed at 196¼ hides in 1086, Kinwardstone Hundred was one of the largest hundreds in Wiltshire and it is likely that this is owed to its former status as a large royal estate based on a *Villa Regalis* at Great Bedwyn, then its largest and most central settlement (Haslam 1980, 58–64). The importance of this estate is evident from its role in the late ninth-century defences of Wessex with the iron-age hillfort of Chisbury believed to be the location of *Cissanbyrig*, referred to in the *Burghal Hidage* list of forts (Brooks 1964, 75–79). This importance continues into the tenth and eleventh centuries as the survival of guild statutes of the early to mid-tenth century testify to its urban status (Whitelock 1979, Cat. No. 39, 429–430). By the mid-eleventh century it was in possession of a mint and had 25 burgesses at the time of the Domesday survey but it seems, like Avebury, to have been ultimately outstripped by Marlborough and Hungerford as an urban focus in the region (Reynolds 2002a, 207).

There are five Anglo-Saxon charters with boundary clauses describing land in Kinwardstone Hundred. These are at Little Bedwyn (S 264), Collingbourne Kingston (S 379), Ham (S 416), Burbage (S 688) and Great Bedwyn (S 756). With the exception of the charter for Burbage, over whose authenticity there is some uncertainty, this group of charters represents a reliable collection of documents (Dumville 1992, 109–110, 112; Kelly 2001, 361–364). The latter four, including the suspected forgery for Burbage, all date from the tenth century whilst the charter for Little Bedwyn is believed to be a reliable tenth-century copy of what was originally an eighth-century grant (Dumville 1987, 167; 1992, 82–83, 109, 112).

The two mentions of 'streets', *strēt gætes* (1.3, SU25NE) and *stratæ* (10.1, SU26NE), are consistent with the Roman roads in this area; connecting *Cunetio* to Winchester to the south-east and the other running due east in the direction of Silchester, via *Spinis* (Thatcham) (Crawford 1953, 69; Margary 1973, nos 43 and 53). A *weall weg* or *wælweg* is referred to towards the south-west corner of the study area and it seems likely that this is referring to a Romano-British route running north–south across the valley (10.1, SU25NW). Peter Fowler has observed how the major ridgeway known further north as the Icknield Way divides up into a series of braided routes as it crosses the valley. This explains, he believes, the numerous gates observed in the standing bank and ditch of Wansdyke as it bounds the southern tips of Fyfield and West Overton parishes through West Woods (2000, 197–200). It may be that this 'British' way is one of many, surviving as parish boundaries and existing north–south routes (such

FIGURE 43 *(opposite)*. Study area 10.2, Wansdyke, Chisbury and the Bedwyn Dykes (contains OS data and OS 1st Edition Six Inch base map © Crown copyright and Landmark Information Group Limited (2018), all rights reserved).

as the 'boundary way') that once formed part of a much wider corridor of movement and as with the case of the Devonian example (4.1 SX74NW), the association with the 'British' implies a recognition of its antiquity on the part of Anglo-Saxon boundary surveyors. Elsewhere, the evidence for the continuation of Wansdyke east beyond the chalk downland to the north of the Vale of Pewsey and through Savernake Forest has been reviewed in detail. The context of this vast linear earthwork as both a defensive and political boundary has been revised, a seventh- to eighth-century date and a much more extensive political boundary (bounding the northern extent of Wessex at this time) has been put forward (Reynolds and Langlands 2006).

The distribution of gates recorded in the Burbage, Great Bedwyn and Little Bedwyn charters along the course of the estate boundaries through Savernake Forest would seem to suggest that some kind of linear boundary persisted from the terminus of Wansdyke, through the forest and connecting with the Bedwyn Dykes. Whilst O.G.S. Crawford (1921) was of the opinion that these gates represented gaps in hedges, the regularity with which these seven gates feature along a five-mile stretch of boundary echo the Roman mile-castle theory put forward by Fowler (2001, 187–191). The charter for Ham describes an area slightly larger than the present day parish and in 1926 it was suggested that this too could represent a continuation of the Wansdyke frontier (10.3) (Major and Burrows 1926, 341–343). In all, the gates in this area, and those seen bounding the chalk downland to the south-east (study area 1) give an impression of a landscape within which movement was heavily monitored and controlled. A similar element that may provide a further insight into how the control and organisation of movement was maintained for people on a local level, is referred to in three separate charters in the region of Ham. A *Peadan stigele* (10.3, SU36SW), *pyddes geate* (SU36SE) and *pædes pape* (SU36SW) may represent the stile, gate and path of the personal name Peada (langscape.org.uk, L 264) but the association with such similar physical entities might also suggest an anglicised version of the Latin *pedes* (foot-traveller, walker). Another example, *Pidebrigg(e)* 1318, referring to Pethybridge in Teignbridge Hundred, has been interpreted as *Pyd(d)a's bridge* or *Pidda's bridge* (Mawer and Stenton 1932, 481), but 'foot bridge' seems a more plausible translation. Of the six references to the Old English *anstigo* (footpath), from the entire corpus of charters used by this project, four appear in this study area (*e.g.* SU36SW) and this further reflects a desire on the part of boundary surveyors to clearly distinguish between those routes viable for cart travel and those suited for pedestrians.

Five of the seven Savernake Forest gates appear in the early charter for Little Bedwyn dated to 788. In being referred to a mere nine years after Offa's defeat of the West Saxon king Cynewulf at Bensington, a campaign that saw the Mercian king take overlordship of Berkshire, north Wiltshire and north Somerset (Stenton 1913, 50), they must surely represent elements of an active political boundary. The remaining two gates are recorded only in later charters but the most western of these, the *sæl gæte* (hall gate) clearly suggests

FIGURE 44 *(opposite)*. Study area 10.3, the Ham Dyke (contains OS data and OS 1st Edition Six Inch base map © Crown copyright and Landmark Information Group Limited (2018), all rights reserved).

an association with a functioning structure (10.2, SU26NW). The selection of Chisbury in Alfred's wider scheme of defence is understandable as the Wessex heartlands at this point could be penetrated from the north via the Icknield Way, the north-east via the Thames and Kennet rivers and from the east along the ridgeway that skirts the downland into Berkshire (referred to as a *herpoðes*, *weg* and *via publica* and discussed in study area 1).

Finally, attention should be drawn to the locations of two important stones. One, Wylbert's stone (10.1, SU25NW), is recorded in the boundary clause for Collingbourne Kingston and lies on the course of the 'British Way', a route that can be traced to the south in an unbroken line, via Amesbury, to Old Sarum. To the north, this route runs through Burbage and Savernake Forest to the site of the Roman town of *Cunetio* and is likely to represent the course of Margary's Roman road number 44. The location of the Cyneward's stone, the stone that gave its name to the Hundred and the likely assembly place, is unknown although the presence of Kinwardstone Farm led the authors of the place-name volume for the county to give a likely position on the boundary between Burbage and Grafton (10.1, SU26SW) (Gover *et al.* 1939, end map). An east–west herepath is preserved in the name of Harepath Farm, which continues west along the valley up to and beyond Swanborough Tump, the meeting place of Swanborough Hundred (Semple and Langlands 2001).

Part 3
DISCUSSION

CHAPTER NINE

Roman roads, wayside markers and gates

The Roman road question

The legacy of Ivan Margary and the *Viatores* – his band of fellow Roman road hunters – is a linear template of Roman roads that has become embedded in landscape folklore, reprinted and regurgitated in studies of the early medieval period (Margary 1948; 1973). It has served not only to furnish the distribution maps of our archaeological, historical and etymological source material but at times, proximity to this network of routes has been seen to provide spatial context and meaning. Chapter 1 reviewed the implications of unconditionally projecting on to the early medieval landscape the network of straight Roman roads and the problems inherent in then attempting to identify their impact on distributions of archaeological and place-name data as if, (a) they were all, including their river-crossings, in serviceable and viable condition and (b) they were the only routes available to the long-distance Anglo-Saxon traveller. In this section we shall review some of the evidence for the fate of the Roman roads defined by Margary and others whilst at the same time exploring some of the evidence for 'Romanised' roads – *i.e.* those roads which are not characteristically straight but may nonetheless have played an important role in the Romano-British and later landscapes.

A number of issues arise in the exploration of the *strǣt* element in local case studies: first and foremost, we do not have a sufficient evidential basis for what the sub-network of Roman roads looked like. Secondly, we don't know, on the very local level, the capacity of Anglo-Saxon surveyors to recognise the antiquity of a route way or its surface. And finally, there are problems of uniformity of *meaning* in the application of Old English terms to physical structures. Whilst it seems to be the case that the *strǣt* elements of major settlement names reflect the presence of a Roman road, the received wisdom is that this rule does not always hold good for boundary marks in Anglo-Saxon charters (Gelling 1997, 153). Margaret Gelling and Ann Cole (2000, 93–94) offer 'main road' as an acceptable rendering in charter boundaries but the risk in such anachronistic interpretations, especially when physical evidence is not at hand to either confirm or dispel, is that we are no closer to establishing an understanding of the term. Where detailed studies exist, it seems most likely that the element *strǣt* in boundary clauses does refer to a road of Romano-British origin and Della Hooke (1981a, 301–307), for example, demonstrates the correlation in enough given examples of known Roman roads to suggest that where it is being used in a location where we have no evidence for a typical Roman road, we should heed the advice that the Anglo-Saxons are giving us and posit the existence of a Roman road. As John Baker (2013, 79) has pointed out, however, for the early medieval period, questions are probably better framed around not what constitutes a Roman road in modern discussion, but what kind of track was considered by Anglo-Saxon observers to be a *strēt*.

What is clear from the study areas is that when Anglo-Saxon boundary surveyors refer to 'streets' there seems to be a recognition of the fact that these routes are of Roman origin. The key Roman roads leading north out of Winchester (2), through St Mary Bourne (1), south-west out of Old Sarum (8) and east out of Exeter (3) are all referred to as 'streets'. However, we are instantly drawn to consider whether, in naming these routes so, the boundary surveyors were alluding to routes that were in active operation or whether it was a phrase used in recognition of their antiquity. What is interesting is that in some places, these Roman roads are referred to as herepaths and this suggests a status or functionality that transcends in importance, in the minds of Anglo-Saxon boundary surveyors, their character as ancient routes. This is most obvious where the Roman road leaves Winchester in a north-west direction (2.2 SU43NW, SU43SE), in the Ebble Valley (7.3 SU02NE) and on the Exeter to Topsham stretch of Roman road (3.1 SX99SW).

With the failure of Silchester as a central place in the post-Roman period, it must be envisaged that the routes radiating from the *civitas* will have fallen redundant. We have seen how the section to Winchester through Stratton Park was overlain by occupational deposits dating to the middle Anglo-Saxon period (Fasham 1981, 167–171). Equally, in study area 1, from an early period it seems that deviations from the course of the first road [RR1] were made both to the north and south for preferred crossings of the Bourne Rivulet (1.1). The survival of the Roman road running south-west from Old Sarum depends very much on the fortunes of the crossings of the Avon and Nadder Rivers (8.1 SU13SW). The presence of a 'Kingsbridge Meadow' on the crossing of the Avon suggests a medieval crossing and one, because of its location, that predates the purported shift of urban focus from the Old Sarum area to the current Salisbury City site. On the continued course of this Roman road through the Ebble Valley it is referred to twice as a 'street' as it forms the boundary between the estates of Stratford Tony and Bishopstone. It is also, however, referred to as a herepath suggesting active use in the Anglo-Saxon period, but the realignment of movement through Stratford Tony on the 'White' or 'Wilton' Way and via Bica's Bridge (7.3 SU02NE) on a course to Wilton suggests that crossings of the Nadder were favoured at Ayleswade and at Bulbridge (8.1 SU12NW, SU03SE) rather than on the course of the Roman road.

It is at the crossing of rivers that the case for Roman road continuity is at its weakest. In every study area the course of a Roman road is obliged to deviate at the point where it is required to negotiate a river crossing and this prompts the obvious question of whether this deviation was carried out at the point of construction, to make use of an existing Iron Age crossing point, or whether this occurred later, with the collapse and ruin of the Roman bridges. In only one instance does the charter boundary clause evidence for Wessex suggest the survival of a Roman bridge into the Anglo-Saxon period and this is the *weala brucge* (British bridge) mentioned in a charter for Brimpton, Berkshire, where the Roman road from Silchester to *Spinae* crossed the River Kennet (S 500). Otherwise, the 'stone heap' of the Laverstock charter (8.1 SU13SE), if we take this to mean a ruinous stone pier, provides an insight into the fate of Romano-British bridges. Three *sceattas* found to the immediate west of this crossing suggest that it may still have been a functioning crossing point (if only as a ford) until the mid-ninth century (Wiltshire SMR numbers: SU13SE405; SU13SE406, although series type not given). The various 'deep fords' that are found in close proximity to Roman road crossing places, such as Deptford on Watling Street and Deptford over the River Wylye where the purported course of the Harroway crosses, suggest that not altogether ideal fording points had to be used by traffic still using these roads. As Christopher Taylor (1979, 97–101) observed, once the crossing of the River Welland on the trajectory prescribed by the course of Ermine Street had been rejected, the road itself fell out of use for much of its course. Only at the very northern extent of Ermine Street in Lincolnshire, in proximity to the Humber, do any metalwork find-spots appear on the line of the Roman road in Kevin Leahy's distribution maps of fifth- to tenth-century finds of Anglo-Saxon metalwork (2003, 139–142, figs 12.1, 12.2 and 12.3).

Figure 45 therefore takes a critical look at the Roman road network in Wessex and on the basis of the evidence from the study areas and more general observations, a 'worst case scenario' is projected for the survival of the Roman road network throughout the early medieval period. The section between Old Sarum and Winchester and the relationship this road has with the Lower Test represents a particularly fruitful avenue of future enquiry in that it appears that over a long time frame, crossing points of the Roman roads at Nursling and Horsebridge were rejected in favour of crossing points at Redbridge, Romsey and Stockbridge. It is clear that only by further detailed analysis and ultimately through archaeological excavation can a much clearer picture be gained of exactly how these routes fell out of use and crucially, when.

In Figure 45 other suggested Roman or 'Romanised' roads have also been included on the basis of certain terms used in the boundary clause evidence. If we were to accept the fact that the use of the term 'street' reflects a consciousness of a Roman road on the part of Anglo-Saxons, its application to routes not previously thought to be of Roman origin may help us to further improve our understanding of the network of Roman roads. In the study areas, further 'streets' occur in the upper reaches of the Ebble Valley (7), to the north of St Mary Bourne (1), running south-west from Bradford-on-Avon (9) and parallel to the coastline of the South Hams (4). In the case of the first two, these can clearly be identified with major ridgeways and it seems likely that such thoroughfares were incorporated into the network of routes that served an estimated population

140 *Alexander Langlands*

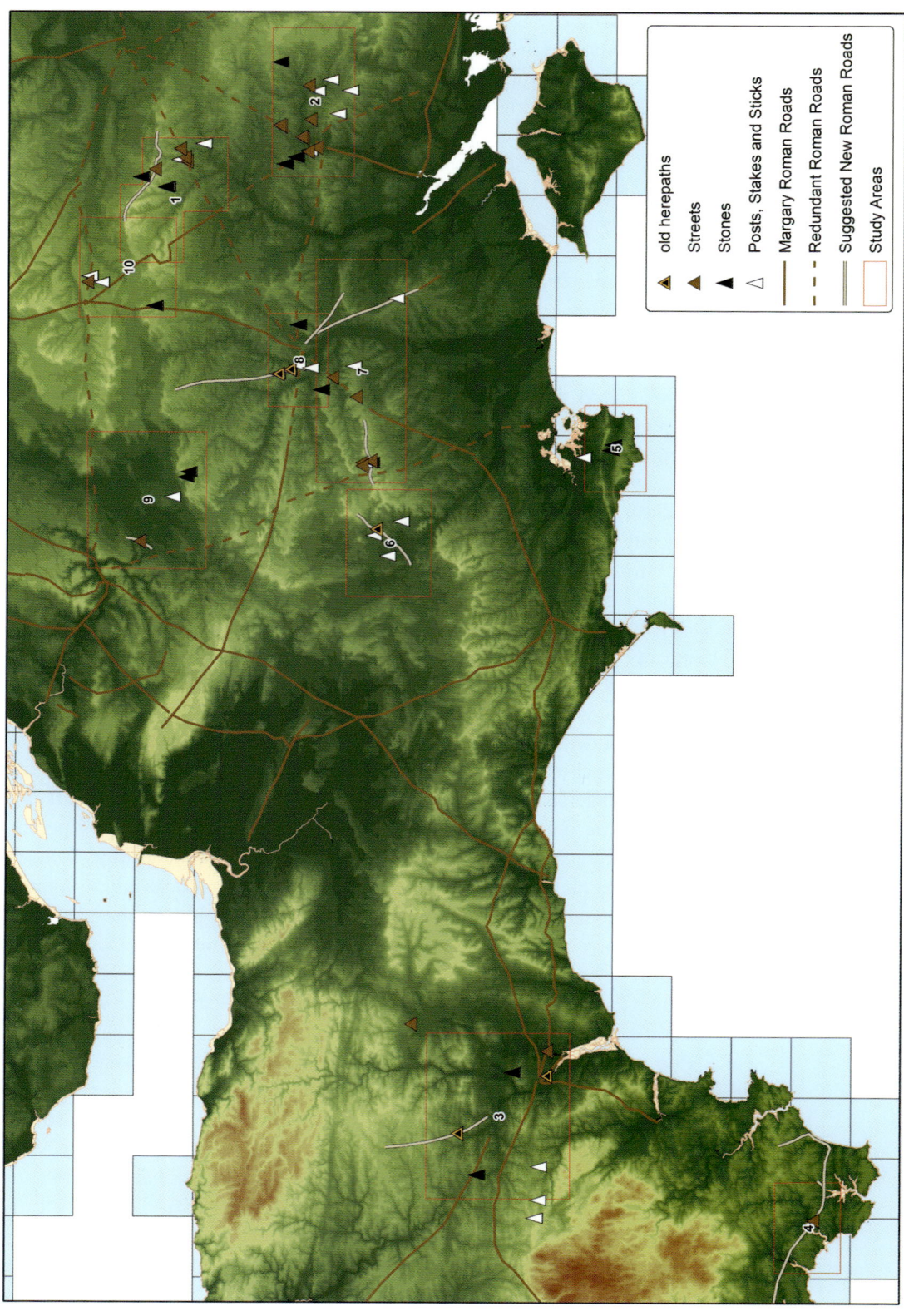

of five million Roman Britons (Fowler 2002, 17). Outside of the study areas a similar situation can be observed on a stretch of the Gloucestershire ridgeway and on the course of the Icknield Way (S 467; S 1208). It seems likely too that the crossing point of the Avon at Bradford was of such importance that it found employment in the Romano-British period and the reference here to a street may represent a road spurred off a conjectural route, of which only the most ephemeral remains have been identified, running from Badbury Rings in Dorset to Bath (Margary 1973, nos 46 and 52). In the South Hams, it may very well be that a route along this course allowed for Cornwall and Devon's rich tin and copper ores and/or the final smelted product to be transported east as either an alternative to, or integrated part of, coastal shipping. Elsewhere it has been observed that the layout of the Roman road network bears a strong relationship in places to the key mining districts of Britain, such as iron in the Weald, lead in Yorkshire, Derbyshire and the Mendips and tin in Cornwall (Margary 1948; 1973, nos 492a and 492b; Shepherd 1993, 274–276). Justifiably, the straight alignments running into Strete from the north and south-south-west along Slapton Sands, might be presumed to indicate the courses of Roman roads, extensions to those first hypothesised in the early part of the twentieth century (Joce 1911; 1912)

A more general analysis in this part of south-western Britain of the relationship between route ways and rich mining areas will only serve better to augment our understanding of the control of mining industries throughout the region in the early medieval period. It may be that the density of herepath references in this period reflect a desire to control a hugely profitable industry as much as the need to protect the relatively exposed peninsula of Dumnonia (pers. comm. Niall Finneran 2013).

It is the references to 'old' herepaths and *stapulas* (posts or columns) that offer the most conjectural support for further Roman roads. In the Salisbury Basin study area (8), the row of three stone posts on the line of a route running north in the direction of *Verlucio* is the clearest indication from the study areas of the survival of Roman milestones. The route they are on is referred to as an 'old' herepath and the use of this term to describe the Exeter to Topsham Roman road (3.1) presents us with the slightest evidence that Anglo-Saxon boundary surveyors identified the antiquity of such routes and perhaps even an ancient obligation for their upkeep. Further 'old' herepaths have therefore been sketched into Figure 45 but the issue of late-Roman legislation for the maintenance of roads and its continued application into the Anglo-Saxon period is reserved for further discussion below. Returning to the 'stone posts' of study area 8, a further example is recorded in the Downton bounds on the course of a herepath (7.4 SU21NW). The trajectory of this herepath due south-south-west joins up with a very short stretch of Roman road identified by Margary, and together the evidence presents us with a route of Roman origin that either crossed the Avon at Downton or continued up the east bank to join with another herepath running through Alderbury. This latter route is itself likely to represent the continuation of another Roman road identified by Margary in the New Forest (Margary 1973, nos 423 and 424).

FIGURE 45 *(opposite)*. Roman roads in early medieval Wessex (contains OS data © Crown copyright (2018)).

Stones, posts and the ambiguity in the terminology used to describe such monuments are discussed in much more detail below but it should be considered that the various references to such edifices in the Anglo-Saxon landscape may very well represent the remnants of a widespread tradition in the Roman Empire of furnishing major thoroughfares with stone waymarkers. References to 'stone posts' may represent explicit descriptions of Roman milestones in the form of the Stinsford example, a worked stone column that survives in what is thought to be in, or very close to, its original location (Farrar 1957; Sedgley 1975, 22). However, we know that many milestones did not necessarily take a cylindrical form and some of the closest surviving examples to study area 8 were recovered, not *in situ*, from excavations at Rockbourne Roman villa and were rectangular in form (Sedgley 1975, 21). It is therefore possible that alongside the generic term 'post', the generic term 'stone' may also be referring to such monuments and it is for this reason that they have been included in Figure 45. Only further mapping of such stones and their relationship with Roman roads, Romanised roads and Anglo-Saxon herepaths would allow further commentary.

In all, Figure 45 paints a very different picture of the extent of the Roman road network in the early medieval period, from the depiction of the network in Figure 4 and of course, neither figure has any of the known Anglo-Saxon routes and other ridgeways projected on to it. What this study has demonstrated is that in many ways the projection of Margary's map of Roman roads on to distribution maps of early medieval phenomena does not do justice to the vast complexity of the issue of survival and furthermore, we can only consider the correlation of archaeological and toponymic distributions in relation to the Roman road network with an awareness of this complexity. One final point needs to be made here that is a further illustration of just how complex the issue of Roman road survival is. It revolves around the notion of 'rebirth', a notion well employed in the context of urban development in the early medieval period (Hodges and Hobley 1988). Essentially, there is a distinct possibility that aspects of the Roman road network were brought back into operation, in the same way that Roman city walls and quaysides were, to play a part in the urban ambitions of late Anglo-Saxon society. Archaeological evidence of this comes from the excavations at East Stratton where middle Saxon occupation layers overlying a Roman road were in turn overlain by flint cobbles believed to correspond to a phase of 'late Saxon road building' (Fasham 1981, 171–172). Tim Tatton-Brown's study of Watling Street identifies a similar sequence – albeit from a different evidence base. In the early and middle Anglo-Saxon periods, he believes that the course of the Roman road fell out of use and that it was not until the resettlement of the Roman walled towns of Canterbury and Rochester during the Viking Ages and more specifically during the peace brought about by Cnut's reign that Watling Street found itself back in service connecting the main urban centres of northern Kent to London (Tatton-Brown 2001, 124–125). The 'Kingsbridge' referred to, albeit at a later date, on the course of the Roman road from Old Sarum heading south-west towards Dorchester as it crosses the Avon (8.1, SU13SW) may very well reflect a later reinstatement.

It is important, therefore, to state here that where we have apparent evidence from the later medieval period for Roman road survival, we must entertain the possibility of phases of redundancy and 'rebirth'. Attention has been drawn to the 'ideological import' of the Roman road network in the medieval period – an 'unacknowledged appropriation of them for a national history' – in Henry of Huntingdon's 1130 *Historia Anglorum*, the *Leges Edwardi Confessoris* and Geoffrey of Monmouth's *Historia regum Britanniae*, and it may be that the implementation of classical ideals in the nation-building projects of the twelfth century actually have their origins in the tenth and eleventh (Allen and Evans 2016, 13).

Wayside markers

The concept of 'landscape' in the social sciences is increasingly linked to notions of experience and engagement and this has been marked in British landscape archaeology by a shift in emphasis away from quantitative and statistical approaches and towards matters of individual human perception (Bender 1993; Darvill 1997). Such an approach requires an intellectual positioning that is receptive to the notion that a landscape can be both a physical entity *and* a form of canvas, or stage, on to which conceptions of the world can be expressed (Gosden and Head 1994, 113; Layton and Ucko 2004, 1). Although the study of medieval travel more generally is marked by the absence of any systematic attempt to explore how travellers found their way from one part of the country to another, we need to be cautious of over-thinking the issue and demanding information on a challenge that might not necessarily have been a reality in the medieval mind (Evans 2016, 139–141). If medieval wayfinding defines and presupposes medieval space, then medieval concepts of space are so profoundly different from our own that it may be a fruitless pursuit to seek wayfinding methods parallel to those of our own (Evans 2016, 147). It is well established that profoundly different worldviews existed throughout the course of human history and these will have impacted upon different ways of constructing, experiencing and inhabiting space (Dewitt 2010).

Wayfinding, therefore, and the types and characters of wayside marker charged with communicating space may have existed within a profoundly different concept of time and space from that of our own. On a practical level, in a world largely devoid of the aerial perspective, we must envisage a cosmology for the Anglo-Saxon world that understands space via a 'mental map' (although for a rare exception see the Anglo-Saxon *Cotton Tiberius* world map, Brown 2007, 146 plate 112). At ground level, mental maps would have been structured around a 'horizontal' perspective wherein a series of vistas would have comprised an understanding of what lay beyond the immediate view-shed. These in turn would have been layered with meaning – for the purposes of memory and identification – and elsewhere for early medieval England it has been argued that the multiple authors of landscapes, through symbolism, monumentalism and place-names with associative meaning, can convey a series of messages to those passing through (Reynolds and Langlands 2011). Nowhere is this more clearly illustrated than in the Icelandic sagas where the narrated journeys of the protagonists are woven with place-specific set pieces in such a way that they read almost like sailing directions (Ohler and Hillier 1989, 42). Whilst, in some cases, such directions are made explicit; listing points of departure, the course, sailing times, and destination, in many cases, key navigational details are embedded in the narrative (Thirslund 1997). If you wanted to find your way, therefore, in the Scandinavian world of the early medieval period, all you had to do was to remember the legends passed down through oral tradition. For later medieval Europe memory was thought to play an important part in wayfinding and the etymological connection between the English *rote* with Latin *rota*, 'wheel' and French *rote*, 'way, route', has been observed as part of a broader connection between remembering and travelling (Evans 2016, 136–137).

So, whilst medieval conceptions of space might be so remote as to be imperceptible to us today, we might be on safer ground to observe more broadly how memory and storytelling overlaps with navigational knowledge, and how the land- and seascape provide the canvas on which to secure the necessary information for the early medieval traveller. This form of mythologising of landscape, one where conceptual frameworks played a role in the formation of both a sense of place and identity in the medieval mind, has been recognised in other parts of early medieval Scandinavia and in Britain (Brink 2001; Semple 2010). For the traveller in early medieval Wessex, to tread the dragon's back (S 496), to encounter Wayland's Smithy (S 564), to step tentatively past Grendel's pit (S 255), to cross the goblin brook (S 387) and to peer down on the Vale of Pewsey from the summit of Woden's barrow (S 272) is to move through a world imbued with the supernatural, with mythological meaning prompting reactions of fear and familiarity.

No evidence from medieval Europe survives to suggest the existence of signposts, in the form of officially sanctioned directional indicators, and it is not until legislation enacted in 1697, as well as the *Highways Act* of 1766 and the *Turnpike Roads Act* of 1773, that a kind of sign-posting emerges that we, today, are more familiar with (Bird 1806, 85; cited in Evans 2016, 139). There are, however, a rich variety of roadside monuments that suggest that information, ideas and opportunities for engagement are being offered to the early medieval traveller – all monuments that can be considered within the framework of the conceptual geographies outlined above.

Stones

The presence of 'stones' in boundary clauses and the -stone element in place-names is a good illustration of the problems of accurately interpreting roadside markers. Attention has already been drawn to the boundary for land granted to the west of Crediton (3.2) that begins *on copelan stan* where today the site is marked by a sculpted granite cross-shaft. Believed to be on or near its original situation, the shaft is decorated with panels of geometric interlace, ring-knotting and a rider figure that are thought to be indicative of Scandinavian influences (Cramp 2006, 42, 82–83). The important thing here is that this cross is not referred to as a 'cross' but as a 'stone'. We are thus left pondering what might actually have existed at other sites where references to stones are made. A more explicit incidence of how clearly the term stone and cross were interchangeable comes from the miracles of St Swithun, as recorded by both Lantfred and Wulfstan. To recapitulate, Lantfred tells us that, 'There is a large, tall, shining stone cross here, put up to the glory of Christ' some three miles out of the city of Winchester and it is likely he was writing within living memory of the translation of St Swithun's bones from outside the west door to a central location in the minster (Lapidge 2003, 319). Wulfstan, writing a generation later informs us that *ibi uexillum quoniam de rupe uestusto erectus sublime crucis*' (a replica in ancient stone of the sublime cross) stood in the same location, provides us with the crucial extra information; *quem lingua 'Petram' uocat Anglia 'Regis'* (which the English tongue calls the King's Stone) (Lapidge 2003, 529). It seems highly likely, from the analysis of boundary clauses in study area 2, that this monument is the same *kinges stane* recorded in the boundary clause of a charter for land at *Worðige*, but even if it is not, the information from both Lantfred and Wulfstan's account is enough to prove that when the Anglo-Saxons speak of stones in the landscape they may very well be referring to sculpted stone crosses and monuments of considerable importance. Attention should also be drawn to the *niwan stan* (new stone) in the boundary clause for an adjacent estate at Crawley (S 381). It is likely that what we have here is another reference to this important landmark.

A similar situation is recorded by William of Malmesbury who tells us that following the death of Bishop Aldhelm, in 709, in the village of Doulting, Somerset, the procession of his funeral cortège was marked at seven-mile intervals by crosses on its journey back (presumably along the course of the Fosse Way) to Malmesbury. Although William was writing at some distance, chronologically, from these events, he is at pains to stress the authenticity of his account and its basis on original documentation. He is explicit when he writes that the stones survived into the landscape of his own time where they were referred to as *biscepstane*s (Preest 2002, 261). These examples, and the ambiguity in the terminology used to describe such monuments, force us to consider that in many places it may not be that simple boundary stones are being referred to in charter boundary clauses and that actually a complex variety of monuments, including highly decorated crosses, were in existence throughout the early medieval landscape of Wessex. We have references to grey stones, great stones, long stones, hollow stones and old stones which no doubt served as convenient and permanent markers against which to set out boundaries, if indeed, they were not moved to their locations for that very purpose. But of a uniform tradition of marking out boundaries with certain types of stones, the evidence is only very slight. From the project study area alone there is only a single reference to a 'boundary stone' (*tham merc stane*) (S 963).

Stones associated with personal names might stand out as potential candidates for boundary markers and one method of exploring this would be to look at charter beneficiaries for land granted alongside locations where personal named markers are recorded. The *Prosopography of Anglo-Saxon England* database allows for all recorded personal names to be searched and whilst the beneficiaries of grants and leases are recorded, as well as charter witnesses, it currently does not hold information on individuals mentioned in boundary clauses. Attempting to find matches in this fashion is, however, a tenuous and often fruitless business. Of all the personal named markers recorded in the project study area (so including posts, stones, roods and stakes), in only two incidences is it likely that a known individual recorded in an early medieval documentary source can be associated with a named boundary mark. The first is *Byrtferths hlawe* (S 543) which may relate to *Byrtferth* the recipient of the Odstock grant (S 400) in Study Area maps 8.2 and 7.3. The second is Beornwulf, who is referred to as the lessee in receipt of 15 hides of land at *æt Eblesburnan*, granted by the community at Winchester in 902 (S 1285). As we saw in study area 7, the only land that Old Minster, Winchester owned in the Ebble Valley at that time was their estate at Bishopstone and the stone referred to in the boundary clauses for this estate (recorded at a later date and at 7.3 SU02NE) is referred to in a contiguous grant of land at *Pyrigean* as *beornolfes stan* (Beornwulf's stone), identified as an estate to the immediate south-west of Wilton (S 586 – not covered in the original study area charters; Grundy 1919, 293–295)

This does not mean that using the *Prosopography of Anglo-Saxon England* in this manner is invalid, in fact, our understanding of the early medieval landscape would only benefit from including the personal names recorded in boundary clauses and identifying spatially any correlations with the existing database of named individuals. In any event, that personal named monuments are more than just boundary markers is suggested by the association of named individuals with stones in other place-names – particularly those places that go on to become hundred-names but that are not recorded on boundaries. In the study areas, Kinwardstone is a fine example of this. Surviving as a farm name to the immediate south-east of Burbage, Cyneweard's stone may have marked the crossing point of the major north–south and east–west aligned routes through the hundred (10.3). Brixton (Surrey), Tibblestone (Gloucs.) (the name meaning '*Þēodbald's* stone') and Ossulston (Middlesex) are just a few examples, from many outside the project study areas, of personally named stones that have lent their names to the hundred for which they are likely to have served as the meeting places.

So it seems likely that certain types of stones, such as the Copplestone, King's Stone and stones with personal associations, sit more comfortably in a grouping that includes crosses, roods and crucifixes (discussed below) and are monuments with a meaning that transcends simple boundary demarcation. John Blair (2005, 479) has observed that such monuments are not 'in the first instance' boundary markers and that if they were, there would be very many more references in the boundary clauses to them. Studies undertaken in Cornwall support this view where, during the eleventh to thirteenth centuries, granite crosses appear to have been set up to mark routes radiating out of church sites (Thomas 1967, 86–100). Few relate to parish boundaries. The case of St Buryan provides an even clearer example. Here, not a single cross is recorded in the charter boundary clause whilst a total of forty-two have been identified on the ground, mostly situated on the course of a route (Hooke 1994b, 22–27). Even when directions do turn up in the historical records, as in the case of an anonymously written English-French phase book dating to the fourteenth century, although heavily stylised, crosses appear to play an important role in the orientation of people rather than as boundary markers (Kristal 1995; Evans 2016, 141–144)

One particular group of markers from the project study area that requires further exploration are the *stænan stapol*s (stone posts) that feature most prominently in study area 8. The use of the term *stapol* is instructive in that it has long been recognised as translating directly as 'post, pillar or column' (Bosworth and Toller 1898, 912). The term occurs frequently as a boundary marker in Anglo-Saxon charters and very often in conjunction with routes. Whilst *ceotan stapole* (S 412), *gæcges stapole* (S 463) and *Finces stapol* (S 619, S 811) (respectively: kite, cuckoo and finch) might feasibly, although not necessarily, be referring to timber posts (perhaps the trunks of dead trees), that the 'stone' qualifier is linked to the *stapole* element in this and other study areas, might suggest that when this landmark is mentioned, a very specific type of monument is being referred to. It is the regular spacing of the stone posts on the old herepath in study area 8 that goes furthest in supporting the notion that *stapolas*, 'posts' or 'columns', are actually Roman milestones that have survived into the late Anglo-Saxon period. The closest comparable monument that can be found today *in situ*, is the stone post that sits on Stinsford Hill almost exactly a mile, on the Roman road, from the gates of the *civitas* of Dorchester (Farrar 1957). A *beatan stapole* (S 382) helps to describe the condition of such columns for, in the Leiden Glossary of circa. 800, the term *Ungeb[e]itne stáne* is glossed in Latin as *non tunso lapide* with both terms meaning effectively, 'unbeaten' or 'unhewn' stone (Toller 1921, 734). In this case then, the 'beaten' *stapole* may very well refer to a column of worked stone. Quite often these landmarks are associated with personal names and we saw in Study Area 6 the locations of a possible two columns called *wigheardes stapele* (Wigheard's post) (6.1, ST81NW and ST82SW). Elsewhere in the corpus of Anglo-Saxon charters *Pinstanes stapole* (S 488, S 511), *Ælfheres stapole* (S 800), *puttan stapul* (S 255) and *pinagares stapule* (S 1032) are referred to but it is difficult to know exactly what the association with an individual might entail. Only further research of these and other named stones might help to elucidate a clearer picture of the function of such edifices as boundary, assembly or way markers. What is clear, however, from the archaeological evidence from the third and fourth centuries is that the Salisbury basin was an area of dense settlement in the Romano-British period (James 2010) and it must be anticipated that a complex and extensive network of routes served the communities living around the area and within the valleys of the Bourne, Avon, Wylye, Nadder and Ebble. The stone posts on the *old* herepath, may well represent the course of a Roman road and the same might be said for the *stenenan stapul*, located on the herepath (7.4, SU21NW). Elsewhere, there is a *stænenan stapole* appearing in a grant of swine pasture in the Weald at a place called Heronden, near Tenterden, through which passes a likely Roman road comprised of a course laid almost entirely in short straight sections (S 1215; Margary 1948, 211). A further *stapol* (7.3, SU12SW) is recorded on the white (or Wilton) way and if we entertain the possibility that such monuments are of Romano-British origin, they may provide the best indicators we have of Roman roads that are otherwise not as obvious as those that adopt the characteristically straight lines in the landscape.

Roods

Ic me on þisse gyrde beluce   and on godes helde bebeode
wið þane sara s[t]ice,   wið þane sara slege,
wið þane grymma gryre,
wið ðane micela egsa   þe bið eghwam lað
and wið eal þæt lað   þe in to land fare.

I entrust myself to this staff, and commend myself to God's guardianship
(for protection) against the pricking of afflictions,
against the blow of afflictions,
against the awful horror,
against the great terror that is hateful to each person,
and against all that evil that invades the land

(The opening lines of *A Journey Charm* printed in Griffiths 1996, 201–203)

In comparison with stones, references to roods in the project study areas are rare and almost entirely confined to the Bradford-on-Avon study area (9). What has been presented in study area 9 is the maximum view for the interpretation of the Old English *rōd* ('rood' as in 'cross') element used in the boundary clauses. Confusion with the Old English *hrēod* (reed), *rōd* (a 'rood' of land) and *rod* (clearing) can easily lead to misinterpretation (Rumble 2006, 29). In the case of the *rodestan* (S 727) we can be fairly certain as elsewhere this place-name, surviving as Radstone in Northamptonshire (recorded in 1086), has been interpreted as 'a stone used as a socket for a rood' (Gover *et al.* 1933, 56–57). As Alexander Rumble stresses, a consideration of the topographical contexts and compound elements is essential to making more assured interpretations of *rōd*, and in Burgred's rood, the personal association and surrounding terrain, along with the marking of a prominent summit, weigh the evidence in favour of a wooden cross marking the way to Bradford-on-Avon. 'The roods' (*ðære rodæ*) that mark *ðære strǣt* on *ða streatan hlywan* (the street to the great refuge) can also be placed in a visible location to traffic crossing the Frome at Farleigh Hungerford but necessarily, the interpretation must remain conjectural. The *rodendich* recorded in the boundary of the Edington charter (9.2 ST95NW) however seems very much more likely to warrant a translation of 'reed(y) dyke' than rood dyke (S 765).

Rumble has drawn attention to a range of other terms that may share a meaning with 'rood'. Whilst the cross on which Christ is crucified is referred to in *The Dream of the Rood* on five occasions as a *rōd*, it is also called a *bēam* and *trēow* and this gave Rumble cause to speculate that, in fact, there may be a significance in the use of such elements in place-names (Rumble 2006, 37–38). The obvious examples for *trēow* would be Hallatrow, Somerset (Helgetrev 1086) and Hallytreeholme, Yorkshire (*Halitreholm* 1175–90) and for *bēam* Rumble draws attention to Bladbean, in Elham, Kent (*Blodebeame* 1226) where he concurs with J.K. Wallenberg's interpretation that this is a reference to a red-oak (Wallenberg 1934, 431). There could, however, be another interpretation of the blood element in this name. Also in *The Dream of the Rood*, we learn that not only was the cross decked with foliage, bejewelled, hung with garments and 'drenched in gold', it was also soaked in blood and at one point is described as shedding its own blood (Swanton 1970, 46, 49). This may provide the rationale behind the *redeston* in the Edington charter (S 765, if it is not a scribal error for *rodeston*), the *red stane* and in particular, the *readan rode* (red rood) of the Winchester study area (2.2 SU43SE). Another alternative possibility is presented in the observation that the 'readan' element, in association with 'ways', may reflect a surface that has been 'prepared' (Cooper 2002, 61). As such then, these 'prepared' stones may reflect other examples of deliberately worked stone markers.

It is probably wrong, therefore, to seek out uniformity in the terminology being used and the manner in which it is applied to the entities being described in such instances. In fact, quite the opposite is likely to be the case; as far as popular practice is concerned, we should anticipate regional variation – both in terms of dialect, spellings and practices. In their respective studies of Anglo-Saxon perceptions to prehistoric burial mounds, Sarah Semple and Della Hooke have both observed the interchangeability of *hlæw* and *beorh* when describing barrows (Hooke 1981b, 2; Semple 1998, 115). There is clearly a lack of distinction (again in the terminology used) to discern prehistoric mounds from early medieval constructions and anthropogenic landscape features from comparable natural topography. One phrase however, that appears fourteen times in boundary clauses and a further four times in place-names, does exhibit a degree of uniformity and this is *cristel-mæl* or 'Christ's image'. Although no examples have been recovered from the project study areas, they are worthy of mention here primarily because they too have been observed to occupy roadside locations. John Blair (2005, 479) has identified two next to fords, one on a headland, five on routes and at least two of the remaining six 'likely to be on routeways'.

Crossroads

A particular aspect of markers that the mapping of charter boundary clauses has identified is their common occurrence with crossroads. This has already been observed in the instance of certain named stones and there are undoubtedly practical considerations for placing such monuments or 'messages' at places where traffic converges. In the case of meeting stones, they form a permanent marker at a site to which people could travel from all around. Accessibility and convenience to the greatest number of 'moot' attendees for stones with such a purpose was undoubtedly a consideration. As far as crosses are concerned, we are reminded of Rumble's observation that such monuments should be seen primarily as wayside edifices at which travellers pray to Christ, with those sited prominently on significant hills or coastal sites serving as both landmarks for travellers as well as Christian symbols in the landscape (Rumble 2006, 39). It is likely that the same rules of visibility apply to execution sites and cemeteries where a roadside location has also been identified (Reynolds 2009a, passim). So far, much of the emphasis has been placed on articulations of belief systems in the landscape but execution sites also represent articulations of power and control, with structures like gallows and heads placed on stakes designed to communicate that message to travellers both alien and familiar to the landscape (Reynolds 2008). Yet, in both instances, is there more to their situation than just a roadside location? Is it the case that their siting at crossroads actually allows us to project back into the early medieval period the later medieval and modern tradition of burying deviants and suicides in crossroad locations? (Daniell 1997, 105–106).

To the veneration of trees, shrines and holy wells can be added worship at crossroads as a practice deplored by the early medieval European church in both sermons and legislation (Flint 1998, 89, 205–207). Martin of Braga, for example, writing his *Reforming the Rustics* in Galicia during the sixth century, is said to have lamented the habit travellers had of carrying stones to cairns at cross-roads for a sacrifice in honour of 'Mercury' (Barlow 1969, 74). Some five hundred years later Burchard of Worms, in his *Corrector*, inveighs against the same practice and also condemns the ritual of ploughmen, herdsmen and hunters secreting enchanted ligatures at crossroads to protect the animals on whose lives they depended (McNeill and Gamer 1990, 334, 331). It is highly likely that such sources influenced the works of Ælfric, whom, writing in the late tenth or early eleventh century, warned against witches who resorted to crossroads to raise the evil dead (Meaney 1984). Similar condemnations can be found in chapter 16 of the *Canons of Edgar*, attributed to Wulfstan II of York who died in 1023 (Whitelock *et al.* 1981, 320). A less demonic aspect to crossroads, but one nonetheless connected with the life course, is the practice observed taking place in early eleventh-century Devon of slaves being ceremonially freed at crossroads after a summertime mass (Radford 1975, 6–7; cited in Blair 2005, 453).

The origins for such behaviour can be found in classical precedent and it is likely that the prevalence and variety of crossroad-related folklore and rituals throughout medieval Europe is based on a tradition with a deep time signature founded on a Roman cultural *milieu*. Some of the evidence Stephen Wilson (2000, 456) has drawn together from the earliest written examples includes two associations with 'dark' deities. Hecate, the Greek goddess of witchcraft, ghosts and magic was invoked at a crossroads in the *Aeneid* and Plato recommended in *The Laws* that 'certain criminals should be buried at a crossroads with a stone over their heads'. More specifically, Wilson suggests that the placing of statues of saints and of crosses at crossroads was a custom potentially continued from the *Lares*. The *Lares*, guardian spirits and deified ancestors, were described by Varro in his *De Lingua Latina*, where he tells of how sacrifices are made to the *Lares Compitales* ('Lares of the crossroads') at crossroads (Kent 1938, Book VI, Chapter 25). One is immediately drawn to consider the personal named stones and their apparent crossroad locations. Increasingly scholars of the early medieval period, inspired by comparable patterns of ritual activity in prehistoric periods, are considering the landscape in terms of the *longue durée* wherein human action is informed and altered by knowledge of and/or the remains of past societies and communities (Semple 2010, 23). In this paradigm it is possible that such monuments went on to become the focus for the practices so reviled by the likes of Ælfric and Wulfstan. The long-term ritual transformation of these sites will be considered (below) but for now, it remains to explore briefly some of the evidence from the project study areas for crossroads and the types of monuments that appear to be associated with them.

Elsewhere the marking of crossroads by the Copplestone and by Beornwin's stone has been explored in depth (Reynolds and Langlands 2011), and from other project study areas evidence supports the case for stones being crucial to the articulation of junctions (Figure 25). A *bræges piþe* stone (SU45NW) may sit at the crossing of the 'honey well way' with a possible 'summerway' route that skirts the foot of the scarp slope parallel to the ridgeway (Grundy 1918, 70–72). Both the King's Stone and the hollow Stone can be seen to mark crossings of the Roman road by east–west ways traversing the downland to the north of Winchester, the latter of which is called the 'London way' (2.2 SU43SE, SU43NE). The King's Stone might also be welcoming traffic coming from the north using the *wic* herepath that converges on the course of the Roman road at this location. It is possible from the reading of two boundary clauses on the Isle of Purbeck that the *weilaite* (ways' meet) (S 534) and *anne stan* (a stone) (S 573) sit at the same location (5.1 SY98SE). The 'stone that lies on the street' almost certainly marks the junction of the major east–west ridgeway with the 'Offa's way/street' that runs up past Winklebury and through the serf's dyke gate (7.2 ST92SE) and Beornwulf's stone also sits on a major east–west aligned ridgeway and marks the crossing of this with a route from Bica's bridge to Wilton (7.3, 8.1 SU02NE).

The crossroad location of the *heafod stoccan* (heads stakes) in the *Chalke* estate has already been discussed in study area 7 but there are indicators of judicial execution and the burial of social outcasts and deviants from other study areas

(S 582). There are a small group of four charters, dated to between 774 and 801, within which feature for the first time detailed perambulations comprised of directional terminology in Latin and actual boundary marks in Old English (S 262, S 267, S 264, S 268). These represent an important set of documents for the study of Anglo-Saxon boundaries, charters and the landscape both because of their dating but also because many of the terms used in Old English are glossed in Latin. This extra information allows for improved interpretations of what would otherwise be at best, enigmatic and at worst mundane landmarks. Two of these charters were covered in the project study areas and in each case, certain clauses are revealing of the character of particular places on both boundaries and at likely crossroads. The first concerns land at Little Bedwyn, the bounds of which are covered in a charter dated to 774, where we learn of a gabulos (gallows) (S 264). This site of execution is recorded as being in close proximity to *illa antiqua monumenta in locum ubi a ruricolis dicitur. æt ðam holen stypbum* (the ancient monuments in the place the locals call 'at the holly [?hollow] stumps'). Today the site is marked by Harrow Farm and, in view of the gallows and the 'ancient monuments', it seems satisfactory to suggest a derivation from Old English *hearg*, a term now thought to denote long-lived localised cult practice peaking in the late Iron Age and Romano-British periods (Semple 2007). The likely location for this monument is the intersection of a significant east–west aligned valley route with the north-west aligned route from Great Bedwyn and Chisbury hillfort to Ramsbury. The course of the *Cunetio* to *Spinæ* Roman road also passed very close to this location (Margary 1973, number 53) and it is likely too that the 'street' of the same charter is referring to this route (10.2 SU26NE).

The second example from one of these early charters is found in a grant of land at Crux Easton dated to 801 (S 268; (Kelly 2000, 31–36). Here we learn of *uno acerbo lapidum quem nos stancestil uocamus* (an acerbic/bitter/sharp stone that we call [in Old English] a 'stone cist'), *a curio habet cothongian*. The second half of this clause has proven difficult to translate with the authors of the *Langscape* (L 268) translations preferring *eurio* (east) as a scribal error for *curio*. The consensus on *cothongian* is a corruption of *hangra* (hanging wood) with *cat(t)* (cat) or *cot* (cottage) (langscape.org.uk, L 269; Gover *et al.* 1939, 341; Kelly 2000, 36). However, the verb *habeo* (to have, hold) creates problems in this translation and a more literal translation, devoid of scribal errors, is offered here. If we see the *acerbo lapidum* as 'embittered' in a wronged and evil sense, it is logical that the 'stone cist' should be, 'by the curate/priest, held to be the bed chamber of the hung'. Kit's Coty (NMR Number TQ 76 SW 4), a megalithic portal dolmen over-looking the Medway provides a comparable link between stone chambered tombs and the *cot* element. The Hellstone in Dorset (NMR Number SY 68 NW 12), the name given to a monument of similar date and structure, provides an analogous link with the presumable damnation the executed individuals of the *cothongian* had confronted. Elsewhere, the Devil's Bed and Bolster (NMR Number ST 85 SW 1), the name applied to the remains of a chambered tomb in Somerset, provides an example of a lingering association with the resting place of the damned and most famously, the *henge* element, as in 'hanging', appears in the name given to Stonehenge, a site known in the seventh century as a place of execution (Pitts *et al.* 2002). The *cothongian* sits at the convergence of a number of routes of which a 'way' and a 'lord's way' is mentioned in the boundary perambulations for the area (1.3 SU45NW).

There are two incidences of the term 'heathen burials' in the project study areas and it is now believed that such features represent not the burial mounds and cemeteries of prehistoric peoples but the burials of early medieval outcasts and felons deprived of burial in consecrated ground and consigned to internment at boundary locations (Reynolds 2002b). For the *hapenum byrgelsum* of the *Chalke* charter, it seems that a location between the hundreds of Downton and Chalke is likely, although they would be some distance (*c.* 1 km, 0.6 miles) from the present-day shire boundary between Hampshire and Wiltshire. They appear to lie at the junction of the Old Sarum to Dorchester Roman road with another major east–west ridgeway (7.3 SU02SE and the 'street' of ST92SE – although not marked on the map). Traffic passing on a north-west/south-east axis from Fordingbridge, Hampshire, to Broad Chalke, Wiltshire, and beyond could also feasibly pass through this point. The other reference to heathen burials comes from the Collingbourne Kingston charter where *þam haeþenan byrgelsan* are much harder to locate. It is possible that they fall on or close to the north–south route from Old Sarum to *Cunetio* (a possible 'Romanised' ridgeway and the course on which both *Wylberhtes Stan* and Cyneweard's stone may have stood 10.3) but without further wide-scale analysis of other routes around the area it is impossible to infer where these burials may have been.

Of course, in making the case for an almost endless number of possibilities for routes through the landscape of early medieval Wessex, one might see the significance of the coincidence of such sites with crossings and junctions as weakened. Yet, in the overlapping of these junctions with liminal areas there may be significance. The association of such sites with death, deviancy and the demonic goes some way to justifying the lines of *The Journey Charm* where it is clearly felt that outside of the protection of the central, the consecrated and the sacred, a *gyrde* (a rod/rood/crucifix) is needed to ward against 'all the evil that invades the land'.

Conversion processes and changing ritual landscapes

Nowhere is the profane and the sacred in the landscape better illustrated than through the evidence for its conversion to Christianity. The range of wayside monuments and symbolism described above makes it clear that the landscape of early medieval Wessex was deeply imbued with messages and meanings conveyed between landscape and traveller. The landscape was sacred, mythologised and manipulated to fit ideological and political frameworks. Messages were therefore being conveyed to all who passed through, whether orally at meeting places, or symbolically at monuments. Thus, the traveller constructed a meaningful space in their mind; a 'mental map' punctuated by symbols that articulated both space and identity. These aspects of perception and place can be further explored through the changes in attitudes and meaning over time towards certain landmarks. We began by looking at the evidence for stones and the ambiguity of the term 'stone', meaning either 'standing stone' or 'stone cross', may very well be the result of an enduring conversion process spanning hundreds of years. It is interesting how Wulfstan referred to the 'King's stone' as being made in 'ancient stone' (Lapidge 2003, 529). Was this a reference to the nature of the stone-type being used or the re-working of an earlier stone monument? Richard Morris entertains the idea that, beyond the obvious use of prehistoric stones for building material, large monolithic orthostats would have been attractive for early medieval sculptors (Morris 1989, 83–84).

If the carving on the Copplestone is of Scandinavian design, is it possible then that the *copelan stan* recorded in a reliable charter of 974 was in fact a standing stone and that a reworking of the stone took place in the reign of Cnut (1015 × 1035), the period when Scandinavian influence in Devon was at its strongest (Yorke 1995, 141–146). That Cnut had a hand in the monumental inscription of the Devonian landscape through the medium of stone monoliths is in evidence from the place-name Knowstone, recorded as *Chenutdestana* in 1086 and *Cnutsstan* in 1220 (Mawer and Stenton 1932, 340). This may be highly speculative, but where the worship of stones is concerned, conversion resonances are strong. Most explicitly, in the *Vita S. Samsonis*, Samson confronted the *simulacrum abominabile* on Bodmin Moor by carving a cross on a nearby stone and entreating the pagan peoples that it should be revered instead (Fawtier 1912, 48–49). Archaeological examples of this practice are known from Brittany where Iron Age *Stele* had been adulterated with later Christian Crosses, most visibly illustrated by the Croas-Men at Lampaul-Ploudalmézean in Finistère (Cunliffe 2001, 346, fig. 8.27). Closer to home, the Long Stone in East Worlington Devon, a four-sided standing stone, has had crosses carved into each face. It sits on the Crediton to South Molton herepath that is served by two 'planked' bridges, connecting the minster of South Molton with the Bishop's seat in Crediton (OS Grid reference SX 277500, 115900). It has also been suggested that the Anglian cross, a tall monolith from Bewcastle in Cumbria, was carved from a salvaged Roman column rather than a result of *ad hoc* quarrying in the seventh century (Eaton 2000, 16).

Whilst we can be confident the crosses marking the funeral procession of Aldhelm's body along the Fosse Way to Malmesbury were a feature in the landscape of William of Malmesbury's time, is the story of how they came about to be taken quite so literally? With a lingering supernatural significance to stones set at crossroads and the clear evidence from this study that Romano-British stone way-markers existed in the landscape well into the tenth century, could it be that the 'crosses' or 'bishop's stones' William informs us of are commandeering a more ancient tradition of reverence towards wayside sacred stones?

This incorporation of earlier stones into later conceptual frameworks would have been an ongoing process. From study area 8, the location of Beornwin's stone is dependent on a new reading, as an anti-clockwise perambulation, of the boundary clause for a charter for land *at Winterburnan* (8.2 SU13SE) (Langlands 2009). The placement of the stone at the north-east corner of the estate is, however, reinforced by a later reference to a monument in this location. In October 1651, *en route* to exile, Charles II retired to Clarendon Palace where, contemplating his fate, he walked to 'Park Corner' where we are informed that the Beckett Cross stood (Beaumont-James and Gerrard 2007, 98–100). Park Corner lies in the very northern tip of Clarendon Park at the angle where the 'fort way' intersects both the Roman road and a west-north-west/east-south-east aligned route (Figure 39). The dedication of the central church in Salisbury to St Thomas, St Thomas's Bridge (on the site of what was once the 'deep ford') and Beckett's cross articulate the popular pilgrim route taken towards the martyr's shrine at Canterbury and it seems only natural that Beornwin's Stone, a monument whose meaning and function may very well have become remote and obscure in the early thirteenth century, found itself incorporated into a later geography of travel.

The ritual significance of trees in the Anglo-Saxon world has been the focus of a number of recent studies (Hooke 2010; Bintley and Shapland 2013) and in many cases trees, as markers, monuments and prominent landscape features, can be seen to bear many of the same characteristics as stones. William of Malmesbury wrote of how Aldhelm, while preaching, struck his ashen staff in the ground where it instantly 'grew to a marvellous size, quickened with sap and covered with bark, having put forth young leaves and beautiful branches' (Preest 2002, 261–262). Even if it is the case that a suitable narrative is being constructed in order to explain the place-name Bishopstrow, Wiltshire (*Biscopestreu*, 1086, Gover *et al.* 1939, 151), where the parish church is dedicated to St Aldhelm, is the ritual significance of Aldhelm's staff commemorating an existing reverence in that place to a sacred ash tree? Whilst reference has already been made to 'hallow' trees, the circumstances surrounding the place-name Cressage in Shropshire is potentially an intriguing example of the long-term ideological significance of a particular place. The earliest surviving record of the place-name is *Cristesache* (1086) meaning 'Christ's Oak' and Margaret Gelling (1990, 102–103) has identified the 'Lady Oak' to the north-west of the present village as a former location for this sacred monument. Here she observes the hulk of an ancient oak supported by a younger tree and goes on to say that 'successive replacements could have been recurring since Saxon times'. Both Gelling and Alexander Rumble (2006, 38–39) speculate that the tree may have carried a crucifix, but it is also important to note the crossroad location of the village. It is clear that trees, like stones, function as meeting places, and as roadside edifices they may also have found themselves marked and symbolised – perhaps as part of a 'conversion' process. There are a number of trees associated with personal names in the study areas. Briefly, and with translations offered, these are: *helmes treowes* (Helm's trees), *beredes trowe* (Bered's tree), *lullyngestrowe* (the people of Lulla's tree), *beornwunne treow* (Beornwyn's tree), *brunwoldes treow* (Brunwold's tree), *egesan treow* (Egsa's tree), *waccas treow* (?watch/lookout person's tree) and *scyldes Treowe* (?the guilty one's tree). Whilst there are no specific elements here such as *cristes* or *hālig* to imply a form of sacredness, in some instances these may, of course, be mere boundary markers. Yet, a greater understanding of the role and function of trees and their relationship to issues of travel and communication can only be gained by expanding the landscape and charter-based approach to a wider study area.

The rich variety of ideologically charged terminology that we find associated with stones, trees, crossroads and wells reflects the types of sacred features that are gradually being incorporated into a Christian ambit and, as such, this may be telling us as much about conversion practices. These were locations where popular belief systems, founded on rituals and folk magic, which were themselves becoming an area of negotiation between normative Christianity and popular belief during, and in the long aftermath of, the conversion period. It is only when we get to the writings of Ælfric and Wulfstan in the eleventh century that we get an open hostility to pagan sites which was previously notably absent (Blair 2005, 481–483). The evidence from the study areas tentatively concurs with Audrey Meaney's 'inclusive practices' whereby an early sacred geography was assimilated into a Christian world (Meaney 1992, 110–111). If we envisage a degree of tolerance for such places and their incorporation into ninth- and tenth-century cultural norms – whether as places for continued reverence or execution – is it the case that roods and *cristel mæls* represent a slightly different Christian geography? In contrast to sacred trees and stones, these are overt Christian symbols. To a degree, they share a uniformity of terminology and probably appearance in terms of materials used. They are likely to have been made of wood (two of the fourteen *cristel mæls* recorded in boundary clauses are associated with oaks and one with a beam) and the term *cristel mæl* (Christ's image) is so literal it has led John Blair to suggest that an actual figure rather than just a cross was being depicted here (Blair 2005, 479, n. 240). For roods and crucifixes, Rumble cautiously (because of the bias in charter distribution) puts forward the idea that in the north and east midlands, Old Norse *kross* and Old English *cros* seem to have replaced *rōd* and in the south *Cristel-mæl* is 'seemingly more common than, or as common as' Old English *rōd* (Rumble 2006, 39–40). Is this a reflection, however, of the growing number of pilgrims on the road in the later Anglo-Saxon period? Whilst we know of pilgrimages being made as early as the seventh century, the rise of popular pilgrimages in the later tenth and eleventh century presents us with a journeying community that, unlike traders, envoys, messengers and the army, were unfamiliar with the landscapes through which they had to travel. Whilst guides (particularly for the blind) are recorded in some of the accounts of these journeys, many people, through their lack of knowledge of regional and national geography, clearly placed themselves in the hands of God when taking to the road. The evidence for the placement of roods and crucifixes doesn't seem to suggest that a crossroads location is important but rather that a roadside location in a visible position is of primary concern (especially in the instance of the Bradford-on-Avon study area). These are not monuments, unlike sacred stones and trees, whose meaning has been refashioned for a local community, but monuments placed anew in the landscape to guide an ever-greater number of lower-status pilgrims to the churches at whose shrines miracle cures was anticipated.

This brings us back to the 'experience' of travelling in the landscape of early medieval Wessex. This section on 'markers' has been an attempt to gain an insight into what it must have been like to have experienced and engaged with the landscape as one moved around it. The various features that have been listed and discussed here were no doubt intended to inform people's concept of space, both physically and conceptually. In 'lived' landscapes of the past we must anticipate the entailing of myths, whether these myths are explicitly known or implicitly understood (Hirsh 2006). For one of Europe's most popular pilgrimages, along the *Camino de Santiago*, the archaeological remains and images along the road highlight the merging of myth and landscape and the construction of tradition (Candy 2009, 130). Further examination of these roadside edifices across early medieval Europe will serve to contribute to a geography of pilgrimage, a growing understanding of which is being derived from archaeological investigation, where it is clearly the case that the proper focus on the 'architecture' of pilgrimage should be on the roads, bridges, hospitals and cemeteries that were as much a part of the enormous physical infrastructure as where the shrines themselves (Graham-Campbell 1994; Stopford 1994). 'Landscape' in this context therefore becomes an act or process that engages with the world. Parallels might be sought in contemporary ethnographic studies where, in the siting of rock-art in hunter-gatherer communities, visibility and a relationship with natural features plays a key role in significance and meaning, especially when incorporated into a knowledge base that is predicated on memory and story-telling (David and Wilson 2002, 6).

Gates and access in the early medieval landscape of Wessex

The application of access analysis to archaeological sites and standing buildings is a growing and fruitful area of study for our understanding of how social space was organised amongst past societies (Gilchrist 1988; Graves 1989; Fairclough 1992; Roffey 2008, chapter 7). Applications of these methods on a grander scale – *i.e.* to the archaeology of landscapes – has been restricted primarily to the archaeological analysis of frontier zones where studies are characterised by their emphasis on cultural contact and zones of 'cross-cutting' social networks (Green and Perlman 1985; Lightfoot and Martinez 1995). One way in which to understand movement in the landscape is to attempt to understand how access was restricted and controlled and the evidence for gates and stiles in the early medieval landscape of Wessex provides an opportunity to explore not only the symbolic but also the practical considerations of controlling the movement of both humans and livestock through the landscape.

It was first suggested that the numerous gates referred to in the charter boundary clauses for grants of land at Little Bedwyn, Great Bedwyn and Burbage represented a continuation of the Wansdyke frontier (Reynolds and Langlands 2006, 20–21). In study area 10 the evidence is set out cartographically and the location of the gates is justified partly on the basis of local place-names and partly on the alignment of the parish boundary. A similar distribution map has attempted to place this sequence of gates in relation to evidence for linear earthworks derived from previous antiquarian investigations and a 2006 LiDAR survey conducted by the forestry commission (Lennon 2010, 285, fig.17). Ultimately this questioned the continued course of Wansdyke through Savernake Forest on the grounds that there is no evidence for a 'large linear feature' and in the critique, attention was drawn to the fact that the term used in the boundary clause to describe the form of the boundary between each gate was *septum*, the Latin for 'fence' or 'hedge', and not *vallum*, meaning 'dyke' (Lennon 2010, 286; S 264).

This is not the place to address the individual issues raised in this excellent review of the evidence but it is important to draw attention to the fact that elsewhere the use of Old English *haga* to describe linear boundaries and enclosures in areas of both dense woodland and wood pasture is common (Hooke 2010, 153–156). Figure 46 illustrates the number of hedges (both *haga* and *septi*) that are referred to in study areas 1 and 10 and it is clear from this evidence that this was an area (in contrast to the other study areas) where physical linear boundaries and gates controlled access and movement in the early medieval period. What needs to be envisaged, however, is that this was likely to have been the case in the late Iron Age and Romano-British period too. In Savernake, for example, a thriving pottery industry, now thought to have its origins in the late Iron Age but peaking in the Romano-British period, is represented by a number of kiln sites located within the dense woodland (Timby 2001). The requirement for a plentiful and well-managed supply of coppice wood for firing and burnishing would have necessitated protective boundaries. The point is also made by Joanna Ramsay and Graham Bathe (2008, 171–174) that where short stretches of dyke are in evidence in this area, they are over the chalk bedrock (rather than the clay) and it is the protection of valuable arable land that is of concern to the dyke builders. There is clearly a density of arable production (thought to be of Iron Age and Roman date, Crutchley *et al.* 2009, 24, fig. 11) in an area to the immediate south of Savernake Forest (on the valley floor in the western part of Figure 46) and it seems likely that this area of arable was bounded by a *haga* referred to in the charters to the immediate north (depicted as light green squares).

Anticipating a frontier laid out between Wessex and Mercia (the main reason to postulate a continued course for Wansdyke), it is highly likely that such a boundary would have been restricted by the existing geography of

FIGURE 46 *(opposite)* 'Hagas', 'Septi', gates and dykes (contains OS data © Crown copyright (2018)).

9. *Roman roads, wayside markers and gates* 159

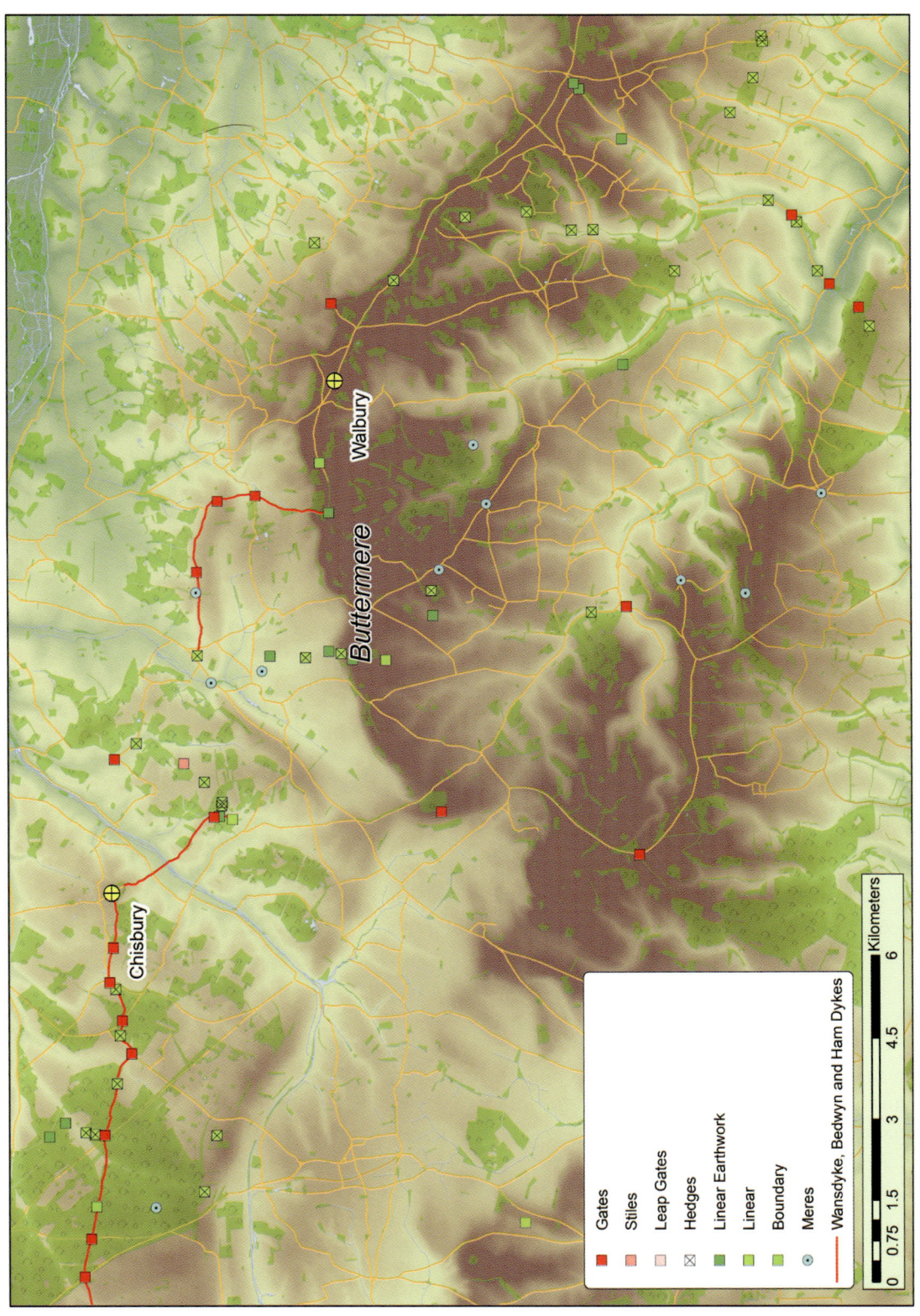

the region. Over the open expanses of the chalk downland the course of a large bank and ditch could have been predetermined. However, through a densely subdivided landscape of enclosed woodland, no such luxury could be afforded and an existing arrangement of linear boundaries would have required negotiation. To seek an earthwork in Savernake Forest is to preconceive the form such a boundary would take on this geology and through this terrain. Most commentators on the dykes in this region have observed that over the clay they are inconsistent in form, but perhaps this inconsistency is borne out of the fact that the chosen method of barrier construction in this region was comprised of *haga* or *septi* which made use of the existing timber and brash resources to create what is known in modern hedging as a 'dead hedge' (Hooke 2010, 155). Although potentially formidable structures, such forms of land division leave little in the way of archaeological evidence.

It is re-iterated here that the Wansdyke frontier fits more comfortably within a seventh- and eighth-century context, a period characterised by a pan-European tradition of drawing up large linear frontiers (Squatriti 2002). Its function and purpose are almost certainly bound up with a sense of emerging 'national' identity and the articulation of power. On the ground level, however, whilst the military functions of such monuments has always been in question, it is useful to consider Ramsay and Bathe's comments that it is only to wheeled traffic that such physical boundaries represent any real obstacle (2008, 174). This is a crucial observation for the purposes of understanding these monuments and their wider function in the landscape during the middle Anglo-Saxon period. Attention has been drawn to the *Peadan stigele* (10.4, SU36SW), *pyddes geate* (SU36SE) and *pædes paþe* (SU36SW), all interpreted as references to pedestrian access, and this is a clear indication of a differentiation made in this region between those paths that were accessible to carts and those that were restricted to the movement of pedestrians alone.

When we consider the other major infrastructure developments of the middle Anglo-Saxon period, at the forefront stand the vast trading complexes – the *wic*s – of which *Hamwic* is Wessex's key site. Royal control of such centres has been presumed to explain their genesis, for the king's social standing during this period – and thus his power – depended heavily on his ability to redistribute wealth amongst his immediate followers (Hodges 1982, 54–56). The link between King Ine (688 × 726) and *Hamwic* has been made explicit and Martin Welch has suggested that its establishment was a direct result of Ine's desire to bring in luxury goods from the Frankish realm (Welch 1985, 16). However, most recently the evidence is pointing more in favour of a greater degree of market function (Naylor 2012, 238–240), and it is perhaps in this context that such linear monuments, designed to restrict traffic, should be seen. If a significant aspect of kingship in middle Anglo-Saxon England – as elsewhere in early medieval Europe – concerns the control of trade within an economy that is now thought to include a greater level of commercialism (Henning 2007, 27–31), it may very well be that these monuments represent steps being taken at the same time to prevent the passing of bulk goods (using carts) outside of a predetermined trading zone or equally, to arrest the influx of cheaper bulk imports. Whether or not we accept the continuation of a linear monument, the gates in this area do exactly that: they restrict the free-flow of wheeled traffic along a north–south corridor of movement that connects the major ridgeways to the south with the Icknield Way to the north.

Archaeological evidence from prehistoric, Roman Iron Age and early medieval Denmark provides extremely useful parallels. It is clear, where conditions allow, that roads were constructed of timber sleepers, brushwood, hurdles and stone, in locations that facilitated the concentration of road traffic into corridors (Jørgensen 1988, 101). Across these axes of movement, particularly the main traffic arteries through the Jutland peninsula, potentially as many as eighty ramparts had been erected, many of which are recorded as several kilometres long (Jørgensen 1988, 106). Olgerdiget and Æ Vold in South Jutland and Trældiget in the hinterland of Kolding Fjord rank amongst the most impressive and are thought to date to the Roman Iron Age (*c.* AD 1 to 400). The Olgerdiget, dated to the middle of the second century AD and at a conceivable length of 30 km, is said to have required some 90,000 poles to complete the stockade (Neumann 1982, 84). Clearly these structures are open to interpretation, but in tandem with the archaeological evidence for constructed routeways, it is highly likely that traffic is being guided to controllable passages in order that customary tolls and duties could be imposed on those wishing to pass through (Jørgensen 2003, 205). Like these southern Scandinavian examples, we must consider that Wansdyke fulfilled a range of functions of which a purely militaristic and political barrier was only a small part. Undoubtedly the socio-cultural bonding of elites with their subjects during the construction phase would have served to embolden a shared identity, but the investment in such a vast project must have been predicated on the promise of long-term benefits in the regulation of trade, and in particular the movement of bulk goods.

One other area where we might consider it important to restrict and control access is in the management of livestock, and there is some circumstantial evidence from the project study areas to suggest that livestock were not only being controlled on a local level but also in their transportation over longer distances. The *lunden weg* (London Way) clearly takes a course that bypasses Winchester. This may be an early sign of the economic pull exerted by London beyond its immediate hinterland and evidence that traders from the south-west were choosing to ignore the financial lure of Winchester for, presumably, greater reward in London. It may also have had something to do with keeping large herds of cattle as far away as convenient from the *urbs* and arable 'inland' of Winchester. Chapters 9, 10 and 11 of Edgar's Code issued at *Wihtbordesstan* are all concerned with witnesses and cattle purchases and cover various eventualities and scenarios that might arise as a result of rustling and illegal trading. In particular, we see a stress placed on witnessing transactions made outside the boroughs (chapters 6, 6.1, 6.2) and the proximity of this chapter of the code to those concerning both 'riding out' to make purchases (chapter 7) and the bringing in of purchased livestock to common pasture for witnessing (chapter 8) (IV Edgar 3, 3.1, 6, 6.1, 6.2, 7, 8, 9; Whitelock 1979, 435–436). This all describes a form a trading quite different, in practical terms, from the trading of goods within the burhs, and the London Way may therefore represent an early form of drove road by which cattle brought up from the West Country were traded and exchanged on a trade and drove route that had London at its terminus.

David Hill (Hill 1981, 116, fig. 199) continues the London Way west past Wilton and on as far as Ilchester (Figure 5). Along this course, the route follows the alignment of later nineteenth-century Ox Droves recorded in early editions of Ordnance Survey maps. North of Winchester, the London Way is referred to as an Ox Drove, and the stretch running west from Wilton as far as the junction with the A303 (a likely continuation of the Harroway) is also referred to as an Ox Drove. Similar Ox Droves, deviating from this 'London Way' to the south-west of Wilton, bound the Ebble Valley to the north and south and converge on a point just outside Shaftesbury, whilst a further spur runs to the south-west towards crossings of the Rivers Iwerne and Stour. In the Shaftesbury study area, there is good evidence of the importance of cattle and dairying to the local economy. A *smeryate* (greasy or butter gate) may be an echo of terminology indicating a form of outdoor butter-making associated with transhumance (Fox 2008, 354–358). Two separate references to a 'cow gate moor' and an *oxene bricge* refer directly to the presence of a bovine-based economy and the *hig weg* discussed in study area 6 indicates the requirement for hay for winter feeding (6.1, ST81NW).

Whilst it is risky to use nineteenth-century references to Ox Droves as indicators of the early medieval movement of livestock, if cattle were being moved over long distances in the tenth and eleventh centuries, they would almost certainly have made use of similar terrain: open downland where the prevalence of ridgeways can keep the potentially hazardous trampling of cattle away from valley bottom settlements, water meadows and arable fields. The 'oxen bridge' has been placed at the point where the nineteenth-century OS records a 'ridgeway lane' crossing the River Stour and this may represent a recognition that this route continued up on to the high ground to the east. Continuing past the meeting place of Six Penny Hundred, referred to as ðies littlen Seaxpennes in the charter for Fontmell (S 419), there is a 'Drove Lane' recorded on the nineteenth-century OS. On the ridgeways to the north and south of the Ebble Valley, where Ox Droves are recorded in the nineteenth century, a number of cross dykes are located across downland spurs. The dating of these is unknown but as we saw in study area 7, the one recorded as the 'serfs' dyke' (7.2 ST92SE) may reflect that at least some are of an early medieval origin and were perhaps constructed or reworked to aid in the channelling of cattle along the ridgeways, again, away from arable and pastoral areas in valley bottoms.

Finally, the gates in the Buttermere and *Æscmere* area and in the Upper Itchen Valley east of Alresford bound two very different types of pasture, downland and woodland respectively. It might not only be the wood pastures identified by Christopher Currie (1994, 116–117) in the Stoneham and New Forest areas that were supplying *Hamwic* with its bovine goods. The analysis of the faunal remains from *Hamwic* have demonstrated that a well-managed and 'productive' hinterland was serving the *emporium* with a large number of high quality beasts for slaughter (Bourdillon 1988, 193; 1994, 122–123) and this hinterland may well have stretched to the upper reaches of the Itchen Valley where eight gates are recorded (four of which fall outside of 2.1 SU63NW). In which case, cattle from this locale could have been driven south-west on one of the many ways that are recorded in the charter boundary evidence intersecting the South Downs Way (2.1 SU52). Thus, *Hamwic* was provided with meat, bone and leather for consumption and processing but the Buttermere area (Map 1.3) may well have been providing the dairy products. Transported to the possible minster at Hurstbourne Priors (perhaps from Upton, down the Bourne Rivulet), various dairy products could then be floated down the River Test from the *stæpas* (landing places) referred to in Map 1.2 (SU44NW).

CHAPTER TEN

Bridges, herepaths, trade routes and the king's peace

In the following chapter the case will be made for herepaths representing purposely-constructed routes and the likely product of a form of military obligation. To arrive at this conclusion the obligation placed on landholders from the mid-eighth century onwards to build bridges will be assessed in relation to the evidence for bridges from the study areas. The character of both the term herepath and the form these routes take in the landscape will be scrutinised with a view to offering an interpretation on their role and function as public works designed to contain the threat posed by Viking (and other) raiding, and as corollaries through which the emerging overland trade of the later Anglo-Saxon period would develop.

The chapter will explore some of the evidence, both from the study areas and other examples, for the origins and development of the herepath network and it will explore how the evidence can help us to establish on whom the burden for maintenance fell. Herepaths were, of course, not the only routes in the landscape and in this discussion it will be demonstrated that charter boundary clauses provide clear indications of a hierarchy of routes of differing function and use – from the local to the national. In the increasingly numerous documentation of the later Anglo-Saxon and immediate post-Conquest period, evidence for a legal status attached to certain roads suggests an emerging 'highway code' and the project study areas will be reviewed for the evidence there is in support of this (Cooper 2000; 2002; 2016).

Chapter 3 reviewed the debates concerning the development of the early medieval economy and considered how the shift from coastal *emporia*, 'productive' sites and minster/estate centres to an economy characterised by a hierarchy of towns will have impacted upon the landscape of travel and communication. In this chapter, therefore, the evidence for trade and trade routes from the project study areas will be presented and related to what we know of urban development and economic trends from the eighth to the eleventh centuries.

Bridge-work, fortress-work but no road-work

By the end of the eighth century, the *Trinoda Necessitas*, a three-fold obligation to undertake work on bridges and forts and to serve in the host army appears to have become a standard feature of landholding in Anglo-Saxon England

(Stevenson 1914). These obligations were seen as burdens from which no one was relieved and they have attracted the attention of numerous commentators concerned with their implementation for the purposes of defending the realm (John 1960, 64–79; Brooks 1971; Abels 1988; Cooper 2006, 24–38). The proximity, in the charters, of the obligation to work on forts with the obligation to construct and repair bridges naturally caused commentators to see the two as, in Nicholas Brooks's words, 'a single military unit'; defended 'bridge-heads' across major rivers (Brooks 1971, 71–72). Whilst there can be little doubt that this approach to the defence of Britain's navigable waterways clearly played a major part in arresting the speed with which the river-borne Vikings could penetrate inland, this neat link between bridges and forts is not without its problems (Coupland 1991). This is because, despite the requirement to build bridges appearing in charters as early as the mid-eighth century, there seems to be very little evidence in documentary sources for a significant number of bridges before the tenth century. To quote Alan Cooper's maxim, we have 'bridge-work but no bridges' (Cooper 2006, 9–38).

There are nine bridges recorded in the project study areas and, analysed in their wider landscape context, together they enable some commentary on a programme of bridge-building proposed by both David Harrison and Alan Cooper to have taken place during the later centuries of the Anglo-Saxon period (Harrison 1992; 2004, 2). The 'king's bridge' recorded in the boundary clause of a charter for land at Sorley, in Churchstow, goes on to lend its name to the fortified town known today as Kingsbridge and is believed to be part of a scheme in Devon within which major bridges were constructed at fortified sites across the heads of estuaries in order to defend against river-borne attack (S 704; Haslam 1984b). If this was the intended purpose, however, we might expect some kind of structure closer to the mouth of the estuary – perhaps in the Salcombe region – and it seems more probable that this bridge is, in fact, facilitating overland movement around the estuary, better connecting the eastern with the western half of the southern part of the South Hams (study area 4.2, Figure 28).

The remaining bridges in this project's study areas are also associated with routes and not directly with forts. The *beoccan* bridge (?beech), planked-bridge, Bica's bridge, Creedy bridge, wood bridge, broom bridge, oxen bridge and the stone bridge are all to be found servicing routes across streams and relatively modest rivers. The *beoccan* bridge of the Sorley charter does not make up a boundary mark in the perambulation but is rather the destination of a route that does. Other commentators, on etymological grounds, have associated it with Bickham Bridge some distance to the north and if this can be substantiated, such a bridge would facilitate the crossing of the Avon River for traffic travelling directly from Modbury to Totnes (4.2 SX75NW) (Rose-Troup 1929, 261–266; Hooke 1994b, 165–168). The planked-bridge to the north of Crediton lies on the course of a herepath and as we have seen, a second Thelbridge (derived from *ðel bricge* meaning 'planked-bridge') appears again as a place-name further north on the same course as it makes its way to South Molton (3.2 SS80SW) (Gover *et al.* 1931, 119; Mawer and Stenton 1932, 395, 412). There are two other examples of planked bridges from Anglo-Saxon charter bounds and these occur as far afield as Kent and Shropshire (S 535, S 723) and in the Shropshire case, the boundary runs '*of þæl bricge to þære heh stræte*', clearly in conjunction with a 'high-street' and likely to be the Roman road that lent its name to Church Stretton. Bica's bridge improves access to Wilton and Shaftesbury (both *Burghal Hidage* forts) for settlements south of the Ebble River (7.1 SU02NE) and the Creedy bridge serves the course of the well-documented herepath east from Crediton (3.1 SS80SW). The stone bridge recorded, potentially as late as the eleventh century, to the immediate north of Corfe and in the gap of the ridge, would have played a crucial role in providing access from the Isle of Purbeck to Wareham, 7 km to the north-west. The 'broom' bridge of the Chilcomb charter survives as Brambridge to the south of Winchester and provides a crossing of the Itchen on the most direct route between the minsters of Romsey and Bishop's Waltham (Hase 1988, 46–47).

Two observations can therefore be made about the bridges in the project study areas. In the first instance, the link between bridges and significant routes, and in particular herepaths, is apparent. This immediately shifts the emphasis away from bridgework representing a form of labour concerned with defensive bridge-heads over navigable rivers and towards structures that were key components on a route network that facilitated movement around the landscape. Of the nine bridges mentioned in the study areas, seven can be seen to either serve a herepath or sit on a route that connects burh to minster, burh to burh or minster to minster. In only one study area do the bridges appear to serve only very minor functions of linking lesser manorial centres either with the wider network of routes or with their own resources in the more remote parts of the estate (study area 6).

The second observation to be made is in the character of these bridges. Four out of the five bridges where the name indicates the material of construction, were made of wood. The instance of the stone bridge at Corfe might be seen as exceptional in that this is an area famed for the availability of good building stone and, perhaps more importantly, the reference to it may well derive from a post-Conquest source (Kelly 1996, 82). Yet even in this situation the term *bricge* might just as well refer to a causeway as much as it does to a structure that actually passes over running water (Blair and Millard 1992). From the project study areas, the 'broom' bridge gives a similar sense of meaning for the term *bricge* with the broom element likely to be referring to a causeway comprised of brush-wood, gorse or broom. Elsewhere the strongest evidence for *bricge* meaning 'causeway' comes from the bounds of Old Swinford in Worcestershire where an *eorthbrycge* (earth bridge) is recorded (S 579). Across the Test the broom bridge finds a parallel in a *risbrigge*, referred to in a charter for Romsey and a derivation, in this instance, from *hrīs* (brushwood) is possible (S 812; Ekwall 1947, 370). Elsewhere, the Old English *persc* element in Piercebridge,

County Durham, is thought to refer to osiers, interpreted as a causeway of faggots across marshy ground (Watts 2004).

Archaeological evidence for causeways dated to the Anglo-Saxon period supports these various forms of timber and brushwood causeway constructions. For example, our *ðel bricge* (planked-bridge), finds physical manifestation in a possible planked timber causeway linking Mersea Island, Essex, to the mainland, inferred from a series of parallel timber piles (Crummy *et al.* 1982). Similarly, in excavations at Scole, Norfolk, a possible causeway consisting of parallel alignments of oak piles, was recovered along the edge of a palaeochannel in the Waveney Valley (Ashwin and Tester 2014, 199). The examples of brushwood causeways in place-names and charter boundary clauses find parallels in the substratum layers of a causeway recovered at Street, Somerset, where a composite construction of stones overlaying brushwood and timber sleepers, bounded by upright stakes of ash and field maple, connected the island of Glastonbury to the north with its estates to the south, via a crossing of the Brue (Brunning 2010). The Old English term *eorthbrycge* (earth bridge) might appropriately be applied to a causeway recovered at St Aldates, Oxford, where the earliest phase of the crossing was comprised of a 4 m-wide clay bank (Durham 1977; Robinson and Wilkinson 2003). 'Wood bridge' and 'beech bridge', as timber constructions, fit alongside references to *stoc* bridges (for Sussex see S 403; for Hampshire see Ekwall 1947, 423), a *beam* bridge (Ekwall 1947, 30), and perhaps *stapul* bridge (S 895) as clear indicators that Anglo-Saxon bridges were primarily wooden structures. In these final instances we might consider the timber piles recovered at Cromwell, indicating a substantial crossing of the Trent, to be a good illustrative example. Likewise, comparisons might be made with the possible bridge (or jetty?) recovered from excavations at Skerne, Humberside, where an earthen causeway was observed leading up to a series of timber post bases (Dent 1984; Graham-Campbell 1989, 74; Salisbury 1995).

'Bridge-work', therefore, despite the apparent link to work on forts in the *trinoda necessitas*, seems, from the charter boundary clause evidence, to be concerned with the improvement and amelioration of passage across low-lying river plains. In Charles the Bald's *Edict of Pîtres* (862–869) there is a suggestion that fortified bridge-head constructions were not his only concern (Coupland 1991). The text stipulates work on *civitates novas* (new cities) and *pontes ac transitus paludium* (bridges and passages across swampy ground) (Boretius and Krause 1897, 321) with the clear implication being that the crossing of the river was as much about building a causeway – a road – across uncertain ground as it was about building the structure that crosses the running water. Notker the Stammerer, writing in the late ninth century praises the implementation of these laws in the time of Charlemagne, referring to the construction of bridges (*pontes*), ships (*naves*) and causeways or 'crossings' (*traiecti*) and the cleaning (*purgatio*) and levelling (and resurfacing?) (*stramentum*) of the roads (*itinerum*) (Haefele 1959, 40; Thorpe 1969, 127). A distinction appears to be made here between ongoing burdens (for which counts and their deputies and lesser

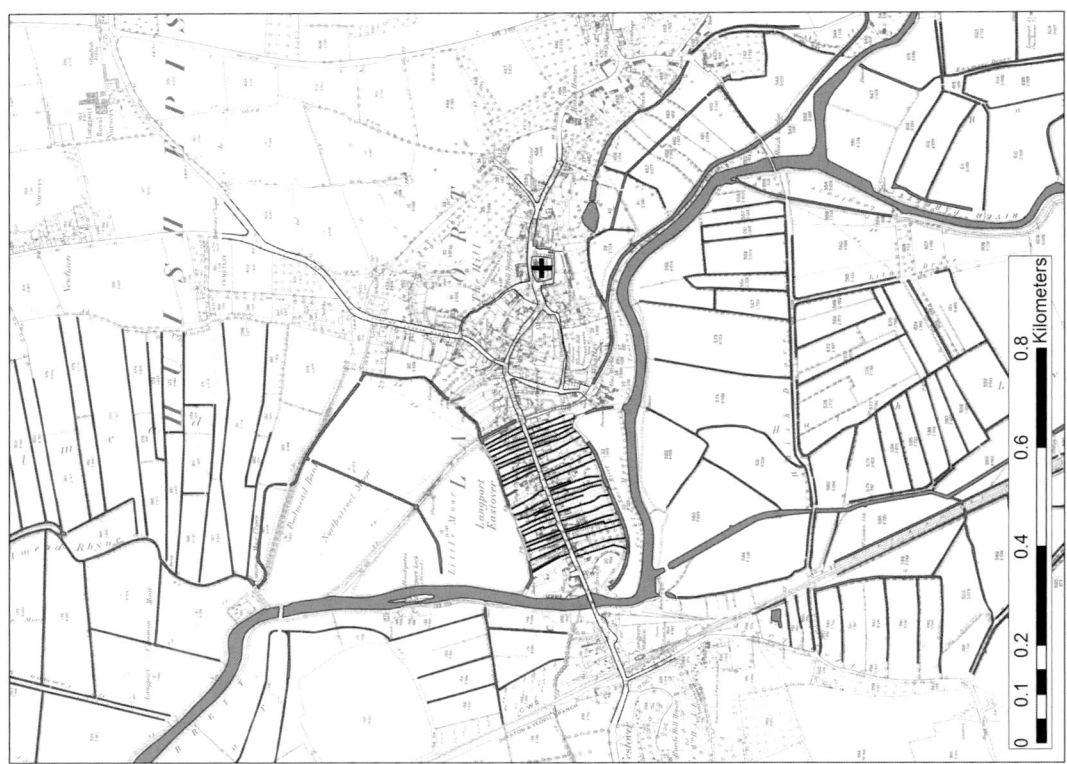
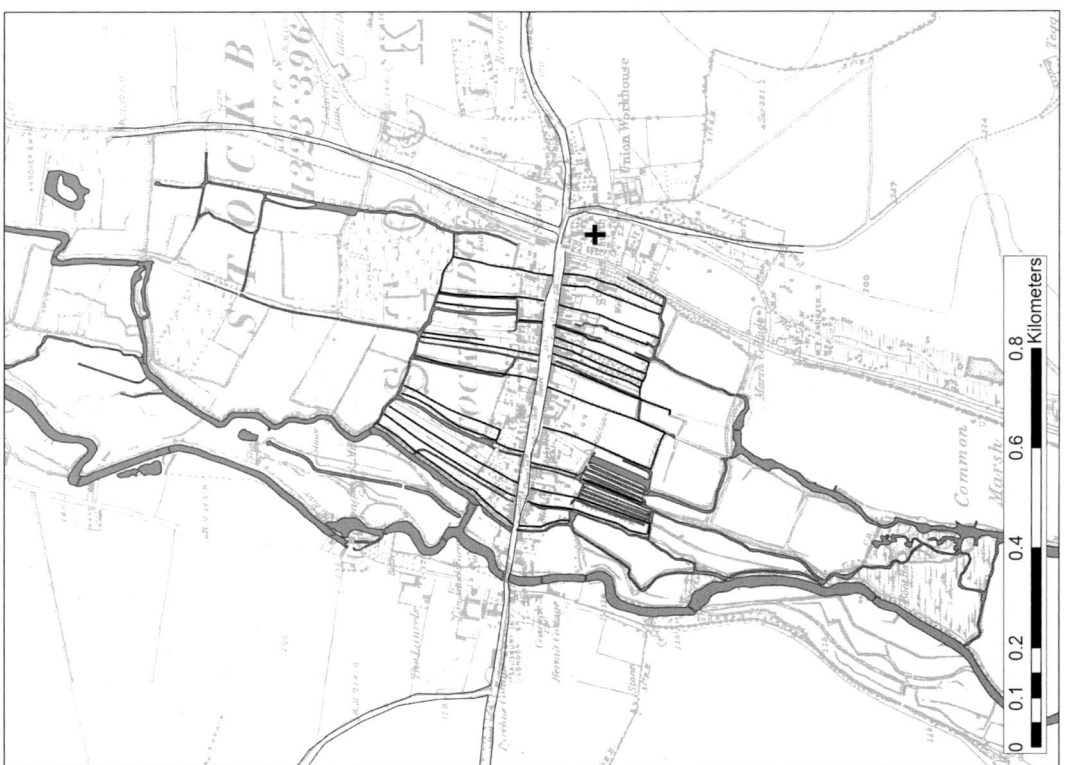

FIGURE 47 *(opposite)*. Stockbridge and Langport Compared (OS 1st Edition Six Inch base map: © Crown Copyright and Landmark Information Group Limited (2018), all rights reserved).

FIGURE 48. Winchester to Wilton, via Stockbridge (contains OS data © Crown copyright (2018)).

officials were responsible) and grand infrastructural projects and major works, especially new constructions, for which no one could be excused, whatever the pretext. Key to both, however, is an emphasis placed as much on the construction of raised roadways as there is on bridges and it seems likely that the Frankish kings were as concerned, at times of crisis, with the increased mobility of troops as they were with the prevention of river-borne attack (Coupland 1991, 6–7). We are reminded that the obligations Charles the Bald imposed on his subjects were described as *iuxta antiquam et aliarum gentium consuetudinem* (according to ancient custom and the custom of other peoples) where the 'other peoples' are believed, by some commentators, to have been the Anglo-Saxons (Nelson 1986, 121, n. 16; Gillmor 1997, 40).

Creating this link between roads and bridges might also help us to better understand and date certain processes of urban development in Anglo-Saxon England. There is an interesting study to be made in the case of Stockbridge, Hampshire (Figure 47). Built on a causeway across the River Test supporting a direct route from Winchester to Old Sarum, the precise origins of the borough are obscure. It is not mentioned explicitly in Domesday but even if the town was in existence in the late eleventh century, the view has been that the causeway upon which it resides could only have been constructed in the Roman period (Hughes 1976, 131; Hinton 1984, 151). However, a body of evidence suggests that

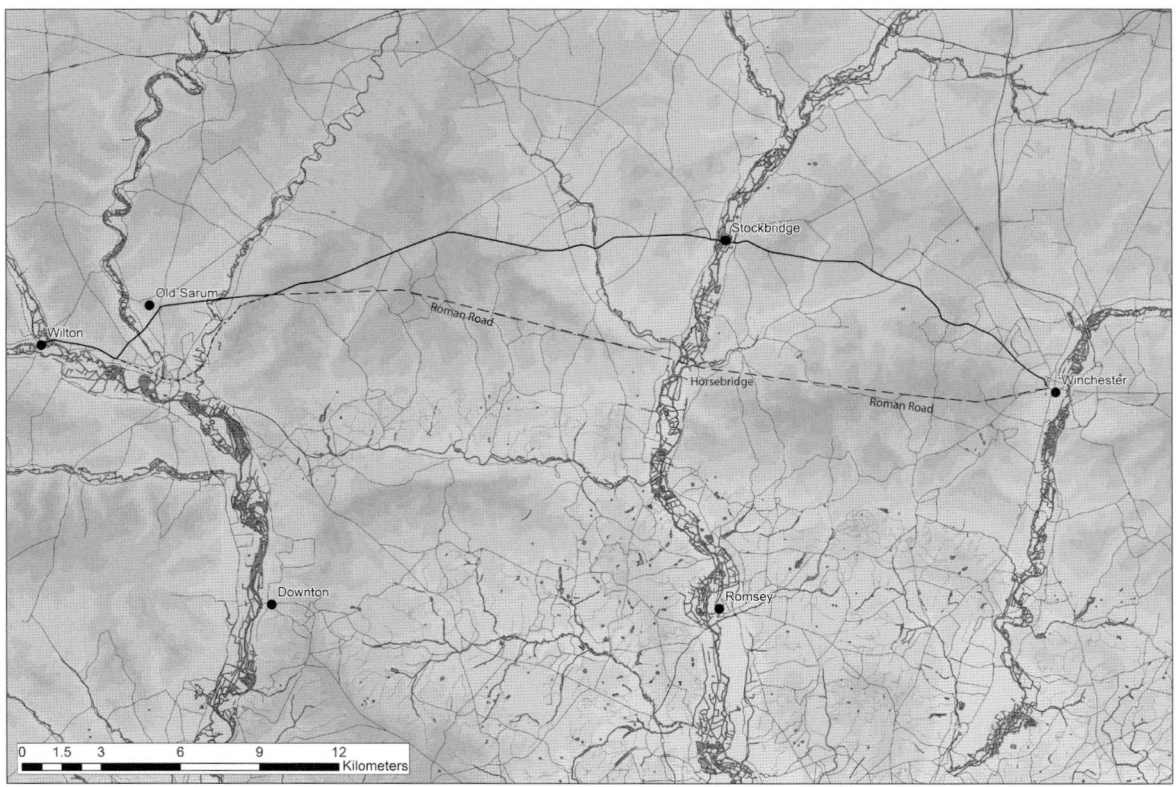

Stockbridge forms part of a major road building project of late Anglo-Saxon date. A connection with the Alfredian campaign of building fortified burhs – in this case one blocking the route up the Test valley – has already been made (Hill 1977, 80–81). However, Stockbridge's origins may be based less on defensive requirements and more on the need for good communications to support emerging administrative and economic ambitions. This is a road that directly connects Winchester with Old Sarum (Figure 48), the latter a site that exhibits many characteristics of urban development and administrative importance in the late Anglo-Saxon period (Langlands 2014). The route opts for a narrower crossing of the River Test to that used by the Roman road between the two Romano-British places, and was perhaps better equipped, by the late Anglo-Saxon period at least, to support the movement of wheeled vehicles than the narrow and composite causeway at Horsebridge, further down river at the crossing made by the Roman road. It is interesting that this proposed late Anglo-Saxon road is known as *Ykeneldestrete/Yknildestrete* in 1279 (Gover *et al.* 1939, 16), and perhaps reflects an attempt to impart a status enjoyed by the Icknield Way proper in the immediate post-Conquest period.

Urban characteristics for Stockbridge emerge in the historical record of the eleventh century with the presence of burgesses, nine and three respectively, in the Domesday entries for Sombourne and Houghton (Williams and Martin 1992, 97, 113), each at opposite ends of a hypothetical borough foundation based on an engineered causeway. There is a late Anglo-Saxon dating for the execution sites at Stockbridge Down and Meon Hill (Reynolds 2009a, 117), both sites that sit on this major highway on either side of the valley and the borough, suggesting that they form part of a broader geography of power. Causeway building on this scale and of this type is archaeologically proven in the case of the Street causeway, Glastonbury (Figure 50), and in this context the grant and confirmation in the late twelfth and early thirteenth centuries of the right to hold a weekly market in Stockbridge at 'Lestrait' and 'Le Strete' is interesting (Hughes 1976, 94; Brunning 2010).

We can also find parallels in Langport, Somerset, a documented burghal construction of the late ninth-century (Figure 47). The name alone suggests that the long causeway that connects both banks of the River Parrett is associated with a planned market place. Like Langport, there are no obvious fortifications at Stockbridge, and it is tempting to see the men from Langport's assigned 600 hides (in the Burghal Hidage) as working on the causeway itself, rather than a rampart earthwork that has, so far, proved elusive (Hill and Rumble 1996, 206–207, and the same might just as well be said of Axbridge). The function of this 'burh' would be, like Stockbridge, the connecting up of major administrative centres, in this case Somerton and Taunton, without having to take the lengthy and circuitous route via Ilchester and Ilminster (Figure 49). Recently, the identification of what has been called a 'High Street' type burh has placed a fresh stress on the economic ambitions, from the outset, for some burhs (Haslam 2016, 211). Stockbridge feasibly sits within this group, and makes a strong case, in conjunction with Langport and other

10. Bridges, herepaths, trade routes and the king's peace   171

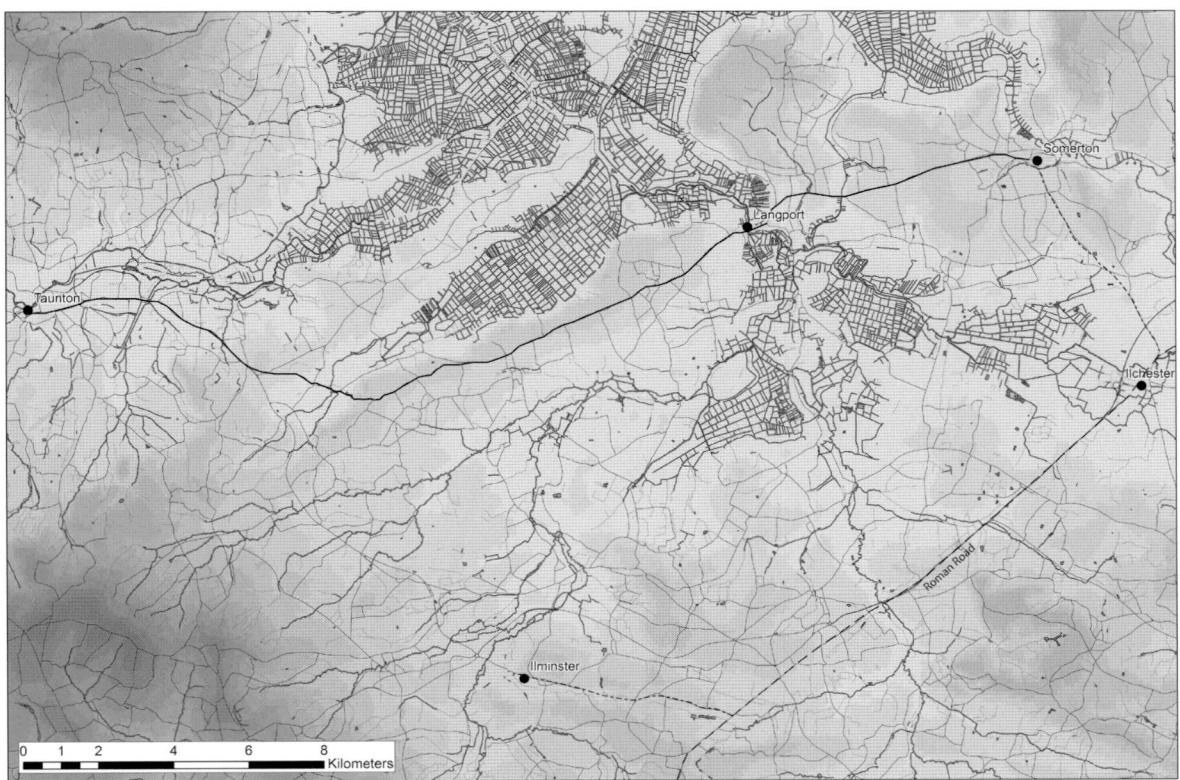

FIGURE 49. Somerton to Taunton, via Langport (contains OS data © Crown copyright (2018)).

towns that owe their origins to substantial causeways, that the taxation system described by the Burghal Hidage might also be being used in the construction of improved routeways throughout the kingdom. In both Stockbridge and Langport there are strong topographical and toponymical parallels with 'The Borough' in Downton, Wiltshire, Boroughbridge, North Yorkshire, and 'Borough High Street', Southwark.

One of the most useful accounts of early medieval bridge building comes from Cogitosus's *Vitae Brigitae*, written in mid-seventh century Ireland (Connolly and Picard 1987, 5). Although writing primarily for the edification of his readers, in the account of a river miraculously changing course there is some information provided on the methods and systems for the organisation of road construction that is of great interest. Chapter 30 of the *Vitae* records how an edict of the king was brought into force throughout the province and that all peoples had to come together to build a solid wide road. Of the road itself we learn that the foundation was to be of tree branches and rocks and some very solid earth works in 'the deep and virtually impassable bog and in the sodden and marshy places through which a large river ran'. The road had to withstand the traffic of chariots, waggons, horsemen and the 'rushing of people' as well as the 'clashing of enemies from all sides'. In terms of organisation, the text informs us that work parties were to be comprised of their own kinship groups and households, each to take charge of a section of road designated to them through the drawing of lots (Connolly and Picard 1987, 23–24). Clearly the section closest to the river was considered the harder draw.

In an early medieval Irish context, broadly, this activity can be seen to fit with what we know of the condition, status and maintenance of roads in the law tracts and other miscellaneous texts (Kelly 1997, 537–544). However, what is being described by Cogitosus might just as easily fit with examples from early medieval Wessex and beyond. The form of construction described is very similar to that employed at Street, Somerset, in the middle Anglo-Saxon period (Figure 50), and to the examples recovered in southern Scandinavia dating from the prehistoric through to the early medieval period (Jørgensen 2003, 202). In terms of organising labour, Cogitosus's account provides insights into how we might envisage the causeway at Langport being constructed, making use of its allocation of 600 hides. Yet, it finds more direct organisational parallels with the construction of major bridges at Rochester and Mainz where we have clear historical references to the division of labour between different groups. 'All of Europe', we are told, 'laboured side by side at this bridge (the arches of the great bridge of Mainz) in orderly cooperation' (Thorpe 1969, 127; and for Rochester see Brooks 1994). The location of the road building project of the *Vitae Brigitae* is interesting too. The swampy ground across which the road is charged with passing echoes strongly the *Edict of Pitres* and both cases force us to consider that the separating out of 'bridge construction' from 'road construction' is potentially a specious exercise and that, in fact, in the majority of occasions when a road might need 'constructing', it is to facilitate passage over very low-lying ground with the ultimate ambition of crossing a water course. In the Old English term 'bridge-work' we have, it is suggested, an implicit reference to what we might today call 'road-work'.

Both the examples from Ireland and southern Scandinavia are insightful in that these areas were never fully under

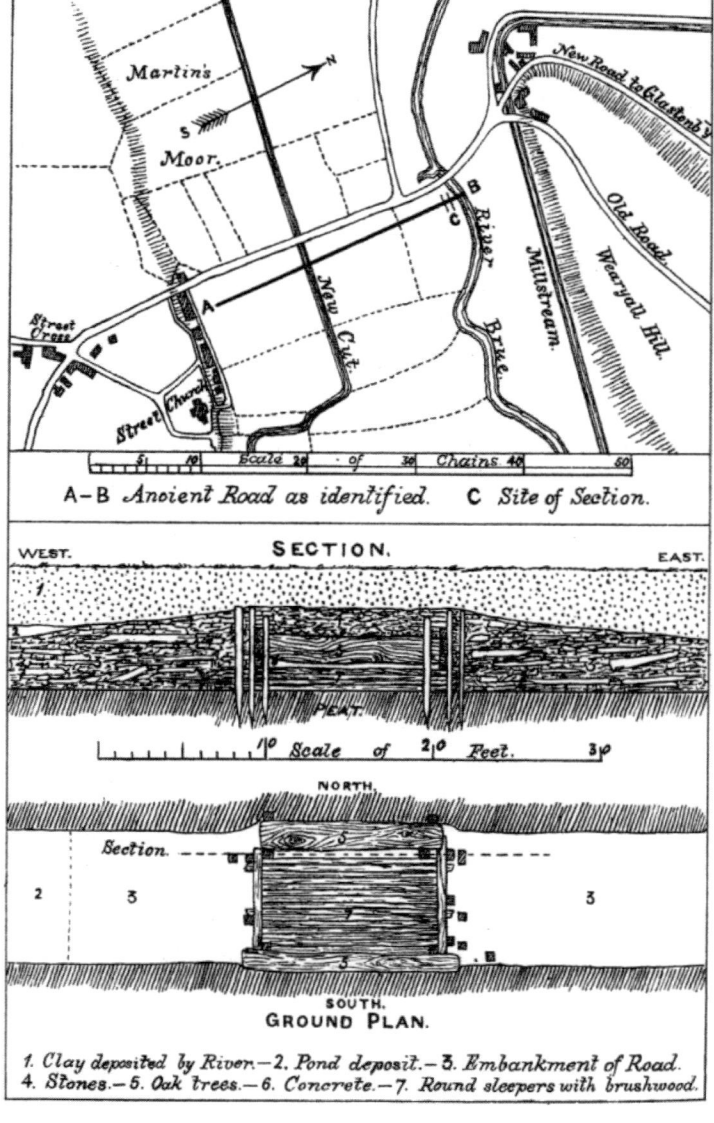

FIGURE 50. The Street causeway, Somerset, showing method of construction (reproduced in Brunning 2010).

the control of the Roman Empire. The underpinning social organisation behind the construction of large public works in both places cannot, therefore, claim derivation from classical practices. The role of the church, in the introduction of classical ideas on how such structures were socially and politically executed, might be suspected in the case of St Brigit's causeway, and the Street causeway, amongst others (discussed below). It seems most fitting, however, to frame bridge-work and the construction of causeways as part of broader social and economic trends and essentially timeless in the manner in which they responded to local and regional needs (Brooks 2002, 14). The most significant development in the argument presented here is that we reduce the importance placed on the references to bridges in what is an *emerging* documentary record: the historical sources alone are simply not a substantial evidence base upon which to draw conclusions on a programme of bridge-building in the early medieval period. *Contra* Alan Cooper's comment that we have 'bridge-work but no bridges', the archaeological examples at Aldates, Mersea, Scole, Street, Skerne and Cromwell – as well as the historically recorded causeway in the *Vitae Brigitae* – all can be seen to have been in place before the early eighth century. The bridge/causeway constructions at Langport and Stockbridge – presumably amongst many others – seem more likely to have their origins in the later ninth, or tenth century, but in all of these cases, these bridges are to be associated with routeways – improving communications through the landscape – and not with forts.

Herepaths and the hierarchy of Anglo-Saxon routes

That the link between the *trinoda necessitas* and the Anglo-Saxon road system has not received a greater degree of investigation is perhaps understandable in view of two seemingly insurmountable obstacles. Firstly, explicit references to work carried out on roads in the Anglo-Saxon period are extremely rare. There is a reference in the Canons of Edgar, in the section entitled 'Of Penitents', to redemptions of penance by gift which include the building of churches, the gift of land to the church, improvement of highways and the building of bridges (McNeill and Gamer 1990, 409–410). A further reference comes from the South Hams charter (S 298; study area 4), where the boundary runs to the ditch 'where the serfs dug the way'. Secondly, where the *trinoda necessitas* appears written in Old English in charters, the term *fyrd* is consistently used as a translation for expeditionary military service and yet, the term *here*- is almost ubiquitous in its association with paths in the Anglo-Saxon landscape. *Fyrd* is used in conjunction with military obligations in Anglo-Saxon charters (S 218; S 333; S 355; S 914; S 1032) but is only associated with routeways in a small number of (Mercian) cases (Baker 2013, 75–85). The dichotomy between *fyrd* and *here* is exacerbated by the *Anglo-Saxon Chronicle*, which consistently refers to the marauding Danish army as the *here* and the defending Saxon forces as the *fyrd*. Thus, with the term *here* comes connotations of lawlessness, raiding and pillaging. Chapter 13 of the laws of King Ine state that: *Ðeofas we hatað oð VII men; from seofon monnum hloð oð XXXV; siððan bið here* (we use the term 'thieves' if the number of men does not exceed seven, 'band of marauders' for a number between seven and thirty-five. Anything beyond this is a 'raid') (Ine 13.1; Attenborough 1922, 41). The *here* in this instance were clearly being associated with thievery, gang-like behaviour and ultimately, something that must be legislated against. This situation has led one commentator to suggest that on no account can the *here-* element in herepaths be associated with an army charged with the maintenance and upkeep of roads (Cooper 2002). Other appearances of the *here-* element in the Anglo-Saxon Chronicle go no further to reconciling the term with the notion of an orderly and disciplined force concerned with the defence of the realm. The *herebeacen* are the war-signals ignited by the Danish as they travelled from their winter camp on the Isle of Wight to Reading, the *here-hyð* is the booty and spoil with which they went on to reward themselves and the *heregild* was the tax raised in an attempt to pay off such lawless banditry (ASC 1006). The last of these though is a tax raised specifically to deal with the issue and what if herepaths are so named because they too were designed specifically to deal with the problem of the *here*?

A closer analysis of the distribution of the term identifies the fact that, for the most part, herepaths recorded in charter boundary clauses and as place-names are restricted to Wessex (Rackham 1986, 259). In Kent they are not nearly as frequent and they are less abundant in the West Midlands where Della Hooke has proposed that whilst they are of 'a limited number', they nonetheless played a 'particular role in the Anglo-Saxon period, one connected with the defence of the kingdom, and were maintained to a standard facilitating the easy movement of troops' (Hooke 1981a, 308). In the historical source material, the term appears almost exclusively in charter boundary clauses and references to it are rare outside of Anglo-Saxon charters. In fact, whilst in Anglo-Saxon charter boundary clauses herepaths are referred to on no less than 292 occasions, a mere three references to them can be found outside of the charters. These appear in the *Book of Daniel* in the *Junius* Manuscript and once each in *Beowulf* and the poem *Judith* (Krapp 1931, 111–132; Dobbie 1953, 3–98, 99–109). We have already seen from the project study areas that the term seems to have been applied to a specific entity, a type of route that uniformly connects the main central places of Anglo-Saxon Wessex. There is also, however, a uniformity in the application of the term itself. Rarely does it come with a qualifier. Of the 79 times it is mentioned in the study areas, on only fifteen occasions is any descriptive terminology applied to it and these are restricted to 'old' (x5), 'broad' (x4), *wic* (x4) and *þeod* (x2). Compare this to 168 'ways' where in 96 cases, a vast range of terms are used to describe the colour, shape, condition, ownership and function of these routes.

Scrutinising in even greater detail the term herepath, we might explore why the *-pæð* element prevails (in all but two cases) over *-weg*. *Pæð* has naturally drawn comparisons with the Greek πάτος (trodden or beaten way), but the occurrence of the original initial *p* in Teutonic is uncertain, making correspondence with the pre-Teutonic *bat-* and a suggested route of Latin *batuĕre* (to beat) the more likely borrowing (Simpson and Weiner 1989d, 337). In either case though, and as with the modern sense of the meaning, a 'path' is something that is trodden and although not formerly 'constructed' it is a purposefully made thoroughfare. 'Way' on the other hand, with an Indo-Germanic root and a sense development influenced by the Latin *via*, perhaps has a more generic meaning of 'a track prepared or available for travelling along; a road, street, lane or path' simply because such routes already existed in the landscape (Simpson and Weiner 1989a, 16). They were open passages, corollaries that needed no maintenance but simply existed and through which movement could pass at will. These routes then are set against the 'paths' that needed treading afresh – maintaining – by the Anglo-Saxons. The predominance of 'ways' on the open downland in, for example, the eastern half of the Shaftesbury study area (6.1) and on the downs to the south-east of Winchester (2.1) along with the repeated association with the qualifier ridge- in charter boundary clauses (x20) indicates something of their character. Whilst the Harro-, Icknield, London, ridge- and 'British' ways are all legacies of an earlier age determined as much by the natural lie of the land, the *pædes* (from Latin *pedes* [foot traveller, walker]), horse, Cutherd's, Strutherd's and the various *here*- paths mentioned in the study areas are all routes beaten out and trodden in a planned and working early medieval landscape (S 756, S 640, S 756, S 534). We are reminded of O.G.S. Crawford's division of all roads into two classes; natural tracks and made roads (Crawford 1953, 60). The distinction between the two is suggested again by Anne Cole's brief assessment of respective gradients where a *weg* is generally much steeper than a *strēt* and usually steeper than a *pæð* (Cole 2008, 346). The steeper gradients of a *weg* may be a general reflection of their initial use for foot and pack travel whilst a concern for newly created paths (even when they incorporate earlier routes) is their suitability for cart travel where steep inclines are more of a concern. In another detailed analysis in a landscape setting, employing least-cost path rather than slope analysis models, Baker and Brookes concluded that rather than being the optimum routes through the landscape, herepaths, in fact, took the character of secondary inter-connecting routes (Baker and Brookes 2011).

It seems, therefore, that what is emerging, both from the landscape evidence and from documentary sources, is evidence for a quite specific entity and one which by name seems concerned with the containment of the threat posed by the marauding *here*. Analysis of the dating of the first widespread appearances of the term in Anglo-Saxon charters initially seems to correspond with that period in the mid-ninth century when the Vikings begin to over-winter in England – a strategy that would require a sustained hoarding of provisions and food supplies. The term first appears in any significant numbers in charters of the 860s, the earliest and most trustworthy of this group being those dated to 868 and 869/870 recording, respectively, land granted by Æthelred, King of Wessex, at Martyr Worthy, Hants and Cheselbourne, Dorset (S 340, S 342). Both these examples are broadly accepted as reliable documents and there is no reason to believe the boundary clauses are not contemporary with the grants. However, it is clear from references to herepaths in charters of an earlier date, such as the Crediton charter of 739 and a grant by Offa of land in Gloucestershire, that the boundary clauses are much later additions (S 255, S 141). There are two comparatively isolated references to herepaths in charters recording grants made by Æthelwulf in 840 and 846 of, respectively, land at Halstock, Somerset (S 290) and in the South Hams, Devon (S 298). What we may be seeing here is the first implementation of the herepath idea and the possible result of Egbert's successful suppression of the combined Viking and British aggression in the south-west of England in the 830s. This might also explain their relative abundance, recorded in later charters, in this exposed part of the kingdom. However, using charter evidence to elucidate a true chronology of herepath origination and development is encumbered by the bias in charter numbers towards the end of the period and the obvious problems of identifying boundary clauses that are contemporary with legitimate documents from those that appear in later copies and forgeries.

Overall, their ubiquity in Wessex, character and distribution in the landscape, and their uniformity in terms of the terminology used to describe them all go some way to suggest that in the herepath system, some kind of kingdom-wide policy and strategy has been implemented in response to the Viking threat. Is it possible we have here a scheme of national defence over which the documentary sources are entirely silent? Accepting the view that herepaths are the product of a planned system of road maintenance for the defence of the realm, we should consider them in relation to another more famous scheme of national defence – the *Burghal Hidage* (Hill 1969; Hill and Rumble 1996).

Much has been made of the spacing of the forts listed in the *Burghal Hidage* and while it is now abundantly clear that many other burhs existed at the time (Baker and Brookes 2013a), there is some sense to the regular spacing of the burhs – particularly in relation to our maintained herepaths and the causeways, embankments and bridges that were a crucial part of them. Let us envisage a situation whereby a signal, a beacon or horn, from a highly developed signalling system (Reynolds 1995; Pepper 1996; Hill and Sharp 1997; Baker and Brookes 2015b) indicates an incoming threat. With no point in Wessex being more than twenty miles from a burh, the safety of the fort walls could be achieved within around seven to twelve hours. Many, in journeying to the local burh, would need to cross watercourses and at any point of the year fords could prove unreliable and dangerous to negotiate – particularly for carts. By improving the roads and, in particular, by improving river-crossings with bridges, carts could more reliably be used and in all weather conditions. Carting allowed very much more produce to be brought into the protection of the burh, and crucially it is here that we see the tactical benefits of an improved road network implemented in conjunction with fortified centres. This system would allow the West Saxon kings to, in effect, starve any invading army and if the *Anglo-Saxon Chronicle*'s account of the year 894 is to be believed, it was in just such a situation that the Viking army had to resort to eating the greater part of their horses. By improving mobility to the designated burhs through implementing a standard of road maintenance, and bridging particularly tricky or unreliable parts of journeys, surplus food (and other resources, such as fire wood) that would otherwise fall into the hands of the invading *here* could be transported to the local burh – at a day's notice. The speed with which the Viking army could penetrate the heartlands of England and return to their ships and winter camps booty-laden might be taken as an indication of a sophisticated level of mobility (for the spectacular but not ultimately damaging raids of 892–895, see Hill 1981, 40–41, figs 60 and 61). At the same time however, it may reflect a desire on the part of the raiding army to return as quickly as possible to a supply base to avert potentially morale-sapping hunger. Ryan Lavelle's model of the relationship between supplies, cohesion and prestige in early medieval campaigns illustrates how food and supplies, whether derived from foraging, centres of collection or purchase, underpins the success of effective military strategy (Lavelle 2010, 179, fig. 5.1).

So, whilst the herepath network almost certainly facilitated response times, in terms of mustering, troop movement and intercepting raiding parties, the above interpretation invites the reader to consider the crucial role herepaths played in the control of resources. Whether hay for horses, livestock for the economy, timber for fuel or food for warriors, improving the route network and, most importantly, providing bridges for the free flowing movement of carted bulk goods, would have gathered up precious supplies away from the unacceptable insecurity of the manor to the fortified sanctuary of the burh. The 'way the serfs dug', recorded in the South Hams charter, allows exactly for this to take place: for the agricultural surpluses to be moved from the relatively exposed manors of Kingston and Bigbury to the security of a centrally designated fortification (in this case Halwell) (for the raiding of this area in 1069 by 'Irishmen', see Thorn and Thorn 1985, 41, n. 17). It may be significant that the South Hams grant is the earliest (surviving) West Saxon charter to contain an immunity clause (*i.e.* immunity from certain obligations but with the reservation of the *trinoda necessitas*, Brooks 1971, 81). The ditch where the serfs dug the way, recorded in 846, was clearly an event that took place within the living memory of those guiding the boundary survey and when Nicholas Howe writes that this is 'evidence of the most mundane local history' and an act perhaps, 'in violation of the customary standards of road maintenance', he arguably could not be more wrong (Howe 2008, 35). In the wider context, if we accept the crucial link between herepaths, the *trinoda necessitas* and the scheme of national defence represented by the burhs, then the serfs' labour may well represent a small but integral part in a campaign that rescued Wessex, ultimately, from the 'crucible of defeat'.

Classical precedent and the notion of highway maintenance

Although the case being presented here is one that links herepaths with the *trinoda necessitas* and the general military obligations placed on society in the ninth and tenth centuries, we have no explicit historical references to such a scheme, and it must therefore remain conjectural. Further support may be found, however, in exploring the evidence from late Roman legislation and its influence on the ideas of Anglo-Saxon rulers in the ninth and tenth centuries. That early medieval kingship drew on classical precedence seems clear from examples across the continent and the parallels between English and continental obligations are clearly a result of contemporary contacts and a shared Germanic and Roman past (Brooks 1971, 69; Nelson 1986; Abels 1988, 53; Cooper 2002, 44).

In particular, the *Theodosian Code*, a compilation of laws dating from the early fifth century, delegated responsibility for public buildings and duties into the hands of local landowners (Mommsen and Krueger 1905a, 593, 601–603 XI.10.2 (370), XI.16.15 (382) and XI.16.18 (390)). The Church sought to evade these obligations, the so-called *sordida munera* ('dirty works' or 'base services'), which included the servicing of the army and the repair of public buildings. In 423, therefore, Emperor Theodosius II decreed that no one, not even *venerandas ecclesias* (venerable churches), should be exempt from the responsibility for the upkeep of roads and bridges (Mommsen and Krueger 1905a, 818; XV.3.6). And this was echoed in 441, in a law issued by Emperor Valentinian III, wherein explicit clarification comes that the obligation rested on land and not on people (Mommsen and Krueger 1905b, 91–92). The idea of the *sordida munera* passed into the *Breviary of Alaric* in Visigothic Spain, although not, as Alan Cooper points out, the specific clause concerning road repair (Cooper 2006, 35, n. 168). Both the *Breviary* and the *Theodosian Code* were well known in Francia – particularly in church circles where clerics made copies and were schooled in the laws (Wood 1993, 166). Thus, when the notion of the *constuetudo antiquam et aliarum gentium* (customs ancient and of other peoples) appears in Charles the Bald's *Edict of Pitres* (862–869) and when Pippin, son of Charlemagne, decreed that repair of churches, making of bridges and repair of streets should be done *sicut antique fuit consuetudo* (as was the ancient custom), these stipulations are almost certainly referring to late Roman legislation (Boretius and Krause 1897, 321–322; Drew 1962, 184). By implementing the *Theodosian Code*, the Carolingians were able to maintain the Roman road network and in practice, this was fundamental to the successful operation of the *tractoria* – the Carolingian re-invention of the Roman *cursus publicus* (Bachrach 2013, 21).

It is entirely possible that these ideas and existing copies of late-Roman legal texts may have influenced the thinking of Wessex's ruling elites in the ninth century and their implementation of a strategy that both defended the realm but that also built capacity through ensuring the prerequisites of a state infrastructure were in place. The exact phrase used to describe one of the subjects of the *sordida munera* in the *Theodosian Code* is *viae publicae et pontium stratarumque* (Mommsen and Krueger 1905a, 818; XV.3.6), and if we take the *-rumque* element to be an adjective of *rus* in the plural masculine genitive case, a literal translation might read 'public ways and rural highway bridges', the latter of which might be seen in opposition to those of the *urbs* and be essentially of a causeway type (discussed above). It should also be questioned, however, whether the institution of Anglo-Saxon kingship was reintroducing such ideas or whether, in certain parts of Britain, these obligations can be traced as a continued arrangement from the late-Roman period. This perennial challenge in the study of early medieval state development is best summarised by Nicholas Brooks (2002, 2):

> To what extent did Anglo-Saxon rulers draw upon powers inherited from Roman or indeed Iron Age polities? Or were they rather, with the aid of seventh-century churchmen, imposing essentially new state structures and new institutions with only the faintest reflections of any Roman or British past?

A recent trend in the study of the fifth to seventh centuries has established from the cultural and political evidence that the west of Britain bore all the characteristics of a late Roman province and a 'failed state' (White 2007; Laycock 2008). If this is the case and *Britannia Prima* can be seen to have successfully operated into the early seventh century, it may very well have seen itself as subject to Theodosian (and Valentinian) legislation and the process of cultural assimilation with Anglo-Saxon England, alongside influences from Merovingian France, may also explain the apparent reappearance of these ideas in the eighth century. In such a scenario, attention should be drawn to the 'old' herepaths of the Crediton and Exeter study area (3), and the possibility that there may have been a recognition of the fact that these were routes at one point maintained for the benefit of a late Roman polity based on Exeter (3.1 SX99SW, 3.2 SS80NW). Equally, the 'old' herepath of the Salisbury study area, potentially furnished with Roman milestones, may again be a reference to the fact that the same hypothetical services that were required to maintain routes in the Anglo-Saxon period had applied back in the fifth and sixth centuries. The argument is, of course, encumbered by the differences of the language used and reconciling the Latin *via publica* with Old English herepath is problematic. However, the faintest suggestion of this link comes from the only reference to a *via publica* in the project study areas where a 'public way' is recorded along the course of the north Hampshire downs ridgeway (1.3 SU45NW). The reference comes from one of the four charters with lengthy Latin directional terminology, dated to 801, and the same route is referred to as a 'street' in a later charter dated to 961 (S 268, S 416). It is, however, the reference to this ridgeway as a herepath to the west of Walbury in a charter reliably dated to 931 that creates the critical, if tenuous, link (S 416). In this instance a *via publica*, an entity that took the appearance at a later date of a 'street', is referred to in the intervening period as a herepath and along with the evidence from the 'old' herepaths there is at least the case to be made for further research along these lines, employing a methodology that explores how the same road is described in different sources along its course. The terms *via publica* or *publica strata* occur in ten other boundary clauses, seven of which predate the tenth century, and analysis of their course in the landscape, how they may be described in other charters and how they relate to a wider geography of civil defence may bear fruits (S 9; S 100; S 187; S 268; S 287; S 1209; S 1267; S 1288; S 1628; S 1629).

Another area that might provide a useful comparison is that part of Mercia that is well served by charter boundary clauses. References to herepaths are few in the Midlands, but it seems logical that in Mercia some kind of organised system of bridge and road maintenance might be reflected in the range of terms applied to different routes. John Baker (2013, 75–85) has observed the occurrence of *fyrd* in compounds with words referring to routeways and in their greater proliferation in the Midlands, proposes dialectical differences that govern, between Mercia and Wessex, the separate toponymic distributions of *fyrd-* and *here-* in compounds with roads. He tentatively suggests that *fyrd-strǣt* is the semantic equivalent in parts of the Midlands of *here-pæð* in Wessex and broaches the possibility that the term reflects a burden of maintenance resting either locally or with the king.

What is interesting, however, is the very small numbers of *fyrd*-related routes that survive. Might we not expect a system as ubiquitous as the herepath network in Wessex? It could be that the few that do survive do so as a result of these being the last survivors of an earlier system, one dating to the eighth century and the age of Mercian supremacy. It may be that, as a consequence, there was already a very developed route network in Mercia and the greater occurrence of the *strǣt* element in the areas of the Midlands that we have good charter evidence for might be an indicator that care was taken, at an earlier period, to ensure well-surfaced roads (Hooke 1981a, 301–307). In this context, *fyrdstræt* might represent a later (?ninth or tenth century) in-filling of this network, to fulfil a role parallel to the herepath system. A cursory analysis suggests that routes with a *fyrd* element appear to stem from even more major routeways. The *fyrdstræt* at Church Stowe, Northants, appears to tap into Watling Street (S 615). The *cynges ferdstrǣte* taps into the Fosse Way (S 1340). A *fyrdstræt* in Worcestershire, recorded in three charters taps into Ryknield Street (S 1590, S 1599, S 1664). They are therefore secondary to much more major routes, of the kind that emerge as the king's special highways in post-Conquest texts, but routes already exhibiting an elevated status in the late Saxon period. The Fosse Way and Ermine Street, for example, are recorded in pre-Conquest charters as *hæn stræt* and *hean strǣte* whilst the Roman road from Caerleon to Wroxeter, has become the *heh strǣte* by the 960s (S 115, S896, S 723, and for further 'high' streets see Cooper 2002, 61). It may not be, therefore, that we need to seek the element *fyrd* for justifying some kind of public service requirement for the upkeep of roads. The *strǣt* element alone, with its greater popularity in Mercian charters, and by analogy with the *pontium stratarumque* of the *Theodosian Code*, may provide us with much of what we need to posit the requirement for work on roads in the *trinoda necessitas* in a Mercian and possible eighth-century context.

Church obligations and herepaths

Anglo-Saxon military obligations first appear in a charter of 749 recording Æthelbald of Mercia's decree, at a council held at Gumley, that church lands were freed from the obligation of all of the regular dues and services owed on land but that they still had to contribute to certain specific public obligations; work on bridges and fortresses (later in the century the burden of 'military watch' is added to create the *trinoda necessitas*) (S 92). One of the main issues to have attracted the attention of scholars in the study of military obligations is the degree to which these mid-eighth-century obligations represented a novel imposition on church lands (and indeed secular lands) or whether they were merely a ratification of burdens that already existed (Stevenson 1914; John 1960; Brooks 1971; Abels 1988; Cooper 2006, 24–38). Analysis of some of the herepaths recorded in the project study areas, whilst not necessarily indicating whether these burdens were novel or ancient impositions on the church, may at least indicate where it was felt, by the tenth century, the burden for the upkeep of roads lay at the very local level. A series of seven charters exist for land in Bishopstone (7.3). Two of these concern a portion of the later parish to the north of the Ebble (S 522, S 640) whilst five describe the bounds of the entire area covered by the later parish (S 229, S 275, S393, S 540, S 891). Only the latest of the five is thought to be acceptable as a reliable account of the restoration, by King Æthelred II to the Old Minster, Winchester of 100 hides at Downton (55 hides) and *Eblesburnan* (*i.e.* Bishopstone, 45 hides) in 997 (S 891; Finberg 1964, 236; John 1965; Hart 1970, 26; Keynes 1980, 101–102). Were it not for the fact that the boundary clauses from the four earlier charters contain minor, although not insignificant differences, they could be dismissed altogether. In one particular boundary clause, an entirely unacceptable fabrication of the tenth century (S 275; Edwards 1988, 148), different terms are used to describe certain features. In two instances 'ways' as they are referred to in the near identical boundary clauses are termed herepaths and further minor differences suggest that two separate perambulations were conducted (S 229, S 393, S 540, S 891). The two charters that describe only the northern half of Bishopstone, one a grant of 947 from King Eadred to Ælfsige, his faithful man, the other of 957 from King Eadwig to Ælfric, his faithful minister, also use the term herepath in place of 'way' (S 522, S 640). It would seem that the use of the term herepath predates the use of the term 'way' as its inclusion in the authentic charters (that is, S 522 and S 640) is earlier than the most reliable survey to include the term 'way' (S 891). However, it would also appear to be the case that the herepaths in this instance are referred to in charters where the beneficiary is a secular individual. Where the church is the beneficiary these routes are referred to merely as 'ways'. The use of the term herepath in the forged charter where Old Minster is the beneficiary, purporting to date to 826, suggests an origin for that boundary clause which was different to those of the other Downton forgeries (S 275). Where it has been suggested that the forger of this charter has used parts of genuine charters from the 820s it may therefore also be that the boundary clause was gleaned from a ninth-century document and that the recipient was a lay individual (Keynes 1994, 1111–1112).

A similar scenario can be observed in the charter boundary evidence that describes the north Hampshire ridgeway in study area 1. We have already seen how a *via publica* is recorded in our earliest charter. In 931, the date of the next reliable charter, this route is called a herepath and the beneficiary is Wulfgar, one of the king's ministers (S 416). In a not so reliable charter, dated to 909 but likely to be a forgery of the eleventh century (S 378; Keynes 1994, 1145), the route is called a 'way' and the beneficiary of the grant is St Peter's, Winchester. In both instances, by the time of the later forgeries it might be considered that the term herepath was becoming obsolete and that there was less necessity to recognise their function in the landscape. This pattern does, however, warrant further research. Is it the case that herepaths appear mainly in charters where a secular individual is recorded as the beneficiary and if so, what are the implications of this? It may very well contribute towards debates about who is drafting the boundary clause and what their relationship to the authors of the charters is (Keynes 2013). Further research would involve actually mapping routes and identifying where particular examples are referred to differently in separate documents to see if there genuinely is a difference between the institutions of church and state in attitudes to the status of certain routes.

Fortress-work and 'street watch'

That the burden of responsibility for the defence of the realm fell heavily on the shoulders of secular individuals – ministers and *thegns* – is illustrated in the archaeological evidence for the emerging manorial centres in the late Anglo-Saxon period. The obligation to build bridges and forts survived as two of a wide variety of obligations owed by freemen to the shire in the thirteenth century. By this time though, they have been commuted to cash payments known as *pontage* and *murage* and the obligation to undertake guard duty becomes a cash payment known as the *wardpenny* (Faith 1997, 99–101). If these customary 'rents', as they came to be known, can be seen to have their origins in the Anglo-Saxon period, is it the case that *streteward*, a thirteenth-century obligation to 'guard the street', represents a similarly ancient obligation to keep watch over the highway and possibly even to see that it is good repair? The process of 'shiring' and defining hundred boundaries to provide for the defence of the realm may represent, Rosamund Faith argues, 'an important stage in the definition and fixing of specific burdens on specific land' so it may be that the late Anglo-Saxon period is when such obligations became fixed (Faith 1997, 101). Of these burdens in the thirteenth and fourteenth centuries it has been observed that, 'there is no indication in the records of their very recent origin. The names given them are all English names with a certain ring of antiquity about them' (Neilson 1910, 48). How ancient these burdens may have been in the thirteenth century can be suggested by certain documents dating from the eleventh century. *Geþyncðo*, concerning *wergilds* and dignities, provides a window into social mobility in the late Anglo-Saxon world and it stipulates that a *ceorl*, provided he is wealthy, possessing 'fully five-hides of land', with a bell-house, burh gate and a seat of office in the king's hall, was entitled to the rights of a *thegn* (Whitelock 1979, Cat. no. 51, 468–469). These entitlements are outlined in more detail in the *Rectitudines Singularum Personarum*, a document dating from the middle years of the eleventh century that lists the rights and ranks of people (Douglas and Greenway 1953, Cat. no. 172, 813–816). In return for a *thegn*'s service consisting of, amongst other things, armed service, equipping a guard ship, guarding the coast and 'military watch', the *thegn* is entitled to 'book-right'. One way of exploring the link between the equation of military watch with the later obligations of *wardpenny* and *Streteward* is to examine the archaeological evidence for '*thegnly*' residences dating from the ninth to the eleventh centuries and their location in relation to the network of Anglo-Saxon communications.

Excavations in the 1970s within the Roman walls of the Saxon Shore fort of Portchester revealed a distinct period of occupation during the tenth and eleventh centuries consisting of phases of high-status halls, stone-based towers, other ancillary buildings and a small fenced cemetery. It is suggested that the whole site, with the exception of the second phase of the tower and the cemetery, came to an end with the building of the Norman keep (Cunliffe 1976). The features of this period of occupation are very much reminiscent of the statutory requirements of *thegnly* status articulated in the *Geþyncðo* and the *Rectitudines*, and Portchester represents the perfect location with which to meet with one's obligation to watch the coast. Because of its unique location and setting, however, Portchester may represent an exceptional example. Other occurrences of high-status sites carrying the same *thegnly* archaeological signatures have been found at far more ordinary locations. At Faccombe Netherton in north Hampshire, for example, excavation exposed successive phases of buildings dating from the beginning of the ninth century (Fairbrother 1990). The site sits not at the centre of its estate (*i.e.* the later parish of Faccombe Netherton) but on the boundary with an estate known as Buttermere in the late ninth century (S 336). Several phases of buildings throughout the tenth and eleventh century, along with the construction of a more substantial retaining earthwork bank and ditch and evidence for high-status metal working all reinforce the identification of Faccombe Netherton as a *thegnly* residence (Reynolds 1999, 136). Importantly, for our purposes, the residence was believed to have been sited in a location suitable for the controlling of the main route through the estate (Fairbrother 1990, 513). Faccombe Netherton is located in a combe referred to in a charter boundary as *faccan cumbes* (Figure 19, SU45NW, the combe to the immediate west of Ashmansworth). It is feasible that the route the fortified residence is controlling is a north–south route, with the crossing of the Kennet at Hungerford the likely northern destination. However, the charters record a *cissan anstigo* (Cissa's footpath) and it may be that this is a reference to a path *en route* to Chisbury, recorded as *Cissanbyrig* in the *Burghal Hidage* (Brooks 1964, 75–79). In which case, Faccombe Netherton is very much keyed into the geography of late Anglo-Saxon mobility and defence, controlling routes between river crossings and local defensive hubs.

Archaeological evidence from Trowbridge has drawn comparisons with Faccombe Netherton (Graham and Davis 1993, 146). The site exhibited evidence of occupation from the middle Anglo-Saxon period but from the tenth century onwards the same distinctively *thegnly* features begin to emerge. These included a church and graveyard and a substantial ditched and banked enclosure. We have already seen how Trowbridge is located on a major route running from the south-east to the crossing of the Avon at Bradford-on-Avon and a possible east–west route across the upper Avon flood plain (9.2 ST85NW/NE). Finally, the best evidence for *thegnly* control of highways comes from excavations undertaken throughout the 1990s at Yatesbury, north Wiltshire, which revealed evidence of what could be interpreted as a late Anglo-Saxon *thegnly* residence (Reynolds 1994). An enclosure some 200 m in diameter straddled a major through-route – known locally as the Harepath – and the place-name, interpreted as the 'gate of the burh', is reminiscent of one of the stipulated requirements of *thegnly* status in the *Geþyncðo*. One key element to the site at Yatesbury is its role in a localised scheme of defence and its position in relation to Silbury, an important signalling site, and the larger burh at Avebury (Reynolds 1999, 92–94).

What seems clear, at least from these Wessex examples, is that a factor in the location of these residences is proximity to, if not immediate control of, a significant thoroughfare. We see this same desire to control major lines of communications in the pattern of land granting in the tenth century – particularly in grants of land to secular individuals. In the middle Trent valley, for example, a series of charters record the granting of a group of estates to Wulfsige the Black in locations that Peter Sawyer has argued control the strategic routes from Derby and Nottingham to Tamworth and Lichfield. This represents, he argues, a scheme designed by Edmund Ironside in order to reassert his control over the territory of the Five Boroughs in the 940s (S 479; S 484; S 1606; Sawyer 1979, 34, 38). We may see the same strategy being employed in the Britford area (study areas 7 and 8). Whilst the king retains control of the crossing point and estate of Britford himself, the surrounding estates that make up the hundred of Cawdon, are all granted to *thegns* of middling importance (Langlands in press).

Whether in the building of *thegnly* residences or the granting of estates, chronologically, the implication is that the routes were already in position for them then to have served as the focus for later royal strategic attention. So, whilst this arrangement is a good archaeological articulation of the burden to perform 'military watch' or *streteward*, it does not necessarily indicate an obligation to maintain and keep in good order the main highways of the realm. By the mid-tenth and eleventh centuries the emphasis on the status of the herepath network may very well have changed from one concerned primarily with dealing with the *here* problem to one that also had as its remit the wider protection and monitoring of people as they moved around the landscape.

The people, the peace and the king's highway

Alan Cooper's analysis of the *Leges Henrici Primi* has demonstrated that many of the laws concerning highways in this legal treatise composed in the early twelfth century can be seen to have their origins in the Anglo-Saxon period (Cooper 2002). In particular, in a prefatory summary of the king's rights we are told that 'All *Herestrete* pertain wholly to the King, and all *cwealm stowa* (killing places), that is places of execution, pertain totally to the king and are in his soke'. Cooper establishes that this connection between the highway, peace and the king's jurisdiction has its origins in at least the mid-tenth century (Cooper 2002, 53). Indeed, this relationship, or at least the connection between highway and execution site, is observed on the Winchester to Old Sarum highway (discussed above in reference to Stockbridge) on which no fewer than four pre-Conquest execution sites have been identified, a distribution interpreted as reflecting royal control (Hill 1937, 258; Reynolds 2009a, 56, 117). Again, classical legal concepts can be seen to have played a significant role in the formation of these ideas across the continent. As well as being concerned with the maintenance, state, repair and dimensions of roads, clauses in the *Theodosian Code* and most of the continental law codes of the early medieval period feature provisions for the protection of strangers, pilgrims, women and children who use the highways (Cooper 2002, 40–42).

From the project study areas some evidence tentatively supports Cooper's back-projection of post-Conquest highway law into the Anglo-Saxon period. A particular phrase that appears in the charter evidence, twice in the study areas and once elsewhere, is *þeod* herepath. A translation might read 'people's herepath' but the interpretation of the qualifier *þeod* is problematic. On a local level, it can simply refer to 'the district occupied by the people' (Bosworth and Toller 1898, 1048). Thus, we might assume that a *þeod* herepath is, perhaps, maintained locally (*i.e.* by local people) for the protection of a local district.

It may be of relevance here that the charters within which this phrase occurs are all of small grants of land. In the study areas the phrase appears as *þone þeod herpað* in a perambulation for the grant of a single hide at Monkton in Wyke, Shobrooke, Devon (3.1 SS80SE) and as *ðæne þeod herpað* in a perambulation for a 2-hide estate at land near Wilton (8.1 SU13SW). In both these instances the term potentially describes a path aligned to the nearest *burghal* forts at, respectively, Exeter and Wilton/Old Sarum. In the third reference, appearing in a boundary clause for a grant of 5 hides at West Buckland, Wellington, Somerset, (S 380) the term appears to be describing a south-west/north-east route connecting Tiverton and Taunton (and a Lyng/Exeter axis is also likely). However, *þeod* is also a term with much deeper connotations, one with poetic resonances and a meaning intimately bound up with a Germanic sense of identity (Bosworth and Toller 1898, 1048). In such a situation, we might view 'the people' here referred to as something more generic and all-encompassing with notions of 'humankind', 'nationhood' and ethnic identity. What, then, if these three references to *þeod* herepaths – albeit a tiny sample – represent a perception, at least in the minds of boundary surveyors, that an added characteristic of these roads was that they were 'for the people'; the roads of a nation where 'the people' as a collective enjoyed the right to go in peace? A similar sense of meaning can be gained from the 'Edway' or 'Edeway' in Hertfordshire, which is thought to have derived from *theod* and is believed to refer to the Icknield Way (Gover *et al.* 1938, 6).

The single reference in all charters to a *folc hearpað* in a grant of land at Grimley, Worcestershire (S 1370 – again, small at only 4 hides), gives the same sense of meaning but creating the link between this idea and the post-conquest evidence for such a notion (discussed below) is justified by one other single reference from a boundary clause. In what is believed to be an authentic charter purporting to date from the reign of King Æthelstan (Finberg 1964, n. 239; O'Donovan 1973, 101, 111), the phrase *þæs frið herpaþes* appears in the boundary clause for land at North Newnton in the Vale of Pewsey, Wiltshire (S 424). William Stubbs, in his *Constitutional History of England*, identified the term *frið* in the context of the Anglo-Saxon legal tradition with notions of public peace and a form of protection that was extended to all people in the kingdom (Stubbs 1903, 198–202). It appears in one of Æthelred's law codes: *And beo man georne ymban friðes bote and ymbe feos bote æghwar on earde and ymbe burhbote and ymbe bric-bote æghwar on earde an æghwilcum ende and ymbe firdunga, áá þonne neod sy, be þam þe man geræde* (And the People are to be zealous about the improvement of the peace, and about the improvement of the coinage everywhere in this country, and about the repair of boroughs [and repair of bridges] in every province and also about military service, according to what is decreed, whenever it is necessary) (V Atr 26.1; Liebermann 1903–1916, 243; Whitelock 1979, 445; Loyn 1984, 163–164). What is intriguing about this law code is the proximity of this 'improvement of the peace' to the *burhbote*, *bric-bote* and *firdunga* (fort-work, bridge-work and service in the host) of the *trinoda necessitas*. What can be meant by 'the peace' in this law? It is a tantalising possibility that our single reference to a *frið* herepath is enough to substantiate the link between herepaths, routes constructed initially to deal with the *here* but ones that went on to provide *frið* to the þeod and *folc* as they travelled and communicated through the landscape of Anglo-Saxon England.

Trade and trade routes

What might we consider was the function of the royally sanctioned peace that emerges explicitly in conjunction with the highway in the post-Conquest law codes but can tentatively be observed in the names of some routes as early as the tenth century? By the later Anglo-Saxon period the concern kings had for the free and unmolested movement of people through the landscape reflects an understanding that such movement facilitated trade and exchange, and therefore royal and ecclesiastical revenue. Edgar, for example, signs off on the *Wihtbordesstan* code noting his pleasure at the zealous upholding of the *frið* amongst his subjects and also in Æthelred's second lawcode, a clause referring to *unfriðland* is followed by a series of clauses concerned with goods, trade ships (*ceapscip*) and men having *frið* (IV Edgar 16; II Atr 1, 2, 2.1, 3, 3.1, 3.2, 3.3; Whitelock 1979, 437, 439–440). In some contexts, it would seem then that this 'freedom' is an explicit protection extended to those who wish to engage in trade (Fell 1983). Such arrangements are likely to have been around as early as the eighth century, as evidenced by the Letter of Charlemagne to Offa (796), which is clear in its expectation for the protection of Frankish traders under English law. Stenton referred to this as the 'first commercial treaty in English history', and whilst it might be safer to describe it as the earliest surviving, it provides a context for the burgeoning cross-channel trade of the eighth and ninth century and may reflect a confirmation of a long-standing agreement (Stenton 1971, 221; Chaplais 1981, 31). Given the very interpersonal content of the letter, however (Story 2003, 195–196), it is questionable as to whether it goes far enough to reflect an independent merchant class, rather than a host of delegates operating directly in the commercial interests of the respective royal households. Alfred and Guthrum's Treaty (878) is evidence that the wider freer movement of traders was valued even if, under such fractious circumstances, it came with conditions. Similar arrangements between the Danes and East Frankish Kings (873) illustrate that, in a wider European perspective, it is clear that such trade arrangements and how they related to political boundaries and settlement were considered important (Jankuhn 1982, 37; Keynes and Lapidge 1983, 171–172; Reuter 2013, 69–70). In Ohthere's account of his travels in Scandinavia, the reason he gives for not entering the territory of the *Beormas* of the White Sea, was *for unfriðe* (Lund 1984, 63) and in all of these examples it is important to consider a sliding scale from diplomatic immunity between monopolistic polities engaged in gift-giving to, at the other end, the free movement of people in a market based economy where revenue is raised at the point of exchange.

Chapter 3 outlined some of the main debates concerning the development of the economy in the early medieval period and in the following sections we will set out to explore the contribution that can be made by the evidence from the physical structures in the landscape, and how they are named. A speculative geography of overland middle Anglo-Saxon trade routes will be proposed, albeit based partially on evidence from charter boundary clauses of the tenth and eleventh centuries. The shift in emphasis from a route network concerned with the *here* to one with an increasingly commercial function is evident from the tenth century and in particular, from the appearance of the term *port strǣt* and *port weg*. This shift will be addressed alongside the evidence from the study areas for planned commercial developments in the later Anglo-Saxon period.

The Age of Emporia

Wic herepaths are mentioned on four occasions in the study areas and occur in one incidence outside at Tarrant Hinton, Dorset (Figure 51, east of Iwerne Minster) (S 429). Of the study area examples, in the region of Downton and Salisbury, links to a geography of middle Anglo-Saxon trading sites were indicated (study areas 7 and 8) and the implication here is that the *wic* element should be associated with '*emporium*' rather than the sense of 'specialised farm or building' (Mills 1998, 407). If we took an interpretation of the term to mean 'the herepath for which the specialised farm was responsible', we might expect occurrences of *burh*-, *tun*-, *minster*- and *ham*- herepaths. Some corroboration can also be found in the *wicstrǣte* recorded in the bounds of land granted at Hendon, Middlesex, and the position of this reference suggests an arterial route running in a south-easterly direction towards *Lundenwic* (S 645). It seems likely therefore that the *wic* element reflects a consciousness on the part of Anglo-Saxon boundary surveyors that these routes at some point were used by traders travelling to and from the major *emporia* of the middle Anglo-Saxon period (Figure 51).

From the project study areas, the *wic* herepath observed heading north out of Winchester, from the King's stone (2.2, SU43NE) is feasibly a continuation of the *wic* herepath in the Highclere and Burghclere bounds on the Hampshire and Berkshire border (SU45NE), reflecting the fact that they both refer to a north–south aligned route connecting Winchester to Oxford and the upper Thames (discussed in more detail below) (S 487; S 565; S 680). The reference from outside the study areas, at Tarrant Hinton, is to a route running roughly parallel to the modern Salisbury to Blandford road (S 429; Grundy 1938, 83). The boundary marks of this clause are particularly well suited to the topography of the present parish boundary and it makes the placement of this *wic* herepath fairly certain (Grundy 1938, 82–86). However, vestiges of this route beyond the parish are difficult to trace and all that can really be said of the short stretch that is identifiable is that it runs on a west-south-west/east-north-east axis with Dorchester as a likely destination.

Figure 51 also depicts the locations of certain 'chapman' place-names that have occurred within the study areas but also some that are known from beyond. The rationale for including these is based, in part, on their apparent relationship to the *wic* herepaths but also because, as we saw in Chapter 3, the term appears in surviving law codes from the seventh century. In Hloþære and Eadric's code of *c.* 685–686, we are told of *cepeman* whose host must hold surety for them if they have stayed for three nights in his home. *Ceapmanna* occur in Ine and Alfred's law codes and the context of them travelling *uppe on londe* (inland) suggests that these were groups who plied their trade on overland routes.

In the study areas there is a record of a *chypmanna ford* in the charter granting one hide of land at Laverstock (S 543) and the same phrase appears as a fourteenth-century place-name – *Chepmannesford* – at the point where the Harroway crosses the Bourne Rivulet (1.2 SU44NW) (Gover 1961, 155). *Ceapmanna* are also mentioned in three other boundary clauses. There is a reference to a *cipemanna dene* in a set of bounds outside the study areas for land in Maddington, Wiltshire (S 1589), and a *ceapmanna del* is recorded in a boundary clause for Crux Easton, Berkshire (1.2, SU45NE). Further evidence

FIGURE 51 *(opposite)*. Wic herepaths and chapmen place names (contains OS data © Crown copyright (2018)).

10. Bridges, herepaths, trade routes and the king's peace

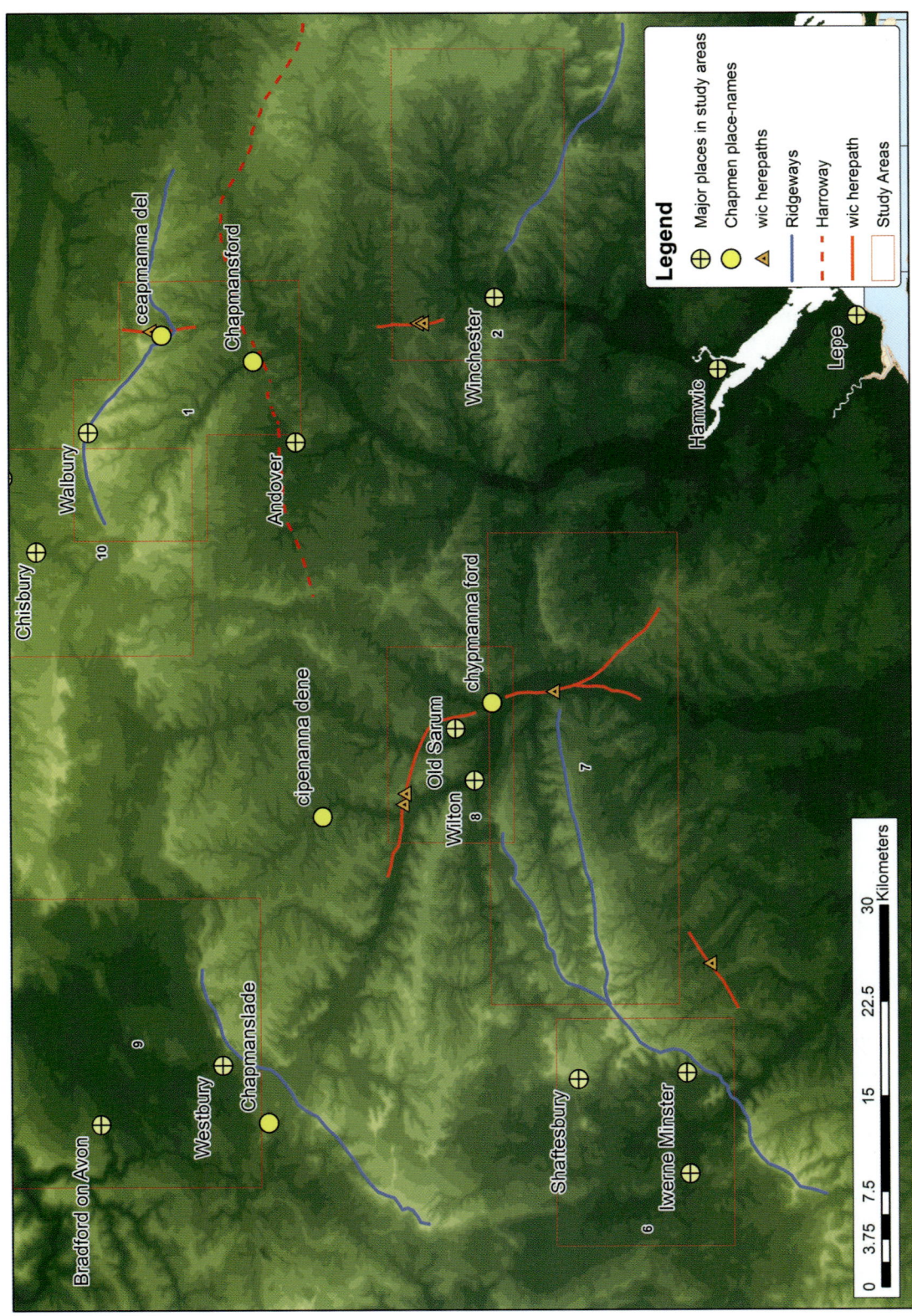

from the period comes in the form of the *ceap manna wyllan* recorded in the Pershore charter (S 786; Stokes 2008) and early place-name records exist for Chapmanslade (*Chipmannesled* 1245) and a *Chapmannescumb* (1327) which has been identified in the parish of Bicknoller, Somerset (Gover *et al.* 1939, xli, 147; Margary 1973, I, 99, 116–117). This does not represent an exhaustive search for *ceapman* place-names and it may be that a more detailed review of the place-name volumes yields more examples. But caution needs to be advised. We saw from the discussion in study area 5 that Chapman's Pool on the Isle of Purbeck, recorded in a tenth-century charter as *schort mannes*, may have its origins in a fourteenth-century local surname and this seems to be the case for the hamlet of Chapmans Well, St Giles on the Heath, Devon, which is 'probably' to be associated with the family of Walter *Chepman* (1330) (Gover *et al.* 1931, 164).

There is, of course, the reverse possibility that the personal names are derived from the names of the places from which they hail, but topographical evidence, and in particular proximity to significant routes, can be brought to bear on the discussion. The *Chep(e)manrewe* recorded in the tithing of Westbury (1476–1500), is the name of a street in Sherborne, Dorset (The 'row belonging to the merchants', Mills 1989, 365). A Chapman's Pit, Kent (TQ 97185917), recorded as the location of an early Saxon inhumation cemetery, is situated on a route believed to be of early medieval date running north to an important middle Anglo-Saxon central place at Faversham (Tatton-Brown 2001, 125; Brookes 2007). Chapmanslade sits on the Bath/Warminster/Old Sarum road, a route considered by Ivan Margary as having likely early origins (Margary 1973, I, 99, 116–117). The *ceap manna wyllan* of the Pershore charter is at a location marking the crossing of the River Avon of a direct route from Worcester to London, and the *Chapmannescumb*, Bicknoller, sits on the main route running south-east out of Watchet in the direction of Taunton (with Ilminster, Crewkerne and Dorchester beyond).

Considering the function of these chapman place-names, it is interesting to note that none of them go on to become towns. Here they differ from the various place-names that retain the *chipping-* element such as Chipping Barnet, Chipping Campden, Chipping Norton, Chipping Ongar, where it is thought to be indicative of pre-Conquest market places (Harmer 1950, 335; and see also 'chupyncliue' (1289), the name that once referred to Shaftesbury's Gold Hill, Mills 1989, 145). A key difference in the *chipping-* and *chapman-* element is that the former are nearly always compounded with a readily formed place-name suggesting that the market function was a secondary designation to an existing settlement. In the character of the slade, the dene, the dell, the pit, the well, the pool and the combe, we have landscape locations that are non-settlement related. They are more indicative of sheltered places and raise some important questions about the character of trade in Anglo-Saxon Wessex and beyond. If we are only prepared to consider these places as active at the time they first appear in the charter evidence of the tenth century, we should perhaps, given the emphasis on the legal restriction of trade to the burhs in the first half of this century, see them only as way-stations; overnight pit-stops for an itinerant merchant class. But if these place-names are vestiges of an earlier eighth and ninth geography of trade and exchange, they might provide some insight into the exchange dynamics between the coastal *emporia* and their hinterlands (Palmer 2003; Costen and Costen 2016). In either case, however, these places potentially tell us something about the manner in which trade developed, more broadly, in the early middle ages. In an economy seen as being almost exclusively initiated, stimulated and controlled by royal, lordly and ecclesiastical interests, we might expect the associated merchant class to have enjoyed the hospitality of their patrons (as we see, for example, in the law code of Hlothære and Eadric). But these apparent roadside camps appear to reflect independence on the part of the trading community and they are reminiscent of the 'niches for self-determined action' that Joachim Henning saw as so crucial to the emergence of free-market activities and the urban economy (2007, 31). Equally, they may form a landlocked parallel to Martin Carver's 'germs of merchant initiative and enterprise', glimpsed, 'in the creek sites of northern coasts' (Carver 2015, 12). Elsewhere it has been suggested that such 'middlemen' – groups who sit outside of the strictures of the majority group's networks and social bonds – are what form the basis for a model of neutral exchange that does not have an impact on, nor is it impacted by, social ties and concepts of honour and prestige (Zenner 1986, 118). Whatever the driver in this 'liberated entrepreneurial phase' conducted by 'independent merchants and workers who traded or practiced a trade for a profit' (Verhulst 1999, 56), it is posited to have occurred in the ninth century in Northern Europe and has been recognised as 'the most important stage in early medieval urban development' (Carver 2015, 13).

Whether legally sanctioned or not, trade may have occurred at these chapmen sites given that they are all in very accessible places. For example, the crossroads location of the *ceapmanna dell*, at the place where the North Hampshire Downs ridgeway crosses the major north–south route from Winchester to Oxford (1.2 SU45NE), stands out as an excellent place for officials to ride out to, in accordance with Ine's laws, to bear witness to transactions. A range of evidence vouches for the vibrancy of a trade route in the early medieval period connecting Winchester (and *Hamwic*) to the south with Oxford and the Upper Thames Valley to the north. In the tenth century the interests of the Old Minster, Winchester in property at *Clere* (Highclere) may reflect a desire to provide a way-station *en route* to the emerging urban centre at Oxford within which it went on, in Domesday Book, to be recorded as having nine *messuages* (S 383; S 565; DB Oxf. B8). That this way-station and thus the need to travel this route was important to the bishops of Winchester as early as the mid-eighth century, is suggested by a charter claiming ownership of the same estate in 749. The location alone on this significant trade route may be a point in favour of this charter which, in its surviving format, although containing clear interpolations, is thought by some commentators to be broadly legitimate in its record of the transaction (S 258; Finberg 1964, 217–218; Yorke 1982, 81).

In study area 8 attention was drawn to the relationship that the *wic* herepaths around the Salisbury area had to a regression analysis distribution of *Hamwic*'s Series H *sceattas* (Metcalf 2003, 41, fig. 4.1). The north–south route from *Hamwic* to the Upper Thames is very clearly articulated through coin finds along its course and in places, these have led commentators to speculate on a possible trade route connecting the two regions. In particular, *Sceatta* coin finds of a type U and J recovered from excavations in *Hamwic* indicate links with a minting place in the Upper Thames Valley (Metcalf 1988, 21–22; 1994, 559). A coin of Offa from Radcot Bridge, comparable with an Offa penny from the site of Martyr's Memorial in Oxford, is also said to indicate this route (Blair 1988c, 223, fig. 90; 1992). Furthermore, Series J *sceattas* – probably originating from the Oxford area – recovered from excavation and metal detecting at Winchester again re-affirm this link with the Upper Thames Valley (Ulmschneider 2000, 43). North of Winchester the likely course of the route is indicated by a silver Frisian *sceatta* and a coin of Offa found near Cranbourne Clump, Wonston, Sutton Scotney (Ulmschneider 2000, 167). Katharina Ulmschneider has suggested that this route may have lead *via* Walbury Camp where a die-linked *sceatta* of Series U type was recovered (Ulmschneider 2000, 100), although it is more likely that this find is indicative of an east–west aligned route, following the course of the North Hampshire Downs ridgeway, discussed above and referred to variously as a *via publica*, herepath and *street*, with its crossing of the Oxford to Winchester route at the site of the *ceapmanna dell*. Even the early importance of Abingdon as an ancient minster site and royal *vill*, before the establishment of an abbey in the mid-tenth century, is thought to be dependent on a major trade route linking the Midlands with Southampton (Rumble 1980, 13).

More widely in Hampshire, the distribution of *Sceatta* coin finds seems to confirm a geography of inland trade restricted to a few major routeways. St Catherine's Hill yielded five continental *sceattas* and other high-status metalwork. The site of an Iron Age hillfort, it is very well connected with the major prehistoric ridgeways of the South and Hampshire Downs and, in sitting just outside of the walls of the Roman city of Winchester, it also enjoyed the access provided by the Roman road network. Two *sceattas* from Warnford, where the South Downs Ridgeway crosses the Meon, two from Twyford, a further two from Otterbourne where the Roman road forks and finally three from *Clausentum* are all tied into this early geography of exchange in middle Anglo-Saxon Hampshire (Ulmschneider 2000, 90–91, 100). Part of Ulmschneider's assessment of the archaeological evidence for the middle Anglo-Saxon material from Hampshire is organised around major routeways. She considers the Wey Valley, the 'Great Northern Ridgeway', the Winchester/Silchester Roman road, the Ports Down Ridgeway, the Chichester/Bitterne Roman road and the South Downs Ridgeway recognising the equal, if not greater impact that prehistoric ridgeways had over Roman roads in the distribution of archaeological material of the middle Anglo-Saxon period (Ulmschneider 2000, 45–48).

This undoubtedly represents a future avenue of enquiry – to explore the exact routes by which middle Anglo-Saxon coinage found itself distributed throughout Wessex. In some of the study areas attention was drawn to where single coin finds of the seventh and eighth centuries were thought to indicate a node on the network of overland trade and the example of Lazarton (6.2), at the foot of Hod Hill, stands out as a very good candidate for what may be as good as it gets as far as a West Saxon 'productive' site is concerned. The place-name element *hōd* meaning 'shelter' aligns the location well with the kinds of landscape locations favoured by our chapmen and crucially, the proximity to a major ridgeway connecting Wilton with Dorchester indicates another viable middle Anglo-Saxon overland route. In Chapter 1, John Blair's theoretical map of inland trans-shipment routes was reviewed (Figure 7) and from it, we can now take the evidence from this research project to indicate some of the exact courses traders between the south coast and the Thames may have taken. The first of Blair's theoretical routes to be addressed is the proposed north–south route from the Itchen estuary to the Thames at Oxford and the references to *wic* herepaths on exactly this course are the clearest indication of this major overland route. A parallel north–south route from the mouth of the Hampshire Avon to the Cricklade/Lechlade stretch of the Thames is also possible, passing through the Salisbury Basin and heading due north. Again, a *wic* herepath is referred to on this course. Finally, the exact routes taken by Blair's suggested trade between Dorchester and London can be suggested by the evidence from the Lazarton site or the *wic* herepath referred to in the bounds of Tarrant Hinton (Blair 2007a, 18, fig. 5). In fact, that this latter route travelled to Dorchester and beyond may force us to consider the possibility that Wyke Regis (*Wike* in 988 and *Kingeswik* in 1242), with its proximity to the natural landing ground of Chesil Beach and harbour of Weymouth Bay, is so named because, like Swanage (*Swanawic*) it represents the location of a middle Anglo-Saxon trading site and not the site of a 'dairy-farm' (S 938; Ekwall 1947, 515; Mills 1977, 267).

Together with the references to chapmen and *wic*-herepaths, the evidence (albeit at this stage selective) from coins and the key role that ridgeways appear to have played in this period, we can tentatively begin to construct an earlier geography of trade in the *Age of Emporia* – but more work needs to be done.

Changes in trading and the emergence of the 'port'

One particular term that concerns traders and trading in the early medieval world is the word 'port'. Whilst the Latin *portus* refers to a harbour, in the Anglo-Saxon sense of the word it can relate to an urban centre of trade at a coastal or inland location and by the eleventh century it had become almost synonymous with the word burh (Tait 1936, 25, 27; Britnell 1996, 12). Unlike *cyping* and *ceapman*, *port* only appears to have been more widely used from the tenth century (Sawyer 1981, 158–162). It features in the laws first in a code of Edward the Elder where *na man ne ceapige butan porte* (no one shall trade except in a port) and later in the laws of King Æthelstan where *ðe mon ceapige butan porte* (one is not to buy outside a port), reiterated again when we are informed *þæt ælc ceaping sy binnon port* (that all trading shall be carried on in a port) (I Ed. 1, II As. 12, 13.1; Attenborough 1922, 114–115, 134–135). There is evidence from the study areas and from examples taken from outside that helps contribute to our understanding of *port*s and their role in the late Saxon economy.

In the charter boundary clause evidence, the compounding of *port* with *strǣts* or *wegs* appears only in documents dated to 960 or after (Cooper 2002, 60, n. 140). Its first association with a routeway, however, can be found in a grant of land made by King Eadwig on the River Nadder to the immediate south-west of Wilton (956 × 959), where the bounds are recorded as running along *þes port her paðes* (S 586). This route is one that runs along the valley from Wilton out to Barford St Martin where it crosses the Nadder and heads due west-south-west to Shaftesbury. In a later charter for land at Ditchampton, immediately alongside the above estate, the same route is referred to as a *port weg* (S 1010). From the study areas, a single instance of a *port strǣt*, and the fact that it occurs in the same location as an earlier herepath (2.2 SU53SW), is another indication that the terminology used to refer to such routes in the Wessex landscape was changing to reflect the emphasis-shift away from routes designated and maintained to counter the threat posed by the *here* to routes that were increasingly taking on a commercial character and an emerging legal status concerned with the protection of trade provided by the king. Alan Cooper's justification for projecting back into the Anglo-Saxon period the legal definition assigned in the *Leges Henrici Primi* to the *via regia* as a route that runs from burh to burh is based on Edward the Elder and Æthelstan's restriction of trade to royal boroughs (I Ew 1; II As 13, 13.1). As we have seen above, the notions of *frið*, *þeod* and the concept of a state-sanctioned peace are all prevalent in late Anglo-Saxon Wessex and as the term herepath slipped into obsolescence so too does the *port weg/strǣt* change in character. This is best indicated by two stand-alone boundary clauses from the archive of Malmesbury Abbey that, as post-Conquest perambulations (though attached to copies of earlier charters), represent the very tail end of the Anglo-Saxon charter boundary clause tradition. In both perambulations two separate routes radiating out from the burh at Malmesbury, routes bearing all the characteristics of our early herepaths and *port wegs*, are referred to as *kingswei* and *kingsweye* respectively and give a final indication of the process of evolution that the early medieval route network had undergone from the ninth through to the twelfth century (S 1577 and S 1585).

In this later shift, however, a critical link between trade and peace is made and the institution of kingship can be seen as arguably central to the promulgation of both to meet one in the same ends. The degree to which late Anglo-Saxon kings are either responding to rising societal wealth or actively setting out to achieve it, is a debate that to explore in any detail is beyond the scope of this chapter. However, what seems clear from the evidence is that a concerted effort to structure the late Anglo-Saxon landscape of Wessex is being made in the interests of a market economy, one that is characterised by 'price-making markets', where producers are incentivised to increase output (Hill 1978b, 217; Jones 1993, 658). We see this most clearly in the concept of the *port* and the use of this term in particular prompts us to consider how much a Roman imperial ideal permeated the thinking of tenth-century kingship. Should we see the *port*-related features of the Anglo-Saxon landscape as indicators of a wider project to stimulate or respond to a growing economy? Of course, this classical idea does not necessarily need to have derived from a first-hand knowledge of the wealth of the Roman Empire as a consequence of the *Pax Romana*. Much closer evidence of the role of the *portus* could be found in the example set by Carolingian Francia in the eighth and ninth centuries where the *portus* sat second in a three-tiered exchange network that had estate centres at its base and the large monopolistic *emporia* at its summit (Verhulst 2000, 105–120; Wickham 2005, 803–805). In comparing eighth- and ninth-century East Anglia with contemporary *Francia*, Grenville Astill has suggested that the lack of *portus* may indicate that the scale of economy on the Frankish model could not be supported in England till the ninth or tenth century (Astill 2011, 266–267). A key aspect to the Carolingian *portus* was its administrative role in an increasingly complex state machinery, and arguably, it is only in the wake of the burh building campaigns of the ninth and early tenth centuries that state development in the south of England at least, can be seen to have reached that level of complexity (Astill 2006, 235). This is when the notion of the *port* appears in the documentary sources for Anglo-Saxon England and a case must exist therefore for an attempted importation of an urban model by the Anglo-Saxon kings.

The Salisbury basin study area allows us to explore the success of this policy in terms of founding a lasting urban centre. The topographical evidence for an earlier settlement and trading focus centred on the crossroads at St Thomas's Church was discussed in study area 8. From the evidence provided by Domesday Book and from various documentary references made in the twelfth century, it seems clear that there were already two 'Old Salisburies' in existence prior to the apparent founding of the new city in 1220 (Langlands 2014). Problems arise in attempting to identify these references with the possible sites, in particular the Salisbury 'market' from which the tolls were granted to the church at Salisbury in 1130 (Crittal 1962, 51–53). However, a *Portwey*, recorded first in 1364, on the line of the Silchester to Old Sarum Roman road can be seen to extend beyond the east gate of the Iron Age hillfort to the southern entrance of a plan-form that morphologically bears similarities to those of the *burghal* foundations at Cricklade, Wareham and Wallingford. The morphology of the Salisbury site and its proximity to an earlier set of earthworks is reminiscent of a similar scenario proposed for Avebury – although on a much grander scale (Reynolds 2001). This evidence supports David Hill's assertion that the burh or 'town' of *Searobyrg* was outside the walls of the hillfort, but it indicates a degree of planning and ambition that is perhaps ill-fitted to the 'emergency burh' moniker that it has been labelled with (Hill 1978b, 223).

Old Sarum has gone on to become the classic example of a 'rotten borough' but exactly when this place 'failed', despite the best efforts of tenth-century kings to coerce trade into its walls, is ultimately dependent on whether we accept the case for an earlier settlement focus – perhaps minster related – at the location of St Thomas's Church and the later medieval market place of Salisbury's cathedral city (presented in study area 8). It is re-iterated here that elsewhere studies have suggested that the success of towns in the tenth to eleventh centuries was dependent on existing communications and minsters founded in the eighth and ninth centuries (Palmer 2003, 50). Furthermore, as Grenville Astill has written, it is the older, pre-burh pattern of trading and assembly places that, 'despite royal efforts to the contrary, continued to determine the social and economic relationships of the majority of the population' (Astill 2006, 254). Taking a much longer-term perspective on the urban developments of the Salisbury Basin therefore, one which embraces a trajectory from the seventh to the thirteenth century, it might be argued that ultimately, the trading site at the major crossroads prescribed by east–west and north–south routes past the church of St Thomas won out as the place eventually settled on as the major market for the region – as it remains today. Crucially in this discussion, it is the evidence from the topography and toponymy of routes that allows us to explore some of these processes in more depth in a landscape context.

Study area 1 established that the Roman road from Silchester to Old Sarum had fallen out of use, at least the stretch as far as Andover. But between Andover and Old Sarum, it is questionable whether this stretch, the stretch that went on to be recorded as the *Portwey* in the fourteenth century, remained in constant use from the Roman period through to the tenth century (when it presumably took the *port* association). Is it the case that, like the Roman roads from Winchester to Silchester and the course of Watling Street between the River Medway and London, the Old Sarum *portway* was also a late Anglo-Saxon re-instatement (Fasham 1981, 171–172; Tatton-Brown 2001, 121–122)? Certainly, when we consider the route by which trade will have moved between study area 1 and study area 8, the line of the ridgeway, and the course of the later medieval road is the most obvious candidate of assured passage between the two with the Chapmansford of study area 1 and the *chypmanna ford* of the Laverstock charter making up two crossing points on a route that ultimately connected London to Dorchester via the Salisbury Basin and Andover. This raises the possibility that the setting out of the *portway* may have been as much at the behest of royal instigation as the laying out of the conjectural burh at the foot of Old Sarum. It may be significant that Æthelstan's *Grately Code*, an 'impressive piece of legislation' (Keynes 1990, 237) and the 'major "official" statement of his reign' (Wormald 1999, 300) was the result of an assembly held on the course of this *portway* between Old Sarum and Andover. Concerned with coinage, minting and the functioning of boroughs, this was a law code set out by one of Anglo-Saxon England's most European-minded kings and it seems credible that the physical edifices of a past great civilisation might be seen, in a show of power to the gathered dignities, to be reinvested with the greatness they enjoyed at the high-point of the Roman *imperium* (Lavelle 2005, 161–162).

CONCLUSION

Wessex and the early medieval world beyond

The case studies presented in this book are of the most detailed and local variety and whilst the discussion in Part 3 has broadened to encompass a regional perspective, it is in the following pages that Wessex itself is presented as a case study, and as a model, for the analysis of the relationship between routes of communication and wider social and political developments across north-western Europe in the early medieval period. Whilst it can always be argued that the south of present day England in the early middle ages was subject to particular and unique circumstances, ones within which Wessex as a political and economic entity emerged, like all other areas of north-western Europe, it was subject to the same broader waves of influence: the northward trajectory of the cross in the sixth and seventh centuries, the zenith of an inter-regional maritime economy in the eighth century, the instability brought about by raiding in the ninth century and the increasing centralisation of power – royal, church and state – in the tenth century. Wessex was also part of a northern European cultural milieu that saw classical ideals blended with Christian practice, interwoven with Germanic custom and radiating out from a Carolingian core. Perhaps most significantly, however, like its neighbours, Wessex's greatest inheritance was a landscape that had been occupied, worked and exploited, and at times more densely so, in the five to six centuries leading up to the period that is the subject of this book. It is hoped therefore that in the studies presented here there is a model – a hypothetical springboard – that can be applied to other analogous areas of northern Europe and beyond. In the first instance, it is entirely appropriate to confirm what many scholars have suspected all along: that it was anything but 'oceans of mud' (Harrison 2004, 222–223) that lay between the places that the Anglo-Saxons of Wessex travelled to and from. The physical means by which people, goods and ideas moved around the early medieval landscape was clearly comprised of a dense network of purposeful routes, proficiently managed so that people of all classes were denied the inconvenience of 'blundering through trackless woods' (Hill 1981, 115) in their need to go about their business. It seems reasonable, therefore, to suggest that the same could be said of Wessex's neighbours and other comparable political and economic entities across early medieval Europe. We should clearly afford ourselves a much less bleak picture of the standards of medieval roads than the popular perception of them allows.

The *via publica* and early medieval roads

There are risks inherent in setting out a Whiggish narrative that charts the changes and developments over time as progressive steps in the direction of the complex, well-ordered and well-administered road network of the later medieval period and beyond, one that by the eleventh century at least was fit for the hypothetical, if questionable, Anglo-Saxon state of the 'maximum' variety. Of this later period, it is often assumed – explicitly and implicitly – that the 'maintenance of roads' is on-going (Maddicott 2010, 18; Sawyer 2013, 182, 105, 231–232), but there is little attempt to systematically address the evidence for work on the actual communications nor, more critically, the dynamic interplay between those that would have them built and maintained and those that would wish to use them. For James Campbell's agents and agencies, the 'maintenance of communications' is seen as essential, yet the discussion is framed only around the evidence for particular offices and ranks charged with the administrative duty of maintaining verbal and written communications throughout the kingdom (Campbell 2000, 218–222). The physical means of communicating – the routeways – and the underpinning social structures required to ensure their upkeep, elements over which the historical sources for the Anglo-Saxon period remain silent, are glossed over.

Understandably, in the scholarship of this period, the classical age and all of its ideas loom large. P.H. Sawyer might be ambitious in his back-projection of the tradition of the four great royal or public roads as 'another feature deriving from the Roman past' (Sawyer 2013, 182) especially if 'the English Kingdoms apparently failed to retain, or to re-institute, Roman concepts of a public obligation to maintain public roads' (Brooks 2002, 14). How does this potential continuity (or discontinuity) become tangible in the evidence, and what are the implications? The reception of classical ideas in the early medieval period was a driver in so many social, political and cultural movements that it is difficult not to see some ambition in the works of Christian polities to reinvest their own frameworks of understanding and practice with Roman legislation, institutions and accoutrements of power, all backed up by the omnipresent magnitude of the remnant physical structures of that age: 'marvellous masonry', 'the works of giants', 'the city crumbled', 'on this bright city … stone buildings stood', and so on (selected lines from 'The Ruin', taken from the translation in Hamer 2015, 3–7). Whilst these elements of design – working towards something in the future, modelled on the past – must have been there amongst the culturally refined rich and powerful, it is equally important to consider elements of circumstance in the grubby business of actually getting an early medieval polity to function. Classical ideas can prove a useful set of tools with which to legitimise control and centralised power, both in the medieval past and in contemporary scholarship of it. On military obligations, for example, whether as novel impositions or timeless burdens, much is made of the legacy of the Roman past (*e.g.* Brooks 1971 on S 92). The reality – the *circumstance* of the age – however, especially when routes of communication are concerned, may have been very different. Alan Cooper's work has consistently and effectively demonstrated the presence, in the later Anglo-Saxon period, of ideas of freedom of movement, of the highway as the King's property and of protection afforded to those who used it (Cooper 2000; 2002; 2016). Had we the sources, we might be able to push these concepts further back and demonstrate an unbroken lineage with the legacy of Rome. Herein lies a critical issue. What genuinely continues from the late Roman period, in institutional form, and what is ideological *renovatio*? Is Bede's comment on the state of travelling overland in Edwin's reign (*HE* Bede II. 16), for example, a reflection of ancient tradition or is this a device employed in the aggrandisement of Edwin as a powerful Christian ruler moulded in the classical idiom? Given the hypothesis put forward by John Blair (2005, 256–261), the presence of early land-locked minsters must be taken as indications of functioning routeways, ones potentially with a form of 'public' status, enjoying the same levels of royal protection as the minster itself. In these and later cases, however, is this really all about re-instating (or maintaining) the *via publica* and all that comes with it in the minds of the late Roman jurists? It is likely that a complex blend of obligation (classically defined or not), personal gain and necessity was at play. There was, perhaps, no one 'obligation' but a multiplicity of negotiated positions within which labour was brought together for mutual gain. Was Glastonbury Abbey forced to undertake the *sordida munera* of bridge construction in order to complete the Street causeway or was it, given its holdings in the Polden Hills to the south, its willing architect?

There is perhaps a need to see in the more philosophical freedoms – the *frið* – of the later Anglo-Saxon period, an unspoken right to travel, a freedom to move. It is one thing to avoid the crime of *stretebroche*, actively inhibiting movement by 'breaking' the street, it is quite another facilitating it via improved river crossings and road surfaces. Somewhere in between, early medieval roads happened. Much has been made in this study of the king's highways – those 'burh to burh' routes – of the fundamental connections they had with the control of trade, and the role of royal protection in ensuring their efficacy. But what of one's right to visit one's daughter, recently married to the farm steward in the neighbouring valley, one's right to drive one's sheep on to one's summer pastures and the right to transport timber from the common wood to the home farm? Highways alone could not have provided for the multiplicity of movements in early medieval life.

Easement is the right of non-possessory use of another's property – a concept first developed in 1913 by Beatrice and Sydney Webb in *The Story of the King's Highway* (1913, 5). In this context, the medieval road – in particular the king's highway – was as much a conception as it was a physical reality. Function over structure allows an abstract and more flexible consideration about passageway (Allen and Evans 2016, 6–8). But how, in reality, does 'right of passage' impact upon the physical structures of the landscape constituted to deal with travellers and traders of all kinds? Without wishing to challenge the stress on the importance of passageway as a notion, it implicitly places the burden of maintenance on those who would not wish for the trampling of their corn, the breaking of their fences, and ingress onto meadow pasture should the road become impassable. Surfaces, bridges, causeways and enclosing fences would all have played a role in constraining and controlling, whilst at the same time ameliorating passage and easement. So there are risks in getting swept up in establishing what of early medieval practice can be seen to be based on classical ideas irrespective of whether these can be proved to have continued unbroken from the early fifth century or whether they are a re-introduction at the hands of Christian learning after the sixth. In early medieval Ireland, a region that resisted the conquest of the Roman legions, it is clear that roads were to be regularly cleaned, ditches re-cut, brash removed from the surface and pot-holes made good. There was also a hierarchy of roads, derived from the terms used to describe them, and that certain roads, and those who travelled on them, enjoyed the protection of the king (Doherty 2015). There is no need here to seek classical precedence. There is a sense of something deeper in these obligations, an undercurrent that runs below what we might consider to be 'Roman' and one that is very likely prehistoric, and better indexed to scales of social organisation and political order (Brookes and Reynolds 2011). These sentiments, especially concerning the units of assessment that ultimately would have been used to levy the labour, 'not quite impossibly, have had an ancestry extending back to the Iron Age kingdoms of the time of Caesar' (Campbell 1995, 45). Nicholas Brooks also concedes that major bridge building projects would have been a factor in earlier societies and that 'some system of bridgework, involving the felling, cutting and transporting of huge quantities of timber and the mobilisation of a substantial workforce, is [therefore] likely to have existed in the pre-Roman Iron Age in Britain, as in Gaul (Brooks 2002, 14).

Critically, it is clearly no longer credible to employ the familiar network of Roman roads as a means to illustrate our maps of early medieval phenomena and less still to provide meaningful commentary on the distributions of archaeological, toponymic and historical data. It is abundantly clear from the study areas, as well as from studies made elsewhere, that these roads were of a specific type and they alone simply do not do justice to what must have a been a highly complex network of routes functioning at all levels – many of which must surely have been in existence in the late Iron Age and beyond. The iconic inter-*civitates* straight Roman roads in Britain were subject to variable rates of survival from the second to the eleventh centuries. This circumstance must be considered in other areas of the post-Roman world. Furthermore, there is the distinct possibility that some Roman roads were 'reborn' as part of a conscious strategy of urban development in the later Anglo-Saxon period – one that made use of the political gain that comes with re-instating the physical edifices of a past great age. By examining the distributions and courses of routeways referred to as streets, *via publica*, and 'old' herepaths, and by plotting occurrences of stones and stone posts, we can explore in more depth the legacy of the classical period on the early medieval landscape of movement and by adopting this approach over a wider study area, and integrating archaeological evidence, we will be in a position to provide a data set hugely significant in its importance to our understanding of continuity and change from the late Roman through to the late Anglo-Saxon periods in a model which may serve well other parts of Europe.

Herepaths, portways and an age of infrastructure

Of early medieval routes the charter boundary clauses provide evidence for a rich variety of character and function. Hay ways, salt ways, wood ways, the mill way, the horse path, the butter mere, the 'smear' gate, oxen bridge and the stone way are just some examples that indicate the uses such routes had in service to the agrarian economy. That they were at times narrow, green, broad, hollow, foul and muddy indicates relative levels of usability. Of the distinctly Anglo-Saxon routes though, one term stands out in particular and this is the ubiquitous herepath. The evidence presented here points distinctly towards a herepath being a particular road with a particular function and subject to a particular set of laws and maintenance. The uniformity of purpose around Winchester in the east and Crediton in the west, and the manner in which they connect up Anglo-Saxon places such as burhs, minsters, manors, look-outs and harbours throughout the other study areas, all suggest central instigation and a level of grand design. This study therefore puts forward the notion that herepaths were routes purposely constructed to deal with the threat posed by the raiding *here*. Under a system of corvée labour, this represented a form of military obligation and it may very well be that the burden of 'bridgework' is, in fact, a direct reference to this. Wessex is dominated by chalk and limestone bedrock, both of which are porous and well-draining. It is only really in the river valleys that causeways would have been required to carry traffic safely from the good going on one side of the valley to firm ground on the other, and the 'bridge', the section that actually crosses the running water, would have been only a small part of much bigger engineering projects. The historical sources may be silent on the burden placed on early medieval society in Wessex to repair and maintain roads, but the landscape archaeology speaks. Alan Cooper's analysis of charter bounds (Cooper 2006, 15), place-names and narrative evidence draws the conclusion that 'the great period of the building of bridges' lay in the later Anglo-Saxon period (*i.e.* post-AD 900). Yet, archaeological evidence very clearly suggests that early medieval polities had the engineering capacity to construct substantial bridges and causeways at an earlier period (Durham 1977; Crummy *et al.* 1982; Salisbury 1995; Robinson and Wilkinson 2003; Brunning 2010; Ashwin and Tester 2014, 199). It is suggested here that to explore this proposition further, it is to the herepath network that attention should turn, in order to seek evidence, archaeological and topographical for, the *pontium stratarumque* ('rural street bridges') and the origins of bridges as civil projects.

For example, the substantial clay embankment and causeway recovered at St Aldates, Oxford, may in fact have been part of the same highway 'project' observed in the references to the *wic* herepath in the corridor of the modern day A34 between Oxford and Winchester. It is not disputed that substantial and significant bridge building endeavours were undertaken in the tenth and eleventh centuries, as the West Saxon dynasty ramped up and extended the burghal project both internally and throughout the newly-conquered territories to the north. But we should be wary about allowing the survival of historical evidence to create a centre of gravity in the later tenth century, pulling in to that period any proposed period of bridge building, and all that it tells us about the political and administrative capacity of the embryonic Anglo-Saxon state. For the age that gave us Offa's Dyke and Wansdyke, there should be no reason to suppose that polities were incapable of extremely large-scale civil projects. Above all else, James Campbell has argued, it is the titanic scale of Offa's Dyke that supports the possibility that there existed complex government in the eighth century: 'much of what is so remarkable about the late Anglo-Saxon state not impossibly has its origins in a past which extends far beyond our written records' (Campbell 1995, 44). There should also be no reason to suspect that more minor projects – composite causeway and bridge constructions – were not being carried out on estates, and inter-connecting urban centres, in the eighth and ninth centuries.

As far as the origins of the herepath system are concerned, the issue is blighted by the familiar bias of having an ever-greater number of documentary sources towards the end of the period and the subsequent temptation to allow this to reflect an introduction and increase in real terms. It is unfortunate in this context that the earliest surviving lengthy Old English boundary clause in original (or near original) form is also the first reliably dated appearance the term herepath makes in the documentary record (S 298). If a significant corpus of detailed boundary clauses without reference to herepaths existed for the period running up to the South Hams charter, we might be able to postulate an introduction of the herepath system broadly contemporary with the first appearance of the *trinoda necessitas* in West Saxon charters of the mid-ninth century. But this is not the case. A very clear avenue of future research would consist of mapping herepath data (both from charter boundary clauses and from place-names) to further understand the character of the system and how it operated and related to what we know of other infrastructural processes in the landscape of Anglo-Saxon Wessex.

One area where an improved understanding of the herepath network stands to make a significant contribution is in the development of the Anglo-Saxon economy from the eighth through to the eleventh centuries. Crucial to this subject is identifying the dynamic played out between the defensive priorities and economic ambitions of late Anglo-Saxon urbanism. In setting about constructing a better network of routes with which to move goods from the relative insecurity of the manorial setting to the sanctuary of a central refuge, to what extent did Anglo-Saxon elites facilitate the urban and economic developments of the later tenth and eleventh centuries? To what extent from the outset may this have been part of the rationale behind the herepath network? This connection between herepaths and trade is most explicit in the term *wic* herepath which, if it is a survival from the eighth century, provides us with an early link between protecting routes and commercial functions. The speculative geography of eighth-century trade presented here has been based, not only on the references to *wic* herepaths, but also on references to 'chapmen', and through the selective analysis of numismatic evidence. Extending this methodology over other study areas – and more comprehensively over Wessex – will allow further elucidation of the lines of communication between the places of production, trade and settlement in eighth-century Wessex. This will only help us further to explore some current themes: the lack of 'productive sites' in the kingdom, the impact of limited water transport in the region, the distributional regression of coinage and the character of trade in Wessex. The major Wessex ridgeways clearly had a role to play during this period and the hypothesis that such watershed routes may have been resorted to by eighth-century traders, instead of the higher-maintenance Roman roads, seems to be borne out by the study areas presented in this book. Again, it is only by mapping this information over a wider study area that we can be more confident in identifying the patterns of overland trade in the *Age of Emporia*.

The trade of the ninth century appears to be characterised by the demise of *Hamwic* and a conjectural 'nadir' before clear evidence emerges in the later tenth century for urban occupation in places like Winchester, Oxford and Southampton. Understanding the herepath network may further help us to shed light on the macro-economic shift in the early medieval period from an 'allocative system', one of gift-exchange and institutionalised redistribution, to a system whereby 'commodities were increasingly exchanged for money in price-making markets' (Hill 1978b, 217; Jones 1993, 658). Analysing the route network in particular will contribute to comprehending the processes by which this shift took place in the landscape. It may actually be that the missing wealth of this 'nadir' period can be found in the infrastructural projects that were undertaken at this time, not just the forts that provided economic resilience but also in a network of routes and bridges that allowed for the greater flow of goods between places of production and central refuges. We might therefore posit an 'Age of Infrastructure', instigated, administered and governed by elites but with the complicity of a self-determined people with an appetite for trade and exchange and the social standing and personal advancement it brings about. Understanding the changes and developments in the network of overland trade routes from the eighth through to the tenth century will allow us to commentate further on the dynamic between top-down royal instigation and the endogenous processes of growth.

As a result of their overstressing in the documentary sources, there has been a tendency in debate over the early medieval economy to place an emphasis on luxury goods exchange. Whilst this may be a form of trade that allows us to connect up far-distant polities, and to reconstruct evocative long-distance routes that served as channels for cultural transmission (McCormick 2001, 501–569), it is a form of trade that is increasingly seen to be not economically significant (Wickham 2005, 701). Again, we have perhaps been swayed by the nature of the survival of historical sources because written evidence, across Europe, for anything other than luxury items is scarce and anecdotal. The hay way, wood way and salt way, amongst other functioning routes recorded in Anglo-Saxon charter boundary clauses, are salutary reminders of the importance of bulk goods. Northern Europe experienced a period of intensification in agricultural production and exploitation, possibly beginning in the eighth century but certainly well-underway in the tenth (Astill and Langdon 1997; Oosthuizen 2007; McKerracher 2018), and it has been suggested that increasing opportunities for exchange was a key driver in this process (Wickham 2005, 287–293). Yet, it is incumbent on us to consider, in light of the research presented here, the role played by a maintained network of routeways and the opportunities these presented for the increased movement of bulk goods. For Anglo-Saxon England, the tolls levied in London during the reign of Æthelred II demonstrate the importance of bulk goods – timber, cloth, fish, whale, wine, hens, eggs, cheese and butter (IV Atr 2; Liebermann 1903–1916, vol. 1, 216–270). It was the 'increasingly significant' ordinary, and not luxury trade, that forms the most part of the exchange between southern England and northern Europe at this time (Sawyer 2013, 232).

Chris Wickham sees a later revival of Mediterranean-wide exchange in the centuries after 1000 as a 'spin-off' of regional economies venturing back into interregional exchange as they 'grew more internally complex' (Wickham 2005, 707). Should we consider this internal complexity to be merely institutional and administrative, or is it *physically* infrastructural? Is it as a result of increasingly complex scales of social organisation in eleventh-century Europe generating a capacity amongst polities to enforce and collaborate in a proactive attitude towards the upkeep and maintenance of overland routes? A transport revolution has been proposed for the twelfth century in northern Europe, predicated on the increased use of horse teams with collars, and of four-wheeled wagons that could carry as much as 600 kg of grain 40 km per day (for the English evidence, see Langdon 1984). As a consequence, land routes, rather than rivers, became more attractive to traders and this is seen as contributing to the success of the Champagne and other inland fairs and to the prosperity of some cities that were not on major navigable rivers (Nicholas 2014, 107). Caution was expressed in Chapter 2 over hypothesising an increased use of carts and carting in the later Anglo-Saxon period: there may be more references to carts then but, again, there are more historical sources. There can be no denying, however, that the improvement of river crossings and road surfaces, allowing safe passage for carts, and therefore facilitating the movement of bulk goods, will have had a huge impact on the growth of the economy. Potentially, then, we might begin to chart, as early as the ninth and tenth centuries, the first phases of an economic boom that had its zenith in the twelfth and thirteenth centuries. Cause and effect, political drivers and social stimuli must play a role in the formulation of any economic developmental model, but the mundane issue of a simple increase in capacity must surely occupy a significant place in the way we think about the growth of the early medieval economy. For a modern day parallel, we need look no further than the profound impact containerisation has had on the global trade in material goods (Broeze 2002; Cudahy 2006). Just as the four-wheeled wagon is seen to have been instrumental in the economic growth of the high medieval period (Hindle 2016, 33), so the two-wheeled will have been in an earlier period. Yet, neither would have been possible without the surfaces upon which to use them. These, it can be argued, were brought about in Wessex through the initiation of a herepath network, and it may be that a large part of the 'emergency conversion' Stephen Jones sees as instrumental to the sophistication of the late Anglo-Saxon economy (Jones 1993), can be found in the infrastructural achievements of the ninth century.

In charter evidence of the later tenth and eleventh centuries we start to see the arrival of a new terminology for certain routes. 'Port ways' and 'king's ways' become standard features of the landscape and in general, they corroborate the evidence for a legal campaign restricting trade to certain 'ports' and affording protection to all people whilst on the road. The changes in name (and function) that are proposed here – from herepath to portway to kingsway – are a reflection of wider attitudes to the highway set out most succinctly by Cooper in his most recent discussion of the king's highway. In the eleventh and twelfth centuries there is a shift, brought about by 'claims of special and private rights' perpetuated by 'royal favour', that saw the highway brought into the king's thrall, 'disposable at his will' (Cooper 2016, 50–51). The increasing emphasis placed on the economic function of the route network of Wessex is reflected in the archaeological evidence for urban occupation in the later tenth and eleventh centuries. However, whilst 'king's ways' and 'highways' might be seen to have a longer period of use as terms to describe the status enjoyed by certain routes, running into the twelfth century and beyond, the term 'port way' appears to have a more limited chronological range and one associated with the concept of the Carolingian *portus* and the urban ambitions of tenth- and eleventh-century kings. The mapping, therefore, of 'port ways' on a larger scale, as well as -port place name elements, might very well serve to contribute further to our knowledge of the processes of urbanisation in later Anglo-Saxon Wessex (and beyond). The term 'port' occurs twenty-six times in the boundary clauses. Of these, it is linked most frequently with *strǣt* (S 219; S 567; S 695; S 883; S 909; S 911; S 1003; S 1297; S 1327; S 1342; S 1380 and S 1393), and only four times with 'way' (S 179; S 673; S 858; and S 1010) with the earliest reliable reference coming from the mention to *per port her paðes* in the grant of land to the immediate south-west of Wilton and dating to 956 (for 959, S 586). It does, however, occur frequently as a place-name and the example of the Andover to

Old Sarum *Portway* is one of a number recorded by the fourteenth century. In the study areas alone, the 'port' element in place-names provides interesting insights into town developments in this period. In Shaftesbury, the name given to the road that runs along the spine of the geological outcrop upon which the medieval town sits is 'Bimport', analogous with the lost street name *Bynport* of Malmesbury (Gover *et al.* 1939, 49). Running perpendicular to the High Street and thought to be a derivation from *binnan* and *port* (within the port) (Mills 1989, 145), it is a further indication of the intention for sites of this stature to serve as both a centre of taxable exchange *and* a fortified refuge. There is clearly a need in these examples, to specify exactly what is in the port and what is outside and, therefore, what is legal and what is not according to the law codes of Edward the Elder and Athelstan. Whilst we must remain cautious on suggesting that there may have been, at the point of inception, one eye on the economic potential of the herepath network, in the *portus* project of the tenth-century, reflected in both the physical and historical evidence, there appears very much to be a planned attitude to roads constructed and maintained in service to the economy. So, perhaps we do not need to wait until Edward I's 1285 Statute of Winchester (chapter V), and the Gough Map, before realising an intended 'national system' (Allen 2016, 81–82) that, driven by urbanisation, emphasises the importance of connecting roads between cities, ports and market towns. The evidence presented here suggests that in the tenth-century portway, and possibly the ninth-century herepath, comprehensive networks of routes, serving a nation and its people – such as the þeod-, *frið-* and *folc-* herepaths – existed not only as ideas, but as implemented realities.

From rivers to roads

The macro-economic picture in the late Antique and early to middle Anglo-Saxon period suggests very much that there was an east and west Britain – both facing different economic spheres (Campbell 1996; Cunliffe 2001; Griffiths 2003; Morris 2004, 422–481; Carver 2005, 499–503). This situation was very likely determined by environmental constraints as much as it was by cultural choices and it tells us a huge amount about the nature of communications in this period. The prevailing winds of the open sea and the natural flow of the rivers towards the coast appear to be the key determinants in a geography of trade that saw polities looking outwards, to opportunities across the sea, on distant shores. In many ways this is an indictment of the road network, or at least the ability to move bulk goods overland at this time. Why build a cart, when you can build a boat? Why take your produce via a broken road, across hazardous fords, on an insecure overland route, when you can float it down stream with ease and trade at a coastal *emporium* that connected you either with the bustling trade of the low-countries or the expansive networks of the Atlantic seaboard?

If seafaring is the means by which most people are moving around in the fourth to seventh centuries, then it makes sense of the location of apparently hermitic monastic foundations. Islands such as Iona, Lindisfarne, Tintagel and Skellig St Michael are anything but remote. They are in fact best connected to engage in the economic prosperity of the age. Of Jarrow, for example, Richard Morris comments (2004, 5–8) that the economic viability of the location is played down by the broader culture amongst early medieval scholars – religiously inclined – who had a vested interest in talking up the monastery as a place of solitude and quiet contemplation. Jarrow, in particular, was a monastery perched over the natural harbour of Jarrow Slake at the meeting of major routeways and was, as such, a regional communications hub.

In northern Europe we see the overwhelming importance of rivers in the growth of the economy in the seventh to ninth centuries. Grain would have travelled down the Rhine to the coast, Wine from Orléans to Tours down the Loire, Salt from Metz to Trier down the Moselle. It is the river networks; the Loire, Seine, Meuse, Moselle and Rhine, that are clearly the nexus through which bulk goods are moving with the consequence that trade and exchange in northern Europe was 'more elaborate than anything we have seen in the Mediterranean by 700' (Wickham 2005, 799–800). It is worth observing here that with the exception of the Saône/Rhone, Hérault and Aude, all other major rivers in France flow out to the western and northern seaboards. The greater part of France's land mass is served by rivers that flow west and north – respectively to the Atlantic seaboard and to the North Sea zone.

Bulk goods require a very different form of conveyance than, say, bullion, gold or silver pennies. Thinking through the mechanics of moving bulk goods requires us to consider the differences between travelling over land or via water, be it seaborne, coastal or riverine transportation. As roads were laid down in the ninth and tenth centuries, carts – for which we have good evidence from at least the tenth century onwards (Figure 9) – could have competed with boats, ships, rafts, barges and punts, and as the inter-regional economy shifted from bullion and luxury goods, to regulated coinage and bulk goods, the attraction of overland opportunities may very well have competed with the riverine and coastal connections that had been so vibrant in the eighth century. Landscapes that may have seemed impassable and distant would have been drawn closer, an emerging network of maintained routes acting like draw strings, pulling tight together adjacent territories that had once been distinct. This is the point at which early medieval polities – and Wessex in particular – break with the constraints of natural forces; the prevailing winds, the long-shore drift and the gravitational pull of the river towards the coast. Unification, the creation of an *Angelcynn* was not just a top-down ideological project but an emerging physical reality as an increasing number of people, goods and ideas exploited new opportunities for increased mobility. Cultural, economic and social interactions are the net result of an improved physical means of communication, and in the case of early medieval England, it is these routes that bonded the internal regions in a way they had not been for centuries, playing a vital part in the emergence of a single polity, a people, a nation and an identity.

Appendix

Table 1. Study area 1 charter boundary clauses.

Sawyer catalogue number	Estate name	Date	Beneficiary
S 268	Crux Easton	801	Lulla, *princeps*
S 336	Buttermere and *Æscmere*	863	Wulfhere, *princeps*
S 359	Stoke (St Mary Bourne and Hurstbourne Priors)	900 but composition *c.* 1050 most likely	Winchester Cathedral
S 378	Whitchurch and Ashmansworth	909 suspicious – possible eleventh-century forgery as above	St Peter's, Winchester
S 416	Ham	931	Wulfgar, minister
S 689	Hurstbourne Tarrant	961 but uncertain authenticity (Kelly 2001, 366)	Abingdon Abbey

Table 2. Study area 2 charter boundary clauses.

Sawyer catalogue number	Estate name	Date	Beneficiary
242	Alresford (1)	Tenth-century fabrication (Edwards 1988, 137–38)	Old Minster
273	Martyr Worthy (1)	825 Genuine but reworked (Edwards 1988, 146–48, 150–53)	Old Minster
284	Alresford (2)	Tenth-century fabrication (Edwards 1988, 148)	Old Minster
304	Martyr Worthy (3)	854 although eleventh-century forgery (Keynes and Lapidge 1983, 232–34)	Old Minster
309	Headbourne Worthy	854 Spurious (Keynes 1994, 1122)	Old Minster
340	Martyr Worthy (2)	868 authentic drafted by royal scribe (Keynes 1994, 1124, 1130)	Hunsige, minister
351	Chilland	939 but later forgery (Keynes 1980, 44, footnote 81)	Heahferth, minister
376	Chilcombe	Late tenth forgery (Dumville 1992, 60)	Bishop of Winchester

(Continued)

Table 2. Study area 2 charter boundary clauses. (*Continued*)

Sawyer catalogue number	Estate name	Date	Beneficiary
385	Tichbourne	909	Community at Winchester
444	Beauworth	938	Old Minster
589	Alresford (3)	956	Ælfric, *fidelis*
660	Bighton	959	New Minster
693	Kilmeston	961	Æthelwulf, minister
695	Easton	961	Old Minster
699	Avington	961	Old Minster
942	Hinton Ampner (1)	990	Old Minster
962	Abbots Worthy	1026 but suspicious	Lyfing, Bishop of Crediton
1007	Hinton Ampner (2)	1045	Bishop of Winchester

Table 3. Study area 3 charter boundary clauses.

Sawyer catalogue number	Estate name	Date	Beneficiary
255	Crediton	739 but bounds eleventh century	Bishop Frothhere
387	Wyke in Shobrooke and Thorverton	924 × 939 but inauthentic – eleventh century	SS Mary and Peter, Exeter
389	Stoke Canon	924 × 939 but inauthentic – eleventh century	St Mary's, Exeter
405	Sandford	924 × 939 but inauthentic – eleventh century	*Familia* at Crediton
433	Topsham	924 × 939 but inauthentic – eleventh century	St Peter's, Exeter
498	Brampford Speke	944 – genuine set of bounds (Rose-Troup 1938)	Athelstan, *comes*
669	Clyst St Mary	961 – forged in eleventh century	Æthelnoth, faithful man
795	Nymed	974 – original	Ælfhere, minister
830	Treable	976 – contemporary	Ælfsige
890	Sandford	997 – original	Ælfwold, bishop
971	Stoke Canon	1031 – original	Hunuwine, minister
1387	Creedy Barton	1016 × 20 – genuine	Beorhtnoth (from Bishop Eadnoth)

(Chaplais 1966, nos 1, 2, 4–6, 11, 22, for a discussion on S386, S387, S388, S389, S433 and his view that they are the work of the same forger in the eleventh century)

Table 4. Study area 4 charter boundary clauses.

Sawyer catalogue number	Estate name	Date	Beneficiary
298	South Hams	846 – original	Æthelwulf to himself
704	Sorley, Churchstow	962 – apparent original	Æthel...e, minister

Table 5. Study area 5 charter boundary clauses.

Sawyer catalogue number	Estate name	Date	Beneficiary
534	Isle of Purbeck	948	Ælfthryth, a religious woman
573	Corfe and Blashenwell (1)	956 – spurious conflation of S 534 and S 632 (Kelly 1996, 82–83)	Wihtsige, minister
632	Corfe and Blashenwell (2)	956	Wihtsige, minister

Table 6. Study area 6 charter boundary clauses.

Sawyer catalogue number	Estate name	Date	Beneficiary
419	Fontmell	932	Shaftesbury Abbey
445	West Orchard	939	Ælfric or Alfred, bishop
502	Hinton St Mary	944	Wulfgar, minister
630	Compton Abbas, Iwerne Minster	956 – uncertain, ?eleventh-century fabrication (Kelly 1996, 86–92)	Shaftesbury Abbey
656	Iwerne Courtney, Thornton	958	Wulfgar, minister
710	East Orchard	963	Ælfsige, minister
764	Sturminster Newton	968	Glastonbury Abbey

Table 7. Study area 7 charter boundary clauses.

Sawyer catalogue number	Estate name	Date	Beneficiary
400	Odstock	928	Byrhtferth, minister
522	Bishopstone (north part)	947	Ælfsige, minister
582	Chalke	955 – uncertain, ?eleventh-century fabrication (Kelly 1996, 86–92)	The nuns of Wilton

(Continued)

Table 7. Study area 7 charter boundary clauses. (*Continued*)

Sawyer catalogue number	Estate name	Date	Beneficiary
635	Homington	956	Wulfric, *proceres*
640	Bishopstone (north part)	957	Ælfric, minister
696	Coombe Bissett	961	Byrnsige, minister
861	Stratford Tony	986	Ælfgar, his minister
891	Bishopstone	997	Old Minster, Winchester

Table 8. Differences in the Easton Bassett boundary clauses, S 630 and S 582.

S 630	S 582	Translations
Arest on offen weg	*Ærest of þare strǣte*	First to Offa's way/from the street
	æt þare ende hit gæþ up on ane furh	at the end it goes up on a furrow
	oð þat hit cymð to þæs hlinches orde	as far as it comes to the lynch end
þanen on þone ellen stub	*to þan ellen stybbe*	then on the elder tree stump
þanen on miclen diches get	*þannen to winterburge geate*	then on the great dyke's gate/to the winter burh gate
þanen on esnes dices get	*þonan to esnadiche geate*	then on the serfs' dyke gate
þanen on stan scylien	*þonne to þan stane*	then on the stone ?shaling/the stone
	þe ligð on þære strǣte	that lies on the street
	7 swa on þane cistel	and so to the cist
þanen on elchene seað	*þonne to ealcan seaðe*	then to the chalk pit
þanen on mapeldere cumb	*of ðam seaðe up on mapuldor cumb*	then to maple tree combe
	þonne 7lang cumbes	then along the combe
	to þæs cumbes heafde	to the combe's head
þanen on empenbeorch	*þonne to ippan beorge*	then to the imps' barrow
þanen on bican pet		then to Bica's pit
þanen on þornwelles	*þonan to ðorn wylle*	then to the thorn well
	7 swa to þan were	and so to the weir
þanen onlang stret	*þonne on ðone here pað*	then on the street/herepath
	west . þonne 7lang here paðes	west, then, along the herepath
eft [on] offenweg		as far as Offa's way
	to þam heafod stoccum þær we ær forleten	to the head stakes where we started

Table 9. Study area 8 charter boundary clauses.

Sawyer catalogue number	Estate name	Date	Beneficiary
492	South Newton	943	Wulfgar, minister
543	Laverstock	946	Ælfsige, gold- and silversmith
766	South Newton	968	Wilton Abbey
767	Bemerton	968	Wilton Abbey
789	Avon (Little Durnford)	972	Wynstan, *cubicularius*

Table 10. Study area 9 charter boundary clauses.

Sawyer catalogue number	Estate name	Date	Beneficiary
727	Steeple Ashton	964	King Edgar to himself
765	Edington	968	Romsey Abbey
867	Westwood	987	Leofwine, *venator*
899	Bradford-on-Avon	1001	Shaftesbury Abbey

Table 11. Study area 10 charter boundary clauses.

Sawyer catalogue number	Estate name	Date	Beneficiary
264	Little Bedwyn	778	Bica, *comes* and minister
379	Collingbourne Kingston	921	Wulfgar, minister
416	Ham	931	Wulfgar, minister
688	Burbage	961 (forged 975 × 1150) (Dumville 1992, 109–10, 112; Kelly 2001, no. 88)	Abingdon Abbey
756	Great Bedwyn	958 or 968	Abingdon Abbey

Abbreviations

Law codes

Abt	Æthelberht of Kent, 602–303.
Hl	Hlothere/Eadric of Kent, 673 × 686.
Wi	Wihtræd of Kent, 695–696.
Ine	Ine of Wessex, 688 × 694.
Af	Alfred's *domboc*, 871 × 899.
I Edw	Edward the Elder, 899 × 925.
II As	Æthelstan's Grately Code, 925 × 939.
II Atr	Æthelred's Treaty with Olaf, 978 × 1016.
IV Atr	Æthelred's Coinage laws, 978 × 1016.
V Atr	Æthelred's Council at Enham, 1008.
II Cn	Cnut's Winchester Code, 1020–1023.
ECf	Edward the Confessor, *c.* 1114.
Hn	Henry I, *c.* 1114.

Other abbreviations

ASC	M. Swanton (ed.) (1996) *The Anglo-Saxon Chronicles*. London: J. M. Dent.
DB	A. Williams and G.H. Martin (eds) (1992) *Domesday Book: A Complete Translation*. London: Penguin Books.
HE	B. Colgrave and R.A.B. Mynors (eds) (1969) *Bede's Ecclesiastical History of the English People*. Oxford: Oxford University Press.
OS	Ordnance Survey.
S	P.H. Sawyer (ed.) (1968) *Anglo-Saxon Charters: An Annotated Bibliography*. London: Royal Historical Society. Available: http://www.esawyer.org.uk/about/index.html.

Bibliography

Abels, R.P. (1988) *Lordship and Military Obligation in Anglo-Saxon England*. Berkeley: University of California.

Abrams, L. (1996) *Anglo-Saxon Glastonbury: Church and Endowment*. Woodbridge: Boydell Press.

Adkins, R.A. & Petchey, M.R. (1985) Secklow Hundred Mound and other Meeting Place Mounds in England. *Archaeological Journal*, 141, 243–251.

Aldsworth, F.R. 1973. *Towards a Pre-Domesday Geography of Hampshire – A Review of the Evidence –B. A. Dissertation*. B. A. Dissertation, University of Southampton.

Algar, D.J. & Hill, G. (1973) Archaeological Register for 1972, Medieval. *Wiltshire Archaeological and Natural History Magazine*, 68, 136.

Allen, V. (2016) When Things Break: Mending Roads, Being Social. *In:* V. Allen & R. Evans (eds) *Roadworks: Medieval Britain, Medieval Roads*. Manchester: Manchester University Press, 74–96.

Allen, V. & Evans, R. (2016) Introduction: Roads and Writing. *In:* V. Allen & R. Evans (eds) *Roadworks: Medieval Britain, Medieval Roads*. Manchester: Manchester University Press, 1–32.

Anderton, M. (ed.) (1999) *Anglo-Saxon Trading Centres: Beyond the Emporia*. Glasgow: Cruithne Press.

Armstrong, J. (1989) Transport and Trade. *In:* R. Pope (ed.) *Atlas of British Social and Economic History since c.1700*. London: Routledge, 96–133.

Ashwin, T. & Tester, A. (2014) *A Romano-British Settlement in the Waveney Valley: Excavations at Scole, 1993–4*. Gressenhall: Norfolk Historic Environment Service.

Astill, G. (2000) General Survey 600–1300. *In:* D.M. Palliser (ed.) *The Cambridge Urban History of Britain, Volume 1: 600–1540*. Cambridge: Cambridge University Press, 27–50.

Astill, G. (2006) Community, Identity and the Later Anglo-Saxon Town: The Case of Southern England. *In:* W. Davies, G. Halsall & A.J. Reynolds (eds) *People and Space in the Early Middle Ages, AD 300–1300*. Turnhout: Brepols, 233–254.

Astill, G. (2011) Exchange, Coinage and the Economy of Early Medieval England. *In:* J. Escalona & A. Reynolds (eds) *Scale and Scale Change in the Early Middle Ages*. Turnhout: Brepols, 253–272.

Astill, G. & Langdon, J. (eds) (1997) *Medieval Farming and Technology: The Impact of Agricultural Change in Northwest Europe*. Leiden: Brill.

Aston, M. (1983) The Making of the English Landscape – the next 25 Years. *The Local Historian*, 15, 323–332.

Aston, M. (1985) *Interpreting the Landscape: Landscape Archaeology in Local Studies*. London: Batsford.

Aston, M. & Lewis, C. (eds) (1994) *The Medieval Landscape of Wessex*. Oxford: Oxbow Books.

Aston, M. & Rowley, T. (1974) *Landscape Archaeology: An Introduction to Fieldwork Techniques on Post-Roman Landscapes*. Newton Abbot: David and Charles.

Attenborough, F.L. (1922) *The Laws of the Earliest English Kings*. Cambridge: Cambridge University Press.

Austin, D. (1990) The 'Proper Study' of Medieval Archaeology. *In:* D. Austin & L. Alcock (eds) *From the Baltic to the Black Sea: Studies in Medieval Archaeology.* London: Routledge, 9–35.

Bachrach, B. (2013) *Charlemagne's Early Campaigns (768–777): A Diplomatic and Military Analysis.* Leiden: Brill.

Bailey, G. (2007) Time Perspectives, Palimpsests and the Archaeology of Time. *Journal of Anthropological Archaeology*, 26, 198–223.

Baker, J. (2013) The Language of Anglo-Saxon Defence. *In:* J. Baker, S. Brookes & A.J. Reynolds (eds) *Landscapes of Defence in Early Medieval Europe.* Leiden: Brepols, 65–90.

Baker, J. & Brookes, S. (2011) From Frontier to Border: The Evolution of Northern West Saxon Territorial Delineation in the Ninth and Tenth Centuries. *Anglo-Saxon Studies in Archaeology & History*, 17, 104–19.

Baker, J. & Brookes, S. (2013a) *Beyond the Burghal Hidage: Anglo–Saxon Civil Defence in the Viking Age.* Leiden: Brill.

Baker, J. & Brookes, S. (2013b) Monumentalising the Political Landscape: A Special Class of Anglo-Saxon Assembly-sites. *Antiquaries Journal*, 94, 147–162.

Baker, J. & Brookes, S. (2013c) Outside the Gate: Sub-Urban Legal Practices in Early Medieval England. *World Archaeology*, 45, 747–761.

Baker, J. & Brookes, S. (2015a) Identifying outdoor assembly sites in early medieval England. *Journal of Field Archaeology*, 40, 3–21.

Baker, J. & Brookes, S. (2015b) Signalling Intent: Beacons, Lookouts and Military Communications. *In:* M.C. Hyer & G.R. Owen-Crocker (eds) *The Material Culture of the Built Environment in the Anglo-Saxon World.* Liverpool: Liverpool University Press, 216–234.

Baker, J., Brookes, S. & Reynolds, A.J. (2011) Landscapes of Governance: Assembly sites in England, fifth-eleventh centuries. *Post-Classical Archaeologies*, 1, 499–502.

Barlow, C.W. (Trans.) (1969) *Iberian Fathers: Martin of Braga, Paschasius of Dumium and Leander of Seville.* Washington: Catholic University of America Press.

Barnatt, J. (2002) *The Bakewell Archaeological Survey.* Bakewell: Peak District National Park Archaeology Service.

Barrow, J. (2012) Way-Stations on English Episcopal Itineraries. *English Historical Review*, 127, 549–565.

Bauch, A. (1984) *Quellen zur Geschichte der Diözese Eichstatt Band 1: Biographien der Gründungszeit.* Eichstatt: Verlag Friedrich Pustet.

Beaumont-James, T. & Gerrard, C. (2007) *Clarendon Park: Landscape of Kings.* Macclesfield: Windgather Press.

Bellavia, G. (2006) Predicting Communication Routes. *In:* J.F. Haldon (ed.) *General Issues in the Study of Medieval Logistics: Sources, Problems and Methodologies.* Leiden: Brill, 185–198.

Belloc, H. (1911) *The Old Road.* London: Constable and Company.

Belsey, V. (1998) *The Green Lanes of England.* Totnes: Green Books.

Bender, B. (1993) Introduction. Landscape: Meaning and Action. *In:* B. Bender (ed.) *Landscape: Politics and Perspectives.* Oxford: Berg, 1–18.

Bender, B. (1998) *Stonehenge: Making Space.* Oxford: Berg.

Beresford, M. (1994) Preface. *In:* M. Aston & C. Lewis (eds) *The Medieval Landscape of Wessex.* Oxford: Oxbow Books, vii–viii.

Biddle, M. (1976a) Towns. *In:* D.M. Wilson (ed.) *The Archaeology of Anglo-Saxon England.* London: Routledge, 99–150.

Biddle, M. (ed.) (1976b) *Winchester in the Early Middle Ages.* Oxford: Clarendon Press.

Biddle, M. & Hill, D. (1971) Late Saxon Planned Towns. *Antiquaries Journal*, 51, 70–85.
Bintley, M.D.J. & Shapland, M.G. (eds) (2013) *Trees and Timber in the Anglo-Saxon World*. Oxford: Oxford University Press.
Bird, J.B. (1806) *The Laws Respecting Highways and Turnpike Roads*. London: W. Clarke and Son.
Blackburn, M. (2003) 'Productive' Sites and the Pattern of Coin Loss in England, 600–1180. *In:* K. Ulmschneider & T. Pestell (eds) *Markets in Medieval Europe: Trading and 'Productive' Sites, 650–850*. Macclesfield: Windgather, 20–36.
Blair, J. (1985) Secular Minster Churches in Domesday Book. *In:* P. Sawyer (ed.) *Domesday Book: A Re-assessment*. London: Edward Arnold, 104–142.
Blair, J. (ed.) (1988a) *Minster and Parish Churches: The local church in Transition 950–1200*. Oxford: Oxbow Books.
Blair, J. (1988b) Minster churches in the landscape. *In:* D. Hooke (ed.) *Anglo-Saxon Settlements*. Oxford: Oxford University Press, 35–58.
Blair, J. (1988c) St Frideswide's Monastery: Problems and Possibilities. *Oxoniensia*, 53, 221–258.
Blair, J. (1992) A Coin of Offa from Radcot Bridge? *Oxoniensia*, 57, 342.
Blair, J. (1994) *Anglo-Saxon Oxfordshire*. Stroud: Alan Sutton.
Blair, J. (2000) Small Towns 600–1300. *In:* D.M. Palliser (ed.) *The Cambridge Urban History of Britain, Volume 1: 600–1540*. Cambridge: Cambridge University Press, 245–270.
Blair, J. (2005) *The Church in Anglo-Saxon Society*. Oxford: Oxford University Press.
Blair, J. (2007a) Introduction. *In:* J. Blair (ed.) *Waterways and Canal-building in Medieval England*. Oxford: Oxford University Press, 1–18.
Blair, J. (2007b) Transport and Canal Building on the Upper Thames, 1000–1300. *In:* J. Blair (ed.) *Waterways and Canal-building in Medieval England*. Oxford: Oxford University Press, 254–286.
Blair, J. & Millard, A. (1992) An Anglo-Saxon Landmark Rediscovered: The *Stan Ford/Stan Bricge* of the Ducklington and Witney charters. *Oxoniensia*, 57, 342–8.
Bonney, D.J. (1969) Two Tenth-Century Wiltshire Charters concerning lands at Avon and at Collingbourne. *Wiltshire Archaeological and Natural History Magazine*, 64, 56–64.
Boretius, A. & Krause, V. (1897) Edictum Pistense. *In:* A. Boretius & V. Krause (eds) *Monumenta Germaniae Historica; Capitularia Regum Francorum II*. Hanover: German Institute for the Study of the Middle Ages, cat. 864, 310–328.
Bosworth, J. & Toller, T.N. (1898) *An Anglo-Saxon Dictionary*. Oxford: Clarendon Press.
Boulay, F.R.H.D. (1961) Denns, Droving and Danger. *Archaeologia Cantiana*, 76, 75–87.
Boumphrey, G.M. (1935) *Along the Roman Roads*. London: George Allen and Unwin Ltd.
Bourdillon, J. (1988) Countryside and town: the animal resources of Saxon Southampton. *In:* D. Hooke (ed.) *Anglo-Saxon settlements*. Oxford: Oxford University Press, 176–195.
Bourdillon, J. (1994) The animal provisioning of Southampton. *In:* J. Rackham (ed.) *Environment and economy in Anglo-Saxon England*. York: Council for British Archaeology Research Report 109, 120–125.
Briggs, K. (2009) The Distribution of Certain Place-name types to Roman Roads. *Nomina*, 32, 43–56.

Brink, S. (2001) Mythologizing Landscape: Place and Space of Cult and Myth. *In:* M. Stausberg (ed.) *Kontinuitäten und Brüche in der Religionsgeschichte*. Berlin: de Gruyter, 76–112.

Britnell, R.H. (1996) *The Commercialisation of English Society*. Manchester: Manchester University Press.

Broeze, F. (2002) *The Globalisation of the Oceans: Containerisation from the 1950s to the Present*. St John's, Newfoundland: International Maritime Economic History Association.

Brookes, S. (2003) The Early Anglo-Saxon Framework for Middle Anglo-Saxon Economics: The Case of East Kent. *In:* K. Ulmschneider & T. Pestell (eds) *Markets in Medieval Europe: Trading and 'Productive' Sites, 650–850*. Macclesfield: Windgather, 84–96.

Brookes, S. (2007) Walking with Anglo-Saxons: Landscapes of the Dead in Early Anglo-Saxon Kent. *Anglo-Saxon Studies in Archaeology & History*, 14, 143–153.

Brookes, S. (2013) Mapping Anglo-Saxon Civil Defence. *In:* J. Baker, S. Brookes & A.J. Reynolds (eds) *Landscapes of Defence in early Medieval Europe*. Leiden: Brepols, 39–64.

Brookes, S. & Reynolds, A.J. (2011) The Origins of Political Order and the Anglo-Saxon State. *Archaeology International*, 13, 84–93.

Brooks, N.P. (1964) The Unidentified Forts of the Burghal Hidage. *Medieval Archaeology*, 8, 74–90.

Brooks, N.P. (1971) The Development of Military Obligations in Eighth- and Ninth-Century England. *In:* P. Clemoes & K. Hughes (eds) *England before the Conquest: Studies in Primary Sources presented to Dorothy Whitelock*. Cambridge: Cambridge University Press, 69–84.

Brooks, N.P. (1974) Anglo-Saxon Charters; the Work of the Last Twenty Years. *Anglo-Saxon England*, 3, 211–231.

Brooks, N.P. (1979) England in the Ninth Century: The Crucible of Defeat. *Transactions of the Royal Historical Society*, 29, 1–20.

Brooks, N.P. (1984) *The Early History of the Church of Canterbury*. Leicester: Leicester University Press.

Brooks, N.P. (1994) Rochester Bridge, AD 43–1381. *In:* N. Yates & J.M. Gibson (eds) *Traffic and Politics: the Construction and Management of Rochester Bridge AD 43–1993*. Woodbridge: Boydell and Brewer, 1–40.

Brooks, N.P. (2000a) The Micheldever Forgery. *In:* N. Brooks (ed.) *Anglo-Saxon Myths: State and Church 400–1066*. London: Hambledon Press, 239–274.

Brooks, N.P. (2000b) Rochester Bridge, AD 43–1381. *In:* N.P. Brooks (ed.) *Communities and Warfare, 700–1400*. London: Hambledon Press, 219–265.

Brooks, N.P. 2002. Church, State and Access to Resources in Early Anglo-Saxon England. *20th Brixworth Lecture, The Brixworth Lectures, Second Series, No. 2*.

Brooks, N.P. & Kelly, S.E. (eds) (2013) *Charters of Christchuch Canterbury, Parts 1 and 2*. Oxford: Oxford University Press.

Brown, A.E., Key, T.R. & Orr, C. (1977) Some Anglo-Saxon Estates and their Boundaries in South-West Northamptonshire. *Northamptonshire Archaeology* 12, 155–176.

Brown, M.P. (2007) *Manuscripts of the Anglo-Saxon Age*. London: The British Library.

Brück, J. (2005) Experiencing the Past? The Development of a Phenomenological Archaeology in British Prehistory. *Archaeological Dialogues*, 12, 45–72.

Brunning, R. (2010) Taming the Floodplain: River Canalisation and Causeway Formation in the Middle Anglo-Saxon Period at Glastonbury, Somerset. *Medieval Archaeology*, 54, 319–329.

Buckberry, J.L. & Hadley, D.M. (2007) An Anglo-Saxon Execution Cemetery at Walkington Wold, Yorkshire. *Oxford Journal of Archaeology*, 26, 309–329.

Bulfield, A. (1972) *The Icknield Way*. Lavenham: Terence Dalton.

Buss, B. (2002) Ebbsfleet Saxon Mill. *Current Archaeology*, 183, 93.

Calkin, J.B. (1953) 'Kimmeridge Coal Money' – The Romano-British Shale Armlet Industry. *Proceedings of the Dorset Natural History and Archaeology Society*, 75, 45–67.

Cambridge, E. (1989) Why did the Community of St Cuthbert Settle at Chester-le-Street? *In:* G. Bonner, C. Stancliffe & D. Rollason (eds) *St Cuthbert, His Cult and His Community to AD 1200*. Woodbridge: Boydell Press, 367–375.

Campbell, A. (ed.) (1973) *Charters of Rochester*. Oxford: Oxford University Press.

Campbell, A. & Keynes, S. (eds) (1998) *Encomium Emmae Reginae*. Cambridge: Cambridge University Press.

Campbell, E. (1996) The Archaeological Evidence for Contacts, Imports, Trade and Economy in Celtic Britain AD 400–800. *In:* K.R. Dark (ed.) *External Contacts and the Economy of Late Roman and Post-Roman Britain*. Woodbridge: Boydell Press, 83–96.

Campbell, J. (1987) Some Agents and Agencies of the Late Anglo-Saxon State. *In:* J.C. Holt (ed.) *Domesday Studies*. Woodbridge: Boydell Press, 201–218.

Campbell, J. (1995) The Late Anglo-Saxon State: A Maximum View. *Proceedings of the British Academy*, 87, 39–65.

Campbell, J. (2000) Some Agents and Agencies of the Late Anglo-Saxon State. *In:* J. Campbell (ed.) *The Anglo-Saxon State*. London: Hambledon Press, 201–226.

Candy, J. (2009) *The Archaeology of Pilgrimage on the Camino de Santiago de Compostela: A Landscape Perspective*. Oxford: Archaeopress.

Carver, M. (2005) *Sutton Hoo: A Seventh-century Princely Burial Ground and Its Context*. London: British Museum Press.

Carver, M. (2015) Commerce and Cult: Confronted Ideologies in 6th–9th-Century Europe. *Medieval Archaeology*, 59, 1–23.

Cathers, K. 2001. *An Examination of the Horse in Anglo-Saxon England*. Unpublished PhD Thesis, University of Reading.

Cave-Penney, H. (2004) *The Archaeology of Wiltshire's Towns: An Extensive Urban Survey: Salisbury*. Trowbridge: Wiltshire County Archaeology Service.

Cessford, C., Dickens, A., Dodwell, N. & Reynolds, A.J. (2007) Middle Anglo-Saxon Justice: the Chesterton Lane Corner Execution Cemetery and Related Sequence. *Archaeological Journal*, 164, 197–226.

Challis, C.E. & Cook, B.J. (1987) Coin Register. *British Numismatic Journal*, 57, 122–152.

Chandler, J. (1983) *Endless Street: A History of Salisbury and its People*. Salisbury: Hobnob Press.

Chaplais, P. (1966) The Authenticity of the Royal Anglo-Saxon Diplomas of Exeter. *Bulletin of the Institute of Historical Research*, 39, 1–34.

Chaplais, P. (1981) *English Diplomatic Practice in the Middle Ages*. London: A.C. & Black.

Clarke, D.M. (1973) Archaeology: The Loss of Innocence. *Antiquity*, 47, 6–18.

Clarke, D.M. (1978) *Analytical Archaeology*. London: Thames and Hudson.

Cochrane, C. (1969) *The Lost Roads of Wessex*. Newton Abbot: David & Charles.

Codrington, T. (1903) *Roman Roads in Britain*. London: Society for Promoting Christian Knowledge.

Cole, A. (2007) The Place-Name Evidence for Water Transport in Early Medieval England. In: J. Blair (ed.) *Waterways and Canal-Building in Medieval England*. Oxford: Oxford University Press, 55–84.

Cole, A. (2008) *Weg*: A waggoner's warning. In: O.J. Padel & D.N. Parsons (eds) *A Commodity of Good Names: Essays in Honour of Margaret Gelling*. Donington: Shaun Tyas, 345–349.

Colgrave, B. (ed.) (1985) *The Earliest Life of Gregory the Great: By an Anonymous Monk of Whitby*. Cambridge: Cambridge University Press.

Colt-Hoare, R. (1812) *The Ancient History of Wiltshire, Vol 1*. London: William Miller.

Connolly, S. & Picard, J.M. (1987) Cogitosus's 'Life of St Brigit' Content and Value. *The Journal of the Royal Society of Antiquaries of Ireland*, 117, 5–27.

Cooper, A. (2000) The King's Four Highways: Legal Fiction meets Fictional Law. *Journal of Medieval History*, 26, 351–370.

Cooper, A. (2002) The Rise and Fall of the Anglo-Saxon Law of the Highway. *Haskins Society Journal*, 12, 39–69.

Cooper, A. (2006) *Bridges, Law and Power in Medieval England, 700–1400*. New York: Boydell and Brewer.

Cooper, A. (2016) Once a Highway, Always a Highway: Roads and English Law, *c.* 1150–1300. In: V. Allen & R. Evans (eds) *Roadworks: Medieval Britain, Medieval Roads*. Manchester: Manchester University Press, 50–73.

Cosgrove, D. (1984) *Social Formation and Symbolic Landscape*. London: Croom Helm.

Cosgrove, D. & Daniels, S. (eds) (1988) *The Iconography of Landscape*. Cambridge: Cambridge University Press.

Costen, M. (1994) Settlement in Wessex in the Tenth Century: the Charter Evidence. In: M. Aston & C. Lewis (eds) *The Medieval Landscape of Wessex*. Oxford: Oxbow Books, 97–113.

Costen, M.D. & Costen, N.P. (2016) Trade and Exchange in Anglo-Saxon Wessex, *c.* AD 600–780. *Medieval Archaeology*, 60, 1–26.

Coupland, S. (1991) The Fortified Bridges of Charles the Bald. *Journal of Medieval History*, 17, 1–12.

Cox, P.W. (1988) A Seventh-Century Inhumation Cemetery at Shepherd's Farm, Ulwell near Swanage, Dorset. *Proceedings of the Dorset Natural History and Archaeology Society*, 110, 37–47.

Cox, R.H. (1927) *The Green Roads of England*. London: Methuen.

Cramp, R. (1975) Anglo-Saxon Sculpture of the Reform Period. In: D. Parsons (ed.) *Tenth-Century Studies: Essays in Commemoration of the Millennium of the Council of Winchester and Regularis Concordia*. Chichester: Phillimore, 184–245.

Cramp, W. (2006) *Corpus of Anglo-Saxon Stone Sculpture: Volume VII: South-West England*. Oxford: Oxford University Press.

Crawford, O.G.S. (1921) Anglo-Saxon Bounds of Bedwyn and Burbage. *Wiltshire Archaeological and Natural History Magazine*, 41, 281–301.

Crawford, O.G.S. (1922) *The Andover District*. Oxford: Clarendon Press.

Crawford, O.G.S. (1924) *Air Survey and Archaeology*. London: H.M.S.O.

Crawford, O.G.S. (1953) *Archaeology in the Field*. London: Phoenix House.

Crawford, O.G.S. & Keiller, A. (1928) *Wessex from the Air*. Oxford: Clarendon Press.

Crick, J. (ed.) (2007) *Charters of St Albans*. Oxford: Oxford University Press.

Crittal, E. (1962) *A History of the County of Wiltshire*. Oxford: Oxford University Press.

Crossley, D. (1997) The Archaeology of Water Power in Britain before the Industrial Revolution. In: E. Bradford-Smith & M. Wolfe (eds) *Technology and Resource Use in Medieval Europe*. Aldershot: Ashgate, 109–124.

Crummy, P., Hillam, J. & Crossan, C. (1982) Mersea Island: the Anglo-Saxon Causeway. *Essex Archaeology and History*, 14, 77–86.

Crutchley, S., Small, F. & Bowden, M. (2009) *Savernake Forest: A Report for the National Mapping Programme*. Portsmouth: English Heritage.

Cubitt, C. (1995) *Anglo-Saxon Church Councils*. Leicester: Leicester University Press.

Cubitt, C. (2009) 'As the lawbook teaches': reeves, lawbooks and urban life in the anonymous Old English legend of the Seven Sleepers. *English Historical Review*, 124, 510, 1021–1049.

Cudahy, B.J. (2006) *Box Boats: How Container Ships Changed the World*. New York: Fordham University Press.

Cunliffe, B. (1974) *Iron Age Communities in Britain*. London: Routledge & Kegan Paul.

Cunliffe, B. (1976) *Excavations at Porchester Castle, Volume 2 (Saxon)*. London: Society of Antiquaries.

Cunliffe, B. (2001) *Facing the Ocean: The Atlantic and its Peoples*. Oxford: Oxford University Press.

Currie, C.K. (1994) Saxon Charters and Landscape Evolution in the South-Central Hampshire Basin. *Proceedings of the Hampshire Field Club and Archaeological Society*, 50, 103–125.

Currie, C.K. (1997) A Possible Ancient Water Channel around Woodmill and Gater's Mill in the Historic Manor of South Stoneham. *Proceedings of the Hampshire Field Club and Archaeological Society*, 52, 89–106.

Currie, C.K. (2007) Early Water Management on the Lower River Itchen in Hampshire. *In:* J. Blair (ed.) *Waterways and Canal Building in Medieval England*. Oxford: Oxford University Press, 242–253.

Daniell, C. (1997) *Death and Burial in Medieval England*. London: Routledge.

Darby, H.C. (1956) The Clearing of the Woodland in Europe. *In:* W.L. Thomas (ed.) *Man's Role in the Changing Face of the Earth*. Chicago: University of Chicago Press, 183–216.

Darby, H.C. (1977) *Domesday England*. Cambridge: Cambridge University Press.

Darvill, T. (1997) Landscapes and the archaeologist. *In:* K. Barker & T. Darvill (eds) *Making English Landscapes*. Oxford: Oxbow Books, 71–91.

David, B. & Wilson, M. (2002) *Inscribed Landscapes: Marking and Making Place*. Honolulu: University of Iowa Press.

Davies, W. (1988) *Small Worlds: The Village Community in Early Medieval Brittany*. Berkeley: University of California Press.

Davison, A. (1990) *The Evolution of Settlement in Three Parishes in South East Norfolk*. Norwich: Norfolk Museums Service.

Deacon, A. (1994) *The Development and Function of Roads: A Case Study*. Undergraduate Dissertation, University College London.

Denison, S. (1998a) Bronze Age Metalled Road near Oxford. *British Archaeology*, 36, 5.

Denison, S. (1998b) Date of Ridgeway. *British Archaeology*, 31, 4.

Dent, J. (1984) Skerne. *Current Archaeology*, 8, 251–253.

Dewitt, R. (2010) *Worldviews: An Introduction to the History and Philosophy of Science*. London: Wiley-Blackwell.

Dobbie, E.V.K. (1953) *Beowulf and Judith*. New York: Columbia University Press.

Doherty, C. (2015) A Road Well Travelled: The Terminology of the Roads in Early Ireland. *In:* E. Purcell, P. Maccotter, J. Nyham & J. Sheehan (eds) *Clerics, Kings and Vikings: Essays on Medieval Ireland in Honour of Donnchadh ó Corráin*. Dublin: Four Courts Press, 21–30.

Douglas, D.C. & Greenway, G.W. (eds) (1953) *English Historical Documents, Volume 2, 1042–1189*. London: Eyre & Spottiswoode.

Downer, L.J. (1972) *Leges Henrici Primi*. Oxford: Oxford University Press.

Draper, S. (2006) *Landscape, Settlement and Society in Roman and Early Medieval Wiltshire*. Oxford: Archaeopress.

Drew, K.F. (1962) The Immunity in Carolingian Italy. *Speculum*, 37, 182–197.

Driscoll, S.T. (1988) The Relationship Between History and Archaeology: Artefacts, Documents and Power. *In:* S.T. Driscoll & M.R. Neike (eds) *Power and Politics in Early Medieval Britain and Ireland*. Edinburgh: Edinburgh University Press, 162–187.

Drury, P.J. & Rodwell, W. (1978) Investigations at Asheldham, Essex: An Interim Report on the Church and the Historic Landscape. *Antiquities Journal*, 51, 133–151.

Dumville, D.N. (1987) English Square Minuscule Script: the Background and Earliest Phases. *Anglo-Saxon England*, 16, 147–179.

Dumville, D.N. (1992) *Wessex and England from Alfred to Edgar: Six Essays in Political, Cultural and Ecclesiastical Revival*. Woodbridge: Boydell and Brewer.

Durham, B. (1977) Archaeological Investigations at St Aldates, Oxford. *Oxoniensia*, 42, 83–203.

Eagles, B. (1994) The Archaeological Evidence for Settlement in the Fifth to Seventh Centuries AD. *In:* M. Aston & C. Lewis (eds) *The Medieval Landscape of Wessex*. Oxford: Oxbow Books, 13–32.

Eaton, T. (2000) *Plundering the Past: Roman Stonework in Medieval Britain*. Stroud: Tempus.

Edwards, H. (1988) *The Charters of the Early West Saxon Kingdom*. Oxford: British Archaeological Reports.

Edwards, J.F. & Hindle, P. (1991) The Transportation System of Medieval England and Wales. *Journal of Historical Geography*, 17, 123–134.

Edwards, J.F. & Hindle, P. (1993) Comment: Inland Water Transportation in Medieval England. *Journal of Historical Geography*, 19, 12–14.

Ekwall, E. (1947) *The Concise Oxford English Dictionary of English Place-Names*. Oxford: Oxford University Press.

Evans, R. (2016) Getting there: Wayfinding in the Middle Ages. *In:* V. Allen & R. Evans (eds) *Roadworks: Medieval Britain, Medieval Roads*. Manchester: Manchester University Press, 127–156.

Everitt, A. (1986) *Continuity and Colonization: The Evolution of Kentish Settlement*. Leicester: Leicester University Press.

Fairbrother, J.R. (1990) *Faccombe Netherton: Excavations of a Saxon and Medieval Manorial Complex*. London: British Museum.

Fairclough, G. (1992) Meaningful Constructions: Spatial and Functional Analysis of Medieval Buildings. *Antiquity*, 66, 348–366.

Faith, R.J. (1994) Tidenham, Gloucestershire, and the Origins of the Manor in England. *Landscape History*, 16, 39–51.

Faith, R.J. (1997) *The English Peasantry and Growth of Lordship*. Leicester: Leicester University Press.

Farley, M.E. & Little, R.I. (1968) Oldaport, Modbury. *Proceedings of the Devon Archaeological Society*, 26, 31–36.

Farmer, D.H. (1983) *The Age of Bede*. London: Penguin Classics, 185–210.

Farmer, D.L. (1989) Two Wiltshire Manors and their Markets. *Agricultural History Review*, 37, 1–11.

Farrar, R.A.H. (1957) The 'Roman Milestone' at Stinsford Cross. *Proceedings of the Dorset Natural History and Archaeology Society*, 79, 110–112.

Farrar, R.A.H. (1962) Miscellaneous Discoveries and Accessions. *Proceedings of the Dorset Natural History and Archaeology Society*, 84, 111–116.

Farrar, R.A.H. (1974) Some Recent Archaeological Discoveries in Dorset. *Proceedings of the Dorset Natural History and Archaeology Society*, 96, 71.

Fasham, P.J. (1981) Fieldwork and Excavations at East Stratton along the Roman Road from Winchester to Silchester *Proceedings of the Hampshire Field Club and Archaeological Society*, 37, 165–188.

Fawtier, R. (Trans.) (1912) *La Vie de Saint Samson* Paris: Bibli. De l'école des Hautes études.

Fell, C. (2007) Perceptions of Transience. *In*: M. Godden & M. Lapidge (eds) *The Cambridge Companion to Old English Literature*. Cambridge: Cambridge University Press, 172–189.

Fell, C.E. (1983) Unfrið: An Approach to a Definition. *Saga Book of the Viking Society*, 21, 85–100.

Finberg, H.P.R. (ed.) (1964) *The Early Charters of Wessex*. Leicester: Leicester University Press.

Finberg, H.P.R. (1970) Supplement to The Early Charters of Devon and Cornwall. *In*: W.G. Hoskins (ed.) *The Westward Expansion of Wessex*. Leicester: Leicester University Press, 23–44.

Fleming, A. (1988) *The Dartmoor Reeves: Investigating Prehistoric Land Divisions*. London: Batsford.

Fleming, A. (1999) Phenomenology and the Megaliths of Wales: a Dreaming too far? *Oxford Journal of Archaeology*, 18, 119–125.

Fleming, A. (2006) Post-Processual Landscape Archaeology: A Critique. *Cambridge Archaeological Journal*, 16, 267–280.

Flint, V.I.J. (1998) *The Rise of Magic in Early Medieval Europe*. Oxford: Clarendon Press.

Forbes, R.J. (1955) *Studies in Ancient Technology*. Leiden: E.J. Brill.

Fowler, P.J. (1964) Cross-ridge Dykes on the Ebble-Nadder Ridge. *Wiltshire Archaeological and Natural History Magazine*, 59, 46–57.

Fowler, P.J. (1998) Moving through the Landscape. *In*: P. Everson & T. Williamson (eds) *The Archaeology of Landscape*. Manchester: Manchester University Press, 25–41.

Fowler, P.J. (2000) *Landscape Plotted and Pieced: Landscape History and Local Archaeology in Fyfield and Overton, Wiltshire*. London: Society of Antiquaries.

Fowler, P.J. (2001) Wansdyke in the Woods: An Unfinished Roman Military Earthwork for a Non-event. *In*: P. Ellis (ed.) *Roman Wiltshire and After: Papers in Honour of Ken Annable*. Devizes: Wilthshire Archaeological and Natural History Society, 179–198.

Fowler, P.J. (2002) *Farming in the First Millennium AD: British Agriculture between Julius Caesar and William Conqueror*. Cambridge: Cambridge University Press.

Fox, H.S.A. (2006) Fragmented Manors and the Customs of the Anglo-Saxons. *In*: S. Keynes & A.P. Smyth (eds) *Anglo-Saxons: Studies Presented to Cyril Roy Hart*. Dublin: Four Courts Press, 78–97.

Fox, H.S.A. (2008) Butter Place-Names and Transhumance. *In*: O.J. Padel & D.N. Parsons (eds) *A Commodity of Good Names: Essays in Honour of Margaret Gelling*. Donington: Shaun Tyas, 352–364.

Fox, H.S.A. (2012) *Dartmoor's Alluring Uplands: Transhumance and Pastoral Management in the Middle Ages*. Exeter: Exeter University Press.

Gelling, M. (1984) *Place-names in the Landscape*. London: Dent.

Gelling, M. (1990) *The Place-names of Shropshire. Part 1*. Cambridge: Cambridge University Press.

Gelling, M. (1997) *Signposts to the Past*. Chichester: Phillimore.

Gelling, M. & Cole, A. (2000) *The Landscape of Place-names*. Stamford: Shaun Tyas.

Gem, R. (1991) Church Architecture. *In:* L. Webster & J. Blackhouse (eds) *The Making of England: Anglo-Saxon Art and Culture, AD 600–900*. London: British Museum Press, 185–188.

Gilchrist, R. (1988) The Spatial Archaeology of Gender: A Case Study of Medieval English Nunneries. *Archaeological Review from Cambridge*, 7, 21–28.

Gillmor, C. (1997) Charles the Bald and the Small Free Farmers. *In:* A.N. Jørgensen & B.L. Clausen (eds) *Military Aspects of Scandinavian Society in a European Perspective, AD 1–1300*. Copenhagen: The National Museum, 38–47.

Good, R. (1979) *Lost Villages of Dorset*. Wimbourne: Dovecot Press.

Gosden, C. (1996) Can we take the Ayran out of Heideggerian? *Archaeological Dialogues*, 3, 22–25.

Gosden, C. & Head, L. (1994) Landscape – A usefully Ambigious Concept. *Archaeology in Oceania*, 29, 113–116.

Gover, J.E.B. (1961) *Hampshire Place-names*. Hampshire Records Office: Unpublished manuscript.

Gover, J.E.B., Mawer, A. & Stenton, F.M. (1931) *The Place-Names of Devon, Part 1*. Cambridge: Cambridge University Press.

Gover, J.E.B., Mawer, A. & Stenton, F.M. (1938) *The Place-Names of Hertfordshire*. Cambridge: Cambridge University Press.

Gover, J.E.B., Mawer, A. & Stenton, F.M. (1939) *The Place-Names of Wiltshire*. Cambridge: Cambridge University Press.

Gover, J.E.B., Mawer, A., Stenton, F.M. & Smith, A.H. (1933) *The Place-Names of Northamptonshire*. Cambridge: Cambridge University Press.

Graham, A.H. & Davis, S.M. (1993) *Excavations in the Town Centre of Trowbridge, Wiltshire, 1977 and 1968–1988*. Salisbury: Trust for Wessex Archaeology.

Graham-Campbell, J. (1989) The Archaeology of the Danelaw: An Introduction. *In:* H. Galinié (ed.) *Les Mondes Normands (VIIIe-XIIe s.) Actes du Deuxième Congrès International d'Archéologie Médiévale (Caen, 2–4 octobre 1987)*. Paris: Société d'Archéologie Médiévale, 69–76.

Graham-Campbell, J. (1994) *The Archaeology of Pilgrimage*. London: Taylor and Francis.

Grat, F., Vielliard, J., Clemancet, S. & Levillain, L. (eds) (1964) *Annales de Saint-Bertin*. Paris: Klincksieck.

Graves, C.P. (1989) *Social Space in the English Medieval Parish Church*. London: Routledge.

Green, S.W. & Perlman, S.M. (1985) *The Archaeology of Frontiers and Boundaries*. Orlando: Academic Press.

Griffith, F.M. & Reed, S.J. (1998) Rescue recording at Bantham Ham, South Devon, in 1997. *Devon Archaeological Society Proceedings*, 56, 109–131.

Griffith, F.M. & Wilkes, E.M. (2006) The Land from the Sea? Coastal Archaeology and Place-names in Bigbury Bay, Devon. *The Archaeological Journal*, 163, 67–91.

Griffiths, B. (1995) *An Introduction to Early English Law*. Hockwold-cum-Wilton: Anglo-Saxon Books.

Griffiths, B. (1996) *Aspects of Anglo-Saxon Magic*. Hockwold-cum-Wilton: Anglo-Saxon Books.

Griffiths, D. (2003) Markets and Productive Sites: A View from Western Britain. *In:* T. Pestell & K. Ulmschneider (eds) *Markets in Early Medieval Europe*. Bollington: Windgather Press, 62–72.

Grimes, W.F. (1951) The Jurassic Way Across England. *In:* W.F. Grimes (ed.) *Aspects of Archaeology in Britain and Beyond: Essays Presented to O.G.S. Crawford*. London: H.W. Edwards, 144–171.

Grinsell, L.V. (1958) *The Archaeology of Wessex*. London: Methuen.

Grundy, G.B. (1917) The Evidence of Saxon Land Charters on the Ancient Road System of Britain. *Archaeological Journal*, 74, 79–105.

Grundy, G.B. (1918) The Ancient Highways and Tracks of Wiltshire, Berkshire and Hampshire, and the Saxon Battlefields of Wiltshire. *Archaeological Journal*, 75, 69–194.

Grundy, G.B. (1919) The Saxon Land Charters of Wiltshire. *Archaeological Journal*, 26, 143–301.

Grundy, G.B. (1920) The Saxon Land Charters of Wiltshire. *Archaeological Journal*, 27, 8–126.

Grundy, G.B. (1921) The Saxon Land Charters of Hampshire with Notes on Place and Field Names. *Archaeological Journal*, 28, 55–173.

Grundy, G.B. (1922–3) Berkshire Charters. *Buckinghamshire, Berkshire and Oxfordshire Archaeological Journal*, 27, 96–102, 137–171, 193–247.

Grundy, G.B. (1924a) Berkshire Charters. *Buckinghamshire, Berkshire and Oxfordshire Archaeological Journal*, 28, 64–80.

Grundy, G.B. (1924b) The Saxon Land Charters of Hampshire with Notes on Place and Field Names. *Archaeological Journal*, 31, 31–126.

Grundy, G.B. (1925) Berkshire Charters. *Buckinghamshire, Berkshire and Oxfordshire Archaeological Journal*, 29, 87–128, 96–220.

Grundy, G.B. (1926a) Berkshire Charters. *Buckinghamshire, Berkshire and Oxfordshire Archaeological Journal*, 30, 48–63, 102–120.

Grundy, G.B. (1926b) The Saxon Land Charters of Hampshire with Notes on Place and Field Names. *Archaeological Journal*, 33, 91–253.

Grundy, G.B. (1927a) Berkshire Charters. *Buckinghamshire, Berkshire and Oxfordshire Archaeological Journal*, 31, 31–62, 111–145.

Grundy, G.B. (1927b) The Saxon Land Charters of Hampshire with Notes on Place and Field Names. *Archaeological Journal*, 34, 160–340.

Grundy, G.B. (1928a) Berkshire Charters. *Buckinghamshire, Berkshire and Oxfordshire Archaeological Journal*, 32, 16–30, 62–68.

Grundy, G.B. (1928b) Saxon Charters of Worcestershire. *Birmingham Archaeological Society Transactions and Proceedings*, 53, 18–131.

Grundy, G.B. (1928c) The Saxon Land Charters of Hampshire with Notes on Place and Field Names. *Archaeological Journal*, 35, 188–196.

Grundy, G.B. (1933a) Dorset Charters. *Dorset Natural History and Archaeological Society*, 55, 239–268.

Grundy, G.B. (1933b) *Saxon Oxfordshire*. Oxford: Oxford Record Society.

Grundy, G.B. (1934) Dorset Charters. *Dorset Natural History and Archaeological Society*, 51, 110–130.

Grundy, G.B. (1935a) Dorset Charters. *Dorset Natural History and Archaeological Society*, 37, 114–139.

Grundy, G.B. (1935b) *The Saxon Charters and Field Names of Somerset*. Taunton: Somerset Archaeology and Natural History Society.

Grundy, G.B. (1935–6) *Saxon Charters and Field Names of Gloucestershire*. Bristol: Bristol and Gloucestershire Archaeological Society.

Grundy, G.B. (1936) Dorset Charters. *Dorset Natural History and Archaeological Society*, 38, 103–136.

Grundy, G.B. (1937) Dorset Charters. *Dorset Natural History and Archaeological Society*, 39, 95–118.

Grundy, G.B. (1938) Dorset Charters. *Dorset Natural History and Archaeological Society*, 40, 75–89.

Grundy, G.B. (1939a) The Ancient Highways of Somerset. *Archaeological Journal*, 96, 226–297.

Grundy, G.B. (1939b) Dorset Charters. *Dorset Natural History and Archaeological Society*, 41, 60–78.

Haefele, H.F. (1959) *Notkeri Balbuli Gesta Karoli Magni Imperatoris*. Berlin: Weidmann.

Hall, T.A. (2000) *Minster Churches in the Dorset Landscape*. Oxford: British Archaeological Reports.

Halsall, G. (2003) *Warfare and Society in the Barbarian West, 450–900*. London: Routledge.

Hamer, R. (ed.) (2015) *A Choice of Anglo-Saxon Verse*. London: Faber & Faber.

Hamerow, H. (2007) Agrarian production and the emporia of mid Saxon England, ca. AD 650–850. *In:* J. Henning (ed.) *Post-Roman Towns, Trade and Settlement in Europe and Byzantium Vol. 1, The Heirs of the Roman West*. Berlin; New York: Walter de Gruyter, 219–232.

Harmer, F.E. (1914) *Selected English Historical Documents of the Ninth and Tenth Centuries*. Cambridge: Cambridge University Press.

Harmer, F.E. (1950) Chipping and Market: A Lexicographical Investigation. *In:* C. Fox & B. Dickens (eds) *The Early Cultures of North-West Europe*. Cambridge: Cambridge University Press, 335–360.

Harris, E.C. (1989) *Principles of Archaeological Stratigraphy*. London: Academic Press.

Harris, E.C., Brown, M.R. & Brown, G.J. (1993) *Practices of Archaeological Stratigraphy*. London: Academic Press.

Harrison, D. (1992) Bridges and Economic Development, 1300–1800. *Economic History Review*, 45, 240–261.

Harrison, D. (2004) *The Bridges of Medieval England: Transport and Society 400–1800*. Oxford: Clarendon Press.

Harrison, S. (2002) Open fields and Earlier Landscapes: Six Parishes in South East Cambridgeshire. *Landscapes*, 3, 35–54.

Harrison, S. (2003) The Icknield Way: Some Queries. *Archaeological Journal*, 160, 1–22.

Hart, C.J.R. (1970) The Codex Wintoniensis and the King's Haligdom. *In:* J. Thirsk (ed.) *Land, Church and People: Essays presented to Prof. H.P.R. Finberg*. Reading: Museum of English Rural Life, 7–38.

Harte, J. (2009) The Devil's Chapels: Fiends, Fear and Folklore at Prehistoric Sites. *In:* J. Parker (ed.) *Written on Stone: The Cultural Reception of British Prehistoric Monuments*. Cambridge: Cambridge Scholars Publishing, 23–35.

Harvey, P.D.A. (1983) Rectitudes Singularum Personarum and Gerefa. *English Historical Review*, 108, 1–22.

Hase, P.H. (1988) The Mother Churches of Hampshire. *In:* J. Blair (ed.) *Minster and Parish Churches: The Local Church in Transition 950–1200*. Oxford: Oxbow Books, 45–66.

Hase, P.H. (1994) The Church in the Wessex Heartlands. *In:* M. Aston & C. Lewis (eds) *The Medieval Landscape of Wessex*. Oxford: Oxbow Books, 47–81.

Haslam, J. (1980) A Middle-Saxon Iron-Smelting Site at Ramsbury, Wiltshire. *Medieval Archaeology*, 24, 1–68.

Haslam, J. (ed.) (1984a) *Anglo-Saxon Towns in Southern England*. Chichester: Philimore.

Haslam, J. (1984b) The Towns of Devon. *In:* J. Haslam (ed.) *Anglo-Saxon Towns in Southern England*. Chichester: Philimore, 249–283.

Haslam, J. (1984c) The Towns of Wiltshire. *In:* J. Haslam (ed.) *Anglo-Saxon Towns in Southern England*. Chichester: Philimore, 87–147.

Haslam, J. (1987) Market and Fortress in England in the Reign of Offa. *World Archaeology*, 19, 76–93.

Haslam, J. (2015) The landscape of late Saxon burhs and the politics of urban foundation. *In:* M. Clegg Hyer & G.R. Owen-Crocker (eds) *The Material Culture of the Built Environment in the Anglo-Saxon World*. Liverpool: Liverpool University Press, 180–277.

Haslam, J. (2016) The Landscape of Late Saxon *Burhs* and the Politics of Urban Foundation. *In:* M.C. Hyer & G.R. Owen-Crocker (eds) *The Material Culture of the Built Environment in the Anglo-Saxon World*. Liverpool: Liverpool University Press, 181–277.

Hassall, J.M. & Hill, D. (1970) Pont de l'Arche: Frankish Influence on the West Saxon Burh? *Archaeological Journal*, 127, 188–195.

Hayman, G. & Reynolds, A.J. (2005) A Saxon and Saxo-Norman Execution Cemetery at 42–54 London Road, Staines. *Archaeological Journal*, 162, 215–255.

Heidegger, M. (1962 (1927)) *Being and Time*. Oxford: Wiley Blackwell.

Henning, J. (2007) Early European Towns. The Development of the Economy in the Frankish Realm Between Dynamism and Deceleration AD 500–1100. *In:* J. Henning (ed.) *Post-Roman Towns, Trade and Settlement in Europe and Byzantium Vol. 1, The Heirs of the Roman West*. Berlin; New York: Walter de Gruyter, 3–40.

Herring, P. (1996) Transhumance in medieval Cornwall. *In:* H.S.A. Fox (ed.) *Seasonal Settlement*. Leicester: Leicester University Press, 35–44.

Hesse, M. (1992) Fields, Tracks and Boundaries in the Creakes, North Norfolk. *Norfolk Archaeology*, 41, 305–324.

Hewitt, R. (2010) *Map of a Nation: A Biography of the Ordnance Survey*. London: Granta.

Higham, R. (2008) *Making Anglo-Saxon Devon*. Exeter: The Mint Press.

Hill, A.D.B. (1910) The Saxon Boundaries of Downton, Wiltshire. *Wiltshire Archaeological and Natural History Magazine*, 36, 50–56.

Hill, D. (1969) The Burghal Hidage: The Establishment of a Text. *Medieval Archaeology*, 13, 84–92.

Hill, D. (1978a) The Origin of the South Saxon Towns. *In:* P. Brandon (ed.) *The South Saxons*. Chichester: Phillimore, 174–189.

Hill, D. (1978b) Trends in the Development of Towns during the Reign of Ethelred II. *In:* D. Hill (ed.) *Ethelred the Unready: Papers from the Millenary Conference*. Oxford: British Archaeological Reports, 213–226.

Hill, D. (1981) *An Atlas of Anglo-Saxon England*. Oxford: Blackwell.

Hill, D. (1998) Anglo-Saxon Technology: The Oxcart. *Medieval Life: The Magazine of the Middle Ages*, 10, 13–18.

Hill, D. & Rumble, A.R. (1996) *The Defence of Wessex*. Manchester: Manchester University Press.

Hill, D.H. & Sharp, S. (1997) An Anglo-Saxon Beacon System. *In:* A.R. Rumble & A.D. Mills (eds) *Names, Places and People: An Onomastic Miscellany in Memory of John McNeal Dodgson*. Stamford: Paul Watkins, 157–165.

Hill, N.G. (1937) Excavations on Stockbridge Down 1935–1936. *Proceedings of the Hampshire Field Club and Archaeological Society*, 13, 247–259.

Hill, R. (1977) The Borough of Stockbridge. *Proceedings of the Hampshire Field Club and Archaeological Society* 33, 79–88.

Hindle, B.P. (1976) The Road Network of Medieval England and Wales. *Journal of Historical Geography*, 2, 207–221.

Hindle, B.P. (1978) Seasonal Variations in Travel in Medieval England. *Journal of Transport History* 4, 170–178.

Hindle, B.P. (1982a) *Medieval Roads*. Aylesbury: Shire.

Hindle, B.P. (1982b) Roads, and Tracks. *In:* L.M. Cantor (ed.) *English Medieval Landscape*. Abingdon: Taylor and Francis, 193–217.

Hindle, B.P. (1993) *Roads, Tracks and their Interpretation*. London: Batsford.

Hindle, B.P. (2016) Sources for the English Medieval Road System. *In:* V. Allen & R. Evans (eds) *Roadworks: Medieval Britain, Medieval Roads*. Manchester: Manchester University Press, 33–49.

Hinton, D.A. (1984) The Towns of Hampshire. *In:* J. Haslam (ed.) *Anglo-Saxon towns in southern England*. Chichester: Phillimore, 149–165.

Hinton. D.A. (1986) Coins and Commercial Centres in Anglo-Saxon England. *In:* M. a. S. Blackburn (ed.) *Anglo-Saxon Monetary History: Essays in Honour of Michael Dolley* Leicester: Leicester University Press, 1–18.

Hinton. D.A. (1992) Revised Dating of the Worgret Structure. *Proceedings of the Dorset Natural History and Archaeology Society*, 114, 258–259.

Hinton. D.A. (1997) The 'Scole-Dickleborough Field System' Examined. *Landscape History*, 19, 5–13.

Hinton. D.A. (2000) The Large Towns 600–1300. *In:* D.M. Palliser (ed.) *The Cambridge Urban History of Britain, Volume 1: 600–1540*. Cambridge: Cambridge University Press, 217–243.

Hinton, D.A. & Webster, C.J. (1987) Excavations at the Church of St Martin, Wareham, 1985–86, and 'Minsters' in South-East Dorset. *Proceedings of the Dorset Natural History and Archaeology Society*, 109, 47–54.

Hippisley-Cox, R. (1914) *The Green Roads of England*. London: Methuen.

Hirsh, E. (2006) Landscape, Myth and Time. *Journal of Material Culture*, 2, 151–165.

Hodder, I. & Orton, C. (1976) *Spatial Analysis in Archaeology*. Cambridge: Cambridge University Press.

Hodges, R. (1982) *Dark Age Economics: The Origins of Towns and Trade, AD 600–1000*. London: Duckworth.

Hinton, D.A. (1989) *The Anglo-Saxon Achievement*. London: Duckworth.

Hinton. D.A. (2000) *Towns and Trade in the Age of Charlemagne*. London: Duckworth.

Hodges, R. & Hobley, B. (eds) (1988) *The Rebirth of Towns in the West AD 700–1050*. London: Council for British Archaeology.

Hogg, A.H.A. (1979) *British Hill-Forts: An Index*. Oxford: British Archaeological Reports.

Hooke, D. (1977) The Reconstruction of Ancient Routeways. *The Local Historian*, 12, 212–220.

Hooke, D. (1978) Early Cotswold Woodland. *Journal of Historical Geography*, 4, 333–341.

Hooke, D. (1980) The Hinterland and Routeways of Late Saxon Worcester: the Charter Evidence. *In:* M.O.H. Carver (ed.) *Medieval Worcester: An Archaeological Framework*. Worcester: Transactions of the Worcestershire Archaeological Society, 38–49.

Hooke, D. (1981a) *Anglo-Saxon Landscapes of the West Midlands: the Charter Evidence*. Oxford: British Archaeological Series.

Hooke, D. (1981b) Burial Features in West Midland Charters. *Journal of the English Place-name Society*, 13, 1–40.

Hooke, D. (1981c) The Droitwich Salt Industry: an Examination of the West Midland Charter Evidence. *In:* D. Brown, J. Campbell & S.C. Hawkes (eds) *Anglo-Saxon Studies in Archaeology and History*. Oxford: British Archaeological Reports, 123–169.

Hooke, D. (1981d) Open-Field Agriculture – The Evidence from the Pre-Conquest Charters of the West Midlands. *In:* T. Rowley (ed.) *The Origins of Open-field Agriculture*. London: Croom Helm, 64–111.

Hooke, D. (1982) West Midlands Charters and Anglo-Saxon Topography. *West Midlands Archaeology*, 15, 52–57.

Hooke, D. (1983) *The Landscape of Anglo-Saxon Staffordshire: the Charter Evidence*. Keele: University of Keele.

Hooke, D. (1985a) *The Anglo-Saxon Landscape: the Kingdom of the Hwicce*. Manchester: Manchester University Press.

Hooke, D. (1985b) Village Development in the West Midlands. *In:* D. Hooke (ed.) *Medieval Villages: A Review of Current Work*. Oxford: Oxford University Committee for Archaeology, 125–154.

Hooke, D. (1986) *Anglo-Saxon Territorial Organization: the Western Marches of Mercia*. Birmingham: University of Birmingham.

Hooke, D. (1988) Early Forms of Open-Field Agriculture in England. *Geografiska Annaler. Series B, Human Geography*, 70, 123–131.

Hooke, D. (1989a) Early Medieval Estate and Settlement Patterns: the Documentary Evidence. *In:* M. Aston, D. Austin & C. Dyer (eds) *The Rural Settlements of Medieval England*. London: Batsford, 9–30.

Hooke, D. (1989b) Pre-Conquest Woodland: its Distribution and Usage. *Agricultural History Review*, 37, 113–129.

Hooke, D. (1990) *Worcestershire Anglo-Saxon Charter-Bounds*. Woodbridge: Boydell Press.

Hooke, D. (1992) Early Units of Government in Herefordshire and Shropshire. *Anglo-Saxon Studies in Archaeology and History*, 5, 47–64.

Hooke, D. (1994a) The Framework of Early Medieval Wessex. *In:* M. Aston & C. Lewis (eds) *The Medieval Landscape of Wessex*. Oxford: Oxbow Books, 83–95.

Hooke, D. (1994b) *Pre-Conquest Charter-Bounds of Devon and Cornwall*. Woodbridge: Boydell Press.

Hooke, D. (1999) *Warwickshire Anglo-Saxon Charter Bounds*. Woodbridge: Boydell Press.

Hooke, D. (2007) Uses of Waterways in Anglo-Saxon England. *In:* J. Blair (ed.) *Waterways and Canal Building in Medieval England*. Oxford: Oxford University Press, 37–54.

Hooke, D. (2010) *Trees in Anglo-Saxon England*. Woodbridge: Boydell Press.

Hoskins, W.G. (1952) The Making of the Agrarian Landscape. *In:* W.G. Hoskins & H.P.R. Finberg (eds) *Devonshire Studies*. London: Jonathan Cape, 289–334.

Hoskins, W.G. (1955) *The Making of the English Landscape*. London: Hodder and Stoughton.

Hoskins, W.D. (1959) *Local History in England*. London: Longman.

Howe, N. (2008) *Writing the Map of Anglo-Saxon England: Essays in Cultural Geography*. New Haven; London: Yale University Press.

Hughes, M.F. (1976) *The Small Towns of Hampshire*. Southampton: Hampshire Archaeological Committee.

Jackson, A. (1972) Medieval Exeter, the Exe and the Earldom of Devon. *Transactions of the Devonshire Association*, 104, 57–79.

Jackson, R. (2000) An Anglo-Saxon Watermill and Wellington. *Historic Environment Today: Herefordshire Council's Historic Environment Newsletter*, 3, 1.

Jacobsson, M. (1997) *Wells, Meres and Pools. Hydronymic Terms in the Anglo-Saxon Landscape*. Uppsala: Acta Universitatis Upsaliensis.

James, D.J. (2010) Settlement in the Hinterland of Sorviodunum. *Wiltshire Archaeological and Natural History Magazine*, 103, 142–180.

Jankuhn, H. (1982) Trade and Settlement in Central and Northern Europe up to and during the Viking Period. *Journal of the Royal Society of Antiquaries of Ireland*, 112, 18–50.

Jarvis, K. & Maxfield, V. (1975) The Excavation of a 1st-century Roman Farmstead and a Late Neolithic Settlement, Topsham, Devon. *Proceedings of the Devonshire Archaeological Society*, 33, 209–265.

Joce, T.J. (1911) An Ancient British Trackway. *Devonshire Association Transactions*, 43, 262–268.

Joce, T.J. (1912) The Exeter and Dartmouth Road. *Devonshire Association Transactions*, 43, 597–604.

John, E. (1960) *Land Tenure in Early England*. Leicester: Leicester University Press.

John, E. (1965) The Church of Winchester and the Tenth-Century Reformation. *Bulletin of the John Rylands University Library of Manchester*, 47, 404–429.

Johnson, M. (2006) *Ideas of Landscape*. Oxford: Blackwell.

Jones, E. (2000) River Navigation in Medieval England. *Journal of Historical Geography*, 26, 60–75.

Jones, G. (1972) Post-Roman Wales. *In:* H.P.R. Finberg (ed.) *The Agrarian History of England and Wales, Volume 1: 43–1042*. Cambridge: Cambridge University Press, 283–301.

Jones, R. & Hooke, D. (2003) Methodological Approaches to Medieval Rural Landscapes. *In:* N. Christie & P. Stamper (eds) *Medieval Rural Settlement, Britain and Ireland, AD 800–1600*. Macclesfield: Windgather, 31–42.

Jones, S.R.H. (1993) Transaction Costs, Institutional Change, and the Emergence of a Market Economy in Later Anglo-Saxon England. *Economic History Review*, 46, 658–678.

Jørgensen, A.N. (2003) Fortifications and the Control of Land and Sea Traffic in the Pre-Roman and Roman Iron Age. *The Spoils of Victory: The North in the Shadow of the Roman Empire*. Copenhagen: Nationalmuseet, 194–209.

Jørgensen, M.S. (1988) Vej, vejstrøg og vejspaerring. Jernalderens landfaersel in Jernalderens Stammesamfund. *In:* P. Mortensen & B. Rasmussen (eds) *Jernalderens Stammesamfund. Fra Stamme til Stat i Danmark*. Aarhus: Aarhus universitetsforlag, 101–116.

Jusserand, J.J. (1889) *English Wayfaring Life in the Middle Ages*. London: T. Fisher Unwin

Keays-Young, J. (1930) The Eadmund-Ælfric Charter 944 AD. *The Review of English Studies*, 6, 271–283.

Keen, L. (1979a) Hanford, Anglo-Saxon Coins. *Proceedings of the Dorset Natural History and Archaeology Society*, 101, 138.

Keen, L. (1979b) Stourpaine, Saxon Coins. *Proceedings of the Dorset Natural History and Archaeology Society*, 101, 140.

Keen, L. (1979c) Worth Matravers, Durotrigian Stater. *Proceedings of the Dorset Natural History and Archaeology Society*, 101, 143.

Keen, L. (1983) Saxon, Carolingian and Medieval Coins. *Proceedings of the Dorset Natural History and Archaeology Society*, 105, 151.

Keen, L. (1984) The Towns of Dorset. *In:* J. Haslam (ed.) *Anglo-Saxon Towns in Southern England*. Chichester: Philimore, 203–247.

Kelly, F. (1997) *Early Irish Farming: A Study Based Mainly on the Law-Texts of the 7th and 8th centuries AD*. Dublin: School of Celtic Studies, Dublin Institute for Advanced Studies.

Kelly, S.E. (1990) Anglo-Saxon Lay Society and the Written Word. *In:* R. Mckitterick (ed.) *The Uses of Literacy in Early Medieval Europe*. Cambridge: Cambridge University Press, 36–62.

Kelly, S.E. (1992) Trading Privileges from the Eighth Century. *Early Medieval Europe*, 1, 3–28.

Kelly, S.E. (ed.) (1995) *Charters of St Augustine's Abbey, Canterbury and Minster-in-Thanet*. Oxford: Oxford University Press.

Kelly, S.E. (ed.) (1996) *Charters of Shaftesbury Abbey*. Oxford: Oxford University Press.

Kelly, S.E. (ed.) (1998) *Charters of Selsey*. Oxford: Oxford University Press.

Kelly, S.E. (ed.) (2000) *Charters of Abingdon Abbey, Part 1*. Oxford: Oxford University Press.

Kelly, S.E. (ed.) (2001) *Charters of Abingdon Abbey, Part 2*. Oxford: Oxford University Press.

Kelly, S.E. (ed.) (2004) *Charters of St Paul's, London*. Oxford: Oxford University Press.

Kelly, S.E. (ed.) (2005) *Charters of Malmesbury Abbey*. Oxford: Oxford University Press.

Kelly, S.E. (ed.) (2007) *Charters of Bath and Wells*. Oxford: Oxford University Press.

Kelly, S.E. (ed.) (2012) *Charters of Glastonbury Abbey*. Oxford: Oxford University Press.

Kent, R.G. (1938) *Varro on the Latin Language*. Harvard: Harvard University Press.

Keynes, S. (1980) *The Diplomas of King Æthelred 'the Unready' 978–1016: A Study in their Use as Historical Evidence*. Cambridge: Cambridge University Press.

Kelly, S.E. (1990) Royal Government and the Written Word in Late Anglo-Saxon England. *In:* R. Mckitterick (ed.) *The Uses of Literacy in Medieval Europe*. Cambridge: Cambridge University Press, 226–257.

Kelly, S.E. (1991) *Facsimiles of Anglo-Saxon Charters*. London: British Academy.

Kelly, S.E. (1994) The West Saxon Charters of King Æthelwulf and his Sons. *English Historical Review*, 111, 1109–1149.

Kelly, S.E. (2002) *An Atlas of Attestations in Anglo-Saxon Charters*. Cambridge: Department of Anglo-Saxon, Norse, and Celtic, University of Cambridge.

Kelly, S.E. (2013) Church Councils, Royal Assemblies and Anglo-Saxon Royal Diplomas. *In:* G. Owen-Crocker & B. Schneider (eds) *Kingship, Legislation and Power in Anglo-Saxon England*. Woodbridge: Boydell Press, 17–180.

Keynes, S. & Lapidge, M. (1983) *Alfred the Great: Asser's 'Life of King Alfred' and Other Contemporary Sources*. Harmondsworth: Penguin.

Kitson, P.R. (1995) The Nature of Old English Dialect Distributions, mainly as exhibited in the Charter Boundaries. *In:* J. Fisiak (ed.) *Medieval Dialectology*. Berlin; New York: Walter de Gruyter, 43–135.

Krapp, G.P. (1931) *The Junius Manuscript*. New York: Columbia University Press.

Krapp, G.P. & Dobbie, E.V.K. (eds) (1961) *The Exeter Book*. New York: Columbia University.

Kristal, A.M. (ed.) (1995) *Maniéres de Langage (1396, 1399, 1415)*. London: Anglo-Norman Text Society.

Langdon, J. (1984) Horse-hauling, A Revolution in Vehicle Transport in Twelfth- and Thirteenth-Century England? *Past and Present*, 103, 37–66.

Langdon, J. (1993) Inland water transport in medieval England. *Journal of Historical Geography*, 19, 1–11.

Langdon, J. (1995) City and Countryside in Medieval England. *Agricultural History Review*, 43, 67–72.

Langdon, J. (2004) *Mills in the Medieval Economy: England 1300–1540*. Oxford: Oxford University Press.

Langlands, A.J. (2009) Accessing the Past on your Doorstep: A Community Investigation into the Early History and Archaeology of Laverstock, Wiltshire. *Wiltshire Archaeological and Natural History Magazine*, 102, 306–314.

Langlands, A.J. (2014) Placing the Burh in *Searobyrg*: Rethinking the Urban Topography of Early Medieval Salisbury. *Wiltshire Archaeological and Natural History Magazine*, 107, 91–105.

Langlands, A.J. (in press) *Loci* and the Locals: Peasant Agency and the Late Anglo-Saxon State. *In*: J. Escalona, S. Brookes & O. Vesteinsson (eds) *Polity and Neighbourhood in Early Medieval Europe*. Turnhout: Brepols.

Lapidge, M. (1993) *Anglo-Latin Literature 900–1066*. London: Hambledon Press.

Lapidge, M. (ed.) (2003) *The Cult of St Swithun*. Oxford: Oxford University Press.

Lavelle, R. (2005) Why Grateley? Reflections on Anglo-Saxon Kingship in a Hampshire Landscape. *Proceedings of the Hampshire Field Club and Archaeological Society*, 60.

Lavelle, R. (2007) *Royal Estates in Anglo-Saxon Wessex: Land, Politics and Family Strategies*. Oxford: Archaeopress.

Lavelle, R. (2010) *Alfred's Wars: Sources and Interpretations of Anglo-Saxon Warfare in the Viking Age*. Woodbridge: Boydell Press.

Laycock, S. (2008) *Britannia – The Failed State: Ethnic Conflict and the End of Roman Britain*. Stroud: History Press.

Layton, R. & Ucko, P.J. (2004) Introduction: Gazing on the landscape and encountering the environment. *In*: R. Layton & P.J. Ucko (eds) *The Archaeology and Anthropology of Landscape: Shaping Your Landscape*. London: Routledge, 1–20.

Leahy, K. (2000) Middle Saxon Metalwork and Coins from South Newbald and the 'Productive site' Phenomenon in Yorkshire. *In*: H. Geake & J. Kenny (eds) *Early Deira, Archaeological Studies of the East Riding in the Fourth to Ninth Centuries AD*. Oxford: Oxbow Books, 51–82.

Leahy, K. (2003) Middle Anglo-Saxon Lincolnshire: An Emerging Picture. *In*: K. Ulmschneider & T. Pestell (eds) *Markets in Medieval Europe: Trading and 'Productive' Sites, 650–850*. Macclesfield: Windgather, 138–154.

Leech, R.H. (2009) Arthur's Acre: A Saxon Bridgehead at Bristol. *Transactions of the Bristol and Gloucestershire Archaeological Society*, 127, 11–20.

Leeds, E.T. & Shortt, H. (1953) *An Anglo-Saxon Cemetery at Petersfinger, near Salisbury, Wiltshire*. Salisbury: South Wiltshire and Blackmore Museum.

Leighton, A.C. (1972) *Transportation and Communication in Early Medieval Europe AD 500–100*. Newton Abbott: David and Charles.

Lennon, B. (2010) The Relationship between Wansdyke and Bedwyn Dykes: A Historiography. *Wiltshire Archaeological and Natural History Magazine*, 103.

Lewis, C., Mitchell-Fox, P. & Dyer, C. (eds) (1997) *Village, Hamlet and Field: Changing Medieval Settlements in Central England*. Manchester: Manchester University Press.

Liebermann, F. (1903–1916) *Die Gesetze der Angelsachsen*. Halle: M. Niemeyer.

Lightfoot, K.G. & Martinez, A. (1995) Frontiers and Boundaries in Archaeological Perspective. *Annual Review of Anthropology*, 24, 471–492.

Lilley, K.D. (2000) Mapping the Medieval City: Plan Analysis and Urban History. *Urban History*, 27, 5–30.

Lilley, K. (2017) The Norman Conquest and its Influence on Urban Landscapes. *In:* D. Hadley & C. Dyer (eds) *The Archaeology of the Eleventh Century.* London: Routledge, 30–56.

Lochlainn, C.O. (1940) Roadways in Ancient Ireland. *In:* J. Ryan (ed.) *Féil-Stríbinn Eóin Mic Néill: Essays and Studies Presented to Eoin MacNeill.* Dublin: At the Sign of the Three Candles, 465–474.

Lowe, K.A. (1998) The Development of the Anglo-Saxon Boundary Clause. *Nomina*, 21, 63–100.

Loyn, H.R. (1971) Towns in Late Anglo-Saxon England: The Evidence and Some Possible Lines of Enquiry. *In:* P. Clemoes & K. Hughes (eds) *England before the Conquest: Studies in Primary Sources presented to Dorothy Whitelock.* Cambridge: Cambridge University Press, 115–128.

Loyn, H.R. (1984) *The Governance of Anglo-Saxon England, 500–1087.* London: Edward Arnold.

Loyn, H.R. & Percival, J. (Trans) (eds) (1975) *The Reign of Charlemagne: Documents on Carolingian Government and Administration.* London: Edward Arnold.

Lucas, G. (2005) *The Archaeology of Time.* London: Routledge.

Lund, N. (1984) *Two Voyagers at the Court of King Alfred: The Ventures of Ohthere and Wulfstan Together with the Description of Northern Europe from the 'Old English Orosius'.* New York: William Sessions.

Macdonald, J.E. 2001. *Travel and Communication Network in Late Saxon Wessex: A Review of the Evidence.* Unpublished DPhil, University of York.

Maddicott, J.R. (2000) Two Frontier States: Northumbria and Wessex c. 650–750. *In:* J.R. Maddicott & D.M. Palliser (eds) *The Medieval State: Essays presented to James Campbell.* London: Hambledon Press, 25–46.

Maddicott, J.R. (2010) *The Origins of the English Parliament, 924–1327: The Ford Lectures Delivered at the University of Oxford in Hilary term 2004.* Oxford: Oxford University Press.

Maitland, F.W. (1897) *Domesday Book and Beyond: Three Essays in the Early History of England.* Cambridge: Cambridge University Press.

Major, A.F. & Burrows, E.J. (1926) *The Mystery of Wansdyke.* Cheltenham: Privately published.

Malim, T. & Hayes, L. (2011) When is a 'Roman' Road Roman? An Iron Age Engineered Road at Sharpstone Hill, Bayston, Shropshire. *PAST*, 67, 3–5.

Margary, I.D. (1948) *Roman Ways in the Weald.* London: Phoenix House.

Margary, I.D. (1957) *Roman Roads in Britain.* London: Phoenix House.

Margary, I.D. (1973) *Roman Roads in Britain.* London: Baker.

Martin, E. (1999) Suffolk in the Iron Age. *In:* J. Davies & T. Williamson (eds) *The Iron Age in Northern East Anglia.* Norwich: Centre of East Anglian Studies, 44–99.

Martin, G.H. (1968) The Town as Palimpsest. *In:* H.J. Dyos (ed.) *The Study of Urban History.* London: Edward Arnold, 155–169.

Massingham, H.J. (1936) *The English Downland.* London: Batsford.

Matless, D. (1998) *Landscape and Englishness.* London: Reaktion.

Mawer, A. & Stenton, F.M. (1929–30) *The Place-Names of Sussex, Parts 1 and 2.* Cambridge: Cambridge University Press.

Mawer, A. & Stenton, F.M. (1932) *The Place-Names of Devon, Part 2.* Cambridge: Cambridge University Press.

McCann, J. (1952) *The Rule of St Benedict.* London: Burns Oates.

McCormick, M. (2001) *Origins of the European Economy.* Cambridge: Cambridge University Press.

McKerracher, M. (2018) *Farming Transformed in Anglo-Saxon England*. Oxford: Windgather.

McNeill, J.T. & Gamer, H.M. (1990) *Medieval Handbooks of Penance: A Translation of the Principal 'libri poenitentiales' and Selections from Related Documents*. New York: Columbia University Press.

Meaney, A. (1992) Anglo-Saxon Idolaters and Ecclesiasts from Theodore to Alciun: A Source Study. *Anglo-Saxon Studies in Archaeology & History*, 5, 103–125.

Meaney, A.L. (1984) Ælfric and Idolatry. *Journal of Religious History*, 13, 119–135.

Meaney, A. (1995) Pagan English Sanctuaries, Place-names and Hundred Meeting-places. *Anglo-Saxon Studies in Archaeology & History*, 8, 29–42.

Meinig, D.W. (ed.) (1979) *The Interpretation of Ordinary Landscapes*. New York: Oxford University Press.

Merleau-Ponty, M. (1996 (1945)) *Phenomenology of Perception*. London: Routledge and Kegan Paul.

Metcalf, D.M. (1984a) Monetary Circulation in Southern England in the first half of the Eighth Century. *In:* D. Hill & D.M. Metcalf (eds) *Sceattas in England and on the Continent*. Oxford: British Archaeological Reports, 27–71.

Metcalf, D.M. (1984b) Twenty-Five Notes on Sceattas Finds. *In:* D. Hill & D.M. Metcalf (eds) *Sceattas in England and on the Continent*. Oxford: British Archaeological Reports, 193–205.

Metcalf, D.M. (1988) The Coins. *In:* P. Andrews (ed.) *Southampton Finds Vol. 1: The Coins and Pottery from Hamwic*. Southampton: Southampton City Museums, 17–57.

Metcalf, D.M. (1994) *Thrymsas and Sceattas in the Ashmolean*. London: Royal Numismatic Society and Ashmolean Museum.

Metcalf, D.M. (2003) Variations in the Composition of the Currency at Different Places in England. *In:* T. Pestell & K. Ulmschneider (eds) *Markets in Medieval Europe; Trading and 'Productive' Sites, 650–850*. Macclesfield: Windgather, 37–47.

Miller, S. (ed.) (2001) *Charters of New Minster, Winchester*. Oxford: Oxford University Press.

Mills, A.D. (1977) *The Place-names of Dorset, Part 1*. Nottingham: English Place-name Society.

Mills, A.D. (1989) *The Place-names of Dorset, Part 3*. Nottingham: English Place-name Society.

Mills, A.D. (1991) *Dictionary of English Place-names*. Oxford: Oxford University Press.

Mills, A.D. (1998) *Dictionary of English Place-names*. Oxford: Clarendon Press.

Mommsen, T. & Krueger, P. (eds) (1905a) *Codex Theodosianus, I, Theodosiani Libri XVI cum constitutionibus Sirmondinis*. Berlin.

Mommsen, T. & Krueger, P. (eds) (1905b) *Codex Theodosianus, II, Leges Novellae ad Theodosianum pertinentes*. Berlin.

Moore, C.N. & Algar, D.J. (1968) Saxon 'Grass-Tempered Ware' and Mesolithic Finds from near Petersfinger, Laverstock. *Wiltshire Archaeological and Natural History Magazine*, 63.

Morland, J. (2000) The Significance of Production in Eighth Century England. *In:* I.L. Hansen & C. Wickham (eds) *The Long Eighth Century: Production, Distribution and Demand*. Leiden: Brill, 69–104.

Morris, R. (1989) *Churches in the Landscape*. London: J. M. Dent and Sons.

Morris, R. (2004) *Journeys from Jarrow*. Jarrow Lecture.

Morton, A.D. (ed.) (1992) *Excavations at Hamwic. Vol. 1, Excavations 1946–83*. London: Council for British Archaeology.

Muir, R. (2000) *The New Reading the Landscape: Fieldwork in Landscape History*. Exeter: Exeter University Press.

Naylor, J. (2012) Coinage, Trade and the Origins of the English emporia, ca. AD 650–750. *In:* S. Gelichi and R. Hodges (eds) *From one Sea to Another: Trading Places in the European and Mediterranean Early Middle Ages*. Turnhout: Brepols, 237–266.

Neilson, N. (1910) Customary rents. *In:* P. Vinogradoff (ed.) *Oxford Studies in Social and Legal History*. Oxford: Clarendon.

Nelson, J.L. (1986) The Church's Military Service in the Ninth Century: A Contemporary Comparative View? *In:* J.L. Nelson (ed.) *Politics and Ritual in Early Medieval Europe*. London: Hambledon Press, 117–132.

Nelson, J.L. (2004) Presidential Address: England and the Continent in the Ninth Century: III, Rights and Rituals. *Transactions of the Royal Historical Society*, 14, 1–24.

Neumann, H. (1982) *Olgerdiget, et bidrag til Danmarks tidligste historie*. Haderslev: Haderslev Museum.

Newman, J. & Pevsner, N. (1972) *The Buildings of England: Dorset*. London: Penguin Books.

Newman, P.B. (2011) *Travel and Trade in the Middle Ages*. Jefferson, NC: McFarland.

Newton, A.P. (ed.) (1930) *Travel and Travellers of the Middle Ages*. London: Kegan Paul.

Nicholas, D.M. (2014) *The Growth of the Medieval City: From Late Antiquity to the Early Fourteenth Century*. London: Routledge.

O'Donovan, M.A. (1973) An Interim Revision of Episcopal Dates for the Province of Canterbury, 850–950, II. *Anglo-Saxon England*, 2, 91–113.

O'Donovan, M.A. (ed.) (1988) *Charters of Sherbourne*. Oxford: Oxford University Press.

Ohler, N. & Hillier, T.C. (1989) *The Medieval Traveller* Woodbridge: Boydell Press.

Oosthuizen, S. (1998) Prehistoric Fields into Medieval Furlongs? Evidence from Caxton, South Cambridgeshire. *Proceedings of the Cambridgeshire Antiquarian Society*, 86, 145–152.

Oosthuizen, S. (2003) The Roots of Common Fields: Linking Prehistoric and Medieval Field Systems in West Cambridgeshire. *Landscapes*, 4, 40–64.

Oosthuizen, S. (2007) The Anglo-Saxon Kingdom of Mercia and the Origins and Distribution of Common Fields. *Agricultural History Review*, 55, 153–180.

Palliser, D.M., Slater, T.R. & Patricia-Dennison, E. (2000) The Topography of Towns. *In:* D.M. Palliser (ed.) *The Cambridge Urban History of Britain, Volume 1: 600–1540*. Cambridge: Cambridge University Press, 153–186.

Palmer, B. (2003) The Hinterlands of Three Southern English *Emporia*: Some Common Themes. *In:* K. Ulmschneider & T. Pestell (eds) *Markets in Medieval Europe: Trading and 'Productive' Sites, 650–850*. Macclesfield: Windgather, 48–60.

Pantos, A. (2004) The Location and Form of Anglo-Saxon Assembly-places: Some 'moot points'. *In:* A. Pantos & S. Semple (eds) *Assembly Places and Practices in Medieval Europe*. Dublin: Four Courts Press, 155–180.

Pantos, A. & Semple, S.J. (eds) (2004) *Assembly Places and Practices in Medieval Europe*. Dublin: Four Courts Press.

Parker-Pearson, M. (2012) *Stonehenge*. London: Simon & Schuster.

Pearce, S.M. (1985) Early Medieval Land Use on Dartmoor and its Flanks. *Devon Archaeology*, 3, Dartmoor Issue, 13–19.

Pearce, S.M. (2004) *South-western Britain in the Early Middle Ages*. Leicester: Leicester University Press.

Pearson, M. & Shanks, M. (2001) *Theatre/Archaeology*. London: Routledge.

Pelteret, D. (1985) The Roads of Anglo-Saxon England. *Wiltshire Archaeological and Natural History Magazine*, 79, 155–163.

Pelteret, D. (1995) *Slavery in Early Medieval England From the Reign of Alfred Until the Twelfth Century*. Woodbridge: Boydell and Brewer.

Penn, K.J. (1982) *Historic Towns in Dorset*. Dorchester: Dorset Archaeological Committee.

Pepper, G. (1996) Tothill Street Westminster, and Anglo-Saxon Civil Defence. *London Archaeologist*, 7, 432–434.

Percival, S. & Williamson, T. (2005) Early Fields and Medieval Furlongs: Excavations at Creake Road, Burnham Sutton, Norfolk. *Landscapes*, 6, 1–17.

Pitt-Rivers, A.H.L.F. (1887) *Excavations in Cranborne Chase near Rushmore on the borders of Dorset and Wiltshire*. Rushmore: Privately printed.

Pitts, M., Bayliss, A., Mckinley, J., Budd, P., Evans, J., Chenery, C., Reynolds, A.J. & Semple, S. (2002) An Anglo-Saxon Decapitation and Burial from Stonehenge. *Wiltshire Archaeological and Natural History Magazine*, 95, 131–146.

Pounds, N. (1942) Notes on Transhumance in Cornwall. *Geography*, 27, 34.

Preest, D. (2002) (Trans.) *William of Malmesbury: The Deeds of the Bishops of England (Gesta Pontificum Anglorum)*. Woodbridge: Boydell Press.

Preston-Jones, A. & Langdon, A. (1997) St Buryan Crosses *Cornish Archaeology*, 36, 107–128.

Rackham, O. (1986) *The History of the Countryside*. London: J.M. Dent and Sons.

Rackham, O. (1997) *The History of the Countryside*. London: Phoenix.

Radford, C.a.R. (1975) The Pre-Conquest Church and the Old Minsters of Devon. *Devon Historian*, 2, 2–11.

Rahtz, P.A. (1961) A Roman Villa at Downton. *Wiltshire Archaeological and Natural History Magazine*, 58, 303–341.

Rahtz, P.A. (1964) Saxon and Medieval Features at Downton, Salisbury. *Wiltshire Archaeological and Natural History Magazine*, 59, 124–129.

Rahtz, P.A. & Meeson, R.A. (1992) *An Anglo-Saxon Watermill at Tamworth: Excavations in the Bolebridge Street area of Tamworth, Staffordshire, in 1971 and 1978*. London: Council for British Archaeology.

Rainbird, P. (1998) Oldaport and the Anglo-Saxon Defence of Devon. *Devon Archaeological Society Proceedings*, 56, 153–164.

Rainbird, P. & Druce, D. (2004) A Late Saxon Date from Oldaport. *Proceedings of the Devon Archaeological Society*, 62, 177–180.

Ramsay, J. & Bathe, G. (2008) The Great Inclosure of Savernake with a note on Cross Valley Dykes. *Wiltshire Archaeological and Natural History Magazine*, 101, 158–175.

Ravenhill, W. (1986) The Geography of Exeter Domesday: Cornwall and Devon. In: C. Holdsworth (ed.) *Domesday Essays*. Exeter: University of Exeter, 29–50.

RCHME (1970) *An Inventory of the Historical Monuments in Dorset*. London: HMSO.

RCHME (1974) *An Inventory of the Historical Monuments in Dorset*. London: HMSO.

Reed, M. (1979) Buckinghamshire Anglo-Saxon Charter Boundaries. In: M. Gelling (ed.) *Early Charters of the Thames Valley*. Leicester: Leicester University Press, 168–187.

Reed. M. (1984) Anglo-Saxon Charter Boundaries In: M. Reed (ed.) *Discovering Past Landscapes*. London: Croom Helm, 261–306.

Reed, S., Bidwell, P. & Allan, J. (2011) Excavation at Bantham, South Devon and Post-Roman trade in south-west England. *Medieval Archaeology*, 55, 82–138.

Reilly, B.F. (1988) *The Kingdom of León-Castilla Under King Alfonso VI, 1065–1109*. Princetown: Princetown University Press.

Reuter, T. (2013) *The Annals of Fulda, Ninth-Century Histories, Volume II*. Manchester: Manchester University Press.

Reynolds, A.J. (1994) Compton Bassett and Yatesbury, North Wiltshire: Settlement Morphology and Locational Change. *Papers from the Institute of Archaeology*, 5, 61–69.

Reynolds, A.J. (1995) Avebury, Yatesbury and the Archaeology of Communications. *Papers from the Institute of Archaeology*, 6, 21–30.

Reynolds, A.J. (1997) The Definition and Ideology of Anglo-Saxon Execution Sites and Cemeteries. *In:* G.D. Boe & F. Verhaege (eds) *Death and Burial in Medieval Europe: Papers of the Medieval Europe 1997 Conference*. Zellick: IAP, 34–41.

Reynolds, A.J. (1999) *Later Anglo-Saxon England: Life and Landscape*. Stroud: Tempus.

Reynolds, A.J. (2001) Avebury: A Late Anglo-Saxon burh? *Antiquity*, 75, 29–30.

Reynolds, A.J. (2002a) The Age of the English: The Anglo-Saxon Achievement (AD 450–1100). *In:* J. Pollard & A.J. Reynolds (eds) *Avebury, The Biography of a Landscape*. Stroud: Tempus, 183–238.

Reynolds, A.J. (2002b) Burials, Boundaries and Charters in Anglo-Saxon England: a Reassessment. *In:* S. Lucy & A.J. Reynolds (eds) *Burial in Early Medieval England and Wales*. London: Society for Medieval Archaeology, 171–194.

Reynolds, A.J. (2008) *The Emergence of Anglo-Saxon Judicial Practice: the Message of the Gallows*. Aberdeen: The Centre for Anglo-Saxon Studies, University of Aberdeen.

Reynolds, A.J. (2009a) *Anglo-Saxon Deviant Burial Customs*. Oxford: Oxford University Press.

Reynolds, A.J. (2009b) Meaningful Landscapes: An Early Medieval Perspective. *In:* R. Gilchrist & A.J. Reynolds (eds) *Reflections: 50 Years of Medieval Archaeology 1957–2007*. Leeds: Maney, 409–434.

Reynolds, A.J. & Langlands, A.J. (2006) Social Identities on the Macro Scale: A Maximum View of Wansdyke. *In:* W. Davies, G. Halsall & A.J. Reynolds (eds) *People and Space in the Early Middle Ages, AD 300–1300*. Turnhout: Brepols, 13–44.

Reynolds, A.J. & Langlands, A.J. (2011) Travel *as* Communication: A Consideration of Overland Journeys in Anglo-Saxon England. *World Archaeology*, 43, 410–427.

Rippon, S. *Ipplepen Archaeological Research Project* [Online]. Exeter University. Available: http://ipplepen.exeter.ac.uk/ [Accessed 11th November 2017].

Rippon, S. (1991) Early Planned Landscapes in South East Essex. *Essex Archaeology and History*, 22, 46–60.

Rippon, S. (1994) Medieval Wetland Reclamation in Somerset. *In:* M. Aston & C. Lewis (eds) *The Medieval Landscape of Wessex*. Oxford: Oxbow Books, 239–253.

Rippon, S. (2008) *Beyond the Medieval Village*. Oxford: Oxford University Press.

Rippon, S., Smart, C. & Pears, B. (2015) *The Fields of Britannia*. Oxford: Oxford University Press.

Roach, L. (2011) Hosting the King: Hospitality and the Royal *Iter* in Tenth-Century England. *Journal of Medieval History*, 37, 34–46.

Roberts, B.K. & Wrathmell, S. (2000) *An Atlas of Rural Settlement in England*. London: English Heritage.

Robertson, A.J. (ed.) (1925) *The Laws of the Kings of England from Edmund to Henry I*. Cambridge: Cambridge University Press.

Robinson, F.C. (1984) Medieval, The Middle Ages. *Speculum*, 59.4, 745–756.

Robinson, M. (1992) Environment, Archaeology and Alluvium on the River Gravels of the South Midlands. *In:* S. Needham & M.G. Macklin (eds) *Archaeology Under Alluvium*. Oxford: Oxbow Books, 197–208.

Robinson, M. & Wilkinson, D. (2003) The 'Oxenford': Detailed Studies of the Thames Crossing in St Aldates. *In:* A. Dodds (ed.) *Oxford Before the University: The Late*

Saxon and Norman Archaeology of the Thames Crossing, the Defences and the Town. Oxford: Oxford University Press, 65–134.

Rodwell, W. (1978) Relict Landscapes in Essex. *In:* H.C. Bowen & P.J. Fowler (eds) *Early Land Allotment*. Oxford: British Archaeological Reports, 89–98.

Roffey, S. (2008) *Chantry Chapels and Medieval Strategies for the Afterlife*. Stroud: History Press.

Rollason, D. (1989) *Saints and Relics in Anglo-Saxon England*. Oxford: Blackwell.

Rose-Troup, F. (1929) The New Edgar Charter and the South Hams. *Transactions of the Devonshire Assocation*, 61, 249–280.

Rose-Troup, F. (1938) The Anglo-Saxon Charter of Brentford (Bampton), Devon. *Transactions of the Devonshire Assocation*, 70, 253–275.

Roskams, S. (ed.) (2000) *Interpreting Stratigraphy: Papers Presented to the Interpreting Stratigraphy Conference 1993–1997*. Oxford: British Archaeological Reports.

Rowley, T. (ed.) (1981) *The Origins of Open Field Agriculture*. London: Croom Helm.

R. P. S. Consultants (2002) *A41 Aston Clinton Bypass: Site B- Lower Icknield Way Post Excavation Assessment*. Unpublished Report: R. P. S. Consultants.

Rumble, A.R. (1980) HAMTUN alias HAMWIC (Saxon Southampton): The Place-Name Traditions and their Significance. *In:* P. Holdsworth (ed.) *Excavations at Melbourne Street, Southampton, 1971–6*. York: Council for British Archaeology, 7–20.

Rumble, A.R. (2001) Edward the Elder and the Churches of Winchester and Wessex. *In:* N.J. Higham & D.H. Hill (eds) *Edward the Elder, 899–924*. London: Routledge, 230–247.

Rumble, A.R. (2002) *Property and Piety in Early Medieval Winchester: Documents Relating to the Topography of the Anglo-Saxon and Norman City and its Minsters*. Oxford: Clarendon Press.

Rumble, A.R. (2006) The Cross in English Place-names: Vocabulary and Usage. *In:* C.E. Karkov, S. Larratt-Keefer & K.L. Jolly (eds) *The Place of the Cross in Anglo-Saxon England*. Woodbridge: Boydell Press, 29–40.

Sage, A. & Allan, J. (2004) The Early Roman Military Defences, Late Roman Burials and Later Features at the Topsham School, Topsham. *Proceedings of the Devon Archaeological Society*, 62, 1–43.

Salisbury, C. (1995) An Eighth-Century Mercian Bridge over the Trent at Cromwell, Nottinghamshire, England. *Antiquity*, 69, 1015–1018.

Sawyer, P.H. (1968) *Anglo-Saxon Charters: An Annotated List and Bibliography*. London: Royal Historical Society.

Sawyer, P.H. (1977) Kings and Merchants. *In:* P.H. Sawyer & I.N. Woods (eds) *Early Medieval Kingship*. Leeds: University of Leeds, 139–58.

Sawyer, P.H. (ed.) (1979) *Charters or Burton Abbey*. Oxford: Oxford University Press.

Sawyer, P.H. (1981) Fairs and Markets in Early Medieval England. *In:* N. Skyum-Nielsen & N. Lund (eds) *Danish Medieval History: New Currents*. Copenhagen: Museum Tusculanum Press, 153–168.

Sawyer, P.H. (1983) The Royal tun in Pre-Conquest England. *In:* P. Wormald (ed.) *Ideal and Reality in Frankish and Anglo-Saxon Society*. Oxford: Basil Blackwell, 273–299.

Sawyer, P.H. (2013) *The Wealth of Anglo-Saxon England*. Oxford: Oxford University Press.

Schreiber, H. (1962) *Merchants, Pilgrims and Highwaymen: A History of Roads through the Ages*. New York: G.P. Putman's Sons.

Scott, I.R. (1993) *The Evidence from Excavations for the Late Iron Age, Roman and Saxon Occupation in Romsey*. Romsey: Test Valley Archaeological Trust Reports.

Scott, I.R. (1996) *Romsey Abbey, Report on the Excavations 1973–1991. Vol. 1: The Excavations on the Abbey*. Stroud: Hampshire Field Club Archaeological Society.

Scull, C. (1997) Urban centres in pre-Viking England. *In:* J. Hines (ed.) *The Anglo-Saxons from the Migration Period to the Eighth Century*. Woodbridge: Boydell and Brewer, 269–298.

Sedgley, J.P. (1975) *The Roman Milestones of Britain*. Oxford: British Archaeological Reports.

Semple, S.J. (1998) A Fear of the Past: the Place of the Prehistoric Burial Mound in the Ideology of Middle and Later Anglo-Saxon England. *World Archaeology*, 30, 109–126.

Semple, S.J. (2004) Locations of Assembly in Early Anglo-Saxon England. *In:* A. Pantos & S. Semple (eds) *Assembly Places and Practices in Medieval Europe*. Dublin: Four Courts Press, 135–154.

Semple, S.J. (2007) Defining the OE *hearg*: A Preliminary Archaeological and Topographic Examination of *hearg* Place-Names and their Hinterlands. *Early Medieval Europe*, 15, 364–385.

Semple, S.J. (2010) In the Open Air. *In:* M. Carver, A. Sanmark & S. Semple (eds) *Signals of Belief in Early England*. Oxford: Oxbow Books, 21–48.

Semple, S.J. & Langlands, A.J. (2001) Swanborough Tump. *Wiltshire Archaeological and Natural History Magazine*, 94, 249–267.

Shennan, S., Gardiner, J. & Oake, M. (1985) *Experiments in the Collection and Analysis of Archaeological Survey Data: The East Hampshire Survey*. Sheffield: University of Sheffield.

Shepherd, R. (1993) *Ancient Mining*. London and New York: For the Institution of Mining and Metallurgy by Elsevier Applied Science.

Sherratt, A. (1996) Why Wessex? The Avon River Route and River Transport in Later British Prehistory. *Oxford Journal of Archaeology*, 15, 211–234.

Simpson, J.A. & Weiner, E.S.C. (eds) (1989a) *The Oxford English Dictionary*. Oxford: Clarendon Press.

Simpson, J.A. & Weiner, E.S.C. (1989b) *The Oxford English Dictionary*. Oxford: Clarendon Press.

Simpson, J.A. & Weiner, E.S.C. (eds) (1989c) *The Oxford English Dictionary*. Oxford: Clarendon Press.

Simpson, J.A. & Weiner, E.S.C. (eds) (1989d) *The Oxford English Dictionary*. Oxford: Clarendon Press.

Skeat, W.W. (1871) *The Gospel According to Saint Mark in Anglo-Saxon and Northumbrian Versions*. Cambridge: Cambridge University Press.

Slater, T.R. (1991) Controlling the South Hams: the Anglo-Saxon *Burh* at Halwell. *Transactions of the Devonshire Association for the Advancement of Science, Literature and Art*, 123, 57–78.

Smith, A.H. (1956 (reprinted 2008)) *English Place-Name Elements Parts 1 and 2, with addenda and corrigenda*. Nottingham: English Place-name Society.

Squatriti, P. (2002) Digging Ditches in Early Medieval Europe. *Past and Present*, 176, 11–65.

Stacey, N.E. (2001) *Surveys of the Estates of Glastonbury Abbey, c. 1135–1201*. Oxford: Oxford University Press.

Stacey, N.E. (2006) *Charters and Custumals of Shaftesbury Abbey, 1089–1216*. Oxford: Oxford University Press.

Stenton, F.M. (1913) *The Early History of the Abbey of Abingdon*. Reading: University College.

Stenton, F.M. (1936) The Road System of Medieval England. *Economic History Review*, 7, 1–21.
Stenton, F.M. (1971) *Anglo-Saxon England*. Oxford: Oxford University Press.
Stevenson, W.H. (1904) *Asser's Life of King Alfred*. Oxford: Clarendon Press.
Stevenson, W.H. (1914) Trinoda Necessitas. *English Historical Review*, 29, 689–703.
Stewart, I. (1984) *The Early English Denarial Coinage, c. 680–750*. Oxford: British Archaeological Reports.
Stokes, P.A. (2008) King Edgar's Charter for Pershore (AD 972). *Anglo-Saxon England*, 37, 31–78.
Stopford, J. (1994) Some Approaches to the Archaeology of Christian Pilgrimage. *World Archaeology*, 26, 57–72.
Story, J. (2003) *Carolingian Connections: Anglo-Saxon England and Carolingian Francia, c. 750–870*. Aldershot: Ashgate.
Stubbs, W. (1903) *The Constitutional History of England*. Oxford: Clarendon Press.
Swanton, M. (1970) *The Dream of the Rood*. Manchester: Manchester University Press.
Swanton, M. (ed.) (1996) *The Anglo-Saxon Chronicles*. London: J.M. Dent.
Symonds, L.A. (2003) *Landscape and Social Practice: the Production and Consumption of Pottery in Tenth-Century Lincolnshire*. Oxford: Archaeopress.
Symonds, L.A. & Ling, R.J. (2002) Travelling Beneath Crows: Representing Socio-Geographical Concepts of Time and Travel in Early Medieval England. *Internet Archaeology*, 13.
Symons, T. (1953) *The Monastic Agreement of the Monks and Nuns of the English Nation*. London: Nelson.
Tait, J. (1936) *The Medieval English Borough: Studies on its Origins and Constitutional History*. Manchester: Manchester University Press.
Talbot, C. (1954) *Anglo-Saxon Missionaries in Germany*. London: Sheed and Ward.
Tatton-Brown, T. (1997) The Church of St Thomas of Canterbury. *Wiltshire Archaeological and Natural History Magazine*, 90, 101–109.
Tatton-Brown, T. (2001) The Evolution of 'Watling Street' in Kent. *Archaeologia Cantiana*, 121, 121–133.
Taylor, C.C. (1979) *Roads and Tracks of Britain*. London: J.M. Dent and Sons.
Taylor, C.C. (1980) The Making of the English Landscape – 25 Years on. *The Local Historian*, 14, 195–201.
Taylor, C.C. (1988a) The Colonization of Medieval England: Introduction. *In:* W.G. Hoskins (ed.) *The Making of the English Landscape Rev. Edn*. London: Penguin, 67–69.
Taylor, C.C. (1988b) The English Settlement: Introduction. *In:* W.G. Hoskins (ed.) *The Making of the English Landscape Rev. Edn*. London: Penguin, 40–42.
Teulon-Porter, N. (1949) Shaftesbury (St Peter), Layton House. *Proceedings of the Dorset Natural History and Archaeology Society*, 71, 67.
Teulon-Porter, N. (1950) Further Discoveries at Mampits Lane near Shaftesbury. *Proceedings of the Dorset Natural History and Archaeology Society*, 72, 94.
Thacker, A. (1992) Monks, Preaching and Pastoral Care in Anglo-Saxon England. *In:* J. Blair & R. Sharpe (eds) *Pastoral Care before the Parish*. Leicester: Leicester University Press, 137–170.
Thirslund, S. (1997) Sailing Directions in the North Atlantic Viking Age (from about the year 860 to 1400). *Journal of Navigation*, 50, 55–64.
Thomas, C. (1967) *Antiquities of Cambourne*. St Austell: H. E. Warne.
Thomas, J. (1993) The Politics of Vision and the Archaeologies of Landscape. *In:* B. Bender (ed.) *Landscape: Politics and Perspectives*. Oxford: Berg, 19–48.

Thorn, F. & Thorn, C. (eds) (1985) *Domesday Book: Devon*. Chichester: Phillimore.
Thorpe, L. (1969) *Einhard and Notker the Stammerer: Two Lives of Charlemagne*. London: Penguin.
Tilley, C. (1994) *A Phenomenology of Landscape: Places, Paths and Monuments*. Oxford: Berg.
Tilley, C. (1999) *Metaphor and Material Culture*. Oxford: Blackwell.
Tilley, C. (2004a) *The Materiality of Stone: Explorations in Landscape Phenomenology*. Oxford: Berg.
Tilley, C. (2004b) Round Barrows and Dykes as Landscape Metaphors. *Cambridge Archaeological Journal*, 14, 185–203.
Timby, J. (2001) A Reappraisal of Savernake Ware. *In:* P. Ellis (ed.) *Roman Wiltshire and after: Papers in honour of Ken Annable*. Devizes: Wilthshire Archaeological and Natural History Society, 73–84.
Timperley, H.W. & Brill, E. (1970) *The Ancient Trackways of Wessex*. London: J.M. Dent and Sons.
Toller, T. (1921) *An Anglo-Saxon Dictionary Supplement*. Oxford: Oxford University Press.
Turner, D.J. (1980) The North Downs Trackway. *Surrey Archaeological Collections*, 72, 1–13.
Turner, S. (2004) Coast and Countryside in 'Late Antique' South-west England, AD. c.400–600. *In:* R. Collins & J. Gerrard (eds) *Debating Late Antiquity in Britain, AD 300–700*. Oxford: BAR British Series, 25–32.
Turner, S. (2006) *Making A Christian Landscape: The Countryside in Early Medieval Cornwall, Devon and Wessex*. Exeter: University of Exeter Press.
Turner, S. & Gerrard, J. (2004) Imported and Local Pottery from Mothecombe: Some New Finds Amongst Old Material at Totnes Museum. *Devon Archaeological Society Proceedings*, 62, 171–175.
Ulmschneider, K. (2000) *Markets, Minsters and Metal-Detectors: The Archaeology of Middle Saxon Lincolnshire and Hampshire Compared*. Oxford: Archaeopress.
Ulmschneider, K. (2003) Markets around the Solent: Unravelling a 'Productive' Site on the Isle of Wight. *In:* K. Ulmschneider & T. Pestell (eds) *Markets in Medieval Europe: Trading and 'Productive' Sites, 650–850*. Macclesfield: Windgather, 73–83.
Ulmschneider, K. & Pestell, T. (2003) Introduction: Early Medieval Markets and 'Productive' Sites. *In:* K. Ulmschneider & T. Pestell (eds) *Markets in Medieval Europe: Trading and 'Productive' Sites, 650–850*. Macclesfield: Windgather, 1–11.
Verhulst, A. (1999) *The Rise of Cities in North-West Europe*. Cambridge: Cambridge University Press.
Verhulst, A. (2000) Roman Cities, Emporia and New Towns (Sixth – Ninth Centuries). *In:* I.L. Hansen & C. Wickham (eds) *The Long Eighth Century: Production, Distribution and Demand*. Leiden: Brill, 105–120.
Vermeulen, F. & Antrop, M. (eds) (2001) *Ancient Lines in the Landscape: A Geo-Archaeological Study of Protohistoric and Roman Roads and Field Systems in Northwestern Gaul*. Leeven: Peters.
Wade-Labarge, M. (1982) *Medieval Travellers: The Rich and the Restless*. London: Hamish Hamilton.
Wallenberg, J.K. (1934) *The Place-names of Kent*. Uppsala: Lundequistska Bokhandein.
Ward, A. (1999) Transhumance and Place-names: An aspect of early Ordnance Survey Mapping on the Black Mountain Commons, Carmarthenshire. *Studia Celtica*, 32, 335–348.

Watson, B. (2001) The Late-Saxon Bridgehead. *In:* B. Watson, T. Brigham & T. Dyson (eds) *London Bridge: 2000 Years of a River Crossing.* London: Museum of London Archaeology Service, 52–60.

Watts, M. (2006) *Watermills.* Princes Risborough: Shire.

Watts, V. (2004) *The Cambridge Dictionary of English Place-names.* Cambridge: Cambridge University Press.

Webb, S. & Webb, B. (1913) *The Story of the King's Highway.* London: Longmans, Green and Co.

Welch, M. (1985) Rural Settlement Patterns in the Early and Middle Anglo-Saxon Periods. *Landscape History,* 7, 13–25.

Wessex Archaeology. 1993. St John's Hospital, Wilton, Wiltshire: Archaeological Evaluation – Unpublished Report. Salisbury: Wessex Archaeology.

Wessex Archaeology 1996a. New flats, St John's Hospital, Wilton: Archaeological Excavation – Post-Excavation assessment – Unpublished Report. Salisbury: Wessex Archaeology.

Wessex Archaeology 1996b. Old George Mall, Salisbury, Wiltshire: Archaeological excavations 1994–1995 – Unpublished Report. Salisbury: Wessex Archaeology.

White, L. (1967) Technology in the Middle Ages. *In:* M. Kranzberg & C.W. Pursell (eds) *Technology in Western Civilisation.* New York: Oxford University Press, 66–79.

White, P. (2003) *The Arrow Valley, Herefordshire: Archaeology, Landscape Change and Conservation.* Hereford: Hereford Archaeology.

White, R.H. (2007) *Britannia Prima: Britain's Last Roman Province.* Stroud: Tempus.

Whitelock, D. (1966) Review of H.P.R. Finberg's *Early Charters of Wessex. English Historical Review,* 81, 100–103.

Whitelock, D. (ed.) (1979) *English Historical Documents, Volume 1, c. 500–1042.* London: Eyre Methuen.

Whitelock, D., Brett, M. & Brooke, C.N.L. (1981) *Councils and Synods, with Other Documents Relating to the English Church, AD. 871–1204.* Oxford: Oxford University Press.

Wickham, C. (2005) *Framing the Early Middle Ages: Europe and the Mediterranean, 400–800.* Oxford: Oxford University Press.

Williams, A. & Martin, G.H. (eds) (1992) *Domesday Book: A Complete Translation.* London: Penguin Books.

Williams, G. (2013) Military and Non-Military Functions of the Anglo-Saxon Burh, c. 878–978. *In:* J. Baker, S. Brookes & A.J. Reynolds (eds) *Landscapes of Defence in Early Medieval Europe.* Turnhout: Brepols, 129–163.

Williams, H. (1999) Placing the Dead: Investigating the Location of Wealthy Barrow Burials in Seventh-Century England. *In:* M. Rundkvist (ed.) *Grave Matters: Eight Studies of First Millennium AD Burials in Crimea, England and Southern Scandinavia.* Oxford: British Archaeological Reports, 57–86.

Williamson, T. (1987) Early Co-axial Field Systems on the East Anglian Boulder Clays. *Proceedings of the Prehistory Society,* 53, 419–431.

Williamson, T. (1998) The 'Scole-Dickleborough Field System' Revisited. *Landscape History,* 20, 19–28.

Williamson, T. (2003) *Shaping Medieval Landscapes: Settlement, Society, Environment.* Macclesfield: Windgather Press.

Williamson, T. (2008) Co-axial Landscapes: Time and Topography. *In:* P. Rainbird (ed.) *Monuments in the Landscape.* Stroud: Tempus, 123–135.

Wilson, D.M. & Hurst, J.G. (1958) Medieval Britain in 1957. *Medieval Archaeology,* 2, 183–213.

Wilson, D.R. (1987) Reading the Palimpsest: Landscape Studies and Air-photography. *Landscape History*, 9, 5–26.

Wilson, S. (2000) *The Magical Universe: Everyday Ritual and Magic in Pre-Modern Europe*. London: Hambledon.

Winterbottom, M. & Thomson, R.M. (eds) (2007) *William of Malmesbury's Gesta Pontificum Anglorum*. Oxford: Clarendon Press.

Witney, K.P. (1976) *The Jutish Forest: a Study of the Weald of Kent from 450 to 1380 AD*. London: Athlone Press.

Wood, I. (1993) The Code in Merovingian Gaul. *In:* J. Harries & I. Wood (eds) *The Theodosian Code*. Ithaca: Gerald Duckworth, 161–177.

Wood, I. (1995) Northumbrians and Franks in the Age of Wilfrid. *Northern History*, 31, 10–21.

Wormald, P. (1999) *The Making of English Law: King Alfred to the Twelfth Century*. London: Blackwell.

Wright, G. (1988) *Roads and Trackways of Wessex*. Buxton: Moorland.

Wylie, J.W. (2007) *Landscape*. London: Routledge.

Yarnham, R. (2010) *How to Read the Landscape*. London: A & C Black Publishers Ltd.

Yorke, B.A.E. (1982) The Foundation of the Old Minster and the Status of Winchester in the Seventh and Eighth Centuries. *Proceedings of the Hampshire Field Club and Archaeological Society*, 38, 75–83.

Yorke, B.A.E. (1984) The Bishops of Winchester, the Kings of Wessex and the Development of Winchester in the Ninth and Early Tenth Centuries. *Proceedings of the Hampshire Field Club and Archaeological Society*, 40, 61–70.

Yorke, B.A.E. (1995) *Wessex in the Early Middle Ages*. Leicester: Leicester University Press.

Zenner, W.P. (1986) The Jewish Diaspora and the Middleman Adaption. *In:* E. Levine (ed.) *Diaspora: Exile and the Contemporary Jewish Condition*. New York: Shapolsky, 117–132.